Understanding Genocide

Understanding Genocide

The Social Psychology of the Holocaust

Edited by
Leonard S. Newman
Ralph Erber

OXFORD
UNIVERSITY PRESS

2002

OXFORD
UNIVERSITY PRESS

Oxford   New York
Auckland Bangkok Buenos Aires Cape Town Chennai
Dar es Salaam Delhi Hong Kong Istanbul Karachi Kolkata
Kuala Lumpur Madrid Melbourne Mexico City Mumbai Nairobi
São Paulo Shanghai Singapore Taipei Tokyo Toronto

and an associated company in Berlin

Library of Congress Cataloging-in-Publication Data
Understanding genocide : the social psychology of the Holocaust / edited by Leonard
S. Newman and Ralph Erber.
p. cm.
Includes bibliographical references and index.
ISBN 0-19-513362-5
1. Holocaust, Jewish (1939–1945)—Social aspects.   2. Holocaust, Jewish
(1939–1945)—Psychological aspects.   3. Holocaust, Jewish (1939–1945)—Influence.
4. Social sciences—Philosophy.   I. Newman, Leonard S., 1961– .   II. Erber, Ralph.
D804.3 .S597 2002
940.53'18—dc21   2001052394

Block quotation on pages 101–102 is reproduced from *Lieutenant Birnbaum: A Soldier's Story*, by
Meyer Birnbaum with Yonason Rosenblum, with permission from the copyright holders Artscroll/
Mesorah Publication, Ltd.

9 8 7 6 5 4 3 2 1

Printed in the United States of America
on acid-free paper

To our families

Preface

The idea for this book evolved over the course of two meetings (1997 and 1998) of the Social Psychologists of Chicago (SPOC). At those meetings, we individually presented papers that were later expanded into our chapters in this book. Besides discovering a common interest in the central themes of this volume, we also found that we shared a concern that social psychologists were not making their voices heard in public debates about genocide and the Holocaust. At the time, there was much public and academic discussion of two monographs that are cited quite a bit in this book: Christopher Browning's *Ordinary Men* and Daniel Goldhagen's *Hitler's Willing Executioners*. The discussion centered around what caused Holocaust perpetrators to act as they did, with special attention devoted to how perpetrators construed their own behavior and the extent to which they had been affected by powerful situational forces. What was being discussed, in other words, was the social psychology of the Holocaust. Unfortunately, when any social-psychological research was cited, it tended to be quite dated. And much to our distress, few actual social psychologists seemed to be entering into the public discourse.

We resolved to do something about that state of affairs and set out to see whether contemporary work being done by social psychologists could speak to the issues that were being (and continue to be) so passionately debated by students of the Holocaust. We were not disappointed. The first concrete result of our efforts was a symposium at the annual meeting of the Society of Experimental Social Psychology, in Lexington, Kentucky, in October 1998 ("Social-Psychological Perspectives on Genocide: Understanding Perpetrator Behavior"). Two other contributors to this volume (Irv Staub and Bob Zajonc) also participated in that symposium, along with John Darley. The next result of our efforts is the book you are holding in your hands. Needless to say, it will not answer all your questions about why one group of people would resolve to exterminate their neighbors. But we do believe that when you finish reading the chapters in this volume, you will have gained a deeper understanding of the personal, social, and cultural factors that can interact in such a way as to trigger the horrors of genocide.

Preface

This book went into production less than a month after the tragic events of September 11, 2001. Before the dust of the former World Trade Center settled, many instant analysts offered "explanations" for the attacks. Jerry Falwell blamed homosexuals and the American Civil Liberties Union; Noam Chomsky attributed them to revenge for the U.S. 1998 missile strike on Khartoum; and Norman Finkelstein cited American support for Israel as the cause. These explanations do little to help us understand the complex nature of what motivated the actual perpetrators to go through with their mission, but preventing future atrocities of this kind will in part depend on developing an understanding of the psychological factors involved in the planning and execution of such massacres. Of course, it is not clear that the September 11 attacks can be categorized as "genocide"; nonetheless, many of the processes described by the contributors to this volume could apply to mass killers of any sort.

We would like to thank the people at Oxford University Press for their interest in this project, especially our editors, Phillip Laughlin (who helped us get started) and Catharine Carlin (who saw it to completion). During our work on this book, Len Newman's research program was supported by grants from the National Science Foundation (SBR-9809188) and the National Institutes of Mental Health (R01 MH58876). Finally, we would also like to thank our many colleagues who over the last few years have inspired and motivated us with their interest in and enthusiasm for our plans for this book. Those colleagues include Peg Birmingham, John Darley, Bella DePaulo, Maureen Wang Erber, Susan Fiske, Paul Jaskot, Nancy Lipsitt, John Pryor, Glenn Reeder, Steve Scher, Clive Seligman, Linda Skitka, Chuck Suchar, Midge Wilson, and Phil Zimbardo.

Contents

Contents

Contributors

ROY F. BAUMEISTER, Case Western Reserve University
THOMAS BLASS, University of Maryland, Baltimore County
CHRISTOPHER R. BROWNING, University of North Carolina at
    Chapel Hill
AMY M. BUDDIE, State University of New York at Buffalo
RALPH ERBER, DePaul University
DIETER FREY, Universitaet Muenchen
PETER GLICK, Lawrence University
JEFFREY KRETSCHMAR, Miami University of Ohio
ARMAND LAUFFER, University of Michigan
DAVID MANDEL, University of Victoria
ARTHUR G. MILLER, Miami University of Ohio
CATHERINE MUNIER, Loyola University Chicago
LEONARD S. NEWMAN, University of Illinois at Chicago
DAPHNA OYSERMAN, University of Michigan
HELMUT REZ, Universitaet Muenchen
MARK SCHALLER, University of British Columbia
CHRISTINE M. SMITH. Grand Valley State University
ERVIN STAUB, University of Massachusetts, Amherst
PETER SUEDFELD, University of British Columbia
R. SCOTT TINDALE, Loyola University Chicago
MICHELLE WASSERMAN, Loyola University Chicago
ROBERT ZAJONC, Stanford University

Understanding
Genocide

Introduction

Christopher R. Browning

In the first decade after the Holocaust, attempts at understanding the perpetrators focused for the most part on the questions of individual psychological makeup, on the one hand, and a specifically German iniquity, on the other. The Nuremberg trials provided a closer look at both the prominent Nazi leaders and the top-echelon functionaries, such as the *Einsatzgruppen* leaders, "euthanasia" doctors, incriminated generals, and ministerial state secretaries, who had survived the war and been captured.[1] The work of Adorno and others focused on the cluster of individual traits—conceived of as the "authoritarian personality"—that would have predisposed others in German society to embrace the Nazi cause and commit mass murder on its behalf.[2] Others traced the fatal effect of Prussian/German traditions of militarism, authoritarianism, and anti-Semitism.[3]

In the early 1960s the search for understanding the Holocaust perpetrators turned from explanations focused on the psychological analysis of individual perpetrators and the exceptionalism of German history to the social-psychological analysis of group behavior. The impetus for this change derived, in my opinion, from three major events. First, in 1961, Raul Hilberg published his monumental study, *The Destruction of the European Jews*, which portrayed the Nazi Final Solution as essentially an administrative and bureaucratic process. Hilberg argued that the perpetrators "were not different in their moral makeup from the rest of the population. The German perpetrator was not a special kind of German." Rather, the perpetrators represented "a remarkable cross-section of the German population," and the machinery of destruction "was structurally no different from organized German society as a whole."[4] Above all, Hilberg argued for an inherent structure of bureaucratic persecution that moved through the stages of identification, confiscation, concentration, and extermination, and that by implication had little to do with the

3

individual psychological traits, anti-Semitic convictions, or national character of the perpetrators.[5]

Second, in 1963, Hannah Arendt published *Eichmann in Jerusalem: A Report
on the Banality of Evil*. Influenced by Hilberg's book and the defense strategy
of Eichmann, Arendt portrayed him as a nonideological, petty bureaucrat duti-
fully carrying out the policies of the regime he served and too mindless even
to understand fully the criminality of those policies. Most historians would
now agree, I think, that Arendt had uncritically accepted Eichmann's misrep-
resentation of himself, and that he was in fact a Nazi activist, motivated by
both his ideological identification with the regime and his unquenchable
ambition.[6] But the fact that Eichmann was not the "banal bureaucrat" that
he pretended to be does not discredit the notion that so many of the Holocaust
perpetrators—the proverbial "desk murderers"—were exactly that. Arendt had
arrived at a powerful insight that the ability of a state to organize mass murder owes much to the accommodation and compliance of petty and dutiful
civil servants, even if she misunderstood her star example. The "banality of
evil" is a concept that survives her historical shortcomings.

Third, virtually simultaneous with the publications of Hilberg and Arendt,
Stanley Milgram conducted his famous "obedience to authority" experiments
and disseminated his initial conclusions. Milgram's experiments have been
both praised and criticized by many, and they are discussed again, of course,
in many of the contributions to this book. Concerning their impact on the
search for understanding the Holocaust perpetrators in the 1960s, however,
two factors must be mentioned here. In the face of the constant claims made
by perpetrators on trial that they had been forced to obey orders, Milgram's
experiments reconceptualized a crucial issue by shifting the focus away from
coerced obedience to noncoerced, situationally induced deference to authority. (In this regard it should be noted that Milgram included the state's power
to legitimize and disseminate ideology as a factor that helped to define the
"situation.") And the fact that his subjects were both randomly selected and
non-German lent his conclusions undeniably universalistic implications.

In the 1970s and 1980s, the lonely, pioneering work of Raul Hilberg and a
few others was followed by a growing wave of historical scholarship. The bulk
of these works that were devoted to studying the perpetrators (as opposed to
those studying the victims and bystanders) focused on the decision and policy-
making processes, the structures and functioning of the Nazi regime, and the
plethora of institutions and professions beyond the notorious SS that had
played a crucial role in one way or another. While the centrality of anti-
Semitism to Hitler's psyche and ideology was not seriously questioned, increasingly this was seen as inadequate to explain the capacity of the dictator
to harness so many others to the enterprise of mass murder. The focus shifted
away from Hitler at the top and the actual killers at the bottom to the institutions, political processes, and bureaucratic personnel in between. Discussions

of motivation shifted from anti-Semitism to other contributing factors: power-struggle calculations, ambition and careerism, the segmenting and routinizing of participation that obviated a sense of individual responsibility, and a broader ideological framework of racism and eugenics that targeted a multitude of victims beyond the Jews.[7]

By the 1990s, the study of what had once been a shamefully neglected but central event in the twentieth century had reached such proportions that it was being disparaged by some with epithets such as "Shoa business" and "Holocaust industry."[8] Despite such criticisms, scholarly research has continued unabated. Several historiographical developments occurred that are highly relevant to the issue of understanding the perpetrators. First, there has been renewed attention to the crucial role of Nazi ideologues as transmitters and legitimizers of anti-Semitic policies, and of fanatically anti-Semitic SS men in key positions as vital personnel in the implementation of the mass murder.[9] Awareness of this corrective trend in scholarship has not been fully appreciated for several reasons. The cutting-edge scholarship in this regard has been published so far only in German but not yet in English.[10] Furthermore, this trend has been virtually eclipsed by the publicity and controversy surrounding the second historiographical trend in the study of perpetrators in the 1990s.

These more recent works focused on the men who actually committed the face-to-face killings. Two books, one by myself and another by Daniel Jonah Goldhagen, involved case studies of the same hitherto obscure but now notorious Nazi killing unit, namely, Reserve Police Battalion 101.[11] Some conclusions in our two accounts were a matter of consensus. The conscripted, middle-aged reserve police of this unit were randomly selected and neither well trained nor especially indoctrinated for their task; they could be characterized as both "ordinary" and representative. Those who found themselves in such units and nonetheless declined to kill were not forced to do so and did not suffer any significant repercussions, much less punishment, for their refusal. Conspicuous and all too numerous among those who did kill where those who did so with frightening eagerness. (In Goldhagen's account there is also a major emphasis on the gratuitous cruelty of the killers.)

On the other hand, a number of issues were contested. Did the eager and gratuitously cruel killers constitute a crucial minority or an overwhelming minority? Were those who sought to evade participation in the killing a minute and insignificant minority, or did they constitute between 10% and 20% of the unit? Were the killers solely motivated by a unique German "eliminationist" anti-Semitism culturally imprinted over centuries? Or were institutional, organizational, and situational factors indispensable to explaining rank-and-file behavior? Did the bulk of the killers come to their task already culturally programmed to kill Jews with "gusto," or did the environment of fighting a race war and imposing racial imperialism, on the one hand, and the task of killing itself, on the other, significantly transform most of these men over time?

Also at issue in the debate was the degree to which the insights and findings of social psychology better equip the scholar to resolve these questions. To help make sense of the materials I had gathered and the narrative I had constructed, I turned to the studies of Stanley Milgram on deference to authority and Philip Zimbardo on adaptation to role expectation and the intoxicating and corruptive effect on some of unfettered power over others. I also emphasized what struck me as the equally important factor of pressure for conformity to the group, especially in the circumstances of an isolated paramilitary unit in occupied enemy territory for which there were in effect no countervailing influences or support for nonconforming behavior outside the unit itself. Goldhagen deemed my use of social psychological concepts as both an academically dubious explanation of the perpetrators' behavior and a morally suspect exoneration of their "individual responsibility" and "choice."

I was resorting to the literature of social psychology now several decades old.[12] The book in hand has the merit of making readily accessible to both scholars and the reading public those recent developments in the discipline of social psychology that the various authors deem relevant to understanding not only the perpetrators but also other aspects of human behavior during the Holocaust. It is not my task to summarize the various contributions that follow, but I would at least briefly note some of the issues discussed that strike me as particularly relevant to recent debates. Some of the authors explore the continuing and dynamic interaction between cognition and attitude, on the one hand, and situation, on the other, and reject the notion that either can be seen as an "unmoved mover" of human behavior. Gratuitous cruelty is understood not only as a reflection of initial attitude (of hatred and contempt for the victim) but also as the product of an escalating process of harm-doing and devaluation of the victim, in which people are changed by what they do. Through the concept of "pluralistic ignorance," it is argued that the attitudes of individuals within a group cannot necessarily be inferred from collective behavior and conformity to a perceived group norm.

Finally, the strong tendency of many to see social psychological explanations as deterministic and individually exonerating is explored. However, no definitive answer is found for the dilemma of the scholar who finds the insights of social psychology crucial in attempting to explain human behavior in the Holocaust while rejecting the exonerating "spin" many readers will inevitably attribute to the resulting interpretations. But the Holocaust was a man-made event—the result of human beliefs and behavior. The contributions of social psychology that help us understand how human beliefs are formed and behavior shaped must not be ignored.

NOTES

1. G. M. Gilbert, *Nuremberg Diary* (New York: Farrar, Straus and Giroux, 1947).

2. T. W. Adorno, E. Frenkel-Brunswik, D. J. Levenson, and R. N. Sanford, *The Authoritarian Personality* (New York, Harper and Row, 1950).

3. This is reflected not only in popular works, such as the best-selling *Rise and Fall of the Third Reich* by William Shirer (New York: Simon and Schuster, 1960), but also in A. J. P. Taylor's *The Course of German History* (New York: Coward McCann, 1946).

4. Raul Hilberg, *The Destruction of the European Jews*, revised and expanded edition (New York: Holmes and Meier, 1985), pp. 1011, 994.

5. However, when asked on occasion if only Germans could have perpetrated the Holocaust, Hilberg seemed to resist the logic of his own argument and wishfully answered, "I hope so."

6. For the most recent and important scholarly study of Eichmann and his entourage, see Hans Safrian, *Die Eichmann Männer* (Vienna: Europaverlag, 1993). For a study of the staff of Eichmann's "Jewish desk" in the Gestapo in Berlin, see Yaacov Lozowick, *Hitlers Burokraten* (Zurich: Pendo, 2000).

7. For a summary of Holocaust scholarship as of the late 1980s, see Michael Marrus, *The Holocaust in History* (Hanover, NH: University Press of New England, 1987).

8. The two most recent critical works in this vein are Peter Novick, *The Holocaust in American Life* (Boston: Houghton Mifflin, 1999), and Norman Finkelstein, *The Holocaust Industry* (London: Verso, 2000). The former is a substantive though controversial study of the rise of "Holocaust consciousness" in American culture; the latter dismisses virtually all Holocaust scholarship as politically motivated and worthless.

9. A prime example of the former is Ulrich Herbert, *Best: Biographische Studien über Radikalismus, Weltanschauulng und Vernuft 1903–1989* (Bonn: Dietz Verlag, 1996). A prime example of the latter is Dieter Pohl, *Nationalsozialistische Judenverfolgung in Ostgalizien 1941–1944* (Munich: R. Oldenbourg Verlag, 1996). Pohl emphasizes both the broad consensus among all the German occupiers behind the mass murder of the Galician Jews and the key role played by a relatively small group of notorious police officials. Pohl is one among a number of young German scholars studying regional aspects of the Holocaust and emphasizing the importance of the initiatives of local German officials.

10. Two works will change this: Yehuda Bauer, *Reexamining the Holocaust* (New Haven: Yale University Press, 2001); and Michael Thad Allen's forthcoming study of the engineers and businessmen of the Economic and Administrative Main Office of the SS.

11. Christopher R. Browning, *Ordinary Men: Reserve Police Battalion 101 and the Final Solution in Poland* (New York: HarperCollins, 1992); Daniel Jonah Goldhagen, *Hitler's Willing Executioners: Ordinary Germans and the Holocaust* (New York: Knopf, 1996).

12. The primary exception was Erwin Staub, *The Roots of Evil: The Origins of Genocide and Other Group Violence* (Cambridge: Cambridge University Press, 1989), published just as I began writing my book. Unfortunately, I did not avail myself of Herbert C. Kelman and V. Lee Hamilton, *Crimes of Obedience: Toward a Social Psychology of Authority and Responsibility* (New Haven, CT: Yale University Press, 1989) until later.

Part I

BECOMING A PERPETRATOR

1

The Psychology of Bystanders, Perpetrators, and Heroic Helpers

Ervin Staub

What leads groups of people or governments to perpetrate genocide or mass killing? What are the characteristics and psychological processes of individuals and societies that contribute to such group violence? What is the nature of the evolution that leads to it: What are the motives, how do they arise and intensify, how do inhibitions decline?

A primary example in this article will be the Holocaust, the killing of between 5 and 6 million European Jews by Nazi Germany during World War II. Other examples will be the genocide of the Armenians in Turkey in 1915–1916, the "autogenocide" in Cambodia between 1975 and 1979, the genocide in Rwanda in 1994, and the disappearances and mass killing in Argentina, mainly between 1976 and 1979. Many of the same influences are also present both in the widespread uses of torture and in terrorist violence.

In the United Nations charter on genocide the term denotes the extermination of a racial, religious, or ethnic group. Although not included in the charter, and although some scholars call it politicide (Harff & Gurr, 1990), the destruction of a whole political group is also widely regarded as genocide (Kuper, 1981). In mass killing, the boundaries of the victim group are less well defined, and the elimination of a whole racial, religious, or ethnic group is not intended. For example, in Argentina the victims included Communists, people seen as left leaning, and liberals who wanted to help the poor or supported social change. Usually, although not always, mass killings have fewer victims. The Holocaust, the killings of the Armenians, and the killings in Rwanda were genocides; the killings in Cambodia were genocidal but with less well defined group boundaries, in that Khmer as well as members of minority groups were killed; the disappearances in Argentina were a mass killing. Genocides and mass killings have similar psychological and cultural origins.

This chapter will focus on the psychology and role of both perpetrators and bystanders. Bystanders to the ongoing, usually progressively increasing mistreatment of a group of people have great potential power to influence events. However, whether individuals, groups, or nations, they frequently remain passive. This allows perpetrators to see their destructive actions as acceptable and even right. As a result of their passivity in the face of others' suffering, bystanders change: They come to accept the persecution and suffering of victims, and some even join the perpetrators (Staub, 1989a, 1989b, 1999a, 2000).

All of us are bystanders to many events—neither actors nor victims but witnesses. We witness discrimination and the fate of the homeless. We have known about torture in many countries, the death squads in Guatemala and El Salvador, the use of chemical weapons by Iraq to kill its own Kurdish citizens while our government and many others supported Iraq, the imprisonment of dissidents in mental hospitals in the Soviet Union (Bloch & Reddaway, 1977, 1984), and the nuclear policies of the United States and the USSR. Examination of the role of bystanders in genocides and mass killings may enlighten us about our own role as bystanders to others' suffering, and to policies and practices that potentially lead to the destruction of human beings.

Another focus of this chapter is the psychology of those who attempt to save intended victims, endangering their own lives to do so. Bystanders, perpetrators, and heroic helpers face similar conditions and may be part of the same culture: What are the differences in their characteristics, psychological processes, and evolution?

BRIEF REVIEW

A conception is presented in this chapter of the origins of genocide and mass killing, with a focus on how a group of people turns against another group, how the motivation for killing evolves and inhibitions against it decline. The conception identifies characteristics of a group's culture that create an enhanced potential for a group turning against others. It focuses on difficult life conditions as the primary activator of basic needs, which demand fulfillment. Conflict between groups is another activator. The pattern of predisposing cultural characteristics intensifies the basic needs and inclines the group toward fulfilling them in ways that turn the group against others. As they begin to harm the victim group, the perpetrators learn by and change as a result of their own actions, in ways that make the increasing mistreatment of the victims possible and probable. The perpetrators come to see their actions as necessary and even right. Bystanders have potential influence to inhibit the evolution of increasing destructiveness. However, they usually remain passive and themselves change as a result of their passivity, becoming less concerned about the fate of the victims, some of them joining the perpetrators.

THE PSYCHOLOGY OF PERPETRATORS

Violence against a subgroup of society is the outcome of a societal process. It requires analysis at the level of both individuals and society. Analysis of the group processes of perpetrators, an intermediate level, is also important.

Instigators of Group Violence

Difficult Life Conditions and Basic Human Needs

Why does a government or a dominant group turn against a subgroup of society? Usually difficult life conditions, persistent life problems in a society, are an important starting point. They include economic problems such as extreme inflation, or depression and unemployment, political conflict and violence, war, a decline in the power, prestige, and importance of a nation, usually with attendant economic and political problems, and the chaos and social disorganization these often entail.

Severe, persistent difficulties of life frustrate powerful needs, basic human needs that demand fulfillment. Certain "predisposing" characteristics of the culture and social organization tend to further intensify these needs (Staub, 1989a, 1996, 1999b). These include needs for security, for a positive identity, for effectiveness and control over important events in one's life, for positive connections to other people, and for a meaningful understanding of the world or comprehension of reality. Psychological processes in individuals and social processes in groups can arise that turn the group against others as they offer destructive fulfillment of these needs.

Germany was faced with serious life problems after World War I. The war and defeat were followed by a revolution, a change in the political system, hyperinflation, the occupation of the Ruhr by the French, who were dissatisfied with the rate of reparation payments, severe economic depression, conflict between political extremes, political violence, social chaos, and disorganization. The intense conflict between political extremes and the collapse of traditional social mores were both manifestations and further causes of life problems (Craig, 1982; A. DeJong, 1978). Intense life problems also existed in Turkey, Cambodia, Rwanda, and Argentina (Staub, 1989a, 1999a). For example, in Argentina, severe inflation, political instability, and repression, followed by wide-scale political violence, preceded the policy of disappearances: the kidnapping and torture of tens of thousands of people and the killing of at least 9,000 but perhaps as many as 30,000 people (Nunca Mas, 1986).

The inability to protect oneself and one's family and the inability to control the circumstances of one's life greatly threaten security. They also deeply threaten identity or the psychological self—self-concept, values, beliefs, and ways of life—as well as the need for effectiveness and control. The need for

13

comprehension of reality (Epstein, 1980; Janoff-Bulman, 1985, 1992; Staub, 1989a), and a conception of the world, one's place in it, and how to live is frustrated as the social chaos and disorganization render the existing views of reality inadequate. The need for connection to other people and the group is frustrated at a time when people need it most, by the competition for resources and self-focus that difficult life conditions foster. Finally, people need hope in a better future. These psychological needs join material ones, such as the need for food and physical safety, and rival them in intensity and importance. Since the capacity to control or address life problems and to satisfy material needs is limited, the psychological needs become predominant in guiding action (Staub, 1989a, 1996, 1999b, in press).

The motivations just described can be satisfied by joining others in a shared effort to solve life problems. But constructive solutions to a breakdown in the functioning of society are difficult to find and take time to implement. Certain cultural-societal characteristics, present in most societies but to greatly varying extents, add to the likelihood that these needs will be fulfilled in ways that turn the group against another group—that create a predisposition for group violence.

In Germany a two-step process led to the genocide. The difficult life conditions gave rise to psychological and social processes, such as scapegoating and destructive ideologies, which are described later. Such processes do not directly lead to genocide. However, they turn one group against another. In Germany, they brought an ideological movement to power and led to the beginning of an evolution, or steps along the continuum of destruction, also described later. Life conditions improved, but guided by ideology, the social processes and acts of harm-doing they gave rise to continued to intensify. In the midst of another great social upheaval, created by Germany, namely, World War II, they led to genocide.

Group Conflict

Another instigator that frustrates basic needs and gives rise to psychological conditions in individuals and social processes in groups that may lead to genocide is conflict between groups. The conflict may revolve around essential interests, such as territory needed for living space. Even in this case, however, psychological elements tend to make the conflict intractable, such as attachment by groups to a particular territory, unhealed wounds in the group, or prior devaluation and mistrust of the other.

Or the conflict may be between superordinate or dominant groups and subordinate groups with limited rights and limited access to resources. Such conflicts deeply affect the needs for security and positive identity, as well as other basic needs. They have often been the originators of mass killing or genocide since World War II (Fein, 1993). When group conflict turns into war and the other predisposing conditions are present, mass killing or genocide becomes especially likely (Harff, Gurr, & Unger, 1999). In Rwanda, preceding the genocide by Hutus of Tutsis in 1994, there were both difficult life conditions and conflict between groups, a combination that is an especially intense instigator. Starting in 1990, there was also the beginning of a civil war (des Forges, 1999; Staub, 1999a).

Cultural-Societal Characteristics

Cultural Devaluation

The differentiation between in-group and out-group, us and them, tends by itself to give rise to a favoring of the in-group and relative devaluation of the out-group and discrimination against its members (Brewer, 1978; Tajfel, 1982; Tajfel, Flament, Billig, & Bundy, 1971). Devaluation of individuals and groups, whatever its source, makes it easier to harm them (Bandura, Underwood, & Fromson, 1975; Duster, 1971).

A history of devaluation of a group, negative stereotypes, and negative images perpetuated in the products of the culture, its literature, art, and media "preselects" this group as a potential scapegoat and enemy (Staub, 1989a). In Germany, there had been a long history of anti-Semitism, with periods of intense mistreatment of Jews (Dimont, 1962; Girard, 1980). In addition to early Christian theological anti-Semitism (Girard, 1980), the intense anti-Semitism of Luther (Hilberg, 1961; Luther, 1955–1975), who described Jews in language similar to that later used by Hitler, was an important influence. Centuries of discrimination and persecution further enhanced anti-Semitism and made it an aspect of German culture. Even though at the end of World War I German Jews were relatively assimilated, anti-Semitism in the *deep structure* of German culture provided a cultural blueprint, a constant potential, for renewed antagonism against them. In Turkey, deep-seated cultural devaluation of and discrimination against Armenians had existed for centuries. In Rwanda, there was intense hostility by Hutus toward Tutsis, as a result of prior dominance by Tutsis.

At times devaluation of the potential victims is the result of a newly emerging ideology that designates a group as the enemy. The ideology usually draws on existing differentiations and divisions in society. For example, in Cambodia, there had been a long-standing rift between the city, inhabited by those who ruled, the officialdom, the aristocracy, and the educated, and the country, with its peasant population (Chandler, 1983; Etcheson, 1984). The Khmer Rouge ideology drew on this division, defining all city dwellers as actual or potential enemies (Staub, 1989a).

This is a probabilistic conception, with different elements enhancing or diminishing the likelihood of one group turning against another. Not all probabilities become actualities. For example, intense anti-Semitism had existed at least in parts of Russia before the revolution of 1917. While it was perhaps not as embedded in the deep structure of the culture as in Germany, it did create the potential for Jews to become scapegoats or ideological enemies. Deep divisions had also existed between rulers and privileged members of society, on the one hand, and the peasants and workers, on the other. The ideology that guided the leaders of the revolution led them to focus on this latter division.

Respect for Authority

Overly strong respect for authority, with a predominant tendency to obey authority, is another important cultural characteristic. It leads people to turn to authorities, old or new, for guidance in difficult times (Fromm, 1965). It leads them to accept the authorities' definition of reality, their views of problems and solutions, and stops them from resisting authorities when they lead them to harm others. There is substantial evidence that Germans had strong respect for authority that was deeply rooted in their culture, as well as a tendency to obey those with even limited authority (Craig, 1982; Girard, 1980). German families and schools were authoritarian, with restrictive and punitive child-rearing practices (Miller, 1983; Devereux, 1972). Strong respect for authority has also characterized the other societies that engaged in genocide or mass killing, such as Turkey, Cambodia, and Rwanda, although in some cases it was especially strong in the subgroup of the society that became the perpetrator, as in Argentina, where the military was both the architect and the executor of the disappearances (Nunca Mas, 1986).

A Monolithic Culture

A monolithic society, in contrast to a pluralistic society, with a small range of predominant values and/or limitations on the free flow of ideas, adds to the predisposition for group violence. The negative representation of a victim group and the definition of reality by authorities that justifies or even necessitates the victims' mistreatment will be more broadly accepted. Democratic societies, which tend to be more pluralistic, are unlikely to engage in genocide (Rummel, 1994), especially if they are "mature" democracies, with well-developed civic institutions (Staub, 1999a).

German culture was monolithic: It stressed obedience, order, efficiency, and loyalty to the group (Craig, 1982; Staub, 1989a). As I noted earlier, the evolution of the Holocaust can be divided into two phases. The first one brought Hitler to power. During the second phase, Nazi rule, the totalitarian system further reduced the range of acceptable ideas and the freedom of their expression. In the other cases, the societies, and at times particularly the perpetrator groups in them, such as the military and paramilitary groups in Argentina, were also monolithic. In the frequent cases of genocide or mass killing when the political-ideological system was highly authoritarian and even totalitarian, monolithic tendencies were further intensified.

Cultural Self-Concepts

A belief in cultural superiority (that goes beyond the usual ethnocentrism), as well as a shaky group self-concept that requires self-defense, can also contribute to the tendency to turn against others. Frequently the two combine, a belief in the superiority of one's group with an underlying sense of vulnerability and weakness. Thus the cultural self-concept that predisposes to group violence can be complex but demonstrable through the products of the culture, its literature, its intellectual and artistic products, its media.

The Germans saw themselves as superior in character, competence, honor, loyalty, devotion to family, civic organization, and cultural achievements. Superiority has expressed itself in many ways, including proclamations by German intellectuals of German superiority and of their belief in Germany's right to rule other nations (Craig, 1982; Nathan & Norden, 1960; Staub, 1989a). Partly as a result of tremendous devastation in past wars (Craig, 1982; Mayer, 1955) and lack of unity and statehood until 1871, there was also a deep feeling of vulnerability and shaky self-esteem. Following unification and a brief period of strength, the loss of World War I and the intense life problems afterward were a great blow to cultural and societal self-concept.

The combination of a sense of superiority with weakness and vulnerability seems to have been present in Turkey, Cambodia, and Argentina as well. In Argentina, progressively deteriorating economic conditions and political violence deeply threatened a belief in the specialness and superiority of the nation, especially strongly held by the military, and an elevated view by the military of itself as protector of the nation (Crawley, 1984). In both Cambodia and Turkey, a past history of empire and national glory were deeply embedded in group consciousness (Staub, 1989a). The existing conditions sharply contrasted with the glory of the past. Difficult life conditions threaten the belief in superiority and activate the underlying feelings of weakness and vulnerability. They intensify the need to defend and/or elevate the self-concept, both individual and cultural.[1]

To a large extent, people define themselves by belonging to groups (Mack, 1983), which makes their social identity important (Tajfel, 1982; Turner, 1987). Group self-concepts become especially important in difficult times as the inability to deal with life problems threatens personal identity. Over time, the group's inability to help fulfill basic needs and societal disorganization also threaten group self-concept, people's vision, and the evaluation of their group.

Unhealed Wounds Due to Past Victimization

Another important cultural characteristic that contributes to a sense of vulnerability is a past history of victimization. Just like victimized individuals (Herman, 1992; McCann & Pearlman, 1990), groups of people who have been victimized in the past are intensely affected. Their sense of self is diminished.

They come to see the world and people in it, especially outsiders, individuals as well as whole groups, as dangerous. They feel vulnerable, needing to defend themselves, which can lead them to strike out violently. Healing by victimized groups is essential to reduce the likelihood that they become perpetrators (Staub, 1998, 1999a).

The limited evidence, as yet, indicates that the effects of group victimization are transmitted through the generations. This is suggested both by the study of individual survivors and their offspring, and group culture. For example, Craig (1982) has suggested that long-ago wars in which large percentages of the German population were killed led to the strongly authoritarian tendencies in Prussian and then German society. People in authority became especially important in providing protection against danger.

A History of Aggressiveness

A history of aggression as a way of dealing with conflict also contributes to the predisposition for group violence. It makes renewed aggression more acceptable, more normal. Such a tradition, which existed in Germany before World War I, was greatly strengthened by the war and the widespread political violence that followed it (Kren & Rappoport, 1980). It was intense in Turkey; it existed in Cambodia as well (Chandler, 1983), intensified by tremendous violence during the civil war between 1970 and 1975; it expressed itself in repeated mass killing of Tutsis in Rwanda (des Forges, 1999); and it existed in Argentina, intensified by the mutual violence between guerrilla groups, right-wing groups and the government preceding the disappearances (Staub, 1989a).

In Germany, an additional predisposing factor was the presence of war veterans. We now know about the existence and prolonged nature of posttraumatic stress disorder in Vietnam War veterans. The disorder was probably widespread among German veterans who had similar experiences—direct combat, a lost war, and lack of appreciation by society. Decline in self-esteem, loss of faith in the benevolence of the world and in legitimate authority, and a search for alternative authority are among the characteristics of this disorder in Vietnam veterans (Card, 1983; Egendorf, Kadushin, Laufer, Rothbart, & Sloan, 1981; Wilson, 1980; see also Herman, 1992). In Germany, they would have intensified needs created by the difficult life conditions and added to the guiding force of cultural predispositions. For example, they would have given special appeal to alternate authority and a movement directed against traditional authority.

Turning Against Others: Scapegoating and Ideology

Scapegoating and ideologies that arise in the face of difficult life conditions or group conflict are means for satisfying basic needs. However, they offer destructive satisfaction of basic needs in that they are likely to lead to harmful actions against others.

In the face of persistently difficult life conditions, already devalued out-groups are further devalued and scapegoated. Diminishing others is a way to elevate the self. Scapegoating protects a positive identity by reducing the feeling of responsibility for problems. By providing an explanation for problems, it offers the possibility of effective action or control—unfortunately, mainly in the form of taking action against the scapegoat. It can unite people against the scapegoated other, thereby fulfilling the need for positive connection and support in difficult times.

Adopting nationalistic and/or "better-world" ideologies offers a new com-prehension of reality and, by promising a better future, hope as well. But usually some group is identified as the enemy that stands in the way of the ideology's fulfillment. By joining an ideological movement, people can relin-quish a burdensome self to leaders or the group. They gain connection to others and a sense of significance in working for the ideology's fulfillment. Along the way, members of the "enemy" group, usually the group that is also scapegoated for life problems, are further devaluated and, in the end, often excluded from the moral realm. The moral values that protect people from violence become inoperative in relation to them (Staub, 1989a).

The ideology that the Nazis and Hitler offered the German people fit Ger-man culture. Its racial principle identified Aryans, and their supposedly best representatives, the Germans, as the superior race. The material needs of the German people were to be fulfilled (and their superiority affirmed) through the conquest of additional territories, or living space. The ideology identified Jews as responsible for life problems and as a primary barrier to the creation of a pure, superior race. Later Jews were also identified as the internal enemy that joined the external enemy, the Soviet Union, to destroy Germany (Dawidowicz, 1975; Hilberg, 1961; Kren & Rappoport, 1980). In the *Fuhrerprinzip,* the leadership principle, the ideology prescribed obedi-ence and offered the guidance of an absolute authority.

Ideology has been important in all the other instances of genocide as well. We may differentiate between "better-world" ideologies, which offer a vision of a better future for all human beings, and nationalistic ideologies, which promise a better life for a nation (Staub, 1989a). Although the German ideol-ogy was nationalistic, it had better-world components, in that racial purity was supposed to improve all humanity—except, of course, the impure, who were to be destroyed or subjugated.

In Turkey, the genocide of the Armenians was guided by a nationalistic ideology: pan-Turkism. Part of this was a vision of a new Turkish empire. In Cambodia, the genocide was guided by a Communist better-world ideology but with intense nationalistic components. To create a world of total social equality, all those privileged by their position, wealth, or education had to be eliminated or totally subjugated. In Rwanda, "Hutu power," the total elevation of Hutus over Tutsis, was a form of ideology (des Forges, 1999; Staub, 1999a). In Argentina, the mass killings partly evolved out of a conflict of interest between more and less privileged groups. However, the perpetrators of the mass killing were also protecting their worldview and subscribed to an intense anti-Communist ideology and visions of a Christian society (Staub, 1989a).

SELF-SELECTION AND THE SELECTION OF PERPETRATORS

Those who supported Hitler at the start, by voting for him, were quite heterogeneous with regard to class and occupation (Abraham, 1987; Platt, 1980). Initially, those who were perpetrators of violence were SA and SS members, and over time, increasingly SS members. They were joined by others as the evolution of violence progressed. A by now well-known example of this is the German auxiliary police, who were sent to kill Jews before the machinery of killing in the concentration and extermination camps was established (see Browning, 1992; Goldhagen, 1996). Some people in areas occupied by the Germans, like the Ukraine, Lithuania, and Latvia, also joined in the killing (Goldhagen, 1996), probably motivated by a combination of factors, including hostility toward the Soviet Union, of which they were part, which led them to join its enemy, the Germans; deep-seated anti-Semitism; and subservience to the occupiers and conquerors and the desire to gain their favor.

Members of the SS, who were central in the killing process, had strong authority orientation, along with a preference, and perhaps need, for a hierarchical system (Dicks, 1972; Steiner, 1980) that was even stronger than the general German orientation to authority. This may have been partly the result of self-selection (Staub, 1989a), partly of special training in obedience (Kren & Rappoport, 1980), partly of learning by doing (see later discussion). Other characteristics of SS members were belief in Nazi ideology and a preference for military-type activities (Steiner, 1980). The early SS joined Hitler to serve as his bodyguards at political meetings. Fighting political opponents was their first major task. Those who joined had to accept, if not welcome, violence.

The importance of ideology was also evident in the selection of ideologically devoted Nazi doctors for the euthanasia program, where they were the direct perpetrators of murder, and for the extermination camps, where they directed the killing process (Lifton, 1986). Given a cultural devaluation, the people who are attracted to an ideology that elevates them over others and promises them a better world need not be *personally* prejudiced against a devalued group that is designated as the enemy. They might have greater needs aroused in them by life problems or might carry more of the cultural predispositions that shape motivation and guide modes of dealing with them. However, in research concluded in 1933 on SS members, although not all respondents reported personal anti-Semitism, most of them were openly and viciously anti-Semitic (Merkl, 1980). The SS members who expressed the most intense anti-Semitism tended to be in leadership positions (Merkl, 1980).

The Role of Obedience

Since the dramatic experiments of Stanley Milgram (1965, 1974), obedience to authority has been viewed as a crucial determinant of the behavior of perpetrators. The importance of obedience is also suggested by the training that direct perpetrators receive in fostering submission to authority, whether the SS (Kren & Rappoport, 1980) or torturers in Greece (Gibson & Haritos-Fatouros, 1986; Haritos-Fatouros, 1988). It is suggested by the self-selection for the SS of individuals oriented to obedience (Dicks, 1972; Steiner, 1980) and the greater obedience in the Milgram experiments (Elms & Milgram, 1966) of high scorers on the F Scale, a measure of the "authoritarian personality." In Greece, the authorities selected especially obedient—as well as ideologically sympathetic—military police recruits for training as torturers (Gibson & Haritos-Fatouros, 1986; Haritos-Fatouros, 1988).

However, many of the direct perpetrators are usually not simply forced or pressured by authorities to obey. Instead, they *join* leaders and decision makers, or a movement that shapes and guides them to become perpetrators. Decision makers and direct perpetrators share a *cultural-societal tilt*. They are part of the same culture and experience the same life problems; they probably respond with similar needs and share the inclination for the same potentially destructive modes of their fulfillment. Many who become direct perpetrators voluntarily join the movement and enter roles that in the end lead them to perpetrate mass killing.

The Role of Leaders

Leaders who propagate scapegoating and destructive ideologies are often seen as acting to gain followers or consolidate their following. Even Gordon Allport (1954) suggested that this was the case with Hitler. However, leaders are members of their group, affected by the instigators that affect the rest of the group and by cultural characteristics that predispose the group to violence. For example, in previously victimized groups the leaders, like the rest of the population, tend to carry unhealed wounds. It is this joining of the needs and inclination of populations and leaders that creates great danger of mass killing or genocide.

While groups often turn to leaders with the potential to generate violence in difficult times, and while leading the group toward constructive resolution of life problems and group conflicts can be difficult and dangerous, except under the most extreme conditions leaders still have the potential to try to do so. Instead, unfortunately, leaders and elites often propagate scapegoating and destructive ideologies, use propaganda against devalued groups and "enemies," and create paramilitary groups or other institutions that become instruments of violence (Staub, 1999b).

LEARNING BY DOING, EVOLUTION, AND STEPS ALONG THE CONTINUUM OF DESTRUCTION

Mass killing or genocide is usually the outcome of an evolution that starts with discrimination and limited acts of harm-doing. Harming people changes the perpetrators (and the whole society) and prepares them for more harmful acts.

In a number of studies with children, my associates and I found that involving children in efforts to help other children—for example, having them spend time making toys for poor, hospitalized children or teaching younger children—increased their later helping behavior (Staub, 1975, 1979, 1986). Prior helping (Harris, 1972) and even the expressed intention to help (W. DeJong, 1979; Freedman & Fraser, 1966) also increase adults' later helping. Similarly, harming others increases the degree of harm people subsequently inflict on others. When "teachers" shock "learners" who make mistakes on a task, teachers who set their own shock levels increase the intensity of shock over trials (Buss, 1966; Goldstein, Davis, & Herman, 1975). This is the case even with control for the learner's error rate (Goldstein et al., 1975).

People learn and change as a result of their own actions (Staub, 1979, 1989a). When they harm other people, a number of consequences are likely to follow. First, they come to devalue the victims more (Berkowitz, 1962; Goldstein et al., 1975; Sykes & Matza, 1957; Staub, 1978). While in the real world devaluation normally precedes harm-doing, additional devaluation makes greater mistreatment and violence possible. Just-world thinking (Lerner, 1980; Lerner & Simmons, 1966) may be an important mechanism in this. Assuming that the world is just, and that people who suffer must have brought their fate on themselves by their actions or character, ironically, perpetrators are likely to devalue people they themselves have harmed. The self-perception of perpetrators is also likely to change (Bem, 1972; Grusec, Kuczynski, Rushton, & Simutis, 1978; Staub, 1979). They come to see themselves as able and willing to engage in harmful, violent acts—against certain people, and for good reasons, including higher ideals embodied in an ideology.

Personal goal theory (Staub, 1980) suggests moral equilibration (Staub, 1989a) as another mechanism of change. When a conflict exists between moral value(s) and other motives, people can reduce the conflict by replacing the moral value with another value that either is less stringent or is not a moral value but is treated like one. Eisenberg (1986) reported research findings that support such a process: Cost and other conditions led both children and adults to shift to less evolved moral reasoning. The Nazis replaced respect for the lives of certain people with the values of racial purity, and obedience and loyalty to leaders.

Consistent with this model, in Nazi Germany there was a progression of "steps along a continuum of destruction." First, Jews were thrown out of government jobs and the military, then from other important positions. They were pressured into selling their businesses and later were forced to sell. Marriage and sexual relations between Jews and Aryan Germans were prohibited. Having lost all their property, earning their livelihood with menial jobs, and identified by yellow stars, the Jews were moved into ghettos. In addition to sporadic violence against them, there was organized violence (e.g., the Kristallnacht, in 1938). Many Jews were taken to concentration camps (Dawidowicz, 1975; Hilberg, 1961) before mass extermination.

Steps along a continuum of destruction often start long before those who lead a society to genocide come to power. In Turkey, the legal rights of Armenians and other minorities were limited for centuries. Armenians were the frequent victims of violence. From 1894 to 1896, over 200,000 Armenians were killed by special troops created mainly for this purpose (Greene, 1895; Toynbee, 1915). In Rwanda, about 50,000 Tutsis were killed in 1959, with massacres of large numbers of Tutsis in the early 1960s and 1970s and sporadic killings of smaller numbers after that (des Forges, 1999; Prunier, 1995).

Harm-doing and violence normally expand. Even when torture was part of the legal process in Europe, in the Middle Ages, over time the circle of its victims enlarged. First it was used only with lower-class defendants, later also with upper-class defendants, and then even with *witnesses,* in order to obtain information from them (Peters, 1985). In Germany, in addition to the increasing mistreatment of Jews, other forms of violence, such as the euthanasia program and the killing of mentally retarded, mentally ill, and physically deformed Germans (Davidowicz, 1975; Lifton, 1986)—who in the Nazis' view diminished the genetic quality of the German race—contributed to psychological and institutional change and the possibility of greater violence. In Rwanda, in addition to Tutsis, Hutus who were seen as politically moderate or as not supportive of the leadership were also targeted (des Forges, 1999). In the course of the genocide, some Hutus were killed for personal reasons, and in addition to Tutsi women, some Hutu women were also raped.

In both Argentina and Cambodia, the form of the evolution was not simply increasing violence against the victim group but a cycle of increasing violence between opposing parties. In Cambodia, the Khmer Rouge and government forces fought each other with increasing brutality from 1970 to 1975. In Argentina, left-wing guerrilla groups abducted and killed people, blew up buildings, and created chaos, while right-wing death squads were killing people identified as left-wing enemies. In both cases one of these parties became the perpetrator of extreme violence. The circle of victims was tremendously enlarged beyond those who participated in the initial cycle of violence.

In the course of this evolution, the perpetrators exclude the victims from the moral universe. Moral principles become inapplicable to them (Staub,

1989a). The prohibitions that normally inhibit violence lose force. The killing of the victims can become a goal in its own right. Fanatic commitment develops to the ideology and to the specific goal of eliminating the victims. Even goals basic to persons and groups, like self-protection, come to be subordinated to this "higher" goal (Staub, 1989b; von Maltitz, 1973), which becomes the dominant guide to action. There is a reverse of morality, so that killing becomes the right thing to do. The example of terrorist groups shows that even life itself can be subordinated when overriding fanatic commitment has developed to a murderous cause.

Group processes come to dominate the psychology of perpetrators. Embedded in a group, trained in submission to authority, and further indoctrinated in ideology, people give up individual decision making to the group and its leaders (Milgram, 1974; Zimbardo, 1969). The "We" acquires substantial power, in place of the "I." With the boundaries of the self weakened, there will be emotional contagion, the spread of feelings among group members (Milgram & Toch, 1969; Staub, 1987; Staub & Rosenthal, 1994), and shared reactions to events. The members' perception of reality will be shaped by their shared belief system and by the support they receive from each other in interpreting events. Deviation from the group becomes increasingly unlikely (Staub, 1989a; Toch, 1965).

As a whole society moves along the continuum of destruction, there is a *resocialization* in beliefs, values, and standards of conduct. New institutions emerge that serve repression, discrimination, and the mistreatment of identified victims. They represent new realities, a new status quo. Paramilitary groups develop into institutions of murder (des Forges, 1999). For example, in Guatemala a civilian group was created, "who killed and abducted on the orders of G-2," the intelligence division of the Guatemalan army. This group acquired a life of its own and also began to initiate killings (Nairn & Simon, 1986).

THE PSYCHOLOGY OF BYSTANDERS

In the face of the increasing suffering of a subgroup of society, bystanders frequently remain silent, passive—both *internal* bystanders and *external* ones, other nations and outside groups (Staub, 1989a, 1999a). Bystanders also learn and change as a result of their own action—or inaction. Passivity in the face of others' suffering makes it difficult to remain in internal opposition to the perpetrators and to feel empathy for the victims. To reduce their own feelings of empathic distress and guilt, passive bystanders will distance themselves from victims (Staub, 1978). Just-world thinking will lead them to see victims as deserving their fate, and to devalue them. While in Cambodia the population was completely brutalized, in Turkey and Germany, and initially in Argentina, the majority accepted, if not supported, the perpetrators' actions. In Rwanda, a small but significant percentage of the population participated in killings.

Most Germans participated in the system, in small ways such as using the Hitler salute (Bettelheim, 1979) and through organizations and group activities. Moreover, as bystanders, most Germans were not just passive: They were *semiactive participants*. They boycotted Jewish stores and broke intimate relationships and friendships with Jews. Many benefited in some way from the Jews' fate, by assuming their jobs and buying their businesses. Repeatedly the population initiated anti-Jewish actions before government orders, such as businesses' firing Jewish employees or not giving them paid vacations (Hilberg, 1961).

The German population shared a societal tilt with perpetrators—the cultural background and difficult life conditions, and the resulting needs and the inclination to satisfy them in certain ways. This might have made the Nazi movement acceptable to many who did not actually join. Moreover, after Hitler came to power, the lives of most Germans substantially improved (Craig, 1982): They had jobs and they were part of a community in which there was a spirit of togetherness and shared destiny.[2]

Their passivity, semiactive participation, and connections to the system had to change the German people, in ways similar to the changes in perpetrators. Consistency theories, and specifically balance theory (Heider, 1958), suggest that given Hitler's hatred for the Jews, the Germans' gratitude to and admiration of Hitler (Craig, 1982) would have intensified their anti-Jewish attitudes. The majority apparently came to accept and even support the persecution of Jews (Staub, 1989a). Others became perpetrators themselves.

The Berlin Psychoanalytic Institute

Some members of the Berlin Psychoanalytic Institute provide an example of bystanders who became perpetrators (Staub, 1989b). Many members left Germany. Those who remained presumably had at least tolerance for the Nazi system from the start. Over time, they changed. They accepted a new name, the Goering Institute, and a new head, the cousin of the second-ranking Nazi, Herman Goering. They were silent when Jewish colleagues were removed (and used ideologically based euphemisms to refer to them—e.g., not pure Germans). Some of the members advanced ideas or reinterpreted psychoanalytic concepts to support the Nazi ideology (Friedrich, 1989). Ideas, such as the theory of sluggish schizophrenia used in the Soviet Union to place dissidents in mental hospitals (Bloch & Reddaway, 1977), can be important steps along the psychological continuum of destruction. In Germany, the evolution of ideas about eugenics before Hitler came to power formed a basis of the euthanasia program (Lifton, 1986) and probably contributed to the Nazi ideology itself. In the end some institute members participated in the euthanasia program, and some became perpetrators in the extermination of Jews (Lifton, 1986; Staub, 1989a).

In the other instances as well, bystanders were either passive or supportive of perpetrators. In Argentina, the violence by guerrilla groups created fear in the population. When the military took over the government, a recurrent event in Argentina during the post–World War II years, the population initially supported the kidnappings the military began. Discomfort and protests, limited by the fear that the military generated, began only much later, as it became apparent that anybody could become a victim. In Turkey, much of the population either accepted or supported the persecution of Armenians (Staub, 1989a). In Cambodia, once the Khmer Rouge won the civil war and the killings and the use of people in slave labor began, most people were part of either the perpetrator or the victim group.

Other Nations as Bystanders

Fear contributed to the passivity of internal bystanders, in Germany and elsewhere. External bystanders, other nations and organizations outside Germany, had little to fear, especially at the start of Jewish persecution, when Germany was weak. Still, there was little response (Wyman, 1984). In 1936, after many Nazi atrocities, the whole world went to Berlin to participate in the Olympics, thereby affirming Nazi Germany. American corporations were busy doing business in Germany during most of the 1930s.

Christian dogma was a source of anti-Semitism in the whole Western world. It designated Jews as the killers of Christ and fanned their persecution for many centuries in response to their unwillingness to convert (Girard, 1980; Hilberg, 1961). It was a source of discrimination and mistreatment, which led to murder and further devaluation. In the end, profound religious-cultural devaluation of Jews characterized many Christian nations.

In addition, people outside Germany were also likely to engage in just-world thinking and to further devalue Jews in response to their suffering in Germany. The German propaganda against Jews also reached the outside world. Moscovici's (1973, 1980) research suggests that even seemingly unreasonably extreme statements about attitude objects have influence, if initially not on behavior, then at least on underlying attitudes. As a consequence of these processes, anti-Semitism increased in the Western world in the 1930s, in the United States reaching a peak around 1938 (Wyman, 1968, 1984).

These were some of the reasons for the silence and passivity. Among other reasons for nations to remain passive in face of the mistreatment by a government of its citizens are their unwillingness to interfere in the "domestic affairs" of another country (which could be a precedent for others interfering in their internal affairs) and the economic (trade) and other benefits they can gain from positive relations with the offending nation (Staub, 1999a).

At the time of the genocide of the Armenians, Turkey was fighting in World War I. Nations already fighting against Turkey in the war, perhaps not surprisingly, did speak out against the atrocities. As Turkey's ally, Germany might have been able to exert influence on Turkish policy, but it did not try to do so (Trumpener, 1968). At the time of the disappearances in Argentina, most nations of the world were silent. The Carter administration did speak out against the policy and helped some people in danger, but it took no serious action, such as a boycott, against the Argentine government.

Rwanda presents a recent, disturbing example of international passivity. The civil war began in 1990, with the Rwandan Patriotic Front, a small group of Tutsis who were refugees from prior violence against Tutsis or their descendants, entering the country as a military force. The French immediately began to provide military aid to the government. France continued its aid in subsequent years without protesting the occasional killings of hundreds of Tutsi peasants. Before the genocide began in April 1994, there were warnings of impending violence by human rights organizations. The commander of United Nations peacekeepers received confidential information that a genocide was being planned and asked his superiors permission to destroy arms that were being assembled. He was instructed to do nothing. After the genocide began, most of the UN peacekeepers were withdrawn. The United States and other nations went to extreme lengths to avoid the use of the term *genocide*, while about 700,000 Tutsis were killed over a period of 3 months, between two thirds and three fourths of the total Tutsi population. Apparently the purpose in not using the word *genocide* was to avoid invoking the UN Genocide Convention and thereby the moral obligation to respond (des Forges, 1999; Gourevitch, 1998).

Silence and passivity change bystanders, whether they are individuals or whole nations. They can diminish the subsequent likelihood of protest and punitive action by them. In turn, they encourage perpetrators, who often interpret silence as support for their policies (Staub, 1989a; Taylor, 1983). Complicity by bystanders is likely to encourage perpetrators even more.

THE POWER OF BYSTANDERS

Could bystanders make a difference in halting or preventing mass killing and genocide? Some lines of research and the evidence of real events indicate bystanders' potential to exert influence.

Whether or not one person verbally defines the meaning of a seeming emergency as an emergency greatly affects the response of other bystanders (Bickman, 1972; Staub, 1974). When bystanders remain passive, they substantially reduce the likelihood that other bystanders will respond (Latane & Darley, 1970; Staub, 1978).

Real-life events also show the influence of bystanders, even on perpetrators. In Denmark, the climate of support for Jews apparently influenced some German officials. They delayed deportation orders, which gave the Danish population the time needed to mount and complete a massive rescue effort, taking the approximately 7,000 Danish Jews to neutral Sweden in small boats. In Bulgaria, the actions of varied segments of the population, including demonstrations, stopped the government from handing over the country's Jewish population to the Germans (Fein, 1979). Even within Germany, in spite of the Nazi repression, the population could exert influence. When the euthanasia program became known, some segments of the population protested: the Catholic clergy, some lawyers' groups, the relatives of people killed, and those in danger. As a result, the official program of euthanasia killing was discontinued (Dawidowicz, 1975; Lifton, 1986). There was little response, however, to the mistreatment of Jews. Added to anti-Semitism and other cultural preconditions, the *gradual* increase in mistreatment would have contributed to passivity.

Hitler's attitude also indicates the potential power of bystanders. He and his fellow Nazis were greatly concerned about the reactions of the population to their early anti-Jewish actions, and they were both surprised and emboldened by the lack of adverse reactions (Dawidowicz, 1975; Hilberg, 1961). As I have noted, the population even initiated actions against Jews, which further shaped Nazi views (Staub, 1989a) and stimulated additional official "measures" (Hilberg, 1961).

In the French Huguenot village of La Chambon, under the leadership of their pastor, André Troucme, the inhabitants saved several thousand refugees, a large percentage of them children (Hallie, 1979). The behavior of the villagers influenced members of the Vichy police. Telephone calls to the presbytery began to inform villagers of impending raids, which enabled them to send the refugees into the neighboring forest. The deeds of the village doctor, who was executed, and his words at his trial influenced a German major, who in turn persuaded a higher officer not to move against the village (Hallie, 1979).

There is also evidence that the practice of torture diminishes in response to negative publicity and reactions by "external bystanders." This was demonstrably the case in South American countries (Stover & Nightingale, 1985). But frequently there is resistance to taking action not only within nations but also in smaller institutions. The practice of putting dissidents into mental hospitals had continued for a long time in the former Soviet Union. A detailed case history showed the resistance of the International Medical Association to condemn this practice (Bloch and Reddaway, 1984). Often organizations, while they may encourage their members to act, do not want to act as institutions, even when their weight and influence are needed. Lack of punitive action or even of condemnation by important bystanders, or support by some, may negate the efforts of others and encourage and affirm perpetrators.

In Iran, after the fundamentalist revolution, the persecution of the Baha'i, a long-persecuted community, has intensified. Over 200 Baha'i were executed in a short period of time. Representations by Baha'i living in other countries to their own governments and to the international community led to UN resolutions, as well as resolutions by individual nations condemning the persecution of the Baha'i in Iran. This led to a cessation of further executions (Bigelow, 1993), although they resumed on a much smaller scale in the 1990s. The international boycott of South Africa apparently also had important influence, which contributed to the abolition of apartheid and the change in government.

By speaking out and taking action, bystanders can elevate values prohibiting violence, which over time perpetrators had come to ignore in their treatment of the victim group. Most groups, but especially ideologically committed ones, have difficulty seeing themselves, having a perspective on their own actions and evolution (Staub, 1989a). They need others as mirrors. Through sanctions bystanders can also make the perpetrators' actions costly to them and induce fear of later punitive action. The earlier bystanders speak out and act, the more likely that they can counteract prior steps along the continuum of destruction or inhibit further evolution (see Staub, 1989a; 1999a). Once commitment to the destruction of a group has developed, and the destruction is in process, nonforceful reactions by bystanders will tend to be ineffective.

THE RANGE OF APPLICABILITY OF THIS CONCEPTION

The conception presented in this chapter can be applied, with modifications, to many forms of mistreatment by groups of members of other groups. It can be used in a tight, even predictive, manner, or as a framework theory that offers understanding. To use it in prediction (and therefore hopefully in prevention), the degree to which the components are present in a specific instance—the level of difficult life conditions and of relevant cultural characteristics, the point at which the group is located on a continuum of destruction, and the activities of bystanders—must be carefully assessed (Staub, 1992c, 1999a). The theory needs to be appropriately modified as it is applied to varied forms of group hostility, in varied contexts. The history of a group, relationships between groups, and the form and nature of any group conflicts must be assessed, and the influences specified here examined in relation to the specific and particular context.

In certain cases difficult life conditions may increase the likelihood of a group turning against others, but they are not central starting points. Even group conflict, where each side wants something from the other, may not be important. The motivation for violence may not originate in the frustration of basic needs described earlier. This is primarily the case when genocide or mass killing develops out of self-interest, as in the destruction of the Ache Indians in Paraguay in the service of the economic development of the forests that were their home. In cases of mass killing or genocide of indigenous peoples (Hitchcock & Twedt, 1997), self-interest is often a central motive.

29

However, difficult life conditions and a history of conflict between groups still make such violence more likely. Intense devaluation of the victim group, which is often present in extreme forms, and other cultural characteristics are central contributors.

In certain cases of group conflict, including what has recently been called *ethnopolitical violence*, "ideologies of antagonism" (Staub, 1989a, 1992a, 1999a) may be a cultural condition that easily gives rise to the motivation for violence. This refers to the outcome of a long history of hostility and mutual violence. Such ideologies are worldviews in which another group is perceived as an implacable enemy, bent on one's destruction. The welfare of one's own group is best served by the other's demise. Economic or other gains by the antagonist group can be experienced as a threat to one's own group and/or group self-concept and can activate hostile motives. While a history of hostility and violence can create a realistic fear of the other, usually the extremely negative view of the other is resistant to changes in reality. The group's identity or self-definition has come to include enmity toward the other. Ideologies of antagonism seemed to have roles in the start or maintenance of violence in the former Yugoslavia, between Israelis and Palestinians, and in Rwanda. They can have an important role even if only a segment of a population holds the ideology.

Difficult life conditions are also not primary initiators of hostility and war that are based on essential conflicts of interest. The beginning of the Palestinian-Israeli hostility is an example of this, with the two groups claiming the same territory as living space. While the conflict of interests has been real, certainly much more so than in a case like the Falklands War, negotiation resulting in compromise that fulfills the essential needs of both groups (Rouhana & Kelman, 1994) was slowed by psychological elements such as identification by both groups with a particular territory and perceptions or beliefs about the other that, among some part of the membership, probably amounted to ideologies of antagonism.

Using the theory presented here, for example, considering cultural characteristics other than devaluation by itself, which is a defining characteristic of racism, as well as instigating conditions, can help us better understand racism. It can help us understand other types of violence as well, for example, youth violence (Staub, 1996) and the unnecessary use of force by police against citizens (Staub, 1992, 2002). Police violence involves intense us-them differentiation and the devaluation of citizens by the police, an evolution of increasing violence with changes in norms and standards as part of the group's culture, and passive bystanders (which includes fellow officers and superiors). It is intensified by difficult life conditions (Staub, 1992, 2002).

Much of the theory is also applicable to terrorism. Terrorism is violence by small groups against noncombatants. It occurs in response to difficult life conditions and/or group conflict which frustrate basic needs, reduce opportunities and hope, create perceptions of injustice, and the experience of having been wronged. At times, great culture change and the inability of people to integrate tradition with new ways of life play a role. The impact of culture change is especially great on people living in societies that are both traditional and repressive.

Small terrorist groups are often less radical at the start. They may begin trying to bring about political and social changes working within the political system (McCauley & Segal, 1989). Over time, they become more radical, due to a combination of the difficulty in bringing about change and dynamics within the group, with members affirming their status and identity by advocating more extreme positions in the direction of already established ideology. The ideology, which is invariably present, becomes more radical, and the devaluation of and hostility toward the ideological enemy more intense. The violence, once it begins, intensifies.

When the theory requires some adjustment appropriate to types of violence and context, many elements of it are still usually present in generating group violence. These minimally include a history of devaluation of the other, the evolution of destructiveness (which has sometimes occurred over a long period preceding a flare-up of current antagonism), and the role of bystanders. Usually, some form of destructive ideology and then ideological justification for violence also exist. A further qualification of the theory in certain instances, such as deep-seated ethnic conflicts, would be that when groups have already progressed far along the continuum of destruction, it is more difficult for bystanders to exert influence.

OTHER VIEWS OF INTERGROUP CONFLICT

We do not have psychological theories of the origins of group violence to compare with this theory. There are, however, varied theories of intergroup relations and conflict. Realistic group conflict theory (LeVine & Campbell, 1972) emphasizes conflicts over scarce, tangible resources. Frustration-aggression-displacement theory (LeVine & Campbell, 1972) identifies frustration within the group as a source of scapegoating and hostility toward other groups. Psychocultural interpretation theory (Volkan, 1988) points to dispositions in groups that lead to threats to identity and fears of survival, which interfere with the resolution of ethnic conflict. Social identity theory (Tajfel, 1982; Turner, 1987) has stressed that individuals' identity is to a substantial degree a social identity, based on membership in a group. Social categorization, the classification of individuals into different categories, leads to stereotyping and discrimination. The desire for a favorable social comparison is an important motive that leads to elevation of one's group by diminishing and discriminating against others. This enhances group self-concept and individual self-esteem.

31

Aspects of these theories are congenial to the theory presented here, with realistic group conflict theory, which in its basic form assumes that conflict is purely over real, material resources, as well as power, without considering psychological elements, the least congenial. The present theory, which may be called *sociocultural motivation theory,* focuses on a multiplicity of interacting influences, with intense group violence as their outcome. These include cultural dispositions, life conditions, and group conflict. While life conditions and group conflict create frustration and the experience of threat, rather than conceptualizing the result as displacement, the theory identifies the basic human needs this gives rise to, as well as how they are satisfied.

While the social nature of individual identity is important, except when the role of prior devaluation or an ideology of antagonism is predominant, it is not social comparison but other motives that are regarded as central in leading a group to turn against others. The essential and unique aspects of the present theory include focus on change or evolution in individuals and groups, the potential of bystanders to influence this evolution, and the necessity to consider how a multiplicity of factors interact.

THE PSYCHOLOGY OF HEROIC HELPERS

In the midst of violence and passivity, some people in Germany and Nazi-occupied Europe endangered their lives to save Jews. To do so, helpers of German origin had to distance themselves from their group. Some rescuers were marginal to their community: They had a different religious background, were new to the community, or had a parent of foreign birth (London, 1970; Tec, 1986). This perhaps enabled them to maintain an independent perspective and not join the group's increasing devaluation of Jews. Many rescuers came from families with strong moral values and held strong moral and humanitarian values themselves, with an aversion to Nazism (London, 1970; Oliner & Oliner, 1988). Many were "inclusive" and regarded people in groups other than their own as human beings to whom human considerations apply (Oliner & Oliner, 1988). Interviews with rescuers and the rescued indicate that individual rescuers were characterized by one or more of the three primary motivators that have been proposed for altruistic helping: a value of caring or "prosocial orientation" (Staub 1974, 1978, 1995), with its focus on the welfare of people and a feeling of personal responsibility to help; moral rules or principles, the focus on living up to or fulfilling the principle or rule; and empathy, the vicarious experience of others' suffering (London, 1970; Oliner & Oliner, 1988; Tec, 1986). These were often accompanied by a hatred of Nazism.

Marginality in relation to the perpetrators or to the dominant group does not mean that rescuers were disconnected from people. In the largest study to date, Sam and Pearl Oliner (1988) found that rescuers were deeply connected to their families and/or other people. They described a large proportion (52%) of rescuers as "normocentric," or norm centered, characterized by "a feeling of obligation to a special reference group with whom the actor identified and whose explicit and implicit values he feels obliged to obey." Some normocentric rescuers were guided by internalized group norms, but many followed the guidance of leaders who set a policy of rescue. Some belonged to resistance groups, church groups, or families that influenced them. In Belgium, where the queen and the government-in-exile and church leaders set the tone, most of the nation refused to cooperate with anti-Jewish policies, and the underground actively helped Jews, who as a result were highly active in helping themselves (Fein, 1979). But normocentric influence can lead people in varied directions. In Poland, some priests and resistance groups helped Jews, while other priests encouraged their communities to support the Nazi persecution of Jews, and some resistance groups killed Jews (Tec, 1986).

Many rescuers started out by helping a Jew with whom they had a past relationship. Some were asked by a Jewish friend or acquaintance to help. The personal relationship would have made it more likely that altruistic-moral motives as well as relationship-based motives would become active. Having helped someone they knew, many continued to help.

Even in ordinary times a feeling of competence is usually required for the expression of motivation in action, or even for its arousal (Ajzen, 1988; Bandura, 1989; Staub, 1978, 1980). When action endangers one's life, such "supporting characteristics" (Staub, 1980) become crucial. Faith in their own competence and intuition, fearlessness, and high tolerance for risk are among the characteristics of rescuers derived from interviews both with rescuers and with the people they helped (London, 1970; Oliner & Oliner, 1988; Tec, 1986).

Although this is less supported by a body of evidence, it seems that some rescuers were adventurous and pursued risky, dangerous activities in their earlier lives (London, 1970). Adventurousness might reduce the perceived risk and enhance the feeling of competence to help. According to personal goal theory, it may also partly transform the risk to potential satisfaction, adding a source of motivation.

Heroic helpers are not born. An analysis of two specific cases shows the roots and evolution of heroism. The many-faceted influences at work can be seen in the case of Raoul Wallenberg, who saved the lives of tens of thousands of Hungarian Jews (Marton, 1982). Wallenberg was a member of a poor branch of an influential Swedish family. He had wide-ranging travel and work experience and was trained as an architect. In 1944, he was the partner of a Hungarian Jewish refugee in an import-export business. He had traveled to Hungary several times on business, where he visited his partner's relatives. Earlier, while working in a bank in Haifa, he encountered Jewish refugees arriving from Nazi Germany, which was likely to arouse his empathy. In 1944, he seemed restless and dissatisfied with his career.

On his partner's recommendation, Wallenberg was approached by a representative of the American War Refugee Board and asked to go to Hungary as a Swedish diplomat to attempt to save the lives of Hungarian Jews who were then being deported to and killed at Auschwitz. He agreed to go. There was no predominant motive guiding his life at the time, like a valued career, which according to personal goal theory would have reduced his openness to activators of a conflicting motive. The request probably served to focus responsibility on him (Staub, 1978), his connection to his business partner and his partner's relatives enhancing this feeling of responsibility. Familiarity with Hungary and a wide range of past experience in traveling, studying, and working in many places around the world must have added to his feeling of competence. In Hungary, he repeatedly risked his life, subordinating everything to the cause of saving Jewish lives (Marton, 1982).

Wallenberg's commitment seemingly increased over time, although it appears that once he got involved, his motivation to help was immediately high. Another well-known rescuer, Oskar Schindler (Keneally, 1982), clearly progressed along a "continuum of benevolence." He was a German born in Czechoslovakia. In his youth, he raced motorcycles. As a Protestant, he left his village to marry a Catholic girl from another village. Thus, he was doubly marginal and also adventurous. Both his father and his wife were opposed to Hitler. Still, he joined the Nazi Party and followed the German troops to Poland, where he took over a confiscated factory and, using Jewish slave labor, proceeded to enrich himself.

However, in contrast to others in a similar situation, Schindler responded to the humanity of his slave laborers. From the start, he talked with them and listened to them. He celebrated birthdays with them. He began to help them in small and large ways. In some rescuers, the motivation to help followed witnessing the murder or brutal treatment of a Jew (Oliner & Oliner, 1988). Schindler had a number of such experiences. His actions resulted in two arrests and brief imprisonments from which he freed himself by invoking real and imaginary connections to important Nazis. Both Schindler and Wallenberg possessed considerable personal power and seemed to enjoy exercising this power to save lives.

To protect his slave laborers from the murderous concentration camp Plaszow, Schindler persuaded the Nazis to allow him to build a camp next to his factory. As the Soviet army advanced, Schindler moved his laborers to his hometown, where he created a fake factory that produced nothing, its only purpose to protect the Jewish laborers. In the end, Schindler lost all the wealth he had accumulated in Poland but saved about 1,200 lives.

Like perpetrators and bystanders, heroic helpers evolve. Some of them develop fanatic commitment to their goal (Staub, 1989a). The usual fanatics subordinate themselves to a movement that serves abstract ideals. They come to disregard the welfare and lives of at least some people as they strive to fulfill these ideals. I regard some of the rescuers as "good fanatics," who completely devoted themselves to the *concrete* aim of saving lives.

Probably in every genocide and mass killing there are heroic helpers, but there is a significant body of scholarship only on rescuers of Jews in Nazi Europe. In Rwanda, as well, there were Hutus who acted to save Tutsis. A very few spoke out publicly against the killings, and some or perhaps all of these were killed (des Forges, 1999). In 1999, I interviewed a few people who were rescued and one rescuer in Rwanda, enough only to gain some impressions (Staub, 2000; Staub & Pearlman, 2001). Rwanda is a highly religious country, and while some high-level church leaders betrayed the Tutsis and became accomplices to genocide (des Forges, 1999; Gourevitch, 1998; Prunier, 1995), it seems from the reports of those who were rescued that some of the rescuers acted out of religious motives, living up to religious ideals. (Research by Oliner and Oliner [1988] suggested that about 15% of rescuers of Jews acted out of religious motives.) Another impression that came out of the interviews was that perhaps because of the horrible nature of the violence in Rwanda, where in addition to the military and paramilitary groups with many very young members, some people killed neighbors and some even betrayed members of their own families who had a Tutsi or mixed ethnic background, some of those who were rescued did not trust the motives or character of their rescuers. They could not quite believe that these motives were truly benevolent rather than based on some kind of self-interest.

The research on rescuers of Jews and other information suggest that over time the range of concern of engaged helpers usually expands. For example, the Mothers of the Plaza del Mayo in Argentina began to march in the plaza to protest the disappearances of their own children. They endured persecution, and some were kidnapped. However, as they continued to march, they developed a strong commitment to universal human rights and freedom (Staub, 1989a), a concern about the persecution and suffering of people in general.

THE OBLIGATION OF BYSTANDERS

We cannot expect bystanders to sacrifice their lives for others. But we can expect individuals, groups, and nations to act early along a continuum of destruction, when the danger to themselves is limited, and the potential exists for inhibiting the evolution of increasing destructiveness. This will only happen if people—children, adults, whole societies—develop an awareness of their common humanity with other people, as well as of the psychological processes in themselves that turn them against others. Institutions and modes of functioning can develop that embody a shared humanity and make exclusion from the moral realm more difficult. Healing from past victimization (Staub, 1998), building systems of positive reciprocity, creating crosscutting

35

relations (Deutsch, 1973) between groups, and developing joint projects (Pettigrew, 1997) and superordinate goals can promote the evolution of caring and nonaggressive persons and societies (Staub, 1989a, 1992b, 1999a).

NOTES

This chapter is a revised and updated version of "The Psychology of Bystanders, Perpetrators, and Heroic Helpers," which appeared in the *International Journal of Intercultural Relations 17* (1993): 315–341. Portions of that paper are reprinted here with the permission of Elsevier Science.

1. In Cambodia, especially, the focus on past national glory may have been not so much an expression of a feeling of superiority as a defense against feelings of inferiority. The glory of the Angkor empire faded hundreds of years earlier, and in the intervening centuries Cambodia was frequently invaded by others and ruled for very long periods by Vietnam and France.

2. In June 1987, I gave a lecture at the University of Trier, in Germany, on the psychology of genocide. I asked my hosts beforehand, and they kindly arranged for me a meeting with a group of older Germans who lived under Hitler—20 individuals aged 60 to 75. In our 4-hour-long discussion, these people repeatedly and spontaneously returned to the satisfactions they experienced under Hitler. They could not keep away from it. They talked about far more than just the material security or the existence of jobs and a livelihood. The camaraderie and feelings of community sitting around campfires, singing songs, and sharing other experiences of connection and group spirit stood out in their memories.

REFERENCES

Abraham, D. (1987). *The collapse of the Weimar Republic.* New York: Holmes and Meier.

Ajzen, I. (1988). *Attitudes, personality and behavior.* Chicago: Dorsey Press.

Allport, G. (1954). *The nature of prejudice.* Reading MA: Addison-Wesley.

Bandura, A. (1989). Human agency in social cognitive theory. *American Psychologist, 44,* 1175–1184.

Bandura, A., Underwood, B., & Fromson, M. E. (1975). Disinhibition of aggression through diffusion of responsibility and dehumanization of victims. *Journal of Research in Personality, 9,* 253–269.

Bem, D. 1. (1972). Self-perception theory. In L. Berkowitz (Ed.), *Advances in experimental social psychology* (Vol. 6). New York: Academic Press.

Berkowitz, L. (1962). *Aggression: A social psychological analysis.* New York: McGraw-Hill.

Bettelheim, B. (1979). Remarks on the psychological appeal of totalitarianism. In *Surviving and other essays.* New York: Vintage.

Bickman, L. (1972). Social influence and diffusion of responsibility in an emergency. *Journal of Experimental and Social Psychology, 8,* 438–445.

Bigelow, K. R. (1993). A campaign to deter genocide: The Baha'i experience. In H. Fein (Ed.), *Genocide watch.* New Haven, CT: Yale University Press.

Bloch, S., & Reddaway, P. (1977). *Psychiatric terror: How Soviet psychiatry is used to suppress dissent.* New York: Basic Books.

Bloch, S., & Reddaway, P. (1984). *Soviet psychiatric abuse: The shadow over world psychiatry.* London: Victor Gollancz.

Brewer, M. B. (1978). In-group bias in the minimal intergroup situation: A cognitive-motivational analysis. *Psychological Bulletin, 86,* 307–324.

Browning, C. R. (1992). *Ordinary men: Reserve Battalion 101 and the final solution in Poland.* New York: HarperCollins.

Buss, A. H. (1966). The effect of harm on subsequent aggression. *Journal of Experimental Research in Personality, 1,* 249–255.

Card, J. J. (1983). *Lives after Vietnam: The personal impact of military service.* Lexington, MA: Lexington Books.

Chandler, D. P. (1983). *A history of Cambodia.* Boulder, CO: Westview.

Craig, G. A. (1982). *The Germans.* New York: New American Library.

Crawley, E. (1984). *A house divided: Argentina, 1880–1980.* New York: St. Martin's.

Dawidowicz, L. S. (1975). *The war against the Jews: 1933–1945.* New York: Holt, Rinehart and Winston.

DeJong, A. (1978). *The Weimar chronicle: Prelude to Hitler.* New York: New American Library.

DeJong, W. (1979). An examination of self-perception mediation of the foot-in-the-door effect. *Journal of Personality and Social Psychology, 34,* 578–582.

des Forges, A. (1999). *Leave none to tell the story: Genocide in Rwanda.* New York: Human Rights Watch.

Deutsch, M. (1973). *The resolution of conflict: Constructive and destructive processes.* New Haven, CT: Yale University Press.

Devereux, E. D. (1972). Authority and moral development among German and American children: A cross-national pilot experiment. *Journal of Comparative Family Studies, 3,* 99–124.

Dicks, H. V. (1972). *Licensed mass murder: A socio-psychological study of some SS killers.* New York: Basic Books.

Dimont, M. 1. (1962). *Jews, God and history.* New York: Signet.

Duster, T. (1971). Conditions for guilt-free massacre. In N. Sanford & C. Comstock (Eds.), *Sanction for evil.* San Francisco: Jossey-Bass.

Egendorf, A., Kadushin, C., Laufer, R. S., Rothbart, G., & Sloan, L. (1981). *Summary findings. Legacies of Vietnam: Comparative adjustment of Vietnam veterans and their peers* (Vol. 1). Washington, DC: U.S. Government Printing Office.

Eisenberg, N. (1986). *Altruistic emotion, cognition and behavior.* Hillsdale, NJ: Erlbaum.

Elms, A. C., & Milgram, S. (1966). Personality characteristics associated with obedience and defiance toward authoritative command. *Journal of Experimental Research in Personality, 2,* 282–289.

Epstein, S. (1980). The self-concept: A review and the proposal of an integrated theory of personality. In E. Staub (Ed.), *Personality: Basic aspects and current research.* Englewood Cliffs, NJ: Prentice-Hall.

Etcheson, C. (1984). *The rise and demise of democratic Kampuchea.* Boulder, CO: Westview.

Fein, H. (1979). *Accounting for genocide: Victims and survivors of the Holocaust.* New York: Free Press.

Fein, H. (1993). Accounting for genocide after 1945: Theories and some findings. *International Journal of Group Rights, 1,* 79–106.

Freedman, J. L., & Fraser, S. C. (1966). Compliance without pressure: The foot-in-the-door technique. *Journal of Personality and Social Psychology, 4,* 195–202.

Friedrich, V. (1989). From psychoanalysis to the "Great treatment": Psychoanalysis under National Socialism. *Political Psychology, 10,* 3–27.

Fromm, E. (1965). *Escape from freedom.* New York: Avon.

Gibson, J. T., & Haritos-Fatouros, M. (1986). The education of a torturer. *Psychology Today, 20,* 50–58.

Girard, P. (1980). Historical foundations of anti-Semitism. In J. Dimsdale (Ed.), *Survivors, victims and perpetrators: Essays on the Nazi Holocaust.* New York: Hemisphere.

Goldhagen, D. J. (1996). *Hitler's willing executioners: Ordinary Germans and the Holocaust.* New York: Knopf.

Goldstein, J. H., Davis, R. W., & Herman, D. (1975). Escalation of aggression: Experimental studies. *Journal of Personality and Social Psychology, 31,* 162–170.

Gourevitch, P. (1998). *We wish to inform you that tomorrow we will be killed with our families.* New York: Farrar, Straus and Giroux.

Greene, F. D. (1895). *The Armenian crisis in Turkey: The massacre of 1894, its antecedents and significance.* New York: Putnam's.

Grusec, J. E., Kuczynski, L., Rushton, J. P., & Simutis, Z. M. (1978). Modeling, direct instruction, and attributions: Effects on altruism. *Developmental Psychology, 14,* 51–57.

Hallie, P. P. (1979). *Lest innocent blood be shed: The story of the village of Le Chambon and how goodness happened there.* New York: Harper and Row.

Harff, B., & Gurr, T. R. (1990). Victims of the state genocides, Politicides and group repression since 1945. *International Review of Victimology, 1,* 1–19.

Harff, B., Gurr, T. R., & Unger, A. (1999, November). *Preconditions of genocide and politicide: 1955–1998.* Paper presented at the Conference on Differing Approaches to Assessing Potential Genocide, Politicides and Mass Killings, Vienna, Virginia.

Haritos-Fatouros, M. (1988). The official torturer: A learning model for obedience to the authority of violence. *Journal of Applied Social Psychology, 18,* 1107–1120.

Harris, M. B. (1972). The effects of performing one altruistic act on the likelihood of performing another. *Journal of Social Psychology, 88,* 65–73.

Heider, F. (1958). *The psychology of interpersonal relations.* New York: Wiley.

Herman, J. (1992). *Trauma and recovery.* New York: Basic Books.

Hilberg, R. (1961). *The destruction of the European Jews.* New York: Harper and Row.

Hitchcock, R. K., & Twedt, T. M. (1997). Physical and cultural genocide of various indigenous peoples. In S. Totten, W. S. Parsons, & I. W. Charny (Eds.), *Century of genocide: Eyewitness accounts and critical views.* New York: Garland.

Janoff-Bulman, R. (1985). The aftermath of victimization: Rebuilding shattered assumptions. In C. R. Figley (Ed.), *Trauma and Its wake.* New York: Bruner/Mazel.

Janoff-Bulman, R. (1992). *Shattered assumptions.* New York: Free Press.

Keneally, T. (1982). *Schindler's list.* New York: Penguin.

Kren, G. M., & Rappoport, L. (1980). *The Holocaust and the crisis of human behavior.* New York: Holmes and Meier.

Kuper, L. (1981). *Genocide: Its political use in the twentieth century.* New Haven, CT: Yale University Press.

Latane, B., & Darley, J. (1970). *The unresponsive bystander: Why doesn't he help?* New York: Appleton-Crofts.

Lerner, M. (1980). *The belief in a just world: A fundamental delusion.* New York: Plenum.

Lerner, M. J., & Simmons, C. H. (1966). Observer's reaction to the "innocent victim": Compassion or rejection? *Journal of Personality and Social Psychology, 4,* 203–210.

LeVine, R. A., & Campbell, D. (1972). *Ethnocentrism: Theories of conflict, ethnic attitudes and group behavior.* New York: Wiley.

Lewin, K. (1938). *The conceptual representation and measurement of psychological forces.* Durham, NC: Duke University Press.

Lifton, R. J. (1986). *The Nazi doctors: Medical killing and the psychology of genocide.* New York: Basic Books.

London, P. (1970). The rescuers: Motivational hypotheses about Christians who saved Jews from the Nazis. In J. Macaulay & L. Berkowitz (Eds.), *Altruism and helping behavior.* New York: Academic Press.

Luther, M. (1955–1975). *Works: On the Jews and their lies* (Vol. 47). St. Louis, MO: Muhlenberg Press.

Mack, J. (1983). Nationalism and the self. *Psychoanalytic Review, 2,* 47–69.

Marton, K. (1982). *Wallenberg.* New York: Ballantine.

Mayer, M. (1955). *They thought they were free: The Germans, 1933–45.* Chicago: University of Chicago Press.

McCann, L. I., & Pearlman, L. A. (1990). *Psychological trauma and the adult survivor: Theory, therapy, and transformation.* New York: Bruner/Mazel.

McCauley, C. R., & Segal, M. D. (1989). Terrorist individuals and terrorist groups: The normal psychology of extreme behavior. In J. Groebel and J. F. Goldstein, *Terrorism.* Sevilla: Publicaciones de la Universidad de Sevilla.

Merkl, P. H. (1980). *The making of a stormtrooper.* Princeton, NJ: Princeton University Press.

Milgram, S. (1965). Some conditions of obedience and disobedience to authority. *Human Relations, 18,* 57–76.

Milgram, S. (1974). *Obedience to authority: An experimental view.* New York: Harper and Row.

Milgram, S., & Toch, H. (1969). Collective behavior: Crowds and social movements. In G. Lindzey & E. Aronson (Eds.), *The handbook of social psychology* (2nd ed.). Reading, MA: Addison-Wesley.

Miller, A. (1983). *For your own good: Hidden cruelty in child-rearing and the roots of violence.* New York: Farrar, Straus and Giroux.

Moscovici, S. (1973). *Social influence and social change.* London: Academic Press.

Moscovici, S. (1980). Toward a theory of conversion behavior. In L. Berkowitz (Ed.), *Current issues in social psychology.* New York: Academic Press.

Nairn & Simon. (1986, June). Bureaucracy of death. *New Republic,* pp. 13–18.

Nathan, O., & Norden, H. (Eds.). (1960). *Einstein on peace.* New York: Avenel Books.

Nunca Mas. (1986). *The report of the Argentine National Commission on the Disappeared.* New York: Farrar, Straus and Giroux.

Oliner, S. B., & Oliner, P. (1988). *The altruistic personality: Rescuers of Jews in Nazi Europe.* New York: Free Press.

Peters, E. (1985). *Torture.* New York: Basil Blackwell.

Pettigrew, T. F. (1997). Generalized intergroup contact effects on prejudice. *Personality and Social Psychology Bulletin, 23,* 173–185.

Platt, G. M. (1980). Thoughts on a theory of collective action: Language, affect and ideology in revolution. In M. Albin, R. J. Devlin, & G. Heeger (Eds.), *New directions in*

39

psychohistory: The Adelphi papers in honor of Erik H. Erikson. Lexington, MA: Lexington Books.

Prunier, G. (1995). *The Rwanda crisis: History of a genocide.* New York: Columbia University Press.

Rouhana, N. N., & Kelman, H. C. (1994). Promoting joint thinking in international conflicts: An Israeli-Palestinian continuing workshop. *Journal of Social Issues, 50,* 157–178.

Rummel, R. J. (1994). *Death by government.* New Brunswick, NJ: Transaction.

Staub, E. (1974). Helping a distressed person: Social, personality and stimulus determinants. In L. Berkowitz (Ed.), *Advances in experimental social psychology* (vol. 7). New York: Academic Press.

Staub, E. (1975). To rear a prosocial child: Reasoning, learning by doing, and learning by teaching others. In D. DePalma & J. Folley (Eds.), *Moral development: Current theory and research.* Hillsdale, NJ: Erlbaum.

Staub, E. (1978). *Positive social behavior and morality: Social and personal influences* (Vol. 1). New York: Academic Press.

Staub, E. (1979). *Positive social behavior and morality: Socialization and development* (Vol. 2). New York: Academic Press.

Staub, E. (1980). Social and prosocial behavior. In E. Staub (Ed.), *Personality.* Englewood Cliffs, NJ: Prentice Hall.

Staub, E. (1986). A conception of the determinants and development of altruism and aggression: Motives, the self, the environment. In C. Zahn-Waxler, M. Cummings, & R. Ianotti (Eds.), *Altruism and aggression: Social and biological origins.* Cambridge, MA: Cambridge University Press.

Staub, E. (1987). Commentary. In N. Eisenberg & J. Strayer (Eds.), *Empathy and its development.* New York: Cambridge University Press.

Staub, E. (1988). The evolution of caring and nonaggressive persons and societies. In R. Wagner, J. DeRivera, & M. Watkins (Eds.), Positive approaches to peace. *Journal of Social Issues, 44,* 2, 800.

Staub, E. (1989a). *The roots of evil: The origins of genocide and other group violence.* New York: Cambridge University Press.

Staub, E. (1989b). Steps along the continuum of destruction: The evolution of bystanders, German psychoanalysts and lessons for today. *Political Psychology, 10,* 39–53.

Staub, E. (1992a). Understanding and preventing police violence. *Center Review, 6,* 1 and 7.

Staub, E. (1992b). Transforming the bystander: Altruism, caring and social responsibility. In H. Fein (Ed.), *Genocide watch.* New Haven, CT: Yale University Press.

Staub, E. (1993). Motivation, individual and group self-concepts, and morality. In T. Wren & G. Noam (Eds.), *Morality and the self.* Cambridge, MA: MIT Press.

Staub, E. (1995). How people learn to care. In P. G. Schervish, V. A. Hodgkinson, M. Gates, & associates (Eds.), *Care and community in modern society: Passing on the tradition of service to future generations.* San Francisco: Jossey-Bass.

Staub, E. (1996). Cultural-societal roots of violence: The examples of genocidal violence and of contemporary youth violence in the United States. *American Psychologist, 51,* 117–132.

Staub, E. (1998). Breaking the cycle of genocidal violence: Healing and reconciliation. In J. Harvey (Ed.), *Perspectives on loss: A source book.* Washington, DC: Taylor and Francis.

Staub, E. (1999a). The origins and prevention of genocide, mass killing, and other collective violence. *Peace and Conflict: Journal of Peace Psychology, 5,* 303–336.

Staub, E. (1999b). The roots of evil: Social conditions, culture, personality and basic human needs. *Personality and Social Psychology Review, 3,* 179–192.

Staub, E. (2000). Mass murder: Origins, prevention and U.S. involvement. In *Encyclopedia of violence in the United States.* New York: Scribner's.

Staub, E. (2000). Genocide and mass killing: Origins, prevention, healing and reconciliation. *Political Psychology, 21,* 367–382.

Staub, E. (2002). *Understanding and preventing police violence.* In S. Epstein & M. Amir (Eds.), *Policing, security and democracy.* Huntsville, TX: Office of Criminal Justice Press.

Staub, E. (in press). *The psychology of good and evil.* New York: Cambridge University Press.

Staub, E., & Pearlman, L. A. (2001). Healing, forgiveness and reconciliation after genocide. In S. J. Helmick & R. L. Peterson (Eds) *Forgiveness and reconciliation.* Radnor, PA: Templeton Foundation Press.

Staub, E., & Rosenthal, L. (1994). Mob violence: Social-cultural influences, group processes and participants. In L. Eron & J. Gentry (Eds.), *Reason to hope: A psychosocial perspective on violence and youth.* Washington DC: American Psychological Association.

Steiner, J. M. (1980). The SS yesterday and today: A socio-psychological view. In J. Dimsdale (Ed.), *Survivors, victims and perpetrators: Essays on the Nazi Holocaust.* New York: Hemisphere.

Stover, E., & Nightingale, E. O. (1985). *The breaking of bodies and minds: Torture, psychiatric abuse and the health professions.* New York: Freeman.

Sykes, G. M., & Matza, D. (1957). Techniques of neutralization: A theory of delinquency. *American Sociological Review, 75,* 664–670.

Tajfel, H. (Ed.). (1982). Social identity and intergroup relations. Cambridge: Cambridge University Press.

Tajfel, H., Flament, C., Billig, M. Y., & Bundy, R. P. (1971). Societal categorization and intergroup behavior. *European Journal of Social Psychology, 1,* 149–177.

Taylor, F. (Ed.). (1983). *The Goebbels diaries, 1939–1941.* New York: Putnam.

Tec, N. (1986). *When light pierced the darkness: Christian rescue of Jews in Nazi-occupied Poland.* New York: Oxford University Press.

Toch, H. (1965*). The social psychology of social movements.* New York: Bobbs-Merrill.

Toynbee, A. J. (1915). *Armenian atrocities: The murder of a nation.* London: Hodder and Stoughton.

Trumpener, U. (1968). *Germany and the Ottoman Empire, 1914–1918.* Princeton, NJ: Princeton University Press.

Turner, J. C. (1987). *Rediscovering the social groups: A self-categorization theory.* New York: Basil Blackwell.

Volkan, V. D. (1988). *The need to have enemies and allies.* Northvale, NJ: Jason Aronson.

Von Maltitz, H. (1973). *The evolution of Hitler's Germany: The ideology, the personality, the moment.* New York: McGraw-Hill.

Wilson, P. J. (1980). Conflict, stress and growth: The effects of war on psychosocial development among Vietnam Veterans. In C. R. Figley & S. Leventman (Eds.), *Strangers at home: Vietnam veterans since the war.* New York: Praeger.

Wyman, D. S. (1968). *Paper walls: America and the refugee crisis, 1938–1941.* Amherst: University of Massachusetts Press.

Wyman, D. S. (1984). *The abandonment of Jews: America and the Holocaust, 1941–1945.* New York: Pantheon.

Zimbardo, P. G. (1969). The human choice: Individuation, reason, and order versus deindividuation, impulse, and chaos. In *Nebraska Symposium on Motivation.* Lincoln: University of Nebraska Press.

2

What Is a "Social-Psychological" Account of Perpetrator Behavior?

The Person Versus the Situation in
Goldhagen's *Hitler's Willing Executioners*

Leonard S. Newman

It is safe to assume that few people would willingly identify themselves as potential mass murderers or ethnic cleansers. As Diamond (1992)
put it, "We'd like to believe that nice people don't commit genocide, only Nazis
do" (p. 277). But mass indiscriminate killings of one racial, ethnic, national,
or religious group of people by another have been a persistent feature of
human history (Diamond, 1992, chap. 16). The twentieth century is arguably
unique in terms of the frequency and scope of such tragedies (Hobsbawm,
1994). In the 1990s alone, a partial list of events that could easily be categorized as genocidal—and that have taken place in full view of a worldwide
audience—would include the violent upheavals in Rwanda (Gourevitch, 1998;
Smith, 1998), Bosnia (Rosenberg, 1998), and Kosovo (Wick & Stone, 1999).
Such a list would also include many other lesser-known tragedies taking place
outside of the media spotlight, such as the mass killings accompanying the
brutal conflict between the Dayaks and Madurese in Indonesia (see Parry,
1998). It is understandable why one might wish to attribute such horrors to
an unfortunate lack of niceness on the part of the perpetrators and leave it at
that. In fact, it is probably difficult to read or hear about accounts of genocide
without at least fleetingly concluding that the killers were twisted and evil
human beings who bear very little resemblance to oneself or one's friends,
neighbors, and loved ones. At the same time, for social scientists to construe
genocide in this way would arguably be "an act of unconditional intellectual
surrender" (Wehler, 1998, p. 97).

Among social scientists, social psychologists in particular would seem to
be well positioned to shed light on the processes that lead individuals and

groups to become perpetrators of genocide. Typical definitions of social psychology are usually very similar to the one offered by Brehm and Kassin (1996) who stated that social psychology is "the scientific study of the way individuals think, feel, desire, and act in social situations" (p. 6). One would hope, then, that social-psychological principles could be applied to the thoughts, feelings, desires, and actions of people in social situations involving the systematic murder of other human beings. But at least one recent analysis of the behavior of genocide perpetrators concluded that "social-psychological explanations" are irrelevant to the goal of understanding such behavior. The focus of that analysis was instead the peculiar characteristics of the perpetrators; in other words, the causal model it promoted was quite consistent with the belief that "nice people don't commit genocide, only Nazis do."

The analysis in question was presented in a book that has done much to promote public debate on genocide in general and the behavior of Holocaust perpetrators in particular. That work, Daniel Goldhagen's *Hitler's Willing Executioners: Ordinary Germans and the Holocaust* (1996), might already be one of the more widely read books on the Holocaust ever published. It has inspired (and continues to inspire) countless reviews, essays, editorials, symposia, and debates in both the mainstream media and academia. In Germany, in particular, Goldhagen's book occasioned much comment (both favorable and unfavorable), and when his publishers sent him on a speaking tour in that country, the appearances were consistently sold out (Elon, 1997).

What was so compelling about Goldhagen's book? Why has it come to play such a major role in framing current discussions of genocide? As a number of commentators have noted, the idea that German anti-Semitism played a central role in the Holocaust is not particularly groundbreaking. Instead, what captured so much attention was Goldhagen's focus. Goldhagen did not write a book about the Nazi leadership and when and why they planned the Final Solution in Europe (i.e., an "intentionalist" analysis). Nor did he write a book focusing on the organizational and technical aspects of the Holocaust, or a monograph describing how impersonal social and economic forces, wartime exigencies, and the nature of the German military bureaucracy all interacted in some way to produce a tragedy that no group of people actually sat down and planned (i.e., a "functionalist" or "structuralist" analysis). Much recent scholarship on the Holocaust falls into those categories (see Browning, 1992b).

Goldhagen's level of analysis was a little different. He focused on the actual immediate perpetrators of the Holocaust. His concern was with the soldiers, policemen, SS men, and even civilians who actually rounded people up, pushed them into cattle cars, brutalized them, forced them to dig their own graves, and shot them. Goldhagen's book is about how the perpetrators felt when they did this; why they behaved the way they did; whether they thought they were doing the right thing; how they explained their acts to themselves; how they understood the situations they were in; and how those immediate situations affected their behavior. In other words (although Goldhagen himself does not define his work in this way), his goal was to develop a social-psychological analysis of perpetrator behavior. In writing about the Holocaust, he focused on the kinds of issues with which contemporary social psychologists generally concern themselves.

Goldhagen (1998) has stated that "mine is a rare study of the Holocaust that incorporates into its interpretations the insights and theories of the social sciences" (p. 136). Unfortunately, despite the nature of his project, his analysis was not very well informed by contemporary social-psychological research and theorizing. One goal of this chapter is to explain how Goldhagen's treatment of social-psychological accounts of behavior was incomplete, because his work is a prominent example of common misconceptions about the social-psychological analysis of the relationship between persons and situations. Much of the discussion will be framed in terms of those misconceptions. Perhaps even more important, though, is the second goal of this chapter: to show how those misconceptions obscure the fact that social-psychological research in the post–World War II era has yielded many insights that can indeed deepen our understanding of perpetrator behavior. A lack of appreciation of those insights not only handicaps our efforts to approach the kinds of issues raised by Goldhagen but also undermines our understanding of the social and psychological factors at work in *any* act of genocide.

A FALSE DICHOTOMY? GOLDHAGEN'S COGNITIVE AND SOCIAL-PSYCHOLOGICAL EXPLANATIONS

First, however, Goldhagen's conclusions about the causes of perpetrator behavior will be briefly reviewed. Central to his analysis is a distinction between what he calls the "cognitive" explanation of perpetrator behavior and what he calls the "social-psychological explanations." What follows is a summary of Goldhagen's cognitive and social-psychological explanations, including his reasons for rejecting the latter.

The "Cognitive Explanation"

In order to account for how seemingly ordinary Germans became Holocaust perpetrators, Goldhagen favored a "cognitive explanation." As detailed in *Hitler's Willing Executioners* (1996), this explanation boils down to not much more than what social psychologists would call *attitude-behavior consistency*. In other words, Goldhagen concluded that the murderous acts committed by many Germans during the campaign to eliminate Jews from European life were simple and straightforward reflections of murderous feelings toward Jewish people. According to Goldhagen, centuries of anti-Semitism in Germany—anti-Semitism that was more intense than anywhere else in Europe—had reached the boiling point. In addition, he claimed that the anti-Semitism found in Germany was a very extreme "eliminationist anti-Semitism," a kind that demanded the total elimination of Jews from German life by any means possible. Once the Nazi Party rose to power, Goldhagen argued, Germans had an opportunity to act on their attitudes. More precisely, once the Nazis eliminated all constraints on the ways in which people could express their eliminationist anti-Semitism, Germans simply followed their hearts and went to work persecuting and killing Jews. Germans "equipped with little more than the cultural notions current in their country," wrote Goldhagen, "would easily become genocidal executioners" (p. 185).

Although many variables moderate and qualify the relationship, social-psychological research does indeed show that attitudes and behavior are often highly correlated (Eagly & Chaiken, 1993). The claim that active participation in the persecution and massacre of Jews was associated with anti-Semitic feelings and beliefs is clearly plausible—and certainly not controversial. But Goldhagen said much more than that. First of all, as already described, he argued that the typical German person during the Nazi era had attitudes toward Jews that were not only unfavorable but so unfavorable as to allow for the killing of Jewish men, women, and children without the slightest degree of ambivalence. Even more provocative, though, is his claim that eliminationist anti-Semitism provides a *necessary and sufficient* explanation for perpetrator behavior. In other words, Goldhagen concluded that the horrors of the Holocaust could not have occurred without such attitudes and, in addition, that no other social or intrapsychic factors played a role in leading people to act on those attitudes. Finally, he argued that eliminationist anti-Semitism is a valid explanation at all relevant levels of analysis. Society, the leadership, institutions, individual people—all, he claimed, were driven by eliminationist anti-Semitism. All participated in the killing of Jews because doing so was consistent with their individual and collective attitudes. These radical conclusions do much to explain why the book has received so much attention and analysis.[1]

Goldhagen marshaled quite a bit of evidence to bolster these arguments, but one fact he emphasized more than others is that many of the police battalions and other groups of people that carried out most of the face-to-face killing in eastern Europe were not made up of men and women who were selected in any careful way for their jobs. They were not assigned their duties because they were known to be especially anti-Semitic, or especially vicious, or especially obedient. They were simply random Germans who happened to be assigned tasks like rounding up all the Jews in a town and shooting them or burning them alive. As Goldhagen (correctly) notes, these people generally carried out these assignments when asked to do so. Why? According to Goldhagen, they did so because they were Germans, and the vast majority of Germans at the time subscribed to eliminationist anti-Semitism.

The "Social-Psychological Explanations"

Just as forcefully as he promoted his cognitive explanation, Goldhagen also rejected the possibility that other psychological or interpersonal forces might have played a role in the creation of Holocaust perpetrators. Goldhagen's attention to these other explanatory factors was in part a response to the work of Browning (1992a), who in *Ordinary Men: Reserve Police Battalion 101 and the Final Solution in Poland* offered a very different perspective on the behavior of the men and women who did much of the face-to-face killing of Jews as the Holocaust unfolded. In particular, Browning emphasized the social-psychological processes of obedience and conformity.

Obedience

In one of the most well-known programs of research in the history of experimental social psychology (and the behavioral sciences in general), Milgram (1974) studied the extent to which ordinary people would follow the directives of an authority figure and inflict harm upon other human beings. Participants in Milgram's experiments were led to believe that they had been recruited for a study of factors promoting learning. As they discovered once the experiment got under way, the specific variable of interest was punishment. Each participant was introduced to another person and told that the two of them would be run through the study together; one of them was to be randomly assigned to the role of "learner," and one to the role of "teacher." The second participant was actually a confederate of the experimenter, and the procedure was rigged so that the confederate was always the learner and the naive participant was always assigned to the role of the teacher.

Participants proceeded to administer a memory test to the learner. Every time the learner made an error, he was to be punished by the teacher, and the punishment was delivered in the form of an electric shock. Furthermore, with each error, the shocks supposedly increased in severity. The first switch on the instrument panel of the "shock generator," labeled "Slight Shock," was said to deliver a 15-volt jolt. Subsequent switches (with labels such as "Strong Shock," "Intense Shock," and "Danger: Severe Shock") were arranged in 15-volt increments, culminating in 450 volts (labeled "XXX"). Within a brief period (and as scripted by Milgram), the learner began to protest and demand that the experiment be terminated. As the experiment continued, these preliminary protests gave way to more intense expressions of discomfort, culminating in agonized screams and, finally, an eerie silence. Throughout the procedure, the experimenter was on hand to urge the participant to continue with the study. Neither force nor threats were involved; participants were pressured with simple verbal directives (e.g., "you must continue"; "the experiment requires that you go on"). In fact, participants were free to call a halt to the proceedings at any time. Milgram systematically varied many features of this basic experimental situation (e.g., the proximity of the learner and the authority figure, the presence of dissenting peers), and many of these experimental manipulations significantly affected the behavior of the participants. Overall, though, the most important finding was that, in general, levels of obedience were alarmingly high. In the most frequently cited study, a full 65% of participants administered the complete sequence of electric shocks. Milgram thus demonstrated that normal people are capable of engaging in harmful and inhumane behavior simply because an authority figure asks them to do so.

Milgram's studies, it has been suggested, present a model for how seemingly ordinary individuals could be absorbed into antisocial activities, including the perpetration of genocidal killings (see Blass, 1992; A. G. Miller, 1986). Browning (1992a) even referred to one notorious massacre of Polish Jews by German policemen as "a kind of radical Milgram experiment that took place in a Polish forest with real killers and victims rather than in a social psychology laboratory" (pp. 173–174). Goldhagen, however, decisively rejected that analogy. Accepting the relevance of Milgram's work, he argued, would mean accepting the idea that Holocaust perpetrators were reluctant killers grimly carrying out their orders. He provided quite a bit of vivid evidence to support his argument that such a characterization would be inaccurate. Specifically, he pointed out that there is little evidence that any German soldier or policeman was ever punished or even seriously threatened with punishment for refusing to participate in killing operations; that it was actually possible to request *not* to participate, although few did; that, instead, many more volunteered to help massacre Jews; that those who did so seemed proud of what they were doing, and even sent family and friends photographs of themselves in action solving the "Jewish Problem"; and that throughout the war, German soldiers and policemen seemed to go above and beyond the call of duty and not just kill Jews but also insult, humiliate, and torture them. Therefore, Goldhagen concluded that the concepts of obedience and coercion are irrelevant for understanding perpetrator behavior. (See also Fenigstein, 1998, and Mandel, 1998, for very different but also critical analyses of the relevance of Milgram's work for understanding perpetrator behavior.)

Conformity

The other social-psychological variable that Goldhagen critically analyzed is conformity pressure. Research has consistently revealed that people will often say and do things that they believe to be wrong or misguided—or *not* say and do things that they feel are appropriate—when they believe that their feelings, beliefs, or preferences are discrepant from those of other people who will be observing and evaluating their behavior. Asch's (1956) experiments provided some of the most compelling examples of conformity pressure. In

Asch's studies, participants were presented with a simple perceptual task. For each trial of the experiment, the task was to decide which of three "comparison" lines matched a fourth "standard" line in length. Each participant was joined by what they thought was a group of other volunteers, but the other participants were actually confederates of the experimenter. Those confederates were coached to make perceptual judgments that were quite obviously incorrect, leaving actual participants in the uncomfortable position of having to either contradict the unanimous (but incorrect) judgments of their peers or stand out as the lone dissenters. In the most frequently cited of his studies, Asch found that close to 40% of all judgments were conforming, and three quarters of participants conformed at least once.

In his own analysis, Browning (1992a) hypothesized that conformity pressures played an important role in turning otherwise average and unremarkable groups of German men into mass murderers. He doubted that many soldiers and policemen arrived at the front with great enthusiasm for mass executions of civilians; instead, he emphasized the salience of group norms to be tough and to do one's share of whatever "dirty work" was assigned. Furthermore, he suggested that individuals might have reasonably assumed that bowing out of killing operations would be seen by the group as a sign of cowardice, selfishness, and perhaps even moral condemnation of the other men. In sum, Browning concluded that pressures to conform to group norms and avoid being ostracized could go a long way toward explaining why groups of soldiers, policemen, and other German Holocaust perpetrators could have gone along with operations that they did not all approve of individually.

Goldhagen (1996), however, argued that appealing to conformity pressures to account for perpetrator behavior is not only wrong but actually illogical. The reasoning used to reach that conclusion was very simple. In his own words,

> The notion that peer pressure, namely the desire not to let down one's comrades or not incur their censure, could move individuals to undertake actions that they oppose, even abhor, is plausible even for the German perpetrators, but only as an account of the participation of some *individuals* in the perpetration of the Holocaust. It cannot be operative for more than a few individuals in a group, especially over a long period of time. If a large segment of a group, not to mention the vast majority of its members, opposes or abhors an act, then the social psychological pressure would work to *prevent*, not to encourage, individuals to undertake the act. If indeed Germans had disapproved of the mass slaughter, then peer pressure would not have induced people to kill against their will, but would have sustained their individual and collective resolve to avoid killing. . . . The explanation is self-contradictory when applied to the actions of *entire groups* of Germans. (pp. 383–384)

49

In other words, Goldhagen argued that when conformity pressure is aroused in a group of people, the people in that group will generally end up conforming to majority opinions. Therefore, if German soldiers and policemen were less than enthusiastic about mass murder, he said, then groups of such people would have conformed to that sentiment. That, of course, is not what happened. Since the Holocaust occurred, Goldhagen concluded, the majority of people in those groups must have been in favor of participating in genocide.

The Person Versus the Situation

Thus, Goldhagen concluded that obedience and conformity pressures played no roles in shaping the behavior of Holocaust perpetrators. Given his general approach to analyzing the effects of situational factors on people and their behavior, it is perhaps not surprising that he reached these conclusions. Goldhagen evaluated what he called the social-psychological explanations by contrasting them to what he called the cognitive explanation. In doing so, he essentially isolated two sets of factors—dispositional ones (i.e., attitudes) and contextual ones (i.e., obedience and conformity)—and pitted them against each other. He felt that the evidence clearly showed that dispositional factors were the more important determinants of perpetrator behavior and thus concluded that the cognitive explanation was the correct one.

This general approach echoes an old controversy in personality and social psychology that came to be known as the "person-situation" debate. Over 30 years ago, a number of researchers (especially Mischel, 1968) mounted forceful critiques of the idea that broad personality traits and other dispositional factors could be used to accurately describe and predict the behavior of individuals. These critics did not claim that there is no stability in human behavior (although, as discussed by Shadel & Cervone, 1993, this is a point not always appreciated by reviewers of the literature). But among the points they did make was that what people do, say, and feel is far more context-specific than typically recognized. What followed was many years of research and debate centered on the issue of whether traits or situations are more important determinants of behavior (for summaries of the relevant research and issues, see Caprara & Cervone, 2000; Mischel, 1990; Pervin, 1984; Ross & Nisbett, 1991).

Ultimately, social and personality psychologists concluded that the person-situation dichotomy is an artificial one, and that trying to determine which set of variables accounts for more variance in behavior is not just difficult but actually conceptually vacuous. For example, one problem with trying to apportion power to person and situation factors is that the two interact in complicated ways (Blass, 1993; Endler & Magnusson, 1976). A given situation can have quantitatively and qualitatively different effects on people as a function of the dispositions they bring to those situations. Note, however, that even that idea treats dispositional and situational factors as preexisting static entities that combine to affect behavior in predictable ways. The interrelationship between a person and the situations he or she encounters is even more tangled than that. To foreshadow some points to be made at greater length later, situations do not only interact with dispositional factors to affect behavior, they also shape and change those dispositions; people do not just react to situations, they also affect and shape situations (although they are not always aware of the extent to which they do so); and, finally, "situations" themselves do not even objectively exist but need to be cognitively constructed by the people they then go on to affect.

In sum, Goldhagen's analysis missed the dynamic relationship between persons and situations that is central to social-psychological theory and research. To be sure, Goldhagen is not to be faulted for falling into a conceptual trap that long preoccupied social and personality psychologists themselves. The point is simply that any even partially satisfying social-psychological analysis of the Holocaust requires an appreciation of the complicated ways in which people and social contexts interact and mutually transform each other.

RECONSIDERING THE ROLE OF SITUATIONS

Goldhagen's emphasis on a peculiarly German eliminationist anti-Semitism as the necessary and sufficient explanation for the behavior of German Holocaust perpetrators has been questioned on a number of grounds other than the ones emphasized in this chapter. Some have challenged the assertion that anti-Semitism in Germany in the first half of the twentieth century was any more virulent than it was in other European countries (Wehler, 1998). Others have pointed out that much of the persecution, killing, and other violent activity involving face-to-face contact with Holocaust victims was actually delegated to non-Germans (Latvians, Lithuanians, Ukrainians, etc.). Although these accomplices of the Nazis were not burdened by a legacy of German eliminationist anti-Semitism, they were by all accounts not distinguished by a lack of brutality in the execution of their duties (Aschheim, 1996; Finkelstein & Birn, 1998). Still another set of critics have cited other episodes of genocide in which behaviors that were arguably as brutal as those engaged in by German Holocaust perpetrators were carried out by people who clearly did not have long-standing or deeply ingrained negative (let alone eliminationist) attitudes toward their victims (Aschheim, 1996; Browning, 1998; see also Smith, 1998).

Nonetheless, Germans during the Nazi era had been indoctrinated for years with a relentless barrage of anti-Semitic propaganda, and the claim that the average German of that time was predisposed to feel extreme antipathy toward Jews is certainly not in dispute. What is at issue, instead, is whether that fact in and of itself rules out the possibility that other factors and psychological processes—factors and processes that we ignore at our peril—also played a significant role in creating willing executioners. Although Goldhagen's assessment of the evidence led him to rule out the importance of social-psychological factors, a reconsideration of that evidence suggests that intense preexisting hatred toward the victims of one's genocidal activities may not be sufficient *or* necessary to produce the kind of unspeakable violence that characterized the Holocaust.

How Situations Affect People

Goldhagen vividly demonstrated that Holocaust perpetrators often acted as they did—and, in many cases, engaged in even more brutality than was asked or expected of them—without any authority figures directing their activities, and without any coercion whatsoever. He thus concluded that situational factors played no role in the generation of such behavior. Instead, he argued, preexisting attitudes can entirely explain perpetrator behavior. Goldhagen's analysis, however, could have benefited from an appreciation of a basic and important principle supported by over 40 years of social-psychological research; that is, while attitudes do indeed give rise to behavior, it is also the case that one's behavior affects one's attitudes and beliefs. And if one's behavior—the very behavior that shapes one's attitudes—is at some point affected by one's social context, then clearly, isolating a given behavior and trying to categorize it as "caused by the situation" or "caused by one's attitudes and dispositions" is a fruitless exercise. In sum, what is missing from Goldhagen's approach—and from *any* approach that treats situational pressures as static independent variables—is an appreciation of the dynamic relationship between people, their behavior, and their social contexts that characterizes contemporary social-psychological analyses of behavior.

These abstract principles can be more clearly illustrated by means of a reconsideration of Goldhagen's dismissal of the effects of situational pressure on people who became Holocaust perpetrators. It would be hard (and foolish) to argue with the assertion that German Holocaust perpetrators were part of a violently anti-Semitic society and that many of them were predisposed to persecute Jews. Goldhagen, however, goes further and argues that because of their attitudes, from the moment perpetrators were sent to the front, they were perfectly comfortable with engaging in activities such as shooting people through the head, burying them alive, and even killing infants. As previously noted, he bases that argument primarily on accounts of perpetrators enthusiastically brutalizing and killing Jews without having to be ordered or even encouraged to do so.

Even if they had attitudes that many readers of this chapter would find to be quite abhorrent, however, it is unnecessary to assume that when perpetrators reported for police or military duty, they already had the cognitive makeup of the genocidal killers they became.[2] In fact, all that might have been necessary for the transformation is that they were prepared or led by their circumstances to play *any* role in anti-Jewish operations. The latter assumption is arguably quite reasonable. One might imagine that German recruits and volunteers newly arrived on the eastern front were quite motivated to carry out their duties effectively and do whatever was asked of them to advance their country's interests. There is also no reason to doubt Browning's (1992a) speculation that the newly mobilized men saw their ability to function effectively within their units as a test of their strength and character. Furthermore, like all soldiers, not just German ones, they were part of a system in which the expectation was that one would follow the orders of superior officers. Given these considerations, it is unfortunately not at all surprising that German soldiers and policemen very quickly found themselves participating in operations aimed at dealing with what they had been encouraged to see as the "Jewish Problem." And once they started playing *any* role in roundups, deportations, and executions, they were on their way to becoming the kinds of sadistic perpetrators that Goldhagen described. That tragic outcome was, in retrospect, quite predictable, even if one were to assume that the kinds of activities in which they ultimately engaged were gross violations of their normal standards for behavior.

The *cognitive dissonance* literature shows that when people are led to engage in behaviors that violate their normal standards, they will be motivated to change their attitudes and beliefs to reduce the discrepancy between their behavior and their cognitions. The classic demonstration of this phenomenon is a frequently cited study by Festinger and Carlsmith (1959). Participants in that experiment first engaged for an extended period of time in some hideously boring tasks (e.g., repeatedly turning 48 pegs on a board a quarter of a turn clockwise). When they were about to be excused from the study, the experimenter surprised them with one more request. He explained that one point of the study was to examine the effects of expectations on performance; therefore, he asked participants to help him out by telling the next scheduled participant that the study was really very exciting and enjoyable. Some participants were promised $1.00 for lying; others were promised $20.00. Regardless of the reward, virtually all complied with the experimenter's request and agreed to help out by misrepresenting the nature of the study to another person.

The key outcome measure followed: Participants were asked to report how much they had actually enjoyed the task. Those who had been paid $1.00 reported that they had, after all, found the tedious tasks to be quite fun. Why would they say such a thing? According to cognitive dissonance theory (Festinger, 1957), when people detect inconsistencies between their attitudes (e.g., the experiment was boring) and their behaviors (e.g., I just told someone that it was wonderful), they will experience pressure to resolve the discrepancy. One way to eliminate the dissonance is to change one's attitudes. This is what participants in Festinger and Carlsmith's study did. After all, denying that the dissonance-producing behavior had occurred would have been quite difficult. Another way participants could have dealt with the dissonance would have been to decide that they were, after all, manipulative liars who always behave in such a manner. Needless to say, that would not have been a very appealing dissonance reduction strategy.

Also as predicted by dissonance theory, the people who were promised $20.00 to lie were far less likely to subsequently claim that they had found the study to be enjoyable. These participants could easily justify their behavior, for who would not have complied with the experimenter's request for such a grand sum? They experienced little dissonance. Participants in the $1.00 payment condition, of course, would not have been able to convince themselves that such a paltry amount was all it took to get them to violate their moral standards. Their dishonest behavior was insufficiently justified, and so attitude change was the only available path to dissonance reduction. Many other studies have also confirmed that subtle pressure to behave in counterattitudinal ways—*induced compliance*—is much more likely to lead to dissonance and attitude change than heavy-handed attempts to manipulate behavior.

People's behavior, then, changes what they think and feel. Furthermore, Cooper and Fazio (1984) reviewed the empirical evidence and concluded that induced compliance is especially likely to cause attitude change when people's behaviors have aversive consequences that they feel personally responsible for bringing about. Playing a role in the death of a person who did one no harm would seem to fall into this category. In fact, other studies show that hurting another person is indeed the kind of behavior that can result in dissonance and attitude change. Research by Brock and Buss (1962) and Goldstein, Davis, and Herman (1975), among others, found that when people aggressed against others (e.g., by administering electric shocks in the context of "learning studies" similar to the one staged by Milgram), the way they perceived the people they aggressed against then changed. They derogated their victims after hurting them and saw them as deserving of punishment. This general finding—that people come to believe that others deserve any suffering that is imposed on them—is robust enough that it has come to be known as the *just world phenomenon* (Lerner, 1980). Herbert (1998) clearly articulated this idea in his discussion of the German population's acceptance of Nazi era anti-Semitic policies. He noted that "to the extent that this acceptance spread, so too, did the conviction grow that there must be just cause behind the persecution of the Jews, since anyone getting this kind of punishment could certainly not be entirely innocent" (p. 112).

To resolve dissonance, attitudes not only can change but also can change in such a way that they encourage repetition of the action that caused the dissonance. In the case of a Holocaust perpetrator, that would have meant dehumanizing one's victims and convincing oneself that they presented a terrible threat to Germany and Europe. What Goldhagen (1996) recounted was arguably the culmination of these processes: perpetrators engaging in violent persecutory behavior without any authority figures directing their activities, and without any coercion whatsoever. Unfortunately, it is also not surprising to read about the escalation of brutality that Goldhagen found for individual perpetrators. Staub (1989, 1996) calls this the "continuum of destructiveness," while Bandura (1999) refers to it as "gradualistic moral disengagement." Justifying and rationalizing what one does leads one to do more of it and do it more easily. Derogation leads to brutality, brutality is justified, even more brutal behavior follows, and the violence can escalate all the way to genocide.[3]

Goldhagen (1996), like many other commentators, makes much of the fact that German soldiers or policemen were not literally forced to take an active role in the attempted extermination of the Jews, and he notes that there is little evidence that any of them were ever punished for refusing to do so. This, of course, could be used as evidence in support of the hypothesis that Holocaust perpetrators did what was in their hearts to begin with. But, as already discussed, it is subtle situational pressure, not excessive pressure or inducement, that promotes attitude change (as exemplified by the difference between the $1.00 and $20.00 conditions of the Festinger and Carlsmith study). The dissonance literature indicates that people who engage in brutality in response to pressures that they would have to admit they could have resisted are precisely the people one would expect to progress through the continuum of destructiveness.

Other paths to dissonance reduction were also available to Holocaust perpetrators. For example, they could have relabeled the very behavior that was causing the dissonance, and done so in a way that made the behavior seem consistent with other important attitudes and values. There are many different ways to categorize a given behavior (Vallacher & Wegner, 1987). For example, even a seemingly simple action like "cutting down a tree" could also be identified and summarized as "swinging an ax," "getting exercise," "gathering firewood," "maintaining the ecological balance," or even "contributing to the destruction of a forest." Similarly, an action like "murdering a Jewish child" can also be flexibly labeled. Norfolk and Ignatieff (1988) suggested that genocide

> is actually a kind of longing for utopia, a blood sacrifice in the
> worship of an idea of paradise. What could be more like paradise
> on earth than to live in a community without enemies? To create a
> world with no more need of borders, for watch-posts, a world freed

> from fear in the night and war by day? A world safe from the
> deadly contaminations and temptations of the other tribe? . . .
> What could be more seductive than to kill in order to put an end to
> all killing? (p. 125)

As noted by Bandura (1999) in his discussion of moral disengagement, "Investing harmful conduct with high moral purpose not only eliminates self-censure, but it engages self-approval in the service of destructive exploits" (p. 196). Indeed, in Nazi Germany "the rationales behind mass murder were linked to the resolution of various dangers or threats that could be warded off by 'liquidating' the Jews: the 'cleansing of the hinterland' on the eastern front or the 'roundup of partisan nests,' the elimination of the black market or of diseases, the punishment of sabotage and of assassination of German soldiers, or just the extermination of Bolshevism" (Herbert, 1998, p. 114). Such recontextualizing of behavior, of course, could have served to reduce dissonance. "Killing innocent people" would undoubtedly have been discrepant with perpetrators' values; "building a better world for my family," on the other hand, would clearly not have been.[4]

Goldhagen (1996) himself took note of some of the high-minded ways in which Holocaust perpetrators talked about their brutal and murderous behavior. But he attributed those justifications to "the perversity of the Nazified German mind" (p. 213), and not to normative psychological processes. Fenigstein (1998), in his own assessment of the role of obedience pressure in the Holocaust, also presented the perpetrators' beliefs that the extermination of the Jews was "right and just, a source of great personal, national, and racial pride," as an alternative explanation for their behavior. Because of the prevalence of these beliefs, he argued, the Holocaust had "almost nothing to do with conscience, morality, and obedience pressures" (p. 72). What Fenigstein failed to consider, however, was that perpetrators' categorization of their actions might have been an effect as well as a cause of their behavior, and that situational pressures and constraints—including obedience pressures—could well have played a role in giving rise to that behavior. This, then, is another example of the difficulties inherent in pitting situational and cognitive-dispositional forces against each other and not considering the dynamic relationship between the situation, persons, and behavior.

In sum, simply identifying incidents in which people engaged in brutality without any obvious situational pressure is not sufficient evidence for concluding that situational factors were irrelevant to what they did. Of course, accepting the importance of the psychological processes discussed here does not necessitate downplaying the importance of the fact that the perpetrators lived in a society in which they were bombarded with anti-Semitic propaganda that encouraged them to dehumanize Jews. But at the same time, acknowledging the fact that the perpetrators lived in a society in which they were bombarded with anti-Semitic propaganda does not rule out the importance of these psychological processes. Social psychologists would indeed suggest that situational pressure could play a role in producing genocidal behavior, but their account of how it could do so involves psychological processes that Goldhagen did not consider.

PEOPLE AFFECT SITUATIONS—AND ARE NOT ALWAYS AWARE OF IT

Another problem with conceptualizing a situation as a static entity that independently affects behavior is that such an analysis ignores the fact that people do not only react to situations; they also influence and even create them (Snyder & Ickes, 1985). For example, one might attribute the dominant behavior of a person within a group to the submissiveness of his or her interaction partners, but that simple situational attribution would not take into account the possibility that the individual's dominant personality actually *elicited* the submissive behavior in the other people. Similarly, although some people might seem to have low self-esteem because they are constantly being put down by others, it is also the case that some of them play a role in creating such a social environment by subtly seeking and eliciting feedback to confirm their already poor self-images (Swann, 1990).

Clearly, it is difficult for an observer to disentangle all the reciprocal influences that people and situations have on each other. Perhaps more surprising, though, is just how poorly people appreciate how their own behavior can shape their social contexts. Social actors do not always appreciate or acknowledge the extent to which they affect situations—including how they affect the other people in those situations—even when their influence would seem to be obvious.

A study by Gilbert and Jones (1986) provided a compelling demonstration of this attributional bias. In general, when people are asked to figure out the causes of another person's behavior, they do not pay enough attention to the situation that person is in. Instead, people seem to be drawn to internal or personality attributions for behavior. Known as the "fundamental attribution error" or "correspondence bias" (Gilbert & Malone, 1995; Jones, 1990; Ross, 1977), this is one of social psychology's most well known and robust findings. In some of the classic studies, for example, people see someone literally ordered to express an opinion. When they are asked afterward to report what they think that person's true beliefs were, they typically conclude that he or she really held the opinion expressed (e.g., Jones & Harris, 1967). The correspondence bias occurs in such cases even though it is quite clear that an opinion was expressed only under duress. Gilbert and Jones took this basic experimental paradigm one step farther and tested whether people would still commit the fundamental attribution error if *they themselves* were the people who were forcing someone else to express an opinion. One might expect that if an individual is the active agent controlling others' behavior, whether that behavior involves expressing an opinion or anything else, then the individual will be able to fully appreciate how the constrained people cannot be judged or evaluated on the basis of their behavior.

Participants in Gilbert and Jones's study of *perceiver-induced constraint* were asked to interview other people about their opinions on a variety of social and political issues. The catch was that the participants were also given the job of signaling to the people they were interviewing whether they should make a conservative response or a liberal one. Some participants, as instructed by the experimenters, signaled for mostly liberal answers; other participants signaled for mostly conservative ones. In addition, these answers were being read from a script provided by the experimenters, and the participants were well aware of that fact. Given that setup, it is hard to imagine that one could learn anything meaningful about another person. On average, though, participants who heard mostly conservative responses from the interviewee rated him or her as being conservative, and those who heard mostly liberal responses concluded that he or she must be liberal.

Gilbert and Jones (1986) thus found that even when people had no particular incentive to be biased, they still failed to take into account how their own behavior affected others even though the their influence was about as obvious as it could be. What if people are actually *motivated* not to take into account their own influence? Perpetrators of genocide degrade people and make them almost less than human by starving them, terrorizing them, and forcing them to live in desperate conditions in prison camps, concentration camps, and refugee camps. An implication of the Gilbert and Jones (1986) research is that perpetrators might then turn around and *justify* their treatment of their victims by pointing out how degraded and less than human they are, even though they themselves brought about that wretched state. Indeed, Rudolph Hoss, the commandant of the Auschwitz concentration camp, reportedly remarked to a visitor that the camp's inmates

> "are not like you and me. You saw them yourself; they are different. They look different. They do not behave like human beings." It had never occurred to Hoss that he had created the conditions that reduced the prisoners to the level of rats scraping and fighting for every crumb of bread. Beset by malnutrition and disease, how could they have looked like average human beings when the camp was devised to reduce the human being to his bare animal state? (Paskuly, in Hoss, 1992, p. 198)

Similarly, the philosopher Beryl Lang has written about how very often, before the Nazis exterminated Jews, they first reduced them to a "subhuman state" through "systematic brutality and degradation." This, he argued, made killing them more "palatable," because it is easier to kill a person once he or she no longer resembles a human being. Interestingly, Lang argues that this was a conscious strategy, because it would have been inconceivable that the perpetrators could have ignored the fact that they themselves had reduced their victims to the pathetic state they were in before their deaths (Rosenbaum, 1998, p. 213). But, again, research on perceiver-induced constraint reveals that people do not always account for situational constraints on behavior, even when they themselves have constructed the situation. Thus, perpetrators could have focused on the degraded and pathetic state of their victims as justification for both their past and their future victimization, even though the perpetrators were actually responsible for their wretched state.

Goldhagen's (1996) analysis could also have benefited from an understanding of how people often seem unaware of the extent to which they have created the social situations to which they then respond. In his description of the brutal Helmbrechts work camp set up by the Nazis in 1944, he recounted how the female prisoners were deprived of access to latrines and instead forced to use buckets in their barracks. Even worse, not enough buckets were provided for the Jewish prisoners, so, predictably, the buckets frequently overflowed, leading to a terrible stench in the barracks. The guards' response was nightmarish yet predictable: "As if the permanent stench was not itself a sufficient form of punishment, the camp's guards beat the Jewish women daily, including the seriously ill, ostensibly for the soiling of their barracks. Yet they would not provide the Jews with the additional buckets that would have altered the conditions producing these 'punishments'" (Goldhagen, 1996, p. 341). In other words, the Germans "'punished' the Jews for things which the Germans themselves guaranteed that the Jews could not avoid doing" (p. 342). Goldhagen's use of the word *ostensibly* and his mocking quotations around the word *punishment* suggest that he believed the guards were fully aware of the grotesque absurdity of their behavior. There is, however, no reason to assume that. Given how far the guards had already traveled along the continuum of destructiveness, they were certainly not motivated to make situational attributions for the prisoners' appearance and behavior. As counterintuitive and even horrifying as it might seem, they could well have felt that it was only natural that they should respond in such a punitive way to the filthy and animal-like behavior with which they felt they were confronted.

Clearly, participating in genocide is a long way from making a fellow student read conservative and liberal attitude statements. However, the research on perceiver-induced constraint (see also Gilbert, Jones, & Pelham, 1987; Ginzel, Jones, & Swann, 1987) reveals that it is psychologically possible to remain blind to how one affects and even shapes the behavior of other people. Thus, not only can perpetrators of genocide judge victims based on their behavior and appearance, and not only can they do so without taking into account how circumstances affected that behavior and appearance, but they are capable of doing so even when *they themselves* create those circumstances.

SITUATIONS ARE CONSTRUCTED BY PEOPLE

Goldhagen's analysis of perpetrator behavior would have been enriched by yet another of social psychology's bedrock principles. When he addressed the hypothesis that situational forces affected perpetrator behavior, Goldhagen adopted an implicit definition of "situations" that was arguably a bit too literal. Some situations, especially those defined by physical parameters, have relatively direct effects on human behavior and can more or less be reified; for example, earthquakes, hurricanes, and extreme temperatures can be expected to have fairly uniform effects on people. In the case of most meaningful human behavior, however, what people respond to is not an *objective* situation but the situation as they *perceive* and cognitively *construct* it. Ross and Nisbett (1991) called this the "principle of construal" and identified it as one of the principles that serve as a foundation for the field as a whole. In their words, "The impact of any 'objective' stimulus situation depends upon the personal and subjective meaning that the actor attaches to that situation. To predict the behavior of a given person successfully, we must be able to appreciate the actor's construal of that situation—that is, the manner in which the person understands the situation as a whole" (p. 11).

This principle has important implications for Goldhagen's conclusion that the idea that conformity pressure could have affected perpetrator behavior is not only wrong but actually illogical. As discussed previously, Goldhagen argued that if German soldiers and policemen in World War II found themselves in groups where most of their peers were uncomfortable with participating in genocide, then conformity pressure would have actually worked to dissuade the group from killing. Indeed, at first glance it is hard to imagine how such a situation could actually lead the opposite to occur. However, the objective attitudes of group members are not as important as *subjective* representations of their attitudes. Furthermore, people are not always so successful at figuring out what other group members believe and feel, a phenomenon known as *pluralistic ignorance* (Miller & Prentice, 1994). The norms that people perceive and conform to might not really accurately represent other group members' actual attitudes and beliefs. D. T. Miller and Prentice (1994) provided an especially clear example of this phenomenon in their discussion of Matza's (1964) study of juvenile delinquents:

> Matza argued that the individual members of juvenile gangs actually lacked a firm commitment to their antisocial behavior, at least initially. In fact, each of the youths in the gang was privately very uncomfortable with his own behavior. But because the youths

were unwilling to express their reservations publicly, they each appeared to the others as fully committed to, and comfortable with, the group's delinquency. The facade of toughness thus created "a system of shared misunderstandings," which, in turn, led to a level of antisocial behavior that no individual member fully embraced. (p. 543)

Experimental research shows that people also do not appreciate how their *own* behavior, affected as it is by what they believe are other people's preferences and beliefs, can actually contribute to and magnify the overall pluralistic ignorance within the group (Vorauer & Miller, 1997). In other words, people's collective efforts to blend in and conform to a norm can actually reinforce the power of an illusory norm that actually has no counterpart at the level of individuals within the group—this despite the fact that no one individual appreciates his or her role in enforcing that norm. This, of course, is another example of how people can affect social situations without being aware of it (see previous section).

There is no direct evidence that pluralistic ignorance played a role in the creation of Holocaust perpetrators, and little evidence that the norms that developed in German police and military units were not simply direct reflections of group members' initial attitudes. But research documenting the phenomenon of pluralistic ignorance indicates that the effects of conformity pressure on perpetrators must be taken very seriously. In addition, pluralistic ignorance has been found to be most likely when people avoid expressing their true feelings because of their fears of embarrassment, public censure, and social isolation (Miller & Prentice, 1994). As Browning (1992a) argued, those German policemen and soldiers who declined to participate in massacres could well have been concerned about being ostracized by the other people in their battalions if they opted out of the "dirty work." Being ostracized and isolated was probably not an appealing prospect for a person stationed out of his or her country in the middle of a hostile population during a brutal war.

In general, the effects of a "situation" cannot be determined unless we understand how the people in that situation construed it. Behavior can thus be affected by people's perceptions of others' attitudes and beliefs even if those perceptions are inaccurate. Related to that, the attitudes of group members cannot be directly inferred from the collective behavior of the group. It should be emphasized that an application of this principle to the case of Holocaust perpetrators does not require the assumption that the members of killing squads were really pacifists at heart. It does, however, suggest that even in this kind of a situation conformity pressures could have led to behavior that was more extreme in terms of its violence and cruelty than would have been initiated by a person *not* subject to those pressures. In sum, social psychologists would indeed suggest that conformity might have played a role in producing genocidal behavior, but their account of how it could do so involves subtle psychological processes that Goldhagen did not consider.

CONCLUSION

When the book *The Rape of Nanking* (Chang, 1997) was released, at least one reader suggested that the reason that the photos taken of the massacre by the Japanese are so shocking is that "it's obvious they are enjoying the killing. Looking at those faces, I see that those young soldiers don't think there is anything abnormal about what they are doing." In contrast, he said, "I think of Germans during the Holocaust carrying out orders to kill with a cold sullenness" (Grossman, 1997, p. 5). Similarly, Joffe (1998) suggested that "our standard view of the Holocaust is that of a literally dehumanized murder machine—much like a modern car assembly plant—where a handful of inspectors and trouble-shooters supervised an army of robots that precision-slaughtered full-time, twenty-four hours a day" (p. 218).

If it is true that recent Holocaust scholarship has given rise to a stereotyped image of perpetrators as detached from their actions and grimly following orders, Goldhagen's (1996) book deserves much of the attention that it has received. The attempted extermination of European Jewry was accompanied by gratuitous cruelty and at times even a gleeful sadism. "Dehumanized murder machines" do not take pride in their work, but Holocaust perpetrators often did. Indeed, Goldhagen himself notes that the desire to remind people of this fact was what motivated his research (Goldhagen, 1998). By focusing so sharply on perpetrator behavior and by vividly describing certain often-neglected aspects of the Holocaust (e.g., the death marches and the work camps), Goldhagen has made an important contribution to the Holocaust literature.

The treatment of "social-psychological explanations" in *Hitler's Willing Executioners* should also be put in the context of the fact that social psychologists have not been very quick to make their voices heard in recent debates about the causes and consequences of genocide. For many years, the research agenda of social psychologists was profoundly affected by the events of World War II (Jones, 1985). Social psychologists, along with other scholars, were faced with the challenge of explaining the terrible events of that period. The genesis of many classic research programs, such as Milgram's obedience studies and Adorno, Frenkel-Brunswik, Levenson, and Sanford's (1950) work on the authoritarian personality, can be traced to a desire to shed light on the behavior of the perpetrators of the Holocaust, but in recent decades, social psychology's preoccupation with understanding how and why people engage in collective violence has waned quite a bit. To be fair, then, Goldhagen's incomplete summary of what social psychologists have to say about the perpetrators of genocide in part can be attributed to the fact that social psychologists themselves have not made it a priority to spell it out for other people (cf. Darley, 1992; Staub, 1989, 1996).

Goldhagen's book may become required reading for people interested in learning about the Holocaust. Unfortunately, his attempt to understand the psychological processes that gave rise to the kind of horrifying perpetrator behavior that he so vividly described was handicapped by some common misconceptions about how social psychologists conceptualize the relationship between persons and situations. A monocausal framework for understanding genocide cannot do justice to the dynamic interplay between persons and situations that is characteristic of human behavior. The goal of this chapter was to provide some examples of how social psychologists have tackled the complexity of human behavior head-on and, in the process, to show how what they have learned might speak to the kinds of issues with which Goldhagen and other scholars have grappled. Social psychologists have a unique perspective to contribute to attempts to understand the Holocaust in particular and genocide in general. It is a perspective that is subtle, rich, and powerful, but underappreciated. Social psychology does indeed have something to contribute to our understanding of Hitler's willing executioners, and to our understanding of the behavior of the perpetrators of past, present, and (unfortunately) future genocides.

NOTES

I would like to thank Dan Cervone, Ralph Erber, and Thomas Griffin for comments on an earlier version of this chapter. Preparation of the chapter was also facilitated by support from the National Science Foundation under grant SBR-9809188 and the National Institutes of Mental Health under grant R01 MH58876.

1. In clarifying his position, Goldhagen has noted that he does not view eliminationist anti-Semitism as a necessary and sufficient global explanation for the occurrence of the Holocaust. The Holocaust, he points out, was contingent upon "the facts that the Nazis gained power, that they crushed internal opposition, that they conquered Europe, that they created the institutions of killing and organized the slaughter," and other historical events (Goldhagen, 1998, p. 140). Instead, his proposal is that eliminationist anti-Semitism is a necessary and sufficient global explanation for why *individual Germans* who found themselves in the midst of those historical circumstances became Holocaust perpetrators. "With regard to the *motivational* cause of the Holocaust, for the vast majority of perpetrators," he argues, "a monocausal explanation does suffice" (Goldhagen, 1996, p. 416).

2. Many never developed that cognitive makeup. A discussed by Finkelstein and Birn (1998), Goldhagen notes that quite a few men were unable to handle their violent assignments, and "transfers occurred frequently" in the *Einsatzgruppen* (mobile killing units; Goldhagen, 1996, p. 381).

3. Similar processes have been observed in torturers (Conroy, 2000) and prison guards (Conover, 2000). And as discussed by Suedfeld (2000), there is evidence that *kindness* can escalate in a similar way. Some rescuers of Jews during the Holocaust seem to have ini-

tially acted in response to social pressures or a sense of duty but "followed the same foot-in-the-door, gradual escalation of involvement as did the murderers whom they were trying to thwart: starting with small acts of kindness and moving on to greater and greater commitment" (p. 4).

4. Perhaps even more remarkable are cases where perpetrators relabeled the very victims of their violence in order to reduce the dissonance that they might have felt as a result of harming human beings. For example, interviews with a veteran of a Japanese military unit that conducted unethical medical experiments during World War II revealed that he insisted on calling the victims of those experiment "logs" rather than "people" (Blumenthal & J. Miller, 1999, p. A10). And one Holocaust survivor who was forced to dig up the bodies of murdered Jews reported that he and his coworkers were beaten by their German supervisors if they called the people they unearthed anything other than "rags" (Lanzmann, 1995). The Nazi decree that all German Jews assume "Israel" and "Sarah" as first names—thus diminishing the individuality and humanity of those destined for extermination—was possibly another variant of this psychological maneuver.

REFERENCES

Adorno, T. W., Frenkel-Brunswik, E., Levenson, D. J., & Sanford, R. N. (1950). *The authoritarian personality*. New York: Harper.

Asch, S. E. (1956). Studies of independence and conformity: I. A minority of one against a unanimous majority. *Psychological Monographs, 70* (9, Whole No. 416).

Aschheim, S. E. (1996, July/August). Reconceiving the Holocaust? [Review of the book *Hitler's willing executioners: Ordinary Germans and the Holocaust*]. *Tikkun, 11*(4), 62–65.

Bandura, A. (1999). Moral disengagement in the perpetration of inhumanities. *Personality and Social Psychology Review, 3*, 193–209.

Blass, T. (1992). The social psychology of Stanley Milgram. In M. P. Zanna (Ed.), *Advances in experimental social psychology* (Vol. 25, pp. 277–329). San Diego, CA: Academic Press.

Blass, T. (1993). Psychological perspectives on the perpetrators of the Holocaust: The role of situational pressures, personal dispositions, and their interactions. *Holocaust and Genocide Studies, 7*, 30–50.

Blumenthal, R., & Miller, J. (1999, March 4). Japanese germ-war atrocities: A half-century of stonewalling the world. *The New York Times*, p. A10.

Brehm, S. S., & Kassin, S. M. (1996). *Social psychology*. Geneva, IL: Houghton Mifflin.

Brock, T., & Buss, A. (1962). Dissonance, aggression, and the evaluation of pain. *Journal of Abnormal and Social Psychology, 65*, 197–202.

Browning, C. R. (1992a). *Ordinary men: Reserve Police Battalion 101 and the Final Solution in Poland*. New York: HarperCollins.

Browning, C. R. (1992b). *The path to genocide: Essays on launching the final solution*. New York: Cambridge University Press.

Browning, C. R. (1998). Ordinary men or ordinary Germans. In R. R. Shandley (Ed.), *Unwilling Germans? The Goldhagen debate* (pp. 55–73). Minneapolis: University of Minnesota Press.

Caprara, G. V., & Cervone, D. (2000). *Personality: Determinants, dynamics, and potentials*. New York: Cambridge University Press.

Chang, I. (1997). *The rape of Nanking: The forgotten holocaust of World War II.* New York: Basic Books.

Conover, T. (2000). *Newjack: Guarding Sing Sing.* New York: Random House.

Conroy, J. (2000). *Unspeakable acts, ordinary people: The dynamics of torture.* New York: Knopf.

Cooper, J., & Fazio, R. H. (1984). A new look at dissonance theory. In L. Berkowitz (Ed.), *Advances in experimental social psychology* (Vol. 17, pp. 229–266). New York: Academic Press.

Darley, J. M. (1992). Social organization for the production of evil. *Psychological Inquiry, 3,* 199–218.

Diamond, J. (1992). *The third chimpanzee.* New York: Harper Perennial.

Eagly, A. H., & Chaiken, S. (1993). *The psychology of attitudes.* Fort Worth, TX: Harcourt Brace.

Elon, A. (1997, January 26). Germany's Daniel Goldhagen complex. *The New York Times Magazine,* pp. 40–44.

Endler, N. S., & Magnusson, D. (1976). Toward an interactional psychology of personality. *Psychological Bulletin, 83,* 956–979.

Fenigstein, A. (1998). Were obedience pressures a factor in the Holocaust? *Analyse & Kritik, 20,* 54–73.

Festinger, L. (1957). *A theory of cognitive dissonance.* Evanston, IL: Row, Peterson.

Festinger, L., & Carlsmith, J. M. (1959). Cognitive consequences of forced compliance. *Journal of Abnormal and Social Psychology, 58,* 203–210.

Finkelstein, N. G., & Birn, R. B. (1998). *A nation on trial: The Goldhagen thesis and historical truth.* New York: Henry Holt.

Gilbert, D. T., & Jones, E. E. (1986). Perceiver-induced constraint: Interpretations of self-generated reality. *Journal of Personality and Social Psychology, 50,* 269–280.

Gilbert, D. T., Jones, E. E., & Pelham, B. W. (1987). Influence and inference: What the perceiver overlooks. *Journal of Personality and Social Psychology, 52,* 861–870.

Gilbert, D. T., & Malone, P. S. (1995). The correspondence bias. *Psychological Bulletin, 117,* 21–38.

Ginzel, L. E., Jones, E. E., & Swann, W. B., Jr. (1987). How "naive" is the naive attributor? Discounting and augmentation in attitude attribution. *Social Cognition, 5,* 108–130.

Goldhagen, D. J. (1996). *Hitler's willing executioners: Ordinary Germans and the Holocaust.* New York: Knopf.

Goldhagen, D. J. (1998). The failure of the critics. In R. R. Shandley (Ed.), *Unwilling Germans? The Goldhagen debate* (pp. 129–150). Minneapolis: University of Minnesota Press.

Goldstein, J. H., Davis, R. W., & Herman, D. (1975). Escalation of aggression: Experimental studies. *Journal of Personality and Social Psychology, 31,* 162–170.

Gourevitch, P. (1998). *We wish to inform you that tomorrow we will be killed with our families.* New York: Farrar, Straus and Giroux.

Grossman, R. (1997, February 3). From history's shadows comes the chilling, heartbreaking story of the rape of Nanking [Review of the book *The rape of Nanking*]. *Chicago Tribune,* sect. 5, pp. 1, 5.

Herbert, U. (1998). The right question. In R. R. Shandley (Ed.), *Unwilling Germans? The Goldhagen debate* (pp. 109–116). Minneapolis: University of Minnesota Press.

Hobsbawm, E. (1994). *Age of extremes: The short twentieth century, 1914–1991*. London: Michael Joseph.

Hoss, R. (1992). *Death dealer: The memoirs of the SS Kommandant of Auschwitz* (S. Paskuly, Ed.). Buffalo, NY: Prometheus.

Joffe, J. (1998). "The killers were ordinary Germans, ergo the ordinary Germans were killers": The logic, the language, and the meaning of a book that conquered Germany. In R. R. Shandley (Ed.), *Unwilling Germans? The Goldhagen debate* (pp. 217–227). Minneapolis: University of Minnesota Press.

Jones, E. E. (1985). Major developments in social psychology during the past five decades. In G. Lindzey & E. Aronson (Eds.), *The handbook of social psychology* (3rd ed., Vol. 1, pp. 47–108). New York: Random House.

Jones, E. E. (1990). *Interpersonal perception*. New York: Macmillan.

Jones, E. E., & Harris, V. A. (1967). The attribution of attitudes. *Journal of Experimental Social Psychology, 3*, 1–24.

Lanzmann, C. (1995). *Shoah: The complete text of the acclaimed Holocaust film*. New York: DaCapo.

Lerner, M. J. (1980). *The belief in a just world: A fundamental delusion*. New York: Plenum.

Mandel, D. R. (1998). The obedience alibi: Milgram's account of the Holocaust reconsidered. *Analyse & Kritik, 20*, 74–94.

Matza, D. (1964). *Delinquency and drift*. New York: Wiley.

Milgram, S. (1974). *Obedience to authority*. New York: Harper and Row.

Miller, A. G. (1986). *The obedience experiments: A case study of controversy in social science*. New York: Praeger.

Miller, D. T., & Prentice, D. A. (1994). Collective errors and errors about the collective. *Personality and Social Psychology Bulletin, 20*, 541–550.

Mischel, W. (1968). *Personality and assessment*. New York: Wiley.

Mischel, W. (1990). Personality dispositions revisited and revised: A view after three decades. In L. A. Pervin (Ed.), *Handbook of personality theory and research* (pp. 111–134). New York: Guilford.

Norfolk, S., & Ignatieff, M. (1998, autumn). The scene of the crime. *Granta, 63*, 121–150.

Parry, R. L. (1998, summer). What young men do. *Granta, 62*, 83–123.

Pervin, L. A. (1984). *Current controversies and issues in personality* (2nd ed). New York: Wiley.

Rosenbaum, R. (1998). *Explaining Hitler: The search for the origins of his evil*. New York: Random House.

Rosenberg, T. (1998, April 19). Defending the indefensible. *The New York Times Magazine*, pp. 46–56, 69.

Ross, L. (1977). The intuitive psychologist and his shortcomings. In L. Berkowitz (Ed.), *Advances in experimental social psychology* (Vol. 10, pp. 174–221). New York: Academic Press.

Ross, L., & Nisbett, R. E. (1991). *The person and the situation*. New York: McGraw-Hill.

Shadel, W. G., & Cervone, D. (1993). The big five versus nobody? *American Psychologist, 48*, 1300–1302.

Smith, D. N. (1998). The psychocultural roots of genocide: Legitimacy and crisis in Rwanda. *American Psychologist, 7*, 743–753.

Snyder, M., & Ickes, W. (1985). Personality and social behavior. In G. Lindzey & E. Aronson (Eds.), *Handbook of social psychology* (3rd ed., Vol. 2, pp. 883–948). New York: Random House.

Staub, E. (1989). *The roots of evil.* New York: Cambridge University Press.

Staub, E. (1996). Cultural-societal roots of violence: The examples of genocidal violence and contemporary youth violence in the United States. *American Psychologist, 51,* 117–132.

Suedfeld, P. (2000). Reverberations of the Holocaust fifty years later: Psychology's contributions to understanding persecution and genocide. *Canadian Psychology, 41,* 1–9.

Swann, W. B., Jr. (1990). To be adored or to be known? The interplay of self-enhancement and self-verification. In E. T. Higgins & R. T. Sorrentino (Eds.), *Handbook of motivation and cognition* (Vol. 2, pp. 408–448). New York: Guilford.

Vallacher, R. R., & Wegner, D. M. (1987). What do people think they're doing? Action identification and human behavior. *Psychological Review, 94,* 3–15.

Vorauer, J. D., & Miller, D. T. (1997). Failure to recognize the effect of implicit social influence on the presentation of self. *Journal of Personality and Social Psychology, 73,* 281–295.

Wehler, H.-U. (1998). Like a thorn in the flesh. In R. R. Shandley (Ed.), *Unwilling Germans? The Goldhagen debate* (pp. 93–104). Minneapolis: University of Minnesota Press.

Wick, J., & Stone, M. (1999, July/August). The left and Kosovo: Giving ethnic cleansing a chance. *Tikkun, 14*(4), pp. 35–40.

3

Authoritarianism and the Holocaust

Some Cognitive and Affective Implications

Peter Suedfeld and Mark Schaller

THE AUTHORITARIAN PERSONALITY: A BRIEF REVIEW

Of all the relationships between social-psychological or personality constructs and real-life phenomena, that between the original concept of the authoritarian personality, on the one hand, and the propensity to engage in persecution and even genocide, on the other, must surely be among the highest in face validity. How could it be otherwise? The entire research program began with an attempt to understand the roots of anti-Semitism and its role in personality (N. Sanford, 1973) and moved on to incorporate ethnocentric prejudice more generally and then to look at how these patterns were related to other personality tendencies.

The authors of *The Authoritarian Personality* (Adorno, Frenkel-Brunswik, Levinson, & R. Sanford, 1950) included social scientists who had seen Nazism at first hand and had fled from it, and who in fact had launched a theoretical and research enterprise precisely to elucidate some people's susceptibility to the siren call of fascism. The Institute of Social Research in Frankfurt had found that German workers who supported the Social Democratic Party had underlying and perhaps unconscious authoritarian values. The Frankfurt group decided that the superficially powerful labor movement would not effectively oppose Hitler. Showing now-legendary, and possibly unique, trust in their own data, the researchers saved their lives by emigrating almost immediately after the Nazis took power (at a time when most liberals and Jews were still convinced that nothing really bad would happen). Some of the "Frankfurt School" émigrés eventually contributed to the further development of authoritarianism theory and research at the hands of what came to be known as the "Berkeley Group" (N. Sanford, 1973).

After considerable work, combining intensive interviews with a variety of paper-and-pencil measures, a picture of the authoritarian personality emerged.

The trait was causally associated with child rearing and family constellation in early life: with fathers who had been distant, hardworking, dominant, and serious, and mothers who had been moralistic, kind, and self-sacrificing. When grown, the offspring of such couples idealized their parents. They had strong superegos, expressed in punitiveness, ethnocentrism, and orthodox morality; and weak egos, shown by the use of repression, denial, and projection, as well as a tendency to superstition and stereotyping and an emphasis on power and toughness.

Moving beyond their psychodynamic theoretical foundations, the researchers also correlated scores on the various scales of authoritarianism with demographic and other group characteristics. They found negative correlations between authoritarianism, on the one hand, and intelligence, education, and paternal income, on the other. The prototypical test that finally came to be the measure of authoritarianism, the F (for pre-fascism) Scale, identified a complex pattern of personality characteristics: six identifiable categories of high scorers, and five of low. Thus, the later oversimplification in secondary sources (high F equals authoritarian, low F equals nonauthoritarian or antiauthoritarian) loses much of the nuanced analysis and interpretation of the original work (cf. N. Sanford, 1973).

It is pointless to recapitulate in detail the storm that soon broke over the authors' heads. The scale development, and to a lesser degree the interview and projective test components of the research, were harshly—and, to a great extent, correctly—criticized for methodological and psychometric flaws. Prominent among these were susceptibility to response sets and experimenter expectancies, and reliance upon a small norm group characterized by narrow and unrepresentative sampling.

Conceptually, the work was faulted for drawing empirically unwarranted inferences as to the familial causes of the syndrome and for the implication that authoritarianism was limited to adherents of politically conservative, right-wing (fascist) ideologies. Whether the former objection was warranted depends upon one's evaluation of psychodynamic theorizing and epistemology; the latter was perhaps less justified than the critiques of methodology. The original authors recognized that high F scores were not necessarily associated with any particular political view and pointed out the existence of low scorers, supporters of "progressive" policies, who were as rigid and totalitarian as extreme high scorers (Adorno et al., 1950). This datum was among the subtleties lost upon later critics and defenders of the work. It is also worth remembering that the Frankfurt School was not nearly as monolithic in its own political orientation as some subsequent writers have implied (see Stone, Lederer, & Christie, 1993).

Some of these flaws have been corrected since then. There are balanced and reversed versions of the F Scale, and it has been administered to widely differing samples in large numbers. Problems or no problems, the scale has been amazingly popular among subsequent researchers. It (and its variants) often, although not always, correlates in the expected directions with a host of attitudinal and behavioral measures. Some of these were support for extreme right-wing parties and policies in various countries, rigidity in problem-solving tasks, punitiveness in response to experimental scenarios dealing with people accused of crime, and giving higher levels of shock in a Milgram-paradigm experiment. Predicted intergroup differences—between people differing in level of education, willingness to serve in the military, susceptibility to bias in favor of one's own athletic team, belief in President Richard Nixon's innocence during the Watergate scandal, and the like—have also been found (one wonders what the pattern would be for continued trust in President Bill Clinton's innocence in the Monica Lewinsky scandal).

A recent, generally favorable, assessment (Stone et al., 1993) concludes that the evidence supports the causal chain proposed by the theory, as summarized by Duckitt (1989):

1. Strict, punitive child-rearing methods result in
2. Resentment toward authority, which must be repressed and displaced because of fear of that authority and is therefore expressed by
3. The covarying traits constituting the surface personality syndrome and including submissiveness to authority, rigid thinking, a tendency to superstition, intolerance of ambiguity, conventional morality, rejection of weakness and nonconformity, hostility toward out-groups, and aversion to introspective and psychological insights. This syndrome, in turn, is expressed as
4. A set of sociopolitical attitudes and beliefs consistent with support for antiegalitarian, undemocratic, and discriminatory leaders, parties, and policies.

One interesting sidelight is that, just as some critics at the height of the Cold War attacked the original researchers for ignoring left-wing authoritarianism, other critics writing during and since the heyday of the New Left have denied that authoritarianism does exist on the left side of the political spectrum (Stone, 1980). The latter argument is supportable if authoritarianism is defined purely in terms of adherence to the stated aspirations of a political movement, as opposed to its actual practice. For example, (left-wing) communism in principle is egalitarian, while (right-wing) fascism is hierarchical; but in every communist *and* fascist country, social hierarchies have been strictly and often murderously enforced. So have the ruling party's monopolization of power; the suppression of dissidence, opposition, and civil liberties; and the subordination of laws to ideology. If the admirers of Stalin, Mao, Hoxha, Ho

Chi Minh, Kim Il Sung, Castro, et al. do not qualify as authoritarian, then we may need to replace the concept of left-wing authoritarianism with that of left-wing gullibility: personality factors related to a predisposition for supporting oppressive authoritarian regimes that generate demonstrably false democratic and egalitarian propaganda (but cf. Stone & Smith, 1993, for a counterargument).

Even ethnocentrism, supposedly a hallmark of right-wing ideology, has been a prominent feature of communist regimes. Anti-Semitism itself has flourished under communism, from the Soviet suppression of Yiddish literature and Stalin's "Doctors' Plot" to the persecution of Jewish officials and intellectuals in the former satellite countries. The subordination of non-Russian minorities in the former Soviet Union, and of non-Han minorities such as Tibetans in the People's Republic of China, of ethnic Chinese and Montagnards in Vietnam, of ethnic Hungarians under Romania's Ceauşescu regime, of Gypsies throughout central Europe, all give the lie to the argument that left-wing ideologies lead to the elimination of ethnic discrimination.

Redefinitions of Authoritarianism

There have been many attempts to rescue the concept of authoritarianism. In general, these have relied on redefining the construct by changing or deleting some of its original components. One major limitation of such efforts is that none has followed the painstaking, multimodal research methodology that led to the initial formulations, so that they have lost the holistic tracing of parental behavior to personality constellation and adult politics. Another is that the disaggregation of individuals with both high and low F scores into different subtypes has been ignored. The term *authoritarianism* now has so many possible meanings that almost any ideological or other political pattern can be included or excluded at will by picking one's definition.

In perhaps the best-known example, Altemeyer (1988, 1996) has proposed that "right-wing authoritarianism" be defined as submissiveness, conventionality, and self-righteous aggressiveness toward dissenters in support of the traditional rulers and norms of whatever society the person lives in. A devoted Stalinist exhibiting these three traits during Stalin's rule would be a right-wing authoritarian, as would his counterpart Red Guard during the Cultural Revolution, and so on. Thus, communists, normally considered to be left-wing, are conceptually relocated to the extreme Right if they live in a communist-dominated society. The Altemeyer definition excludes people who adhere to movements *opposed* to their society's traditional power structure, even though such people frequently show submissiveness toward their superiors in the movement, conventional values as promulgated by that movement, and self-righteous aggression toward everyone who disagrees with them.

The "authoritarian syndrome" includes the entirety of the Adorno et al. causal model, from childhood experiences to defense mechanisms of the ego

71

and their consequences for personality and ideology. However, Altemeyer and other revisionists (e.g., Pratto, Sidanius, Stallworth, & Malle, 1994) have abandoned many of the conceptual bases as well as the research procedures of Adorno et al. in their versions. Social learning and cognitive style explanations have replaced psychodynamic personality theorizing. These trends have both expanded and diluted the original work, so that the relationship between authoritarianism and participation in the Holocaust or subsequent genocides becomes murkier than ever.

Authoritarianism and the Holocaust

There is one basic question here: Were authoritarian Europeans more likely to become perpetrators in, and supporters of, the Holocaust? It seems like a silly question, with an obvious answer. If the authoritarian personality is defined by obedience to authority and aggressiveness toward deviants and outsiders, plus—in its prototypical version—a specific animus toward Jews, how could it *not* be associated with acceptance of the attempted eradication of the Jewish people by the government in power, in a milieu where anti-Semitism (even if not "eliminationist" anti-Semitism, as Goldhagen, 1996, called it) had been traditional and Jews were historically seen as deviants and outsiders?

Unfortunately, no one administered the F Scale or any of its variants to a representative sample of the people who actually committed the Holocaust— or, at least, to those who were known to have committed it. Analogue scales and analogue-dependent measures—such as support for conservative parties, or for capital punishment, or aversion to homosexuality, or dislike of some other ethnic group—just do not answer the question.

This is a crucial issue. Although some version of authoritarianism may underlie how the individual relates to the occurrence of ethnic persecution (and the construct is probably the most plausible candidate among currently known personality variables), mere prejudice is not the same as participation in, or even agreement with, genocide. Believing that society condones too many immoral lifestyles is not the same as wanting to kill those who practice such lifestyles; the fear that the health care system is heavily burdened by the pointless extension of the lives of comatose or hopelessly senile patients is not the same as advocating that they be murdered. The Nazi death camps were not some banal expression of aversion to Jews and other non-Aryans; they were the embodiment of extreme evil (cf. Kressel, 1996). Does the F Scale measure extreme evil? Probably not, but there are no data to test the hypothesis.

Social Psychology and the Holocaust

It may also be that the hypothesized link between authoritarianism and support for the Nazi genocide is an example of the *fundamental attribution error*, a term that refers to a widespread tendency to attribute people's actions to personality dispositions rather than to external, situational factors. This tendency becomes an error because it is found when we really know it to be unwarranted—for example, when we know that someone's actions are the result of their being in a hurry or of their desire to avoid punishment, or when we hear a diplomat presenting an official position in the role of spokesperson for his or her government. The fundamental attribution error operates even when experimental subjects are specifically told that a speech was randomly assigned to a speaker, who had no hand in preparing the contents and no choice about what to say. Of course, a dispositional attribution is not always an error; in fact, much of the time people do act or speak in harmony with their preferences. This was unquestionably true of the behavior of many leaders and followers of the Nazis.

However, in the Holocaust context generally, one must seriously consider attributions emphasizing external factors rather than (or as well as) dispositional ones. Situational explanations of the Holocaust itself, and of the actions of its perpetrators, abound in political science, history, and economics (see, e.g., Suedfeld, 1998). Such explanations, and experimental analogues incorporating variables that are thought to be significantly relevant to behavior during the Holocaust, also exist in social psychology. Staub's historical analysis (1989) of how social learning and reinforcement can lead to the gradual disinhibition of hurtful behavior is one outstanding example. Laboratory procedures that have been cited as shedding light on the Holocaust include the work of Lewin, Lippitt, and White (1939) on types of leadership; Sherif, Harvey, White, Hood, and Sherif's (1961) Robber's Cave study of intergroup conflict; Haney, Banks, and Zimbardo's (1973) observations of role-consistent behavior in a simulated prison; and, above all, Milgram's (1974) obedience experiments.

All these studies were able to illuminate aspects of interpersonal or intergroup behavior that were relevant to some component of the Holocaust, but none can provide a complete accounting. The psychological literature to a great extent oversimplifies actual history. Realistically, it has to do so: the complexity of life under the Nazis cannot be replicated in the laboratory. In view of the tremendous difference between any laboratory or simulation method and the actual, up-close torture and killing of men, women, and children, the researchers cannot be faulted for the incompleteness of their explanations.

In the real situation, people's roles and behaviors were often inconsistent and subject to diverse and changing influences. Both supporters and opponents of the Nazis were motivated by a wide variety of goals and aspirations (see, e.g., Baumeister, 1997; Proctor, 1999); and, as many survivor narratives demonstrate, people who rescued some Jews persecuted others (as well as sometimes abusing the ones they were sheltering), while some of the worst persecutors, including SS concentration camp guards, succored and saved some Jews (e.g., Dippel, 1996; Gushee, 1994; Hilberg, 1992; Holliday, 1995).

Of course, no single explanation of the Holocaust can be complete. It is clear that such events involve complicated interactions of personal, cultural, and environmental factors. But despite the risks of oversimplification, and despite the imprecise denotative and connotative meanings of authoritarianism, an approach based on the authoritarian personality construct may be of value. The effort requires a careful dissection of the construct, separating its multi-faceted, multilayered complex of variables in order to focus more specifically on particular elements of the authoritarian personality that may help us to understand why the Holocaust happened and why some people but not others chose to perpetrate, while others resisted, the genocide.

We shall look at two aspects of authoritarianism theory that may be relevant to the Holocaust. One is related to chronic patterns of thinking; the other, to pervasive underlying emotions—the two major realms of human psychology.

AUTHORITARIANISM AND COGNITIVE STYLE

According to both classic and contemporary perspectives on the authoritarian personality, authoritarians think differently from nonauthoritarians. The differences pertain not only to *what* they think (e.g., political attitudes and ideologies) but also to *how* they think. This process-based element of authoritarian thinking patterns—cognitive style—has received considerable attention.

Among the major features of how authoritarians think are closed-mindedness, rigidity, categorical (black-or-white, all-or-none) preferences and attitudes, and intolerance of ambiguity. Authoritarians tend to have low need for cognition (they do not enjoy thinking hard), low cognitive complexity (they fail to recognize the legitimacy of alternative perspectives or to find integrative solutions), and high needs for structure and closure (they seize upon quick conclusions and dismiss contradictory ideas; see Budner, 1962; Cacioppo & Petty, 1982; Kruglanski, 1989; Rokeach, 1960; Schroder, Driver, & Streufert, 1967; Suedfeld, 2000; Suedfeld & Tetlock, 2001).

Cognitive-style explanations are extractions from the complex and multi-factor edifice of Adorno et al.'s theory and make no claim to explaining those aspects of high-F personality that are unrelated to information processing. They are intended not to replace authoritarianism theory per se (contrary to the critique of Stone, 1993) but to shed more light on what cognitive psychologists consider one fundamental aspect of authoritarianism. The cognitive style described here, which for the sake of brevity we shall refer to as "simple," is the opposite of the rational, open-minded, flexible, and complex thinking style that social scientists and other commentators often assume to be necessary for morally and pragmatically optimal decisions, attitudes, and behaviors. And, indeed, researchers have found that individuals with low need for cognition and high needs for closure and structure are quicker to form erroneous stereotypes of groups and to apply those stereotypes to individuals (e.g., Neuberg & Newsom, 1993; Schaller, Boyd, Yohannes, & O'Brien, 1995).

However, it is wrong to assume that simple cognitive style leads directly to support for fascism, for the Holocaust, or even for any kind of oppressive attitude (Suedfeld, 1992). Depending on the circumstances, either simple or complex thinking can lead to decisions that are optimal, appropriate, and moral—or the opposite. For example, in pre–Civil War debates on slavery, both Southern sympathizers and radical abolitionists showed less complex thinking than did the advocates of gradual emancipation (Tetlock, Armor, & Peterson, 1994); and, among people with somewhat prejudicial attitudes, higher need for cognition is associated with the perception that acts of racial discrimination by others are rational and justified (Khan & Lambert, 2001). These and similar results suggest that it is worth reexamining the tacit assumption that simple cognitive style was a causal factor in the Nazi genocide.

Cognitive Styles of Perpetrators and Resisters

Individuals who resist ethnopolitical violence do so in many different ways, including political and/or legal action, propaganda, armed force, covert sabotage, or the rescuing of intended victims of violence. We shall refer to all these actions as *resistance*, and to all who participated as *resisters*. There is an intriguing bifurcation in how one can consider in the same breath the perpetrators and resisters of persecutory violence. The temptation is to take a Manichean viewpoint: Perpetrators are evil and resisters are virtuous. Let us temporarily ignore the fact that—as noted previously—perpetrators were sometimes also rescuers (and vice versa), skip over the existence of ambivalent figures such as Oskar Schindler, and dismiss the highly dubious characterizations of the evildoer as merely a banal bureaucrat, abused child, frustrated artist, or sincere although misguided idealist. On the basis of what remains, who can doubt that people like Rudolf Höss, the commandant of Auschwitz-Birkenau, and people like Raoul Wallenberg, the rescuer of Hungarian Jews, were truly opposites? Surely, the difference between them was the difference between evil and goodness.

Compounding this moralism are the inescapably evaluative implications of the social-psychological mechanisms that influence individual behavior. Based on the classic studies of social influence by American and European psychologists (e.g., studies by Asch, Moscovici, and Milgram; see any social psychology textbook), it has been an axiom of Western psychology textbooks and of social analyses that conformity to peer groups and obedience to authority lead easily to violence and hatred, and that the autonomous individual is the best hope for the present and the future. Social scientists have implied that those who are not appropriately independent are likely to become at the very least passive bystanders, if not actually torturers or murderers, by uncritically following group pressure or orders from above. Conversely, we might

75

expect, those who resist evil commands and who stand against group consensus are the good guys: Just read the literature of the Milgram studies, or *Huckleberry Finn*—or rent *Twelve Angry Men* or *To Kill a Mockingbird* at your video store. Parenthetically, some authoritarians can recognize the dimension but assess it quite differently: Jaensch, a Nazi social scientist, asserted that low authoritarianism reflects a decadent lack of clear and strong moral values (cited in Brown, 1965).

It is also quite easy to draw the connection between what we are calling simple cognitive style and the tendency to be conformist to peers and obedient to authority. People who are averse to elaborate information search and processing are more likely to accept and follow the dictates of authority, which are usually unequivocal and definite; resistance to authority or to the group stems from thinking for oneself, a much more cognitively difficult and time-consuming enterprise (Harvey, Hunt, & Schroder, 1961).

Empirically, the F Scale, Dogmatism Scale, and similar measures do in fact tend to correlate positively and significantly with measures of simple cognitive style. But, as Adorno et al. recognized, specific attitudes of authoritarians vary with circumstances. The same is true of simple information processors. It appears that at least one substantial subgroup of resisters to the Holocaust may have been low in cognitive complexity, conformist, and responsive to authority figures—showing at least one significant psychological similarity to their ostensible opposites.

Most resisters probably did not fit Adorno et al.'s profile of the authoritarian personality. For example, few recalled severe physical punishment in childhood (Oliner & Oliner, 1988). Many resisters were motivated by empathy, personal affection, democratic or humanitarian convictions, and so on; and many exhibited personality traits of tolerance, inclusive thinking, independence, and other characteristics incompatible with authoritarianism (Gushee, 1994).

But just because many resisters showed nonauthoritarian characteristics, it does not logically follow that resisters and perpetrators in general differed along all the personality dimensions that typify authoritarianism. From the beginning, researchers (e.g., Oliner & Oliner, 1988) found some relevant similarities as well. Among these was the fact that over 50% of those who engaged in rescuing Jews from the Holocaust were "normocentric"; that is, they participated because some valued person or group expected them to do so. Strongly moralistic parents were especially important role models (London, 1970), just as they were—to the opposite effect—for eventual authoritarians.

In some cases, a respected authority figure such as an anti-Nazi community leader, teacher, mentor, or clergyman exhorted people to help. As Gushee (1994) put it, "Sometimes rescue occurred in submission to church authority" (p. 109)—although most church leaders were passive, or even actively supportive, toward the Nazi persecution of Jews. In still other instances, a preexisting cohesive group performed a "communal rescue" (Huneke, 1989). Well-disciplined members of the Communist Party in several occupied nations engaged in effective sabotage and armed resistance, and—in some countries— in rescuing Jews. For some, resisting the German occupiers and their collaborators was a patriotic duty, which sometimes included thwarting the persecution of Jewish compatriots.

Thus, some resisters exhibited the classic high-F features of obedience and conformity, presumably associated with simple cognitive style, that led perpetrators to join the murderers. Another high-F characteristic, ethnic prejudice and persecution, was also present in the opposition to Nazism: Partisan groups, especially in Eastern Europe, are known to have rejected and sometimes killed Jews who tried to join them, and some people who rescued Jews on the basis of political, patriotic, or religious ideology actually held anti-Semitic views and sentiments.

The argument is, of course, not that perpetrators and resisters are morally equivalent, nor even that they are the same kinds of people. But many of them may have been influenced by shared intellectual predispositions. We propose that the much-denigrated and stereotypically authoritarian characteristics of simple cognitive style and a tendency to conformity and obedience are largely process-based and content-free. In relation to the Holocaust, as in other contexts, whether these characteristics led to collaboration or resistance was steered by situational factors that led to widely different intellectual and emotional *content*—values, attitudes, loyalties—even when the cognitive *structures* (i.e., cognitive styles) were similar. Given the existence of abundant archival materials from both groups, and the availability of a way to score relevant cognitive styles from such materials, the hypothesis is easily testable.

Next, we turn to differences that may be more clearly predictive of different responses to genocide. Fear and perceived vulnerability to danger are considered at length by Adorno et al.; their more pervasive roots in the evolutionary history of the human species may contribute to an affect-oriented examination of Holocaust behavior.

THE FEARFUL AUTHORITARIAN

Aggressive people believe others to be hostile toward them (Staub, 1999). The original theory of authoritarianism links intergroup aggressiveness to such perceptions and to the pervasive fear that they arouse (Adorno et al., 1950). As children, the theory holds, budding authoritarians are afraid of their parents and of being punished if the parents ever discover the child's sexual and aggressive impulses. Children are in fact weak, compared with their parents; recognizing that reality, they are afraid of their own weakness and dependence. Their two main orientations toward outsiders stem from how these fears are handled. To compensate for the fear of being weak, authoritarians exaggerate their own toughness and exalt power as the ultimate good (Kaplan, 1994). Because of their fear of punishment, their forbidden desires are repressed and projected onto others, who are then seen as both immoral and hostile. If those others are weaker than the in-group, they become the targets of contempt and aggression—but they are still feared not because of any objective threat that they pose but because they embody the inner fears of the individual.

Whether or not psychoanalytic theory is the best explanation of this pervasive fear, the key empirical fact is that the authoritarian personality is characterized by feelings of fear and vulnerability. Highly authoritarian individuals are especially likely to perceive that the world is a dangerous place (Adorno et al., 1950; Altemeyer, 1988, 1996). According to Altemeyer, the fear pertains most specifically to social chaos caused by the actions of bad people. Such people therefore have to be suppressed—by force, if necessary.

This notion of the fearful authoritarian clearly resonates with the cultural context within which the Holocaust occurred. The years immediately preceding the Holocaust were characterized by considerable social and economic disorder within Germany (Dippel, 1996; Elias, 1996). The natural tendencies to perceive danger amid this disorder and to fear social chaos were reflected and amplified by Nazi propaganda, which held that "the Jews willfully, actively undermined the order of society, corroding its mores and cohesion, and introduced disorder and disharmony into an otherwise well-integrated whole" (Goldhagen, 1996, p. 65).

Thus, although fear and the perception of danger may not be the most commonly discussed or prototypical facets of the authoritarian personality, a fuller consideration of fear and prejudice, and of their behavioral implications, may contribute to our understanding of authoritarianism and of the Holocaust. Toward that goal, we review three contemporary theoretical perspectives pertaining to fear and its impact on intergroup attitudes and behavior.

These theories fall within the category of "evolutionary psychology," which considers the contexts characterizing the prehistory of the human species. It is perhaps valuable to clarify the broad principles guiding this approach to psychological theorizing. The fundamental assertion is that contemporary psychological processes evolved in part to solve the particular problems imposed by the physical and social environments that characterized our ancestral past. To understand the nature of these processes, it is important to consider specific problems characterizing ancestral populations and to identify specific plausible psychology-relevant adaptations that may have emerged within these populations as means to solve those problems. (Depending on their specific nature, these adaptations may have evolved through biological means, or may have emerged through a process of cultural transmission, or both.) Theories derived through the use of this heuristic necessarily contain two levels of conceptual model: a "historical" model speculating about the emergence of specific psychological adaptations over the course of long spans of time, and a "contemporary" model specifying the operation of these psychological adaptations in current environments. Within the context of this latter model, hypotheses can be identified and tested through traditional psychological methods. These hypotheses may offer interesting and novel explanations of contemporary human cognition and behavior.

Each of the three theories summarized in the following articulates the evolution of psychological processes resulting from specific fears that may have characterized ancestral human populations. More important, each yields predictions concerning contemporary contextual features that may trigger these processes, and so lead to dangerous prejudicial thoughts about and behaviors toward people who are "different." Thus, each offers a unique perspective on social-psychological processes that may help explain individuals' actions during the Holocaust.

Fear of Out-Group Members

Intergroup prejudice can emerge simply from social categorization. Divide individuals into two groups on the basis of even the most arbitrary of distinctions, and those individuals will come to perceive their in-group members more favorably than out-group members (as in the so-called minimal group paradigm; Tajfel, Billig, Bundy, & Flament, 1971). This phenomenon may have its roots in our evolutionary past. The argument is simple: If, as is commonly assumed, our ancestors in the Pleistocene lived in small tribal units, and intratribal interactions were more supportive than interactions between tribes, then it would have been natural for individuals to perceive in-group members more favorably than out-group members. Although intergroup environments have since changed, the tendency to view out-group members uncharitably may be a residue of our past (Campbell, 1965; Fishbein, 1996).

This simple line of reasoning is merely a speculative explanation for the fact that intergroup prejudice exists at all. However, beginning with the same assumptions about the tribal structures of ancestral populations, it is possible to deduce a more detailed theoretical structure that predicts and explains variability in contemporary prejudicial beliefs about out-groups. Such a structure is offered by intergroup vigilance theory (Schaller, 1999). In brief, the logic is as follows.

If, in our ancestral past, unexpected encounters with out-group members posed a threat of violence and physical harm, it would have been functional for individuals to vigilantly avoid such encounters. Consequently, psychological processes that facilitated such vigilant avoidance would also have been functional. One such process would be the tendency to form exaggerated mental representations (e.g., stereotypical beliefs) about the potential dangers posed by out-group members. Over the course of time, the tendency to construct prejudicial beliefs about out-group members would have become increasingly common. The pragmatic consequences of such beliefs were surely minimal (in fact, perhaps nonexistent, or even counterproductive) if intergroup contact posed minimal threat, or if contact was unlikely to occur. Conversely, these beliefs would have benefits if out-group members really did pose a threat, and if unexpected contact was highly probable. Therefore, it would have been adaptive to recognize situational cues relevant to the utility of prejudicial beliefs and behavior, and for such cues to activate those beliefs and behavioral responses.

Even though intergroup encounters have since changed, there is evidence that prejudicial beliefs are indeed triggered by cues signaling the potential for intergroup contact and intergroup threat (Schaller, 1999). These cues include specific features of the social environment (e.g., the relative size and/or proximity of the out-group), the physical environment (e.g., ambient darkness), or one's own psychological environment (e.g., fear, anxiety, perceived vulnerability to danger). This analysis has several implications for understanding the origins of genocide.

1. Prejudicial beliefs about outsiders are likely to be especially pronounced under circumstances that produce fear and feelings of vulnerability. In the Holocaust context, the social, economic, and political upheavals during the 1920s and 1930s may have provided such cues.

2. In attempting to identify others, people are likely to err on the side of "overexclusion." That is, under conditions of perceived vulnerability and fear, ambiguity in the group membership of any individual will be especially likely to be resolved by assuming that individual is an outsider. The Nuremberg Laws may be an illustration of this tendency: Unclear categories, such as converts from Judaism to Christianity, and their children and grandchildren, were legally classified as Jewish. Later, to avoid a failure to identify them as members of the out-group, Jews were legally required to wear the distinguishing yellow star.

3. The resulting prejudicial beliefs are likely to pertain especially to characteristics that connote the potential for intentional threat or harm. Such accusations were constantly leveled at Jews by Nazi propaganda that characterized Jews as both overtly and covertly malicious (the "stab in the back" resulting in German defeat in 1918, collusion with international capitalism and with Bolshevism, a "world Jewish conspiracy," etc.; Rosenbaum, 1998; Yahil, 1990). More generally, "The prevailing general image of the Jews held them to be malevolent, powerful, and dangerous. . . . The danger that they posed, their capacity to inflict harm, was believed by Germans to be colossal" (Goldhagen, 1996, pp. 64–65).

4. Fear-based prejudicial beliefs about out-groups are likely to precipitate behaviors designed to reduce the perceived threat. Heightened vigilance is only the least harmful response. More destructive are acts designed to reduce the threat through forcible removal or extinction of the threatening forces. Total annihilation of dangerous out-groups has been observed in the intergroup

behavior of nonhuman primate species (e.g., Goodall, 1986). So, too, perceptions of danger from an out-group can precipitate intergroup violence and murder among humans (Hass, 1990; Jankowski, 1991). The possibility that such apprehension may play a role in genocide is not far-fetched.

Fear of In-Group Members Who Are Different

Prejudices are also often expressed against certain members of one's own in-group—those who are physically, mentally, or socially different. It is unlikely that these prejudices spring from any fear of intentional harm, but a different theoretical perspective implies that they might be precipitated by a different form of fear rooted in our ancestral past (cf. Neuberg, Smith, & Asher, 2000; Stangor & Crandall, 2000).

In the past, "different" in-group members may have posed an unintentional threat if they carried infectious disease or otherwise undermined the group's chances of survival—for example, by using up scarce resources without being able to contribute needed labor. It would have been functional to avoid encounters with those individuals, and psychological processes that facilitated vigilant avoidance would have been functional as well. One such process would be the tendency to form stereotypical beliefs about the dangers posed by individuals who had morphological characteristics that deviated from the "healthy" norm. As long as some of those characteristics were truly diagnostic of disease or other problems, avoidance-motivating beliefs would have been functional to both other individuals and the group as a whole. Over the course of time, the tendency to construct prejudicial beliefs about odd-looking or oddly behaving individuals would have become increasingly common. There may also have emerged psychological processes through which the tendency to construct prejudicial beliefs about "different" in-group members was triggered by cues diagnostic of the likelihood of threats to one's health (e.g., perceived vulnerability to disease) or the likelihood of contact with one of these individuals (e.g., physical proximity). In addition, feelings of fear or anxiety might also have emerged as general-purpose emotional cues triggering these prejudicial beliefs.

Such responses are common among nonhuman primates. Chimpanzees react with fear when one of their own troop members is sick or injured, and they sometimes respond with brutal aggression toward those individuals (e.g., Goodall, 1986). Recent human history reveals abundant evidence of "different" individuals being forcibly removed and quarantined without legal recourse, whether their affliction is truly infectious (e.g., leprosy) or not (mental disability). Given the tendency to err on the side of overexclusion, it may be that perceived vulnerability may lead individuals to attempt to remove people who are "different" on even the most superficial characteristics. The "euthanasia" program, killing physically and mentally defective patients, was the Nazis' first policy-level demonstration of this principle.

In the context of the Holocaust, the connection between Jews and disease has a centuries-old history in Christian anti-Semitism: "The logic of Europeans' fantastical beliefs about Jews was such that, as Jeremy Cohen concludes, 'it was almost inevitable that Jews were blamed for the Black Death and many of their communities in Germany completely and permanently exterminated'" (Goldhagen, 1996, p. 53). The stereotype of Jews as dirty and as carriers of disease—equated with bacilli, lice, and rats—was a core aspect of Nazi propaganda, and may have triggered the Gentile population's fear of contagion. Such epithets, cartoons, and films exaggerating "Jewish" physical characteristics as opposed to "Aryan" ones, and—as a last resort—the badge of the yellow Star of David, also helped to relocate previously culturally assimilated and frequently physically indistinguishable fellow citizens from the category of "us" to that of "them."

It is noteworthy that even in concentration camps, where sanitary facilities and the opportunity to use them were minimal, the Nazis castigated their captives for their lack of cleanliness and blamed them for getting sick (Bluhm, 1948/1999). The barracks in Birkenau (Auschwitz II) were festooned with slogans such as the German equivalent of "Cleanliness is next to godliness" and similar exhortations to good hygiene—while the camp provided one wash barrack per 7,800 prisoners and one latrine hut per 7,000 (Dwork & van Pelt, 1996). The women's camp of Birkenau had one latrine for 30,000 to 32,000 prisoners, who were allowed to use it only during certain hours, even though most had dysentery. The latrine was a roof and walls enclosing a deep ditch, with planks thrown across it at such close intervals that the users could not avoid soiling each other. As Dwork and van Pelt (1996) write, "With the latrines submerged in excrement, with very little water to be had at very few points, and with mud everywhere, what remained was an inmate population without the means to preserve any outward sign of human dignity" (p. 268)—and the situation was then blamed on the innate filthiness of the prisoners themselves. Indeed, the nature of the camps helped to create an appearance among the camp's inhabitants, "including festering, open wounds, and the marks of disease and illness" (Goldhagen, 1996, p. 176), that fit the characterization of a dangerously contagious population. Thus, the camps not only served as a means to quarantine and eliminate the Jews but also as a means of amplifying the cues triggering Germans' self-protective "need" to do so.

Fear of Death

A third fear-based perspective on prejudice emerges from terror management theory (Solomon, Greenberg, & Pyszczynski, 1991; Greenberg, Solomon, & Pyszczynski, 1997). The focus here is not on danger per se but rather on existential dread.

The logic of the theory holds that the human capacity for abstract symbolic thought brings with it the awareness of our own eventual death and of the evanescence of all we do and are. This realization precipitates a state of existential terror. Over the course of history, substantial components of human culture may have emerged to provide buffers against this terror. Virtually every individual grows up within a cultural context that provides means through which one may feel valued and worthwhile (e.g., through compliance with cultural standards and norms), and through which one might symbolically transcend death (e.g., through religious beliefs in some form of afterlife).

If cultural worldviews play this important role in protecting people against existential terror, it follows that individuals are motivated to defend their own cultural worldviews and to derogate worldviews inconsistent with their own. This motivation may be especially pronounced under conditions in which the usual cultural buffers against terror are breached, destabilized, or endangered, or in which one's own mortality is made temporarily salient for any reason. Dozens of studies have in fact shown that various forms of worldview defense are enhanced under conditions of mortality salience (Greenberg et al., 1997). Most relevant are findings that mortality salience causes individuals to support harsher punishments for individuals who transgress against cultural standards (Rosenblatt, Greenberg, Solomon, Pyszczynski, & Lyon, 1989) and leads to increased prejudice and covert aggression against peoples who ascribe to cultural worldviews different from one's own (reviewed in Greenberg et al., 1997).

Dying for the Fatherland was traditionally a major theme in the German self-concept (Elias, 1996), and a number of factors may have conspired to make mortality especially salient to Germans in the years preceding the Holocaust. The tremendous slaughter of World War I and the deadly influenza pandemic of 1918 killed disproportionately high numbers of young people who ordinarily might have been less sensitive than older persons to concerns about their own eventual death. It would have been difficult to escape the awareness of how fragile life was, especially when facing the high prominence given to remembering the nation's fallen soldiers and the very visible presence of many combat veterans.

In addition, the postwar years of the 1920s and early 1930s were marked not only by destitution but also by upheavals within the sorts of normative structures (e.g., social, moral, and political systems) that might ordinarily provide cultural buffers against terror. The Weimar Republic represented a significant and disconcerting break with traditional top-down governance (Elias, 1996); prewar social and economic arrangements were in flux; new forms of art, music, theater, and literature—considered decadent by many Germans—were flourishing; new relations were emerging between classes, age-groups, and sexes.

Thus, the time may have been characterized both by heightened awareness of death and also by fissures in the cultural structures that normally serve as buffers against the ensuing terror. One common response may have been through the strengthening of a different buffer—the assertion of the intrinsic goodness of one's cultural worldview: "The mere sound of the word *'Deutschland'* seemed for Germans to be laden with associations that were out of the ordinary, with a charisma that bordered on the holy" (Elias, 1996, p. 324). Existential terror among Germans may have been warded off through increased identification with a morally and racially superior, irresistible, unified mass of millions of people within the "Thousand-Year Reich." It may have been warded off further through the derogation and destruction of peoples holding a different, and therefore existentially threatening, cultural worldview.

Nazi propaganda during this time was both a reflection of and a contributor to this process. This propaganda heightened mortality salience by continually harping on the alleged betrayal by "Jew/Bolsheviks" of the heroic dead of World War I, and on the exalted nature of military service and death in battle. "I believe that I have enough energy to lead our people whither it must shed its blood," said Hitler in 1928, in only one of many such speeches (quoted in Weinberg, 1995, p. 51). Other central topics were the purity of the Aryan race, the moral superiority of Aryans, and the moral turpitude of Jews.

The metaphors used in the propaganda may have also served to heighten the salience of mortality. Terror management processes are commonly precipitated by thoughts about what happens to one's own body following death (e.g., post-mortem decomposition and decay). So it is interesting to consider the consequences of anti-Semitic propaganda in Germany, which abounded in "organic metaphors of decomposition" (Goldhagen, 1996, p. 67). Also common within Nazi propaganda were references to Jews as bacilli and vermin, to their "unclean" blood (e.g., the Law for the Protection of German Blood), and to their desire to pollute the purity of the Aryan race (Goldhagen, 1996). Such images focus attention on base corporeal elements of life and so may trigger the processes of terror management (Goldenberg, Pyszczynski, McCoy, Greenberg, & Solomon, 1999).

Fear Among Perpetrators and Resisters

These fear-based perspectives on the Holocaust are speculative, of course, and we must acknowledge certain limitations to each analysis. Although all three identify plausible processes that may influence particular forms of prejudice, only intergroup vigilance theory and terror management theory have been subjected to extensive empirical testing. In any case, as we have said earlier, empirical support in the psychological laboratory cannot guarantee accuracy in generalizing the results to the Holocaust. Such validity can only be determined through a consideration of the complicated context within which the events of the Holocaust occurred and an attempt to answer the question, Would this particular context have triggered the sorts of psychological processes specified by the three fear-based perspectives?

We have briefly indicated some points of fact to suggest that these processes might indeed have been operative, and so may bear further consideration as contributors to the murderous anti-Semitism that characterized the Holocaust.

Of course, there is still a substantial difference between prejudice and genocide. Two of the three fear-based perspectives (the intergroup vigilance and contagion approaches) imply clear motives that tighten the causal connection between prejudice and killing. Terror management theory indicates a less clear connection. On the other hand, terror management theory may have clearer implications for understanding the psychological distinction between perpetrators and resisters. It is to this topic that we now turn.

Fear-based analyses suggest that in Germany, cues triggering these fearful responses facilitated aversion to and hostile actions against Jews—as outsiders, as compatriots who, however, were "different," and in defense against the terror of mortality. Individual tendencies to fear were surely amplified by institutionalized rhetoric. Those who orchestrated the Holocaust used propaganda to create fear cues where no realistic fear was warranted and to make existing fears (such as the terror of dying) more salient. According to some historical accounts, the Nazis merely triggered the expression of long-lasting fear and hatred rather than originating or even greatly increasing those feelings (e.g., Goldhagen, 1996). Even so, not everyone was a supporter of the persecution, much less a willing perpetrator. How can fear-based analyses help to identify underlying differences between perpetrators and resisters?

One answer may lie in individual differences in beliefs about a dangerous world. Those who view the world as relatively safe—either because they consider it benign or because they view themselves as invulnerable—may be relatively insensitive to fear cues that would lead to prejudice and persecution. Conversely, individuals who view the world as a dangerous place may be hypersensitive to cues signaling potential danger and so may be especially likely to respond to perceived sources of danger with extreme, including murderous, prejudice. This specific affect-based reasoning would predict that authoritarians, who are generally fearful, are especially likely to become perpetrators in persecutory programs such as the Holocaust.

Another answer may lie in specific elements of individuals' cultural worldviews. Terror management theory implies that contexts that make mortality salient are likely to lead individuals to defend their own cultural worldviews and to derogate others'. But if tolerance of differences is a core element of one's worldview, then mortality salience may actually lead to greater tolerance for different groups and views. In one study (Greenberg, Simon, Pyszczynski, Solomon, & Chantel, 1992), mortality salience was manipulated among politically conservative or liberal Americans, who were asked to evaluate others with similar or dissimilar political attitudes. When mortality was not made salient, everyone expressed some evaluative prejudice against others who were different. Among conservatives, who were generally less tolerant of differences, mortality salience led to even greater prejudice. However, among liberals—in whose political worldview tolerance of differences is a key element—mortality salience led to decreased prejudice.

This hypothesis is related to the distinction between psychological content and structure, referred to earlier. Even if some Holocaust perpetrators and rescuers may have shared a given level of cognitive rigidity and simplicity, they may have differed in their attitudes toward cultural worldviews distinct from their own and/or in the value they placed on human life. While some individuals might have been impelled by existential fear to attack those with offending worldviews as a means of defending their own cultural standards, others may have responded to the same existential fear by defending their tolerance-based values even more directly. For some rescuers of Jews during the Nazi era, tolerance for different peoples and inclusiveness in the definition of "we" were themselves core themes of the worldview. The increased threat of death may have led such individuals to move beyond mere tolerance, to risk their own lives to save those of the stigmatized and imperiled.

Another group of rescuers were committed Christians, for whom a similar role may have been played by the religious values of the Golden Rule and the sanctity of life (Fogelman, 1994; Oliner & Oliner, 1988). Ironically, many religious rescuers and resisters—including famous clergymen such as Martin Niemöller, Heinrich Grüber, and Karl Barth—evidenced strong anti-Semitic attitudes (Goldhagen, 1996). Nevertheless, such individuals may have perceived that prolonging the lives of fellow human beings, even at personal risk to themselves, was demanded by their (perhaps cognitively simple) belief system, as well as affording a form of vicarious immortality—including the Christian idea of eternal life in heaven. This reaction may have served to reduce existential dread just as the perpetuation of the Third Reich may have appealed to Nazi supporters for similar underlying reasons.

CONCLUSION

We have not answered in any complete way the question about the association between the authoritarian personality and participation in the Holocaust. What is clear is that, in spite of the seductiveness of the idea, there is no simple causal relation, nor even an empirically demonstrated complex one. The reason reflects both a weakness and a strength of Adorno et al.'s original conceptualization of the authoritarian personality. The weakness is that neither the original version nor the reformulations of authoritarianism offer a single coherent psychological construct; rather, each of the different definitions and approaches to authoritarianism represents a multifaceted complex of traits and underlying processes. Inevitably, each specific construct is more relevant to certain behaviors than others. Some of them may help explain the behaviors of perpetrators of genocide, some may not; some may help explain the behaviors of active resisters to genocide, and some may not. As we have indicated, certain prototypical features that appear in the authoritarian personality syndrome may actually underlie the behavior of both perpetrators and resisters, whereas other features may predict the different reactions shown by perpetrators and resisters.

By attending carefully to the subtleties rather than to the stereotypes of authoritarianism, it is possible to view the authoritarian personality in ways that point to interesting and testable hypotheses about individuals' capacities for both awful and awe-inspiring deeds, and to the contextual triggers that turn those capacities into realities. The two facets of authoritarianism that we have elaborated upon represent only a small portion of the possibilities.

One important point is the compatibility among these explanations. We are not suggesting that they are mutually exclusive and that research is likely to find the "correct" one; for example, such factors as Nazi propaganda about Jews being a source of both real and metaphorical infection are supportive of more than one of the hypotheses. What we would strive for is an explanatory model that does justice to the complexity of large-scale historical events. A fuller analysis of the facets and implications of the authoritarian personality construct is necessary to reveal the extent to which different aspects of authoritarianism may have contributed to the perpetration of, and resistance to, the Holocaust.

We feel it is important to make one final comment. The attempt to identify underlying psychological mechanisms that may help to explain the behavior of some perpetrators and some resisters does not, in our view, lead to either exculpation of the former or lessened admiration for the latter. Whatever the causal factors may be, perpetrators chose to participate in a vicious process of mass murder, torture, and persecution; resisters risked (and in some cases knowingly sacrificed) their safety and life in order to help those in extreme need. The possibility that some shared causal factors contributed to these opposed decisions in no way affects the moral standing of the persons who followed either course of action.

REFERENCES

Adorno, T. W., Frenkel-Brunswik, E., Levinson, D. J., & Sanford, R. (1950). *The authoritarian personality*. New York: Harper.

Altemeyer, B. (1988). *Enemies of freedom: Understanding right-wing authoritarianism*. San Francisco: Jossey-Bass.

Altemeyer, B. (1996). *The authoritarian specter*. Cambridge, MA: Harvard University Press.

Baumeister, R. F. (1997). *Evil: Inside human cruelty and violence*. New York: Freeman.

Bluhm, H. O. (1948). How did they survive? Mechanisms of defense in Nazi concentration camps. *American Journal of Psychotherapy, 2*, 3–32. Reprinted as a Classic Article in *American Journal of Psychotherapy, 1999, 53*, 96–122.

Brown, R. (1965). *Social psychology*. Glencoe, IL: Free Press.

Budner, S. (1962). Intolerance of ambiguity as a personality variable. *Journal of Personality, 30*, 29–50.

Cacioppo, J. T., & Petty, R. E. (1982). The need for cognition. *Journal of Personality and Social Psychology, 42,* 116–131.

Campbell, D. T. (1965). Ethnocentric and other altruistic motives. In D. Levine (Ed.), *Nebraska Symposium on Motivation* (pp. 283–311). Lincoln: University of Nebraska Press.

Dippel, J. V. H. (1996). *Bound upon a wheel of fire.* New York: Basic Books.

Duckitt, J. (1989). Authoritarianism and group identification: A new view of an old construct. *Political Psychology, 10,* 63–84.

Dwork, D., & van Pelt, R. J. (1996). *Auschwitz: 1270 to the present.* New York: Norton.

Elias, N. (1996). *The Germans.* New York: Columbia University Press.

Fishbein, H. D. (1996). *Peer prejudice and discrimination.* New York: Westview.

Fogelman, E. (1994). *Conscience and courage: Rescuers of Jews during the Holocaust.* New York: Doubleday.

Goldenberg, J. L., Pyszczynski, T., McCoy, S. K., Greenberg, J., & Solomon, S. (1999). Death, sex, love, and neuroticism: Why is sex such a problem? *Journal of Personality and Social Psychology, 77,* 1173–1187.

Goldhagen, D. J. (1996). *Hitler's willing executioners: Ordinary Germans and the Holocaust.* New York: Random House.

Goodall, J. (1986). *The chimpanzees of Gombe: Patterns of behavior.* Cambridge, MA: Belknap.

Greenberg, J., Simon, L., Pyszczynski, T., Solomon, S., & Chantel, D. (1992). Terror management and tolerance: Does mortality salience always intensify negative reactions to others who threaten one's worldview? *Journal of Personality and Social Psychology, 63,* 212–220.

Greenberg, J., Solomon, S., & Pyszczynski, T. (1997). Terror management theory of self-esteem and cultural worldviews: Empirical assessments and conceptual refinements. *Advances in Experimental Social Psychology, 29,* 61–139.

Gushee, D. P. (1994). *The righteous Gentiles of the Holocaust: A Christian interpretation.* Minneapolis, MN: Fortress.

Haney, C., Banks, C., & Zimbardo, P. (1973). Interpersonal dynamics in a simulated prison. *International Journal of Criminology and Penology, 1,* 69–97.

Harvey, O. J., Hunt, D. E., & Schroder, H. M. (1961). *Conceptual systems and personality organization.* New York: Wiley.

Hass, J. (1990). *The anthropology of war.* Cambridge: Cambridge University Press.

Hilberg, R. (1992). *Perpetrators victims bystanders: The Jewish catastrophe, 1933–1945.* New York: HarperCollins.

Holliday, L. (Ed.). (1995). *Children in the Holocaust and World War II: Their secret diaries.* New York: Washington Square Press.

Huneke, D. (1989). Glimpses of light in a vast darkness: A study of the moral and spiritual development of Nazi era rescuers. In A. R. Eckhardt & A. Eckhardt (Eds.), *Remembering for the future* (Vol. 1, pp. 486–493). Elmsford, NY: Pergamon.

Jankowski, M. S. (1991). *Islands in the street: Gangs and American urban society.* Berkeley: University of California Press.

Kaplan, H. (1994). *Conscience and memory: Meditations in a museum of the Holocaust.* Chicago: University of Chicago Press.

Khan, S. R., & Lambert, A. J. (2001). The effects of contextual and personality variables on the "subjective rationality" of stereotype use. *Basic and Applied Social Psychology, 23,* 43–53.

Kressel, N. M. (1996). *Mass hate: The global rise of genocide and terror*. New York: Plenum.

Kruglanski, A. W. (1989). The psychology of being "right": The problem of accuracy in social perception and cognition. *Psychological Bulletin, 106*, 395–409.

Lewin, K., Lippitt, R., & White, R. K. (1939). Patterns of aggressive behavior in experimentally created "social climates." *Journal of Social Psychology, 10*, 271–299.

London, P. (1970). The rescuers: Motivational hypotheses about Christians who saved Jews from the Nazis. In J. Macauley & L. Berkowitz (Eds.), *Altruism and helping behavior* (pp. 241–250). New York: Academic Press.

Milgram, S. (1974). *Obedience to authority*. New York: Harper and Row.

Neuberg, S. L., & Newsom, J. T. (1993). Personal need for structure: Individual differences in the desire for simple structure. *Journal of Personality and Social Psychology, 65*, 113–131.

Neuberg, S. L., Smith, D. M., & Asher, T. (2000). Why people stigmatize: Toward a biocultural framework. In T. Heatherton, R. Kleck, J. G. Hull, & M. Hebl (Eds.), *Stigma* (pp. 31–61). New York: Guilford.

Newman, L. S., Duff, K. J., & Baumeister, R. F. (1997). A new look at defensive projection: Thought suppression, accessibility, and biased person perception. *Journal of Personality and Social Psychology, 72*, 980–1001.

Oliner, S. P., & Oliner, P. M. (1988). *The altruistic personality: Rescuers of Jews in occupied Europe*. New York: Free Press.

Pratto, F., Sidanius, J., Stallworth, L. M., & Malle, B. F. (1994). Social dominance orientation: A personality variable predicting social and political attitudes. *Journal of Personality and Social Psychology, 67*, 741–763.

Proctor, R. N. (1999). *The Nazi war on cancer*. Princeton, NJ: Princeton University Press.

Rokeach, M. (1960). *The open and closed mind*. New York: Basic Books.

Rosenbaum, R. (1998). *Explaining Hitler*. New York: Random House.

Rosenblatt, A., Greenberg, J., Solomon, S., Pyszczynski, T., & Lyon, D. (1989). Evidence for terror management theory: I. The effects of mortality salience on reactions to those who violate or uphold cultural values. *Journal of Personality and Social Psychology, 57*, 681–690.

Sanford, N. (1973). Authoritarian personality in contemporary perspective. In J. N. Knutson (Gen. Ed.), *Handbook of political psychology* (pp. 139–170). San Francisco: Jossey-Bass.

Schaller, M. (1999). *Intergroup vigilance theory*. Unpublished manuscript, University of British Columbia.

Schaller, M., Boyd, C., Yohannes, J., & O'Brien, M. (1995). The prejudiced personality revisited: Personal need for structure and the formation of erroneous group stereotypes. *Journal of Personality and Social Psychology, 68*, 544–555.

Schroder, H. M., Driver, M. J., & Streufert, S. (1967). *Human information processing*. New York: Holt, Rinehart, and Winston.

Sherif, M., Harvey, O. J., White, J., Hood, W., & Sherif, C. (1961). *Intergroup conflict and cooperation: The Robber's Cave experiment*. Norman: University of Oklahoma, Institute of Intergroup Relations.

Solomon, S., Greenberg, J., & Pyszczynski, T. (1991). A terror management theory of social behavior: The psychological functions of self-esteem and cultural worldviews. *Advances in Experimental Social Psychology, 24*, 91–159.

Stangor, C., & Crandall, C. S. (2000). Threat and the social construction of stigma. In T. Heatherton, R. Kleck, J. G. Hull, & M. Hebl (Eds.), *Stigma* (pp. 62–87). New York: Guilford.

Staub, E. (1989). *The roots of evil: The origins of genocide and other group violence.* Cambridge: Cambridge University Press.

Staub, E. (1999). The roots of evil: Social conditions, culture, personality, and basic human needs. *Personality and Social Psychology Review, 3,* 179–192.

Stone, W. F. (1980). The myth of left-wing authoritarianism. *Political Psychology, 2,* 3–19.

Stone, W. F. (1993). Psychodynamics, cognitive functioning, or group orientation: Research and theory in the 1980s. In W. F. Stone, G. Lederer, & R. Christie (Eds.), *Strength and weakness: The authoritarian personality today* (pp. 159–181). New York: Springer-Verlag.

Stone, W. F., Lederer, G., & Christie, R. (1993). Introduction: Strength and weakness. In W. F. Stone, G. Lederer, & R. Christie (Eds.), *Strength and weakness: The authoritarian personality today* (pp. 3–21). New York: Springer-Verlag.

Stone, W. F., & Smith, L. D. (1993). Authoritarianism: Left and right. In W. F. Stone, G. Lederer, & R. Christie (Eds.), *Strength and weakness: The authoritarian personality today* (pp. 144–156). New York: Springer-Verlag.

Suedfeld, P. (1992). Cognitive managers and their critics. *Political Psychology, 13,* 435–453.

Suedfeld, P. (1998). Theories of the Holocaust: Trying to explain the unimaginable. In D. Chirot & M. E. P. Seligman (Eds.), *Ethnopolitical warfare: Causes, consequences, and possible solutions* (pp. 51–70). Washington, DC: American Psychological Association.

Suedfeld, P. (2000). Cognitive styles. In A. E. Kazdin (Ed.), *Encyclopedia of psychology* (Vol. 2, pp. 166–169). Washington, DC: American Psychological Association and New York: Oxford University Press.

Suedfeld, P., & Tetlock, P. E. (2001). Individual differences in information processing. In A. Tesser & N. Schwartz (Eds.), *The Blackwell handbook of social psychology: Vol. 1, Intraindividual processes* (pp. 284–304). London: Blackwell.

Tajfel, H., Billig, M. G., Bundy, R. P., & Flament, C. (1971). Social categorization and intergroup behavior. *European Journal of Social Psychology, 1,* 149–178.

Tetlock, P. E., Armor, D., & Peterson, R. (1994). The slavery debate in antebellum America: Cognitive style, value conflict, and the limits of compromise. *Journal of Personality and Social Psychology, 66,* 115–126.

Weinberg, G. L. (1995). *Germany, Hitler, and World War II.* Cambridge: Cambridge University Press.

Yahil, L. (1990). *The Holocaust: The fate of European Jewry, 1932–1945.* New York: Oxford University Press.

4

Perpetrator Behavior as Destructive Obedience

An Evaluation of Stanley Milgram's
Perspective, the Most Influential Social-
Psychological Approach to the Holocaust

Thomas Blass

Obedience, as a determinant of behavior, is of particular
relevance to our time. It has been reliably established
that from 1933 to 1945 millions of innocent persons
were systematically slaughtered on command. Gas
chambers were built, death camps were guarded, daily
quotas of corpses were produced with the same
efficiency as the manufacture of appliances. These
inhumane policies may have originated in the mind of a
single person, but they could only have been carried out
on a massive scale if a very large number of people
obeyed orders.

—Stanley Milgram (1963)

During the summer of 1944, the Nazis, under the direction of
Eichmann and with the assistance of their Hungarian allies, were in the process of rounding up the Jews of Budapest and segregating them prior to transporting them in cattle cars to the gas chambers of Auschwitz. Budapest is split
by the Danube River into two parts: Buda and Pest. One day during the roundups, a Jewish mother and her 2-year-old child were taking the trolley from
Pest, where they had been visiting relatives, to Buda, where they were currently living in a recently found apartment. Unlike most of her fellow Jews,
she believed the unbelievable, deadly rumors about what "resettlement for
work in the east" really meant. So rather than remaining in Pest, she obtained

forged Christian identity papers, and moved to Buda, which had been a largely non-Jewish part of the city. The trolley was crossing the bridge between Buda and Pest when the rhythmic clatter of the trolley car's wheels was interrupted by the insistent sound of the child's voice: "Mommy," he asked, "why don't I wear a cap like other Jewish boys?" This was within earshot of many of the other passengers, who included members of the Nyilas, the Hungarian Nazi militia. With a resourcefulness spawned by desperation, the mother quickly turned to her child and said, "This is our stop," grabbed his hand, and got off the trolley—right in the middle of the bridge, quite a distance from their actual destination. Miraculously, no one stopped them.

Why did this mother feel threatened by her fellow Hungarians at that moment, but if her child (who is the author of this chapter) would have made the same remark before the war, she probably would not have taken evasive action? This question, in more general form, is, I believe, one of the primary psychological puzzles underlying the mass destruction of European Jewry: What psychological mechanism transformed the average, and presumably normal, citizens of Germany and its allies into people who would carry out or tolerate unimaginable acts of cruelty against their fellow citizens who were Jewish, resulting in the death of 6 million of them?

The question is especially compelling given the fact that, as some historians of the Holocaust have noted, those who participated in the killings generally did so willingly, not under duress. As the historian Friedlander (1998) states, "In more than thirty years of postwar proceedings, no proof has emerged that anyone who refused to participate in killing operations had been shot, incarcerated, or penalized in any way, except perhaps through transfer to the front—but this, after all, was the destiny of most German soldiers" (p. 248).

Since the question of how apparently normal people could so readily turn into brutal killers is first and foremost a psychological one, it is no surprise that, from the beginning, psychology has been among the disciplines that have tried to account for the Holocaust, beginning with the U.S. Army psychologist Gustav Gilbert, who administered the Rorschach test to the Nazi war criminals awaiting trial in Nuremberg after the war and later wrote about the experience (G. M. Gilbert, 1950).

The purpose of this chapter is to evaluate the adequacy of what has been, arguably, the most influential psychological account of perpetrator behavior during the Holocaust, the social-psychological approach of Stanley Milgram (1963, 1974).

Milgram's theorizing about perpetrator behavior was based on a series of experiments on the dynamics of obedience to authority, which yielded, among others, the startling and well-known finding, first reported in 1963, that 65% of his subjects—ordinary New Haven residents—were willing to punish another person with as much as 450 volts of electric shock at the bidding of an experimenter, despite the fact that the victim did nothing to the subject to merit such severe action and that the experimenter had no special powers to enforce his orders.

The context for the emergence of such extreme obedience was an experiment focusing ostensibly on the effects of punishment on learning. The subject was to teach another person—the learner—a list of word pairs and to punish him with electric shock every time he made an error. The shock machine contained 30 switches, each labeled in 15-volt increments beginning with 15 volts and ending with 450 volts. The shock levels were also marked by verbal designations beginning with "Slight Shock" and ending with "Danger: Severe Shock." The last two switches, corresponding to the 435 and 450 voltage levels, were marked simply and ominously, "XXX." The subject was instructed to begin with the lowest-voltage switch and to increase the shock level, one step at a time, on each subsequent error. Although unbeknownst to the subject, the learner was an actor who made errors on designated trials and was not actually shocked, the experiment was a very real, and typically powerful, experience for the subject, as the following observation by Milgram (1963), reveals:

> Many subjects showed signs of nervousness in the experimental situation, and especially upon administering the more powerful shocks. In a large number of cases the degree of tension reached extremes that are rarely seen in sociopsychological laboratory studies. Subjects were observed to sweat, tremble, stutter, bite their lips, groan, and dig their fingernails into their flesh. These were characteristic rather than exceptional responses to the experiment. (p. 375)

The obedience experiments, funded by grants from the National Science Foundation, were begun in the summer of 1961 and completed about a year later, at the end of May 1962. Milgram announced the completion of his studies in a letter to Claude Buxton, chairman of the Yale Psychology Department. The letter was dated June 1, 1962, and read, in part, as follows: "I wish to announce my departure from the Lindsly-Chittenden basement laboratory. It served us well. Our last subject was run on Sunday, May 27. The experiments on 'obedience to authority' are, Praise the Lord, completed."[1] Four days later, on May 31, the Israeli government, after a lengthy trial, hanged Adolf Eichmann for his role in the Nazis' "final solution of the Jewish problem."

The close juxtaposition of these two events—the completion of the obedience series and the carrying out of Eichmann's death sentence—was quite propitious, since Milgram's concern about the Holocaust was a prime motive for conducting the experiments, as the following passage indicates:

> [My] laboratory paradigm merely gave scientific expression to a
> more general concern about authority, a concern forced upon
> members of my generation, in particular upon Jews such as
> myself, by the atrocities of World War II. . . . The impact of the
> holocaust on my own psyche energized my interest in obedience
> and shaped the particular form in which it was examined.
> (Milgram, 1977, pp. 92–93)

This concern about the suffering of his fellow Jews at the hands of the Nazis can be traced to Milgram's childhood. Milgram was born in the Bronx, New York, on August 15, 1933. His parents, Samuel and Adele Milgram, were both born in Eastern Europe. Samuel had emigrated from Hungary after World War I, while Adele was born in Romania and came to the United States before World War I. During World War II, Samuel still had relatives remaining in Europe, and Stanley was very conscious of his father's concerns about them. He would often recall how his parents listened to the radio to keep up to date on developments in Europe (A. Milgram, 2000). (Milgram's sister, Marjorie, told me that all of their close relatives survived the Holocaust.) And we can see the close identification with his people expressed by Milgram in 1946 in a speech he wrote and delivered at the celebration of his bar mitzvah: "As I come of age and find happiness in joining the rank[s] of Israel, the knowledge of the tragic suffering of my fellow Jews throughout war-torn Europe makes this also a solemn event and an occasion to reflect upon the heritage of my people—which now becomes mine."[2]

Consistent with his goal of shedding light on the Holocaust, Milgram had planned to follow up his American series with some obedience experiments in Germany, as he wrote to Gordon Allport, his former mentor and later colleague at Harvard, in a letter dated October 10, 1960: "Next year I . . . plan to undertake a long series of experiments on *obedience*. While this series will stand by itself as an independent study, it is also preparation for the project on German character—in which comparative experimental measures of 'obedience to authority' will play an important part." He never did the follow-up studies in Germany because, as he told an interviewer (Meyer, 1970), he found such a surprisingly high degree of obedience among his American participants that he "hardly saw the need for taking the experiment to Germany" (p. 73).

At the beginning of the obedience series, Milgram had hired Alan Elms (now at the University of California–Davis) as his first research assistant. Milgram wrote him a letter dated June 27, 1961. Though written in a playful tone, that his colleagues and students say was characteristic, it reveals that Milgram already had an intuitive sense of the broader significance of the research he was embarking on. He wrote:

> The advertisement was placed in the *New Haven Register* and yielded a disappointingly low response. There is no immediate crisis, however, since we do have about 300 qualified applicants. But before long, in your role as Solicitor General, you will have to think of ways to deliver more people to the laboratory. This is a very important practical aspect of the research. I will admit it bears some resemblance to Mr. Eichman's [*sic*] position, but *you* at least should have no misconceptions of what *we* do with our daily quota. We give them a chance to resist the commands of malevolent authority and assert their alliance with morality.

Very few research programs in psychology can match the continuing attention received by Milgram's studies on the dynamics of obedience to authority (see Blass, 1991, 1992, 1999, for reviews). An important factor accounting for this attention is the troubling lesson Milgram derives from it about human nature, that is, just how easily normal people possessing no malevolence can be made to carry out inhumane commands. In particular is the implication that anyone—not just the Nazis and their collaborators—would have been willing participants in the destruction of European Jewry during World War II. Milgram's analysis has been accepted not only by many introductory-level psychology texts but also by more advanced and scholarly treatments, such as Bauman (1989), Berger (1983), Hirsch (1988), Katz (1993), Kelman and Hamilton (1989), Kressel (1996), Miller (1986), Novick (1999), and Sabini and Silver (1980).

Milgram's analysis was especially well received by his fellow experimental social psychologists because—like the historically dominant approach in social psychology (Blass, 1984)—it is situational in its orientation. Milgram's approach is situational in the sense that the external pressures of the moment exerted by an authority—rather than internal instigators of action such as hostility or hatred—are seen as the main determinants of the subject's harsh actions. Further, when the subject relinquishes responsibility to the authority, his or her own actions are no longer under the usual moral constraints, according to Milgram (1967, 1974).

Recognition of the potential value of Milgram's work in relation to the Holocaust has extended beyond academia to the knowledgeable public. For example, we find the following statement in a book review by Marc Fischer of Daniel Goldhagen's controversial book, *Hitler's Willing Executioners: Ordinary Germans and the Holocaust*, which appeared on April 25, 1996, in *The Washington Post*: "[Daniel Goldhagen] now claims he deserves a place alongside Hannah Arendt, Stanley Milgram, Raul Hilberg, and Yehuda Bauer, the great fathomers of the Holocaust." And across the Atlantic, *The Observer* of London carried an insightful article about how far people will go in the name of duty. The writer gives extensive coverage to the obedience research, "the great and terrifying study of obedience by the American . . . Stanley Milgram whose experiments . . . look back to Nazi Germany and forward to today, tomorrow, horribly always" (Gerrard, 1997).

Here is how Milgram described the relevance of his findings for understanding the Holocaust:

> A commonly offered explanation is that those who shocked the victim at the most severe level were monsters, the sadistic fringe of society. But if one considers that almost two thirds of the participants fall into the category of "obedient" subjects, and that they represented ordinary people . . . the argument becomes very shaky. Indeed, it is highly reminiscent of the issue that arose in connection with Hannah Arendt's book, *Eichmann in Jerusalem*. Arendt contended that the prosecution's effort to depict Eichmann as a sadistic monster was fundamentally wrong, that he came closer to being an uninspired bureaucrat who simply sat at his desk and did his job. . . . After witnessing hundreds of ordinary persons submit to the authority in our own experiments, I must conclude that Arendt's conception of the banality of evil comes closer to the truth than one might dare imagine. The ordinary person who shocked the victim did so out of a sense of obligation, a conception of his duties as a subject and not from any peculiarly aggressive tendencies. This is, perhaps, the most fundamental lesson of our study: that ordinary people, simply doing their jobs, and without any particular hostility on their part, can become agents in a terrible destructive process. (Milgram, 1967, p. 5; also, with slight changes, in Milgram, 1974, pp. 5–6)

Although Milgram (1974) recognized that there are "enormous differences of circumstance and scope" between obedience in his laboratory and Nazi Germany, he argues that "a common psychological process is centrally involved in both events" (p. 175). He believes that his experiments speak to all superordinate-subordinate relationships in which people become willing agents of a legitimate authority to whom they relinquish responsibility for their actions. Once having done so, actions are no longer guided by their conscience but by how adequately they have fulfilled the authority's wishes.

Milgram's approach has a good deal of appeal. It is certainly consistent with the litany of "I was only following orders" heard repeatedly at the Nuremberg war crimes trials of the major Nazi leaders at the end of World War II. It also has support from Arendt's analysis of the trial of Adolf Eichmann, who had been in charge of deporting the Jews from all the countries occupied by Germany to the death camps in the east. In her book *Eichmann in Jerusalem: A*

Report on the Banality of Evil (Arendt, 1963), she claimed that Eichmann was a very conventional person, guided largely by a drive to advance his career rather than by hate for his victims.

The impressions of Simon Wiesenthal (1989, p. 66), whose investigative work led to Eichmann's capture by the Israelis, are very similar. He describes Eichmann as "an utterly bourgeois, an utterly normal, almost in fact a socially adjusted, person. . . . He was not driven by blood lust."

One historian even makes a direct connection between some events that occurred during the Holocaust and Milgram's obedience experiments. In his book *Ordinary Men: Reserve Police Battalion 101 and the Final Solution in Poland*, Christopher Browning (1992) describes the activities of a Nazi mobile killing unit that scoured the Polish countryside between 1942 and 1943, searching for Jews. The unit's members ended up murdering 38,000 Jews in cold blood at the bidding of their commanders. Browning makes a detailed comparison between the actions of members of Battalion 101 and those of Milgram's subjects, concluding that "many of Milgram's insights find graphic confirmation in the behavior and testimony of the men of Reserve Police Battalion 101" (p. 174).

The "banality of evil" thesis also finds support in the writings of Hilberg (1980a). Hilberg has pointed out that the Nazis' success in carrying out their destructive plans on such a massive scale was made possible by countless bureaucrats and agencies applying their practiced skills and standard procedures to the task at hand. Among the examples he mentions is the SS being billed by the German railroad for each Jewish deportee it transported.

Consistent with Hilberg are findings of more recent historical research on the conduct of members of specific professions who, when the Nazis came to power, readily assimilated Nazi doctrine and directives into their everyday, normative activities, virtually without missing a beat. Weisberg (1996), a legal historian, studied the behavior of French lawyers and judges under the collaborationist, pro-Nazi, Vichy government, which instituted racial, exclusionary laws that eventually led to the deportation of 75,000 Jews to the Nazi death camps. He writes as follows:

> Legal activity during the full four years of Vichy was pervasive.
> Courts functioned much as they had always functioned, although
> bound by an unusual oath to Vichy's leader, Marshal Pétain. . . .
> Private legal practitioners . . . took up the new materials of racial,
> religious and ethnic ostracism and worked with them in volume
> and without substantial protest. Legal academicians wrote doctoral
> theses and had them published on the subject of the anti-Jewish
> laws, made their reputations as young law professors by discussing
> "neutrally" the stuff of exclusion, tried to explain how French
> constitutional norms could co-exist with laws designed to

97

persecute people *ex post facto* and because of immutable traits or private beliefs. (pp. xviii–xix)

In a similar vein, research by Geuter (1987) reveals that German psychologists generally "ran with the ball" when the Nazis took over. The first anti-Jewish law enacted by Hitler after he came to power, the Law for the Reconstitution of the Civil Service (Hilberg, 1985), led to the dismissal of the Jewish psychologists at universities (including Max Wertheimer, one of the founders of Gestalt psychology). Members of the German Society for Psychology took no action to help their dismissed colleagues. Instead, they requested the authorities to fill the vacated positions quickly to ensure the continued representation of psychology in the affected universities. Geuter notes further that

> the adaptation of psychological theory to National Socialist ideology supports the view that psychology was fully co-opted by the regime, or presented itself for co-optation. . . . Even without official directives for psychology's theoretical development, psychologists took ideological expectations of the subject for granted and attempted by themselves to show the compatibility of their approaches with Nazi ideology. (p. 171)

Milgram was also on solid ground in pinpointing obedience to authority as a possible key to understanding the Holocaust, given the high value placed on it by Nazi ideology and German culture generally. For example, the first of 12 commandments listed in a primer used to indoctrinate Nazi youth was "The leader is always right" (Berger, 1983, p. 25). And many generations of German children grew up on cautionary tales, such as that of Struwwelpeter or Shock-Headed Peter, whose moral was that disobedience could lead to rather drastic, violent consequences.[3]

The adequacy of Milgram's approach rests on two assumptions that bear closer examination. One is that he has demonstrated destructive obedience in the laboratory. In order to argue that the same psychological processes guided both the Nazi bureaucrat or death camp guard and the subject in an obedience experiment, it is first necessary to assess the evidence for the operation of those processes in the Milgram-type experiment itself.

The second assumption underlying the adequacy of Milgram's approach is that his conceptualizations fit the historical facts. Was the obedient Nazi subordinate mechanically carrying out the murderous commands of his leader, without any hate or hostility toward his victims, an accurate characterization of the prototype of the Nazi perpetrator?

Let us look at each of these questions in turn. First, did subjects in a Milgram-type experiment see their actions as destructive, that is, that they were harming and possibly killing the "learner"? A parallel between the actions of Milgram's obedient subjects and the murderous actions of the Nazis is based on the correctness of this assumption. Mixon (1971, 1972, 1979) has differed vigorously with Milgram's contention that his subjects' behavior was a manifestation of destructive obedience. He argues that both subjects' expectations about what is tolerable in a scientific experiment and the experimenter's comments about the shocks being painful but not hazardous reassure the subjects about the safety of the procedures. Although they might expect the learner to be in pain, they do not expect him to be harmed. Subjects became disobedient, according to Mixon, when doubts about the protection of the learner's well-being began to set in.

Support for Mixon's more benign interpretation of the Milgram experiment comes from a series of nonactive role-playing procedures in which a subject is read a description of the obedience experiment up to the point where the learner has pounded on the wall. The listener subject was then asked to describe what he thought happened after this point. By systematically changing the details about the procedure read to subjects, Mixon was able to obtain variations in predicted obedience. These ranged from 0% of the subjects predicting complete obedience when the description they read clearly indicated that the learner was in danger of being harmed to 90% where indications of possible harm were minimized (Mixon, 1971).

On the other hand, some replications of the obedience experiment support Milgram's view that subjects obeyed even when harm to the learner was likely. For example, Ring, Wallston, and Corey (1970) had subjects administer increasingly "painful" sound to a learner. As the learner screamed and sobbed in apparent agony, the experimenter acted as if he had not expected these kinds of reactions. Yet 91% of the subjects were fully obedient—the highest rate of obedience reported in the literature for a standard obedience experiment (see also Mantell, 1971).

To sum up, the evidence on the question of the destructiveness of subjects' actions within the Milgram-type experiment is not wholly uniform. But even if we were to give more weight to the evidence in favor of the destructive view of subjects' behavior, we need to turn to the other side of the potential equation to see how Milgram's model fits the historical details of the Holocaust itself.

As noted earlier, Milgram saw Arendt's "banality of evil" thesis to be consistent with his own findings and conclusions. Yet, a reading of the Holocaust literature can certainly lead one to contest the idea that a cold, emotionless, and dutiful approach (e.g., Eichmann's) was prototypical of the Nazis' behavior. To begin with, Arendt's perception of Eichmann has been challenged. Robinson (1965) points out that Eichmann pursued his goal of shipping as many Jews as possible to the extermination camps with a degree of drive, perseverance, and enthusiasm that was clearly beyond the call of duty.

Furthermore, to intensify their suffering, in many cases large-scale actions against the Jews were timed to coincide with their religious holidays. For example, the deportation of the Jews of Warsaw began on the eve of Tisha B'Av (July 22, 1942), the day of mourning that commemorates the destruction of the Temple in Jerusalem (Bauer, 1982). According to M. Gilbert (1985), "Since the first days of the invasion of Poland in September, 1939, the Germans had used the Jewish festivals for particular savagery: these days had become known to the Jews as the 'Goebbels calendar'" (p. 297). The historical evidence on the spontaneity, inventiveness, and enthusiasm with which the Nazis degraded, hurt, and killed their victims also argues against explaining their behavior as simply responses to an authority's commands despite the perpetrators' abhorrence toward their own actions, and without hate toward their victims. It must have come from within.[4]

There are countless examples. One comes from a description of a witness's testimony at the trial of Klaus Barbie, "the butcher of Lyons": "Simone LaGrange was sent to Auschwitz and, one day, saw her father there. He was in a column of men marching by. She waved and an SS guard asked if that was really her father. 'Then go kiss him, girl,' the guard said. She ran to her father. The guard shot him" (Reeves, 1987, p. A9).

And here is a description by a survivor of the Majdanek concentration camp of the kind of brutalities that routinely took place there:

> [A] customary SS habit was to kick a Jew with a heavy boot. The Jew was forced to stand to attention, and all the while the SS man kicked him until he broke some bones. People who stood near enough to such a victim often heard the breaking of the bones. The pain was so terrible that people, having undergone that treatment, died in agony. (quoted in Bauer, 1982, p. 212)

Another example involves the actions of an *Einsatzgruppe*, or mobile killing unit, in operation in the town of Uman, in the Ukraine. A German army officer described how the Jews of the area were gathered near the airport and surrounded by SS men and other militia. The Jews were ordered to undress, hand over everything they owned, and stand in a line in front of a ditch. They were then shot and thrown into the ditch. The observer stated that no one was overlooked.

> Even women carrying children two to three weeks old, sucking at their breasts, were not spared this horrible ordeal. Nor were mothers spared the terrible sight of their children being gripped by their little legs and put to death with one stroke of the pistol butt or club, thereafter to be thrown on the heap of human bodies in the ditch, some of which were not quite dead. Not

before these mothers had been exposed to this worst of all tortures did they receive the bullet that released them from this sight.

Significantly, the observer noted that the killers worked "with such zealous intent that one could have supposed this activity to have been their lifework" (quoted in Herzstein, 1980, p. 142).

A final example is a heartrending story from the memoirs of Lieutenant Meyer Birnbaum, a Jewish officer who served in the U.S. Army during World War II. At the end of the war, his unit came to Ohrdruff, a concentration camp annexed to Buchenwald. At first they saw no sign of life. They were greeted by a pile of still-warm bodies machine-gunned by the retreating Germans "in a final spasm of hatred." Birnbaum searched for survivors and found two in the typhus ward. They were so weakened they could barely move, and that is what saved them from the fate of their fellow prisoners. They had been far too sick to obey the order to gather in the courtyard, where the others were shot. Both were Jewish; one was a 35-year-old man from Poland, and the other a 16-year-old Hungarian boy. Their first request was for a piece of bread, and they both sobbed uncontrollably as they recalled their murdered families. Birnbaum's narrative then continued:

> After about fifteen minutes of bitter sobbing, the sixteen-year-old suddenly looked at me and asked whether I could teach him how to do *teshuvah* [repent]. I was taken aback by his question and tried to comfort him. "After the stretch in hell you've been through, you don't have to worry about doing *teshuvah*. Your slate is clean. You're alive, and you have to get hold of yourself and stop worrying about doing *teshuvah*," I told him. But my words had no effect. I could not convince him. He kept insisting: *"Ich vill tuhn teshuvah*—I want to do *teshuvah*. Ich muz tuhn teshuvah*—I must do *teshuvah*."
>
> Finally, I asked him, "Why must you do *teshuvah*?" in the hope that talking would enable him to let go of some of the pain I saw in his eyes. He pointed out the window and asked me if I saw the gallows. Satisfied that I did, he began his story:
> *Two months ago one of the prisoners escaped. . . . The camp commandant was furious about the escape and demanded to know the identity of the escaped prisoner. No one could provide him with the information he was seeking. . . . In his fury, the commandant decided to play a sadistic game with us. He demanded that any pairs of brothers, or fathers and sons, step forward. We were terrified of what he might do if we did not comply. My father and I stepped forward.*

They placed my father on a stool under those gallows and tied a noose around his neck. Once the noose was around my father's neck, the commandant cocked his luger, placed it at my temple, and hissed, "If you or your father doesn't tell me who escaped, you are going to kick that stool out from under your father." I looked at my father and told him "Zorgst sich nit—Don't worry, Tatte, I won't do it." But my father answered me, "My son, you have to do it. He's got a gun to your head and he's going to kill you if you don't, and then he'll kick the chair out from under me and we'll both be gone. This way at least there's a chance you'll survive. But if you don't, we'll both be killed."

"Tatte, nein, ich vell dos nit tuhn—I will not do it. Ich hab nit fargessen kibbud av—I didn't forget kibbud av (honoring one's father)."

Instead of being comforted by my words, my father suddenly screamed at me: "You talk about kibbud av. I'm ordering you to kick that stool. That is your father's command."

"Nein, Tatte, nein—No, Father, I won't."

But my father only got angrier, knowing that if I didn't obey he would see his son murdered in front of him. "You talk about kibbud av v'eim [honoring one's father and mother]," he shouted. "This is your father's last order to you. Listen to me! Kick the chair!"

I was so frightened and confused hearing my father screaming at me that I kicked the chair and watched as my father's neck snapped in the noose.

His story over, the boy looked at me . . . as my own tears flowed freely, and asked, "Now, you tell me. Do I have to do *teshuvah*?" (Birnbaum, 1993, pp. x–xi)

But, in some ways, a passage that is most directly at odds with Arendt's "banality of evil" thesis can be found in an introduction to a book (Naumann, 1966) about the trial in Frankfurt from 1963 to 1965 of 22 SS men who served at Auschwitz. The book contains the testimony of witnesses who described the unimaginable acts of torture and murder perpetrated by the defendants. The writer of the introduction reflected on the horrors described in the book: "No one had issued orders that infants should be thrown into the air as shooting targets, or hurled into the fire alive, or have their heads smashed against walls. . . . Innumerable individual crimes, one more horrible than the next, surrounded and created the atmosphere of the gigantic crime of extermination." The author was none other than Hannah Arendt (1966, p. xxiv), giving recognition to the fact that there was another face to the Holocaust than that of the dutiful bureaucrat, and she stated that the Frankfurt trial "in many respects reads like a much-needed supplement to the Jerusalem trial" (p. xx). Thus, while her phrase "banality of evil" has sometimes been adopted to describe the essential nature of Nazi destructiveness, it would seem that Arendt herself had second thoughts about this.

A unique perspective vis-à-vis Arendt's (earlier) view is provided by Lifton (1986) in his in-depth study of the role of the medical profession in carrying out the Nazi program of destruction. He shows how SS doctors were centrally involved in all aspects of the killing process, ranging from providing a scientific aura for the Nazis' "biomedical vision," which saw Jews as deadly germs that had to be cleansed from the tissue of "Aryan" civilization, to the killing of camp inmates via injections to the heart. He relates his findings to Arendt's conclusions as follows:

> Consider . . . Hannah Arendt's celebrated judgment on Adolf Eichmann and the "banality of evil." That phrase has emerged as a general characterization of the entire Nazi project. What I have noted about the ordinariness of Nazi doctors as men would seem to be further evidence of her thesis. But not quite. Nazi doctors were banal, but what they did was not. Repeatedly in this study, I describe banal men performing demonic acts. In doing so—or in order to do so—the men themselves changed; and in carrying out their actions, they themselves were no longer banal. (Lifton, 1986, p. 12)

A final perspective on how Milgram's approach fits the details of the Holocaust is provided by Hilberg (1980b):

> When Milgram performed his experiment at Yale, his model comprised an authority figure and men who did as they were told. How accustomed we are to thinking in these terms about the administrative process in totalitarian systems. The reality, however, was much more complex. The bureaucracy that destroyed the European Jews was remarkably decentralized, and its most far-reaching actions were not always initiated at the top. Officials serving in middle or even lower positions of responsibility were producers of major ideas. Every once in a while, a particular set of recommendations would be approved by a superior and become a policy, authorization, or directive. Such, often enough, was the genesis of an "order." (pp. 100–101)

To sum up, Milgram's approach does not provide a wholly adequate account of the Holocaust. Both the laboratory evidence and the historical details of the destruction of European Jewry raise questions about the degree of fit between Milgram's conceptual model of obedience to authority and the actualities of the Holocaust. Clearly, there was more to the genocidal Nazi program than the dispassionate obedience of the average citizen who participated in the murder of his fellow citizens who were Jewish out of a sense of duty and not malice. At the same time, it could not have succeeded to the degree that it did without the passive or active complicity of Everyman. While Milgram's approach may well account for their dutiful destructiveness, it falls short when it comes to explaining the more zealous hate-driven cruelties that also defined the Holocaust.

But, even with this limitation, Milgram's ideas still possess significant explanatory value vis-à-vis the Holocaust, in several ways. First, the number of Germans *directly* involved in the killings and atrocities was very small, relative to the total population of Nazi Germany, which numbered about 66 million people in 1939 (Mitchell, 1985). Now, although the vast majority did not actually kill Jews, zealously or otherwise, they readily accepted the various decrees, beginning in 1933, that increasingly led to the Jews' economic suffering and social isolation (e.g., dismissal from their jobs, "Aryanization" of their businesses, imposition of curfews, restrictions on their use of public transportation and telephones), and eventually to their annihilation. In this regard, Hilberg (1985) notes that Heydrich, chief of the Security Police, "looked upon the whole German population as a kind of auxiliary police force. They were to make sure that the Jew 'behaved' himself. They were to watch all Jewish movements and to report anything that might be suspicious" (pp. 168–169). He notes further that "when the hour of decision [the deportation roundups] came, few Germans made any move to protect their Jewish friends" (p. 165). Milgram's work certainly speaks to this dutiful complicity of the vast majority of Germans.

Second, Milgram's ideas may also shed some additional light even on the behavior of the cruel Nazi killer who seemed to take delight in his savagery. Milgram argued that two processes are involved in destructive obedience—relinquishing responsibility to the person in charge (which he referred to as "entry into the agentic state") and accepting the authority's definition of the situation or reality. As Milgram (1974) put it: "There is a propensity for people to accept definitions of action provided by legitimate authority. That is, although the subject performs the action, he allows authority to define its meaning" (p. 145). By abdicating responsibility to the commanding authority, the person frees himself from having to decide about the morality of his actions; the authority does that for him. The Nazi leaders' "definition of action" relating to the Jews was to see them not as humans but as "a lower species of life, a kind of vermin, which upon contact infected the German people with deadly diseases" (Hilberg, 1985, p. 20). Thus, while the zeal and inventiveness with which many Nazis hurt, degraded, and killed their Jewish victims suggest that their deep-seated hatred of Jews was the main driving force behind their actions, the two processes suggested by Milgram undoubtedly enabled them to carry them out without a guilty conscience.

Third, one of the distinctive features of the Milgram (1974) obedience paradigm is the sequential nature of the delivery of shocks. The learner's "suffering" intensifies in a gradual, piecemeal fashion. Milgram considered this manner of giving shocks one of the factors "that powerfully bind a subject to his role" (p. 149). The importance of this unfolding process as a facilitator of destructive obedience in Milgram's laboratory has served to alert us to the vital role played by the step-by-step, escalating process that the Nazis used in the victimization of the Jews, as described by Hilberg (1985):

> The process of destruction unfolded in a definite pattern . . . a step-by-step operation. . . . The steps of the destruction process were introduced in the following order. At first the concept of the *Jew* was defined; then the expropriatory operations were inaugurated; third, the Jews were concentrated in ghettos; finally, the decision was made to annihilate European Jewry. Mobile killing units were sent to Russia, while in the rest of Europe the victims were deported to killing centers. . . . It is the bureaucratic destruction process that in its step-by-step manner finally led to the annihilation of 5 million victims. (pp. 53, 47)

Referring to the incremental feature of his experimental procedure, Milgram (1974) said: "The laboratory hour is an unfolding process in which each action influences the next. The obedient act is perseverative" (p. 149). One can hear echoes of this view in Hilberg's (1985) assertion that "a measure in a destruction process [whose sequential nature he had just outlined] never stands alone. . . . It always has consequences. Each step of the destruction process contains the seed of the next step" (p. 54).

But regardless of degree of fit, in trying to find an explanation for the Holocaust, Milgram created a laboratory paradigm that stands out as the foremost example of creative experimental realism, applied to a question of profound social and moral significance. Furthermore, his work has helped maintain and spread an awareness of the Holocaust. There are probably hundreds of thousands of students who first learned about the Holocaust through exposure to the obedience experiments in an introductory psychology course. Some middle school and high school Holocaust curricula contain discussions of the obedience experiments (Saltzman, 2000).

Milgram taught us something profoundly revelatory about human nature—about ourselves—that we did not know before: just how powerful is our propensity to obey the commands of an authority, even when those commands might conflict with our moral principles. And, having been enlightened about our extreme readiness to obey authority, we can try to take steps to inoculate ourselves against unwanted or reprehensible commands.

One important place where this has been happening is in the U.S. Army, which apparently has taken the lessons of Milgram's research to heart and acted on it. On November 29, 1985, a college student doing a research paper on the obedience experiments wrote a letter to West Point, asking if Milgram's research was "considered a vital part of [their] program." In response, she received a letter, dated December 12, 1985, from Colonel Howard T. Prince II, head of the Department of Behavioral Sciences and Leadership. He wrote: "The answer is a definite, yes. All cadets at the United States Military Academy are required to take two psychology courses, General Psychology . . . and Military Leadership. . . . Both of these courses discuss Milgram's work and the implications of his findings."

But there is more. A military psychologist, Lieutenant Colonel Dave Grossman, wrote *On Killing: The Psychological Cost of Learning to Kill in War and Society* (1995), an insightful book about soldiers' resistance to killing and how it is overcome, which draws substantively on Milgram's work. After I read the book, I contacted Grossman to ask him if Milgram's ideas have had any discernible impact on the military. His answer astounded me. He told me that when he was undergoing officer training in the early 1970s, he was shown training films instructing soldiers on how to *disobey* illegitimate orders. He believes that the use of these films was attributable to the My Lai massacre and Milgram's findings (personal communication, May 18, 1999).

NOTES

This chapter is a revised, updated, and expanded version of a portion of an article titled "Psychological Perspectives on the Perpetrators of the Holocaust: The Role of Situational Pressures, Personal Dispositions, and Their Interactions," which appeared in *Holocaust and Genocide Studies*, 1993, Vol. 7, pp. 30–50. By permission of Oxford University Press.

1. Quotations from letters and most information given without citation are from the Stanley Milgram Papers, Yale University Archives, or from Milgram's widow, Alexandra (Sasha) Milgram.

2. I want to express my thanks to Alexandra (Sasha) Milgram for providing me with a copy of this speech.

3. The story of Struwwelpeter, which has usually been published in picture-panel format, begins with a mother telling her young son that she has to go out, that he must stay in the house while she is out, and warns him ominously that, if he disobeys her, she will take him to the tailor. The moment she leaves the house, Struwwelpeter bolts out the door. The mother returns, discovers that her son has ignored her wishes, and drags him to the tailor. The last picture panel in the story shows the boy crying, with fingers severed, dripping blood.

4. Readers familiar with Goldhagen's (1996) controversial book, *Hitler's Willing Executioners: Ordinary Germans and the Holocaust,* will notice a similarity between the point of view I express in this statement and Goldhagen's. For the record, this statement first appeared

verbatim in 1993, in my article in *Holocaust and Genocide Studies* (Blass, 1993), on which this chapter is based—that is, 3 years before the publication of Goldhagen's book.

REFERENCES

Arendt, H. (1963). *Eichmann in Jerusalem: A report on the banality of evil*. New York: Viking.

Arendt, H. (1966). Introduction to B. Naumann, *Auschwitz*. New York: Praeger.

Bauer, Y. (1982). *A history of the Holocaust*. New York: Franklin Watts.

Bauman, Z. (1989). *Modernity and the Holocaust*. Ithaca, NY: Cornell University Press.

Berger, L. (1983). A psychological perspective on the Holocaust: Is mass murder part of human behavior? In R. L. Braham (Ed.), *Perspectives on the Holocaust* pp. 19–32). Boston: Kluwer-Nijhoff.

Birnbaum, M. (with Rosenblum, Y.). (1993). *Lieutenant Birnbaum: A soldier's story*. Brooklyn, NY: Mesorah Publications.

Blass, T. (1984). Social psychology and personality: Toward a convergence. *Journal of Personality and Social Psychology, 47*, 1013–1027.

Blass, T. (1991). Understanding behavior in the Milgram obedience experiment: The role of personality, situations, and their interactions. *Journal of Personality and Social Psychology, 60*, 398–413.

Blass, T. (1992). The social psychology of Stanley Milgram. In M. P. Zanna (Ed.), *Advances in experimental social psychology* (Vol. 25, pp. 277–329). San Diego, CA: Academic Press.

Blass, T. (1993). Psychological perspectives on the perpetrators of the Holocaust: The role of situational pressures, personal dispositions, and their interactions. *Holocaust and Genocide Studies, 7*, 30–50.

Blass, T. (1999). The Milgram paradigm after 35 years: Some things we now know about obedience to authority. *Journal of Applied Social Psychology, 29*, 955–978.

Browning, C. (1992). *Ordinary men: Reserve Police Battalion 101 and the Final Solution in Poland*. New York: HarperCollins.

Friedlander, H. (1998). The T4 killers: Berlin, Lublin, San Sabba. In M. Berenbaum & A. J. Peck (Eds.), *The Holocaust and history: The known, the unknown, the disputed, and the reexamined* (pp. 243–251). Bloomington, IN, and Washington, DC: Indiana University Press and the United States Holocaust Memorial Museum.

Gerrard, N. (1997, October 12). Do as you're told. *The Observer*, p. 3.

Geuter, U. (1987). German psychology during the Nazi period. In M. G. Ash & W. R. Woodward (Eds.), *Psychology in twentieth-century thought and society* (pp. 165–188). Cambridge: Cambridge University Press.

Gilbert, G. M. (1950). *The psychology of dictatorship: Based on an examination of the leaders of Nazi Germany*. New York: Ronald Press.

Gilbert, M. (1985). *The Holocaust: A history of the Jews of Europe during the Second World War*. New York: Holt, Rinehart and Winston.

Goldhagen, D. (1996). *Hitler's willing executioners: Ordinary Germans and the Holocaust*. New York: Knopf.

Grossman, D. (1995). *On killing: The psychological cost of learning to kill in war and society*. Boston: Little, Brown.

Herzstein, R. E. (1980). *The Nazis*. Alexandria, VA: Time-Life.

Hilberg, R. (1980a). The nature of the process. In J. E. Dimsdale (Ed.), *Survivors, victims, and perpetrators: Essays on the Nazi Holocaust.* Washington, DC: Hemisphere.

Hilberg, R. (1980b). The significance of the Holocaust. In H. Friedlander & S. Milton (Eds.), *The Holocaust: Ideology, bureaucracy, and genocide—The San José papers.* Millwood, NY: Kraus.

Hilberg, R. (1985). *The destruction of the European Jews* (Rev. and definitive ed.). New York: Holmes and Meier.

Hirsch, H. (1988). Why people kill: Conditions for participation in mass murder. In H. Hirsch & J. D. Spiro (Eds.), *Persistent prejudice: Perspectives on anti-Semitism.* Fairfax, VA: George Mason University Press.

Katz, F. E. (1993). *Ordinary people and extraordinary evil.* Albany: State University of New York Press.

Kelman, H. C., & Hamilton, V. L. (1989). *Crimes of obedience: Toward a social psychology of authority and responsibility.* New Haven, CT: Yale University Press.

Kressel, N. J. (1996). *Mass hate: The global rise of genocide and terror.* New York: Plenum.

Lifton, R. J. (1986). *The Nazi doctors: Medical killing and the psychology of genocide.* New York: Basic Books.

Mantell, D. M. (1971). The potential for violence in Germany. *Journal of Social Issues, 27*(4), 101–112.

Markle, G. E. (1995). *Meditations of a Holocaust traveler.* Albany: State University of New York Press.

Meyer, P. (1970, February). If Hitler asked you to electrocute a stranger, would you? Probably. *Esquire,* pp. 73, 128, 130, 132.

Milgram, A. (2000). My personal view of Stanley Milgram. In T. Blass (Ed.), *Obedience to authority: Current perspectives on the Milgram paradigm* (pp. 1–7). Mahwah, NJ: Erlbaum.

Milgram, S. (1963). Behavioral study of obedience. *Journal of Abnormal and Social Psychology, 67,* 371–378.

Milgram, S. (1967). Obedience to criminal orders: The compulsion to do evil. *Patterns of Prejudice, 1,* 3–7.

Milgram, S. (1974). *Obedience to authority: An experimental view.* New York: Harper and Row.

Milgram, S. (1977). *The individual in a social world: Essays and experiments.* Reading, MA: Addison-Wesley.

Miller, A. G. (1986). *The obedience experiments: A case study of controversy in social science.* New York: Praeger.

Mitchell, B. R. (1985). *International historical statistics: Europe, 1750–1993* (4th ed). New York: Stockton Press.

Mixon, D. (1971). Further conditions of obedience and disobedience to authority. (University Microfilms No. 72-6477)

Mixon, D. (1972). Instead of deception. *Journal for the Theory of Social Behavior, 2,* 145–177.

Mixon, D. (1979). Understanding shocking and puzzling conduct. In G. P. Ginsburg (Ed.), *Emerging strategies in social psychological research* (pp. 155–176). New York: Wiley.

Naumann, B. (1966). *Auschwitz.* New York: Praeger.

Novick, P. (1999). *The Holocaust in American life.* Boston: Houghton Mifflin.

Reeves, R. (1987, July 13). France's courage. *The Sun* (Baltimore), p. A9.

Ring, K., Wallston, K., & Corey, M. (1970). Mode of debriefing as a factor affecting subjective reactions to a Milgram-type obedience experiment: An ethical inquiry. *Representative Research in Social Psychology, 1,* 67–85.

Robinson, J. (1965). *And the crooked shall be made straight: The Eichmann trial, the Jewish catastrophe, and Hannah Arendt's narrative.* New York: Macmillan.

Sabini, J. P., & Silver, M. (1980). Destroying the innocent with a clear conscience: A sociopsychology of the Holocaust. In J. E. Dimsdale (Ed.), *Survivors, victims and perpetrators: Essays on the Nazi Holocaust* (pp. 329–358). Washington, DC: Hemisphere.

Saltzman, A. L. (2000). The role of the obedience experiments in Holocaust studies: The case for renewed visibility. In T. Blass (Ed.), *Obedience to authority: Current perspectives on the Milgram paradigm* (pp. 125–143). Mahwah, NJ: Erlbaum.

Weisberg, R. H. (1996). *Vichy law and the Holocaust in France.* New York: New York University Press.

Wiesenthal, S. (1989). *Justice not vengeance.* New York: Grove Weidenfeld.

Part II

BEYOND THE INDIVIDUAL:
GROUPS AND COLLECTIVES

5

Sacrificial Lambs Dressed
in Wolves' Clothing

Envious Prejudice, Ideology, and the
Scapegoating of Jews

Peter Glick

The goyim are a flock of sheep and we are their wolves.
And you know what happens when the wolves get hold
of the flock?
—From "The Protocols of the Learned Elders of Zion" (an 1897
anti-Semitic forgery of the alleged minutes of a meeting of the
"rulers of Zion")

Why did the Nazis desire to exterminate a whole people? Why, in
particular, were the Jews chosen as the primary targets of their aggression?
Why did the perpetrators persist and even accelerate their efforts when the
war against the Allies was clearly about to be lost? The social-psychological
concept most often invoked to answer these questions is scapegoating—the
venting of frustrations on an innocent but weak target—a notion that has
become part of popular "folk psychology." Scapegoat theory, however, is not
well integrated into contemporary social psychology, since its foundations are
firmly set in late nineteenth-century views of human irrationality, steeped in
the metaphor of the steam engine (e.g., the belief that energy constantly created by the mind must be "vented" in some fashion) and focused on the role
of "primitive" drives and repressed emotions. The theory sits uneasily among
contemporary models of prejudice informed by the "cognitive revolution" in
psychology, a reaction against drive-based models that replaced the steam
engine metaphor with a computer-based analogy of the mind as a rational,
though imperfect, information processor (Fiske & Taylor, 1991).
     Among social psychologists, scapegoating is treated as a half-remembered
distant relative, trotted out to be included in the family picture of prejudice

theories but kept on the margins and only vaguely recognized. At worst, the scapegoat concept seems like a social-psychological fad that has faded, the all-too-familiar tale of a theory met with an initial flurry of excitement, followed by criticism, disillusionment, and a sharp drop-off of research interest. The theory has a checkered past, coming in for serious criticism soon after its formulation (Allport, 1954; Zawadzki, 1948). Research yielded inconsistent data (see Billig, 1976, chap. 5, for a review), and scapegoating was largely abandoned as an area of empirical study in the late 1960s (for a recent exception to this trend, see D. P. Green, Glaser, & Rich, 1998). The persistence of the scapegoat concept, in both popular and social-scientific discourse, seems to stem more from its intuitive appeal than from direct empirical evidence.

This chapter reexamines the scapegoat concept, distinguishing between two variants of the theory identified by Allport (1954). After explicating and critiquing these classic versions of scapegoat theory, I present an alternative, ideological model of scapegoating. The proposed model seeks to correct scapegoat theory's deficiencies more generally and to provide a greater understanding of the Holocaust more particularly, with special attention to the questions that opened this chapter: Why genocide, and why did the Nazis focus so strongly and so persistently on the Jews?

OVERVIEW OF PROPOSED IDEOLOGICAL MODEL OF SCAPEGOATING

The alternative model presented here proposes that an ideology of envious prejudice is a crucial mediator of scapegoating. It builds upon Tajfel's (1981) and Billig's (1976) arguments that collective aggression is the result of shared ideologies adopted to explain large-scale social events, Mandler's (1975) theory of emotion and cognitive appraisals, and Staub's (1989, this volume) insights into how the needs aroused by difficult life conditions are addressed by ideologies such as National Socialism. In brief, widespread social and economic frustrations are hypothesized to motivate people to seek *plausible causal explanations* at a collective level. Scapegoating ideologies—which blame shared frustrations on a specific group—are adopted by a critical mass of adherents when they offer a psychologically and socially attractive explanation for, and course of action designed to remove, the frustrating conditions. An ideology's attractiveness is jointly determined by prior stereotypes and values (which affect its plausibility and acceptability), as well as its ability to address heightened needs aroused by difficult conditions (Staub, 1989, this volume).

The preceding arguments are largely a synthesis of other theorists' insights, but three crucial implications are developed further here. First, contrary to the original scapegoat hypothesis, the scapegoated group is *not* likely to be any minority that happens to be vulnerable and helpless but rather a group that (though it may be vulnerable in actuality) is believed to be powerful, cunning, and dangerous. Weak, unsuccessful groups are much less likely to be viewed as plausible causes of a dominant group's loss of status and power, their failure at war, or the meltdown of their economy than are successful minorities, who are viewed as wielding power and influence disproportionate to their numbers. Thus, scapegoating is likely to be an *envious prejudice* (Glick & Fiske, 1999, 2001) directed at groups perceived to have dangerous abilities and evil intentions. Perceptions of the target group's malice and power are exaggerated in scapegoat ideologies, such as the Nazi view of Jews as potent and demonic manipulators of the economy (Friedländer, 1997). As a result, the most extreme forms of intergroup discrimination, including genocide, are typically legitimated by perpetrators as acts of self-defense against an implacable foe.

Second, even though scapegoating may be both irrational (in the sense that demonstrably false beliefs are held about the scapegoat) and maladaptive (because violence against the scapegoat fails to remove the frustrations that instigated it), the processes that lead to scapegoating may represent generally rational and adaptive psychological systems (which, under certain circumstances, nevertheless yield irrational and maladaptive results). This view is consistent with a dominant strain in contemporary social-psychological theorizing, which suggests that irrational and destructive behavior need not reflect irrational thought processes or destructive drives (see Nisbett & Ross, 1980). Classic scapegoat theory, which was heavily influenced by Freudian constructs, assumes that extreme behavior, such as the Nazi genocide, must be driven by irrational, unconscious processes (e.g., repressed psychodynamic conflict). Events as horrific and destructive as the Holocaust seem to demand this kind of explanation. How perpetrators understand, justify, or explain their behavior (e.g., Nazi ideology) is, in this view, merely a set of rationalizations, a smoke screen that masks the true causes of behavior (from the perpetrators themselves, as well as from less astute observers). In contrast, the proposed model (though it does not reject all Freudian concepts) views ideology as the proximal cause of behavior. The processes that lead even to extreme forms of scapegoat ideologies may not themselves be inherently irrational or indicative of psychodynamic conflict. Generally adaptive, though imperfect, psychological systems can nevertheless yield grossly maladaptive beliefs and behavior, especially in circumstances of extreme social flux.

Third, once people adopt a scapegoat ideology, increasing ideological commitment can maintain aggression against a scapegoat even if the frustrations that initially generated attraction to the ideology disappear (indeed, if improved social conditions are attributed to the enactment of the ideological program, the lessening of frustrations can actually enhance commitment to a violent ideology). Ideology is not only a necessary mediator between frustrating conditions and scapegoating (Billig, 1976), but ideological commitment develops its own legs once people act on the ideology. As people enact an ideological program, they seek justifications of those actions (Festinger, 1957), and this, in turn, increases both ideological commitment and the probability of future, more extreme behavior. In other words, scapegoat ideologies become self-sustaining as ideologically motivated aggression against the scapegoat creates a cycle of increasing commitment and a progression down a "continuum of destruction" (Staub, 1989, p. 17).

CLASSIC SCAPEGOAT THEORY

Following World War II, the problems of aggression and prejudice, not surprisingly, received heightened attention from social scientists. Many of these theorists sought to combine Freudian concepts with social learning theory and a sophisticated empiricism (e.g., Adorno, Frenkel-Brunswik, Levinson, & Sanford, 1950; Bettelheim & Janowitz, 1950). The most prominent results were two theories directly relevant to understanding the Holocaust: the authoritarian personality (Adorno et al., 1950) and the frustration-aggression hypothesis (Dollard, Doob, Miller, Mowrer, & Sears, 1939). Dollard et al. combined the hypothesis that frustration inevitably results in an instigation to aggress with Freudian concepts—the need for psychic energy to find an outlet, the defense mechanisms of displacement, projection, and catharsis—to create the most frequently cited version of scapegoating. The authoritarian personality and scapegoating are closely related: The former hypothesizes a constellation of personality traits that make an individual particularly prone to displacing aggression onto those in a weaker position (i.e., to scapegoat).

Interestingly, among prejudice researchers, the authoritarian personality and scapegoating experienced a similar trajectory: Both initially generated an impressive amount of research before interest waned in the late 1960s. Both fell victim to methodological and theoretical critiques, as well as a distaste for Freudian concepts concerning drives, irrationality, and defense mechanisms that accompanied the cognitive revolution in psychology (which instead offered an emphasis on stereotyping as a consequence of normal cognitive processes of categorization). Additionally, Staub (1989) suggests that Milgram's (1974) dramatic obedience experiments may have accelerated the demise of interest in motivational and personality approaches to understanding the Holocaust by showing that most people can be induced to become reluctant perpetrators when subjected to the demands of a destructive authority.[1] Finally, increasing concern with racism and sexism, forms of prejudice that social psychologists in the United States viewed as more pressing social problems, resulted in a dramatic decrease in research on anti-Semitism. Because anti-Semitism differs qualitatively from the typical manifestations of these other prejudices in ways that have not been fully appreciated by social psychologists (but which will be articulated later; see also Glick & Fiske, 2001), this shift in emphasis may also have steered researchers away from scapegoating.

Although interest in the authoritarian personality has recently been renewed (Altemeyer 1981),[2] research on scapegoating continues to languish, despite the fact that the concept remains popular in general discourse. Allport (1954) identified two versions of scapegoat theory: One is more purely Freudian, emphasizing psychodynamic conflict (here labeled the *internal conflict* version), whereas the other stresses the role of external frustrating events (Dollard et al., 1939). The latter (here labeled the *external events* version), for which Dollard et al.'s (1939) *Frustration and Aggression* is the foundational work, still borrows heavily from Freud. The next section explicates and critiques these classic versions of scapegoat theory, both more generally and also within the specific context of the Holocaust.

External Events Scapegoating: The Frustration-Aggression Hypothesis

Among social psychologists, the *external events* version of scapegoating is the most accepted. It begins with the frustration-aggression hypothesis (Dollard et al., 1939): Frustrating events create an instigation to aggress against the source of the frustration, an instigation that may or may not be acted upon directly and that may be displaced. Consistent with Freudian theory, Dollard et al. presume that if the instigation is not acted upon, the desire to aggress does not disappear and is likely to "leak out" in some form to release the individual's aggressive energy. In contrast, acting on the aggressive impulses has a cathartic effect and should reduce the need for further aggression (or for substitute outlets for the aggressive energy).

Why would an instigation to aggress not result in action against the source of the frustration? Fear of punishment is theorized to be the primary reason for aggression inhibition. Instead, aggression may be *displaced* onto a target that can be safely aggressed against without aversive consequences—a scapegoat. Much as the child scolded by a parent may displace his or her frustration by kicking the family pet or pounding a younger sibling (because aggression against the powerful parent is deemed unwise), any weak or vulnerable group that happens to be close at hand will serve as a scapegoat. To justify this aggression, undesirable traits are attributed to the target in a process Allport (1954) dubbed *complementary projection*. In this view, unfavorable stereotypes of a targeted group are rationalizations that are caused by, rather than cause, aggressive impulses toward the group. For the most part, these hypothesized processes take place without conscious awareness, that is, the individual has repressed any incipient awareness of hostility toward the true source of frustration and does not realize that his or her rationalizations about the scapegoat are merely a displacement (as conscious realization would defeat the whole purpose of such rationalizations).

117

Internal Conflict Scapegoating: Psychodynamic Conflict and Inherent Aggression

A second classic variant of scapegoat theory can be labeled the *internal conflict* version. This model is more purely Freudian and emphasizes the role of inner psychodynamic conflict and inherent human aggressiveness, with external events being given a more distal role. Freud (1930/1961) hypothesized that social life inevitably sets up continued psychodynamic conflict because all societies demand the repression of the id's impulses. In particular, sexual and aggressive drives are heavily regulated by society. The young child is taught to inhibit aggressive and sexual impulses and is punished when he or she acts inappropriately (according to cultural or parental norms) on these impulses. This inevitably creates frustration and resentment that build up and need to be vented. This view is consistent with the frustration-aggression hypothesis, but the inner-conflict version of scapegoating emphasizes how the inevitable frustrations of childhood socialization shape the individual's personality, whereas the frustration-aggression hypothesis emphasizes the immediate effects of frustration on aggression.

Initially, parents are the direct source of the child's frustrations, but as parental strictures are internalized, one's own superego frustrates the desires of the id. Direct aggression against these sources is typically inhibited. Children repress hatred toward parents for a number of reasons: They are taught that it is unacceptable, parents are also loved, and parents are powerful and might retaliate. The inhibition of the desire to aggress creates psychodynamic conflict as the aggressive energy that is built up finds no direct release. Later, the conflict is primarily an internal one because the individual has adopted the parents' ideals and the superego becomes the immediate source of frustration. This psychodynamic conflict may prompt aggression against the self (in the form of "accidents" or psychopathologies), but because self-hatred and self-punishment are painful, aggression is often directed outward instead, displaced onto an alternative target.

Displacing aggression onto a scapegoat allows the venting of aggressive energy created by internal conflict, and the aggression can be justified by attributing undesirable traits to the scapegoat. Importantly, the traits attributed to the scapegoat will be the very ones that the individual fails to recognize and represses in the self. Because repression is typically inefficient and incomplete, those motives the individual tries to exclude from conscious awareness have an annoying tendency to break through into consciousness. Unwilling to "own" these impulses as part of the self, they are instead attributed to the scapegoat. Allport (1954) refers to this as *direct projection*; an attribute that lies within oneself is attributed to another (e.g., it is others, not I, who have perverse sexual desires). Direct projection is the original, Freudian version of projection and is distinct from what Allport (1954) termed *complementary pro-*

jection (described earlier), in which one seeks explanations or justifications for one's behavior and emotions (e.g., I dislike the Jews, therefore the Jews must have undesirable traits that elicited my dislike). The crucial difference is that complementary projection does *not* involve traits the individual possesses (or strongly fears possessing) that must consequently be expelled from the self.

Direct projection serves the dual function of rationalizing aggressive feelings toward the scapegoat and defending against attributing unacceptable thoughts and motives to the self. For instance, imagine a child who has been taught that sex is dirty and bad. Her parents might punish her severely for overt behaviors they deem sexual, such as touching her genitals. Fear of parental punishment may lead her to engage in these acts only covertly. Once she has internalized the parents' strictures, however, there is no place to hide; her own superego may punish her for mere thoughts of touching her genitals, not just the active behavior. Thus, she attempts to repress her sexual thoughts, to convince herself that she does not have them. Repression, however, demands constant vigilance and is incomplete. Direct projection helps resolve the problem because the unacceptable impulses can be attributed to a scapegoat (*they* are the ones who are sexually depraved). The aggressive impulses arising from her inner conflict not only can be safely displaced onto the scapegoat but also can be rationalized as stemming from the scapegoat's repulsive characteristics.

Comparing and Combining the Classic
Models of Scapegoating

The inner conflict version of scapegoating acknowledges that external social conditions influence the amount of inner conflict individuals experience. Although all societies will promote some degree of psychodynamic conflict (because no society can allow complete freedom for individuals to act on impulse), some are more strict and repressive than others, heightening individuals' frustrations. Thus, authoritarian social norms that require strict obedience from children foster authoritarian personalities who are particularly likely to vent their frustrations on weaker targets (Adorno et al, 1950). What distinguishes the inner conflict from the external events version of scapegoating is that it casts internal psychological sources as the more proximal cause of frustration. External social forces are accorded a distal role, since they have their influence primarily through socialization, shaping the individual's enduring personality (e.g., strict toilet training might explain an adult's subsequent attraction to authoritarian ideologies). Further, because the id constantly generates sexual and aggressive energy, the inner conflict version suggests that frustration is constantly renewed even when external frustrations may be minimal. In contrast, the external events version of scapegoating emphasizes immediate situational factors (e.g., difficult economic conditions) as the proximal cause of frustration.

119

Although the standard versions of scapegoating differ in some respects, they can be viewed as complementary. Figure 5.1 presents a flowchart that captures both sets of processes. In the main, the psychological paths of both explanations can be viewed as similar regardless of whether the contemporaneous cause of frustration is primarily internal or external. With internal conflict, inhibition of aggression occurs because the self is the source of the frustration, whereas in the external events version, inhibition occurs because a powerful external source of frustration cannot be aggressed against with impunity. The major psychological difference is that internal conflict leads to direct projection, whereas external frustration does not (leading only to complementary projection).

In terms of explaining the Holocaust, a combination of the external events and inner conflict versions of scapegoating could be applied. Germany had authoritarian norms of obedience and correspondingly strict parenting styles, creating a population with a high proportion of authoritarian personalities prone to scapegoating to resolve inner conflict. Unable to recognize the true source of their psychodynamic conflicts, Germans targeted the Jews, a group unable to retaliate against aggression, for projection of this inner conflict. Once external conditions—the loss of World War I and the subsequent economic, social, and political collapse—heightened frustration, the combination of internal conflict and external frustrations proved explosive, creating an unprecedented venting of frustration on the Jews.

CRITICISMS OF SCAPEGOAT THEORY

Scapegoat theory has been severely criticized in ways that suggest deficiencies in both classic versions of the concept. Here I review the general criticisms of scapegoat theory, with particular reference to problems the classic versions of the theory encounter as explanations of the Holocaust. These problems fall into three major areas: (a) the choice of the scapegoat, (b) the process of displacement, and (c) the notion of catharsis.

Choice of Scapegoat

As early as 1948, Zawadzki noted that scapegoat theory is inadequate in predicting which minority group will be chosen as a target and in accounting for differences in the intensity of dislike of different minorities. This has continued to be a frequent criticism of scapegoat theory, reiterated by Allport (1954) and later expanded upon by Tajfel (1981) and Billig (1976). Why did the Nazis center their hatred on the Jews, who formed less than 1% of the German population? Both the inner conflict and external events versions of the theory have difficulty with this issue.

The inner conflict version of scapegoating requires the assumption that German culture was overly restrictive and authoritarian even before the

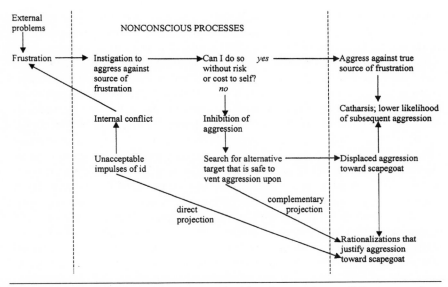

Figure 5.1 Model Incorporating Both Classic Versions of Scapegoating

Nazis—an assumption that has some merit (Staub, 1989). There is also evidence that people with authoritarian personalities were more likely to be attracted to Nazi ideology (Staub, 1989). Whether German norms of authoritarianism created the sort of inner conflict hypothesized by the theory and whether the unacceptable impulses then were projected onto the Jews is impossible to know. In favor of this idea, Bettelheim and Janowitz (1950) note that German stereotypes characterized Jews as sexually depraved, greedy, and conniving—all traits deemed unacceptable in the self and therefore candidates for projection onto others. Even granting this, why were the Jews in particular such a popular choice as a projective screen? Why is it that so many separate individuals' psychic conflicts were resolved by choosing the same target? Why, for example, not attribute sexual depravity to a disliked non-Jewish neighbor?

The external events account also has problems explaining consensus in the choice of target. Widespread frustration might lead to violence, but such aggression would be aimed at a variety of available targets and result in essentially random outbursts of individual violence. "It is too fanciful," Billig (1976) argues, "to imagine that the Germans were kept in an increasing state of emotional arousal for fifteen years, and at the end of this time simultaneously millions happened to rid themselves of these tensions in an identical manner" (p. 150).

121

Berkowitz and J. A. Green (1962; Berkowitz, 1989) attempted to address the problem of choice of scapegoat in a modification of the theory in which additional target characteristics (besides availability and vulnerability) determine who will be scapegoated. Thus, other characteristics of the Jews, their strangeness, visibility, and prior stereotypes about them, explain why they were chosen as victims. Although this modification helps to some degree—in particular, the role of prior stereotypes has widely been acknowledged as crucial to understanding the Holocaust (Friedländer, 1997; Goldhagen, 1997; Staub, 1989)—it still does not sufficiently account for the choice of Jews as scapegoats. Although Nazi propaganda fostered stereotypes of Jews as alien and the Nuremberg Laws instituted measures (most infamously, wearing the yellow Star of David) to render Jews more visible, these events seem as much consequence as cause of Nazi anti-Semitism. In particular, Berkowitz and Green's modification cannot explain why Nazi anti-Semitism was so hostile to Jews who were well assimilated into German society; a striking feature of Nazism was the attempt to root out "racial" Jews who might appear to be no different from most other Germans, even if they were half or quarter Jews, seemingly in contradiction to the principles of strangeness and visibility.

Even the original notion that vulnerable groups are chosen as targets of frustration was questioned early on. Zawadzki (1948) and Allport (1954) both pointed out that minorities often target their frustrations on more powerful majorities. Although the Jews were indeed a vulnerable minority within Germany, German stereotypes of Jews, even prior to the Nazis, did not characterize them as powerless. Christian anti-Semitic stereotypes cast the Jews as potent allies of the Devil who could employ supernatural powers (Goldhagen, 1997; Rubenstein, 1966). The popular anti-Semitic tract "The Protocols of the Learned Elders of Zion" placed Jews at the center of a powerful and dangerous international conspiracy that allegedly manipulated the world economy. Nazi anti-Semitism followed suit. Jews were viewed as being far from helpless, having enough shrewdness, power, money, and influence to cause Germany's defeat in World War I, the subsequent economic depression, and the Russian Revolution. Early actions against Jews were taken with some trepidation because the Nazis feared financial and political retaliation from the international Jewish community (Friedländer, 1997). In terms of perceptions, at least, the Jews were not the most vulnerable target the Nazis could have chosen.

The Process of Displacement

Both classic versions of scapegoat theory propose that aggression is displaced because it is unacceptable to aggress against the real source of the frustration, requiring the aggressive energy to be expended in another way. The scapegoated group is an "acceptable" target because it is perceived to be weak and (in the Berkowitz and Green modification of the theory) already devalued. The stereotypes of Jews outlined here challenge the notion that the Jews were chosen due to perceived vulnerability. A scapegoat theorist might dismiss this criticism by asserting that stereotypes of Jewish influence and power were merely complementary projection, rationalizations of displaced aggression (i.e., a consequence, rather than cause, of Nazi anti-Semitism). Aggressive impulses toward the Jews might have been rationalized by believing that "Jews are powerful and wish to harm us." This projective process, though certainly possible, is rather convoluted, and its verisimilitude is not easily assessed. Additionally, stereotypes of the Jewish menace had a long history in Germany and Europe more generally (Goldhagen, 1997) and cannot be wholly characterized as a response to Germans' post–World War I frustrations.

In general, displacement is not well understood or well researched (Billig, 1976). Most of the research on displacement, moreover, is susceptible to alternative explanations (Baumeister, Dale, & Sommer, 1998). Displacement requires an implicit or nonconscious decision-making process in which the feasibility or desirability of aggressing against the true source of the frustration is weighed. If aggression is thereby inhibited, another poorly understood and poorly researched implicit process by which alternative targets are considered is hypothesized to occur. In the case of the Holocaust, supporters of the Nazis, according to this theory, must have (at least implicitly) recognized that someone or something other than the Jews was responsible for their frustrations, but that this source was not one they could freely aggress against. The obvious sources of German frustrations in the 1920s and 1930s were the victorious Allies in World War I who imposed the Treaty of Versailles. Certainly the Nazis explicitly harbored great ill will toward the Allies. But because the Allies remained powerful and Germany was weak, it was impossible to vent frustrations on them, and, according to the scapegoat view, the Jews were selected as a substitute.

But if this explanation is correct, then why, once Germany was rearmed and powerful and began to attack the true sources of frustration, did the persecution of the Jews accelerate rather than diminish? Why was the Final Solution only concretely planned for after the war began? Most strangely, why did the Nazis continue to devote massive amounts of resources and effort to keeping the death camps operating until the very end of the war, to the detriment of the fight against the Allies? Scapegoat theorists might appeal to the notion that once the war appeared to be lost, the Nazis displaced their aggression with renewed fervor, but this explanation only deepens the mystery of why, early on, when the war against the Allies went well for Germany, the scope and intensity of Nazi persecution of Jews increased. Scapegoat theorists cannot have it both ways. The theory is simply ill suited to accounting for the pattern of behavior over time that the Nazis exhibited.

Catharsis

Whether aggression is expressed toward the true source of frustration or toward a scapegoat, it is thought to be a cathartic release of mental energy that makes subsequent aggression less likely. Both versions of scapegoat theory presume a Freudian model of drives in which drive-based energy seeks an outlet, much like steam in a heated kettle seeks release. The release of energy through aggression should reduce the subsequent need to aggress, until more energy is created, such as by a continuation of external frustrations or inner conflict. The notion of catharsis has had a troubled history in psychology, and it is generally recognized that aggressive behavior tends to make subsequent aggression more, not less, likely (Geen, 1998).[3] In the Holocaust, aggression against the Jews progressed along a continuum of destruction involving increasingly severe forms of persecution, with each step preparing the way for (rather than inhibiting) the next (Staub, 1989). The well-charted history of this continuum, from the Nuremberg Laws to the Final Solution, would seem unambiguously to disconfirm the notion of catharsis. Scapegoat theorists might counter this view by noting that aggression will intensify if frustrations build, and war is a frustrating time. This, however, does not explain why Nazi aggression toward the Jews increased after the 1934 Nazi Party Congress (lovingly presented in Leni Riefenstahl's *Triumph of the Will*) when the Nazis were flush with political and economic successes, war had not yet begun, and material conditions in Germany had greatly improved (Arendt, 1964).

Furthermore, although both classic versions of the theory cast scapegoating as a violent, spontaneous venting of built-up tension (an uncontrollable outburst that results in a cathartic release), part of what is particularly chilling and unique about the Holocaust is that it was such a controlled, regulated, and bureaucratized system of violence. Even Kristallnacht, which was politically engineered to look like a spontaneous outburst of anti-Jewish hatred (of the sort that might be predicted by scapegoat theory), was actually carefully planned and coordinated. Furthermore, Kristallnacht was an unpopular event that frightened many Germans, who (though no friends to the Jews) were upset at the apparent lack of control and wanton destruction of property (Friedländer, 1997).

Although the rounding up, deportation, and killing of Jews allowed many opportunities for spontaneous individual acts of sadism (and Nazi propaganda certainly encouraged people to express hatred toward Jews), Nazi leaders nevertheless went to great lengths to "improve" the methods of killing not only for the sake of efficiency but also to *avoid* turning their soldiers into sadists (Arendt, 1964; Browning, 1998; Staub, 1989). Browning's (1998) study of the "ordinary men" of a police battalion in Poland reveals that officers were concerned for the "spiritual care" of soldiers who were ordered to shoot Jews face-to-face. Among the *Einsatzgruppen* (mobile killing units), the actual killing duties were quickly farmed out, whenever possible, to "helpers" (e.g., Ukrainians) drafted from occupied areas (Browning, 1998). In the camps, shooting was replaced by gassing, and the victims themselves were forced to shove people in the ovens, further insulating German soldiers from direct involvement in the killings. Although psychoanalytically oriented interpreters of the Holocaust such as Richard Rubenstein (1966) see the Nazi regime as "a world without restraints, . . . without impediment" in which aggressive impulses could be satisfied at will, this fails to acknowledge how organized and systemized all behavior, including violence, was in Nazi Germany. For the ordinary German, it seems odd to characterize this supremely totalitarian society as a fantasy world in which gratification of impulses was freely permitted. Hannah Arendt's (1964) acerbic commentary seems more on the mark. "Evil in the Third Reich," Arendt argued, "had lost the quality by which most people recognize it—the quality of temptation. . . . many Germans and many Nazis . . . must have been tempted *not* to murder, *not* to rob, *not* to let their neighbors go off to their doom" (p. 150).

AN ALTERNATIVE: THE IDEOLOGICAL MODEL OF SCAPEGOATING

The shortcomings of the classic versions of scapegoat theory, both more generally and as applied to the Holocaust, suggest that the theory must be reconceptualized. The alternative, ideological model proposed here directly builds upon Mandler's theory of motivational arousal and cognitive appraisals, Tajfel's (1981) and Billig's (1976) insights into the weaknesses of prior scapegoat theory, and Staub's (1989) analysis of the social-psychological roots of genocide. This alternative model questions some of the fundamental assumptions of older versions of scapegoating concerning how and why a scapegoat is chosen and what sustains aggression against the targeted group. Although the proposed model is not inimical to the possible contributions of particular unconscious psychodynamic processes (e.g., projection), it recasts these as possible contributory factors that are not sufficient, necessary, or necessarily central to understanding scapegoating.

Interruption of Goal-Directed Behavior Leads to Meaning Analysis

The ideological model of scapegoating is outlined in Figure 5.2. As in the external events formulation of scapegoating, frustration is hypothesized to begin a process that may eventually elicit aggression against an innocent group. Frustration, as Dollard et al. (1939) argued, is an interruption of goal-directed behavior. This is consistent with Mandler's (1975) theory of emotion. When goal-directed behavioral sequences are interrupted (i.e., one cannot fulfill one's plans), arousal results, preparing the individual for "fight or flight," because

125

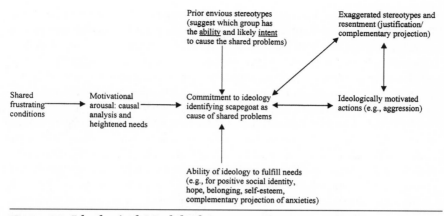

Figure 5.2 Ideological Model of Scapegoating

interruptions may indicate something dangerous or threatening to one's well-being. Additionally, Mandler argued, arousal motivates us to attend to the interruption, to analyze its meaning, and to contemplate how we might alter our behavior to reach our original goals (i.e., to engage in cognitive appraisals).

Mandler views this system as highly adaptive. Much of our behavior can become automatic as we develop successful routines for accomplishing short-term and long-term goals (e.g., after walking a familiar route, a person may have no memory of most of the walk, having negotiated the trip without consciously attending to it). It is only when routine behavior is interrupted that one needs to bring one's full cognitive capabilities to bear to analyze and solve the unexpected problem. The arousal caused by the frustration motivates continuing analysis and action until the source of the problem is addressed, thereby relieving the frustration (and diminishing the arousal). Essentially, Mandler suggests that consciousness evolved, in part, to enable us to engage in effective troubleshooting when obstacles are encountered. This perspective, which holds that frustration motivates conscious thought processes, contrasts with the processes proposed in the classic versions of scapegoat theory, which emphasize unconscious processes and psychodynamic conflict.

If Mandler's theory of emotion is correct, why does scapegoating occur? People who are frustrated by external events should focus their cognitive resources on figuring out the real source of the problem and then act to remove this source. As Allport (1954) noted, displacing aggression onto a scapegoat is counterproductive because it does not relieve the frustration (as actions against the true source might). If people have a generally adaptive response to frustration, why would they aggress against an innocent target? The answer is that generally adaptive processes do not inevitably yield correct or adaptive thoughts and behavior. The system Mandler describes undoubtedly works well for many of the individual frustrations encountered in daily life. For instance, if my car fails to start when I am on my way to an important appointment, the frustration I feel motivates me to diagnose the problem (e.g., recall whether I filled the tank yesterday) and to plot potential courses of action to reach my original goal (e.g., I can walk and get fuel at the station down the street, call a friend for a ride, or catch a bus).

Yet although this system may be effective for dealing with daily personal hassles, frustrations that stem from large-scale events, such as an economic depression, defy simple explanation (their causality involves a tangled web of interacting causes), and the scale of the events often impedes people's ability to find alternative ways to fulfill their goals (e.g., if I lose my job during a depression, there may be no viable alternatives available). Collective frustrations may require collective, rather than individual, responses (Tajfel, 1981). In short, large-scale frustrations in a complex society may pose problems with which a normally adaptive system (which originated in a very different evolutionary environment) is ill suited to cope.

Social Causation and Ideology

Tajfel (1981) and Billig (1976) argue that only large-scale social changes are likely to produce scapegoating of a group. Idiosyncratic frustrations—events that primarily affect one individual, not many—do not lead to widespread, consensual scapegoating. If one individual is frustrated because of conflict in his marriage, another because she has not been promoted at work, and a third because of a tax audit, it is unlikely that these three will all independently decide to blame the Jews. Frustrations that are specific to individuals, not widely shared, typically demand explanations that fit into the context of each of those particular individuals' lives (e.g., problems in one's marriage will be blamed on one's spouse or interfering in-laws, not on an outside social group).

In contrast, if many individuals are affected by the same social changes, such as mass unemployment, they will seek explanations on a group, rather than an individual, level. Tajfel (1981) labeled this "social causation," which he defined as "a search for the understanding of complex, and usually distressful, large-scale social events" (p. 156). The same need to explain and to act to eliminate frustration occurs regardless of whether frustrating events are small-scale and idiosyncratic or widespread and socially shared, but large-scale, shared frustrations require explanation in terms of forces that are deemed capable of causing the events. Although experts may appeal to abstract and complex processes (e.g., economic cycles), such explanations require a high degree of sophistication. Alternatively, people often attribute shared misfortunes to the actions of groups that can plausibly be seen as having caused the difficulties, perhaps because of the group's apparent power (e.g., government bureaucrats' policies have caused economic failure) or other characteristics that seem to connect this group to the frustrating social changes (e.g., an influx of refugees might be blamed for taxing the country's resources).

When many people share the same frustrations, existing social ideologies may be adapted to offer coherent explanations and solutions for the distressing events. New social ideologies are also likely to develop because older ideologies are associated with established political parties and social orders that may be blamed for causing (or failing to prevent) the frustrating circumstances (Staub, 1989). An ideology that is perceived successfully to diagnose the cause of the problems and that offers a plan for their solution has the potential to attract many adherents. If such an ideology identifies a particular social group as the source of the difficulties, that group will be at risk as a target of considerable hostility. This is especially true if the target group is thought to have intentionally caused the frustrating events; people who are perceived as having caused harm intentionally are much more likely to be retaliated against (Geen, 1998). In the end, it is the adoption of a shared ideology that accounts for coordinated (rather than isolated, random, or uncontrolled) aggression against a targeted group. As Billig (1976) noted, "Frustration may seem to trigger-off an aggressive response, but for this response to have any social strength, it must be backed up by an ideology of action. . . . Without the coherence provided by an ingroup ideology, frustrations will merely produce individual actions; these will take diffuse forms and will not be vehicles of mass social change" (p. 156).

Thus, it is not true that any type of frustration will lead to the scapegoating of a social group or that any vulnerable group will serve as a scapegoat. Rather, (a) the frustrations must involve large-scale, shared events that require social, rather than personal, explanations; (b) the groups that are scapegoated will be ones that can plausibly be viewed as causing the events; (c) enough similarly frustrated individuals must adopt a shared ideology that explains their frustrations as being intentionally caused by the targeted group; and (d) this ideology must endorse aggression against the scapegoated group as necessary to solving the problems. In some cases, the causal analysis may be largely correct (e.g., in some countries, believing that government corruption has ruined the economy may be a correct view). The same process, however, can also yield explanations that are plausible to a critical mass of disaffected people but incorrect in their diagnosis and counterproductive in dealing with the underlying problems. Such plausible but misguided explanations may stem at least in part from an inability to fathom the true causes of complex events, as well as an attraction to explanations that serve a variety of social-psychological needs (Staub, 1989). The first step toward understanding which group is likely to be scapegoated, however, is to know when and why a particular group will be perceived as a plausible cause of shared difficulties.

Envious Prejudice and Stereotype Content

Inability to account for the choice of scapegoat has been the most forceful criticism of past scapegoat theory. In the ideological model, prior stereotypes or beliefs about a group must render them a socially and psychologically plausible source of the current frustrating events; it is not true that any vulnerable, culturally devalued group will serve. Thus the ideological model of scapegoating suggests that groups that are seen as powerful and influential (rather than weak and vulnerable) are more likely to be blamed for large-scale, shared frustrations. In addition (and detailed later), some explanations will be culturally and personally more attractive because they fulfill other needs (e.g., an ideology that places blame on oneself or one's own group threatens positive self-image and is therefore less attractive than an ideology that places blame elsewhere).

Consider first why some groups are more likely to be blamed for frustrating social and economic conditions. Heider (1958), in his influential analysis of "folk psychology" (i.e., the manner in which people explain events and actions), noted that when we attribute events to the behavior of a person, we typically assume that the other must have the ability to cause the event and has attempted to bring the event about. For a group to be scapegoated, it must first be perceived as having the *ability* to cause widespread problems, for example, as wielding a great deal of influence. Second, unless the problems are viewed as accidental (a conclusion that people may actively seek to avoid, since it suggests that important events are capricious and uncontrollable; Lerner & Miller, 1978), the targeted group must have had the *intent* to cause the frustrating events. Prior stereotypes informed the Nazis' causal analysis and lent plausibility to the notion that the Jews had both the ability and the intention to cause Germany's woes. Christian anti-Semitism had already cast the Jews as demonic and powerful (Goldhagen, 1997; Rubenstein, 1966; Staub, 1989). As alleged allies of the Devil, Jews were viewed as devious and manipulative, conspiratorial, possessing supernatural abilities, and desiring to harm Christians. Visible Jewish success in banking and the media within Germany fed into a secular equivalent of this stereotype, with powerful Jews seen as exerting dangerous influence over the economy and German culture (Friedländer, 1997). In short, prior stereotypes characterized the Jews as possessing an uncanny ability and a fiendish desire to undermine German society and the economy in a way that stereotypes of alternative targets, such as the Gypsies, did not.

The abilities and intentions attributed to Jews were essential to defining them as a mortal enemy that had to be eliminated. Although other groups were also targeted by the Nazis, the particular vehemence of Nazi ideology concerning the Jews stemmed from the Jews' alleged role in causing Germany's defeat and economic depression. Gypsies, homosexuals, and the physically and mentally handicapped were viewed as weakening Germany, but they were not conceived as being "a superhuman force driving the peoples of the world to perdition" (Friedländer, 1997, p. 100), as Hitler (in a manner quite consistent with earlier German Christian anti-Semites) characterized the Jews. Volpato and Capozza (1998) performed a content analysis of *Mein Kampf*, concentrating on Hitler's racial views. Hitler portrayed the Jews as clever, greedy plotters who dominate the press, international finance, and university positions; as cunning, unscrupulous demagogues and exploiters who are out to destroy and dupe Germans. Although some contradictory images emerge—for example, the Jews are stupid and servile, as well as dictatorial and dominant—the overall picture is of an extremely powerful foe. (The contradictions in Nazi images of Jews are addressed later.)

Is it possible to predict which groups will be stereotyped as dangerous enemies? Susan Fiske and I argue that stereotypes of social groups tend to fall into predictable categories (Fiske, 1998; Fiske, Cuddy, Glick, & Xu, in press; Fiske, Xu, Cuddy, & Glick, 1999) determined by structural relations between groups (Glick & Fiske, 1999, 2001). Groups that are socioeconomically successful, such as Jews or the wealthy, are attributed traits of competence (e.g., viewed as ambitious, clever) that explain the group's success, but, if they are considered to be an out-group (e.g., foreign), such groups are simultaneously viewed as lacking in warmth (e.g., no concern for others, manipulative, self-interested, arrogant) because they are seen as competitors or exploiters. The former set of traits attribute the *ability* to influence the economy and society to the targeted group (i.e., they *can* if they choose to), whereas the latter set of traits suggest that the group may *intend* to do harm (i.e., they are likely to *try* to do so). Thus, groups that are targets of *envious prejudice* are at particular risk of being viewed as intentionally causing economic and social problems. Unfortunately, in recent decades, social psychologists have tended not to study envious prejudices as they turned their attention more exclusively to the treatment of socioeconomically disadvantaged minorities, but it is precisely the socioeconomically successful minorities that may be at most risk of being scapegoated.

Envious prejudices are likely to be at their most acute in situations in which majority group members feel that their social status has shifted downward relative to the status of a minority, a situation likely to create intense feelings of relative deprivation—the resentment that occurs when individuals or groups believe that others' outcomes are unfairly greater than their own (Davis, 1959; Runciman, 1966). In intergroup relations, relative deprivation theory has mainly been applied to understanding how low-status groups come to be dissatisfied with their lot (relative to other groups) and to resent, rather than comply with, the demands of high-status groups. High-status groups, however, may experience relative deprivation when their status or material conditions, like those of Germans after World War I, deteriorate relative to those of other groups. Feelings of entitlement to old privileges can intensify resentment against those who are perceived not to have suffered as much (cf. Olson, 1986). Envious prejudice, therefore, is likely to go hand in hand with a sense of relative deprivation. When, as in Germany, the success of an envied minority group is viewed as illegitimate and as based on exploitation of the majority, majority group members may see violent measures as justifiable in their attempt to regain their "usurped" social position and privileges.

Socioeconomically unsuccessful groups (e.g., the poor) do not evoke feelings of relative deprivation and envy. Stereotypically, they are viewed as incompetent (explaining their lack of success) and are not seen as serious competitors or threats. As long as such low-status groups are kept firmly "in their place," they will continue to be perceived as incompetent but also may be viewed as warm (e.g., friendly, supportive). These groups are the object of *paternalistic prejudice* from the dominant group (see also Jackman, 1994). Such groups are often exploited for cheap labor and to engage in low-level service roles. Paternalistic relationships between dominant and subordinate groups involve a coercive cooperation that is masked by condescending affection on the part of the dominant group toward the subordinate group. The worst forms of paternalistic exploitation are colonization and enslavement (rather than genocide—why kill others when you can enrich yourself on their labor?), which are typically justified by the dominant group with paternalistic ideologies such as the "White man's burden." In *Mein Kampf*, Hitler says little about the "Negroes," who, though clearly perceived as an inferior race, pose no serious threat to Aryans. The major traits attributed to the "Negro" are a lack of culture and a history of being exploited by the Jews (Volpato & Capozza, 1998).

In some cases, socioeconomically unsuccessful groups may be seen as competitors, rather than as cooperative "helpers," if they are deemed to be a drain on resources (rather than a source of cheap labor) or viewed as threatening the integrity of the dominant group. Such groups are the targets of *contemptuous prejudice*. These groups are viewed both as incompetent and as lacking in warmth and may be the target of scapegoating. However, because they are less likely to be seen as capable of intentionally causing the wide-scale frustrations of the dominant social group, they are less likely than successful minorities to be targets of the most severe forms of aggression. Nevertheless, such groups are still at some risk for violence and even genocide if they are viewed as a serious danger. The Nazis' initial institutionalized murder schemes were directed at the mentally and physically disabled, whom the Nazis viewed as weakening the "Aryan race" (Friedlander, 1995).

The different forms of prejudice are summarized in Table 5.1, which shows how two social-structural variables concerning relations between groups—their relative socioeconomic status and whether they are perceived to be positively or negatively interdependent (i.e., cooperative or competitive) with the in-group—can account for the different ways in which groups are stereotyped

131

Table 5.1

Taxonomy of Prejudices Based on the Structural Relations
Between Groups (Based on Glick & Fiske, 2001)

	INTERDEPENDENCE	
RELATIVE STATUS	COOPERATIVE	COMPETITIVE
High	*Admiration*	***Envious Prejudice***
Stereotype	Competent, warm	**Competent but not warm**
Negative emotions		**Envy, fear, resentment, hostility**
Positive emotions	Respect, admiration, affection	**Grudging admiration of abilities**
Behavior	Defer	**Avoid, exclude, segregate, exterminate**
Experienced by	Subordinates toward generous dominants upon whom they are dependent; in-group members toward allies; unchallenged dominants toward their own group	**Dominants whose status is slipping and disadvantaged groups toward successful minorities/dominants**
Low	*Paternalistic Prejudice*	*Contemptuous Prejudice*
Stereotype	Warm but incompetent	Not warm and incompetent
Negative emotions	Disrespect, condescension	Disrespect, resentment, hostility
Positive emotions	Patronizing affection, pity, liking	
Behavior	Personal intimacy but role segregation	Avoid, exclude, segregate, exterminate
Experienced by	Dominants toward subordinates upon whom they are dependent and toward "legitimate" dependents; groups that pose no socioeconomic threat	Dominants toward subordinates who are seen as illegitimate dependents (a perceived drain on social resources)

and how they are treated. The cells of the table represent idealized prototypes. In reality, combinations of the different types of prejudice may be directed at a group. For instance, the Nazis blended paternalistic and contemptuous prejudice in their treatment of the physically and mentally handicapped, who were the first targets of their killing programs. Nazi racial theories helped true believers to view the handicapped as a threat—an unnecessary drain on resources, a threat to racial purity, and "life unworthy of life" (Friedlander,

1995). Yet the Nazis could not completely do away with more paternalistic views of the handicapped and therefore couched their euthanasia program as "mercy killings" in which physicians alleviated the "suffering" of the victims (Friedlander, 1995). The Nazis, however, could not sustain popular support for the euthanasia program, largely because of family ties to the victims, but perhaps also because too many Germans simply did not see the handicapped as a profound threat. Prior paternalistic stereotypes and the lack of any perceived threat from such disadvantaged groups (who, after all, could not be characterized as intentionally seeking to harm Germany) sustained a more benign view of the handicapped.

In contrast, prior envious prejudice toward the Jews made them a socially plausible cause of Germany's problems. To enhance this perception, Hitler emphasized the power and cunning of the Jews (e.g., propagating the myth of the "Protocols of the Learned Elders of Zion"). Even so, the Jews were the target of both contemptuous and envious prejudice as additional motives (addressed later) led the Nazis to also characterize the Jews as lazy, unclean parasites (an image somewhat in conflict with the notion of Jews as ambitious, powerful conspirators). This contemptuous image of Jews as parasites reinforced their status as a threat but allowed Germans to feel superior to, not just resentful of, the Jews. Other groups (e.g., Gypsies) came in for similar contempt. But Jews remained the special obsession of the Nazis because they were also targets of envious prejudice; only the Jews were uniquely attributed with both the power and the intent to ruin Germany.

Ability of Ideology to Serve Heightened Needs

The attractiveness of a scapegoat ideology is not determined solely by its ability to explain frustrating events but by its ability to serve a variety of social-psychological needs heightened by difficult life conditions (Staub, 1989). Some plausible explanations of frustrating conditions may be rejected because they are unpalatable for a variety of reasons. For example, blaming the consequences of defeat on Germany's own militarism, which precipitated involvement in World War I, would have required rejecting cherished cultural values (Staub, 1989). For a demilitarized Germany (in the 1920s and early 1930s), blaming the Allies alone did not suggest an immediate course of action that might alleviate current problems. The process by which psychological needs influence the acceptance of ideologies may well occur without conscious awareness but can be understood without appealing to the problematic psychodynamic processes of aggression inhibition and displacement. In other words, it is not that, at an unconscious level, the true source of widespread frustrations is recognized but repressed but simply that some explanations—whether correct or not—are rendered more plausible and attractive because of preexisting beliefs, values, and needs. Specifically, Staub (1989) emphasizes a host of needs that are frustrated and therefore

133

become more strongly aroused during difficult life conditions: connection with others, self-protection, positive self-esteem and group esteem (the latter being what Tajfel, 1981, refers to as "positive differentiation for the ingroup," p. 156), and optimism for the future. Nazi ideology was attractive to many Germans not only because it offered an explanation for the source of their difficulties but also because it successfully addressed the needs that Staub has identified.

To some extent, the various motivations Staub identifies were easily reconciled with the social explanation function of Nazi stereotypes. Seeing the Jews as the intentional source of Germany's difficulties implied a course of action—eliminating the Jews—that offered hope for a utopian future in which Germany would be an Aryan paradise. Saul Friedländer (1997) labels this "redemptive antisemitism," an anti-Semitism that defines the Jews as a problem and offers a solution that would usher in a *völkish* utopia, the thousand-year Reich. Also, by banding together to accomplish this goal (and the Nazis were masters of the group rally), feelings of social connection were restored, addressing the need for belonging.

Yet some of the social-psychological needs Nazi ideology attempted to fulfill pulled in seemingly opposing directions, resulting in paradoxical Nazi images of Jews. In particular, the need to restore a positive group image and self-images, as well as the need to believe that this putative enemy could be vanquished, dictated that the Jews be seen as ultimately inferior to Aryans. Thus, Jews were simultaneously portrayed as possessing a superhuman potency and will to dominate, yet also as servile, parasitical, and inferior (Volpato & Capozza, 1998), "a subhuman cause of infection, disintegration, and death" (Friedländer, 1997, p. 100). Envious stereotypes of the Jews as influential and powerful but ill intentioned and manipulative allowed the Jews to serve as the explanation for Germany's woes, whereas the contrasting contemptuous stereotype of Jewish inferiority addressed the need to regain a sense of Aryan superiority (allowing the Nazis to restore the positive group image that the loss of World War I had all but demolished). This reassertion of a positive social identity once it has come under threat is predicted by social identity theory (Tajfel, 1981), and Nazi racial (and cultural) theories of Aryan superiority were undoubtedly central to the ideology's attraction for many Germans.

It is important to note that despite the contradictions in Nazi images of the Jews, the "weak," contemptuous image of Jews still casts them as a threat, as breeders of disease and depravity who had "infected" the body of Germany (e.g., the equation of Jews with rats in Nazi propaganda, such as the film *The Eternal Jew*). In *Mein Kampf*, Hitler attempted to reconcile the apparent inconsistencies by arguing that the Jewish conspiracy was only effective because of the secrecy and immoral deceitfulness of the Jews and, ironically, the too-trusting and tolerant (!) character of the Aryan (Volpato & Capozza, 1998). Thus, the insidious manipulation of the Jews would not stand up once unmasked and directly confronted by the culturally, morally, and physically superior Aryan race.

In sum, in the competing marketplace of ideologies, some will be more attractive than others because of their ability to fulfill a variety of needs. Although the first requirement for a scapegoat ideology is that it explains the causes of social ills in a manner that is culturally plausible, people will be more attracted to scapegoat ideologies if they also successfully address a variety of frustrated needs.

Projection in the Ideological Model

Although the ideological model rejects some psychodynamic concepts (e.g., catharsis), it remains hospitable to the notion of projection, both direct and complementary. Direct projection may, in some cases, cause an individual to create or to be attracted to a scapegoating ideology. Hitler, of course, has been endlessly psychoanalyzed, and it is certainly possible, for example, that repressed aggressive and sexual impulses projected (by Hitler and others) onto the Jews partially account for Nazi stereotypes of the Jews' power, manipulativeness, aggression, and sexual depravity. Recent research, however, casts some doubt upon the classic version of direct projection. Newman, Duff, and Baumeister (1997) gathered experimental evidence that defensive projection of undesirable traits occurs, but they suggested that the psychological mechanisms that account for these effects differ from Freudian theory. Specifically, Newman et al. propose that individuals' attempts to suppress any implications that they possess undesirable qualities lead to a "rebound" effect by which these traits become chronically cognitively accessible, with the result that people are prone to see these traits in others. It is not clear from this interpretation why projection would be directed disproportionately at one group of people (i.e., a scapegoat). Newman et al.'s model implies that projection does not discriminate but instead is likely to affect an individual's perception of others regardless of the social category to which others belong.

Even if classical direct projection occurs, the widespread acceptance of National Socialism cannot simply be attributed to individual psychopathologies. As Staub (1989) points out, however important psychodynamic conflict might have been for some individuals' attraction to Nazism or for the origins of Hitler's particular obsessions, obsessed and pathological individuals exist in all societies but are not usually capable of inducing others to follow their lead unless they articulate ideologies that others find attractive. Thus, direct projection of deep-seated psychodynamic conflict is likely to be, at most, a contributory factor rather than a central determinant of widespread commitment to a scapegoat ideology.

Complementary projection, in which stereotypes serve as justifications of anxieties (e.g., I fear, therefore you must be dangerous) is accorded a more prominent role in the ideological model and may help to explain why stereo-

135

types can become as grossly divorced from reality as were Nazi images of Jews. Anxieties thrive under difficult life conditions. When difficult conditions are widespread, anxious individuals seek not only explanations for but also justifications of their shared anxieties, creating fertile ground for the development and transmission of socially shared beliefs that are not backed up by evidence. Festinger (1957) noted how after an earthquake in India, rumors that severe aftershocks were going to occur were quickly disseminated, leading Festinger to conclude that one function of rumors is to justify anxieties. Socially shared stereotypes may function similarly to rumor; indeed, many anti-Semitic beliefs are based in rumor (e.g., that Jews sacrifice Christian children or are at the heart of an economic conspiracy). Preexisting envious stereotypes, which characterize an out-group as powerful and evil, are likely to be magnets for complementary projection when anxieties run high. Additionally, once ideologically motivated aggression begins to take place, it creates the need to rationalize such behavior by believing that the victims somehow deserved their fate. Thus the processes by which perpetrators justify their actions (detailed in the next section) are also likely to involve complementary projection—believing that the victim was not innocent but a threat.

Ideological Commitment: How Ideologies Become Self-Sustaining

Once people become attracted to a scapegoat ideology, their behavior is directly determined by the course of action the ideology dictates. Nazi ideology was the proximal cause of increasing persecution and the eventual attempt to exterminate the Jews; without it, an event like the Holocaust, with its bureaucratized and systematic brutality, could not occur (Billig, 1976; Tajfel, 1981). Commitment to an ideology can sustain scapegoating whether the original frustrations wax or wane. Although the initial attraction to the ideology may be a response to widespread frustrations, once people start to act on the ideology, other social-psychological processes perpetuate and increase ideological commitment. Actions lead to rationalizations in support of those actions, enhancing ideological commitment and propelling perpetrators along an ever-intensifying continuum of destruction (Staub, 1989).

One of the most important principles of social psychology is that people seek to justify their behavior. Part of the appeal of Nazi ideology was, of course, that it offered a course of action—elimination (whether this was in the form of social exclusion, deportation, or, eventually, extermination) of the Jews—as a solution to shared problems. According to cognitive dissonance theory, the more difficult the act, the stronger the need to justify it (Festinger, 1957). For example, the SS required repeated demonstrations of loyalty and willingness to expose oneself to danger, helping to cement the members' commitment to the Nazi regime (Staub, 1989). The more the perpetrators of the Holocaust enacted atrocities in service of their ideology, the more committed they became. For instance, Eichmann's notorious countervailing of Himmler's orders (issued toward the end of the war, when Himmler was eager to appease the Allies) *not* to send Hungarian Jews to the death camps stemmed directly from Eichmann's commitment to Nazi ideology and not, in Arendt's (1964) view, from a personal hatred of Jews. Even small acts can affect commitment. Self-perception theory (Bem, 1967) posits that, to some extent, we infer our beliefs from our actions. The Nazis encouraged (and coerced) small daily acts of support, such as loyalty oaths and the ubiquitous "Heil Hitler" greeting, to increase commitment to the Führer, Reich, and National Socialism. Additionally, seeing others support the regime creates conformity pressure to go along (Asch, 1955; Milgram, 1974).

Thus, even if aggressive behavior has some cathartic effects (as prior theories of scapegoating suggest), aggressive actions tend to increase, rather than decrease, both the probability and the intensity of subsequent aggression. This is because the proximal cause of organized aggression in response to shared frustrations is ideological rather than the result of a direct frustration-aggression link. For example, Green et al. (1998) have shown that there is not a simple correlation between economic or social distress and hate crimes, suggesting that scapegoating requires an ideological component that mediates between frustration and aggression. Because the frustration-aggression link is not direct, but mediated by ideology, the removal of frustrations does not necessarily translate into less aggression. When the Nazis made progress addressing Germany's economic crisis in the 1930s and frustrations were reduced, this did not lead to a lessening of pressure on the Jews. If anything, such successes only increased commitment to the total Nazi program. Once an ideology is adopted, it develops its own legs. The justification of one's own and one's group's actions creates a feedback loop in which aggression against a scapegoat enhances commitment to the ideology and also intensifies negative views of and aggression against the victims.

People attempt to rationalize not only their own behavior but also the behavior of groups they identify with (Pettigrew, 1979; Tajfel, 1981). Once the Nazis were in a position of power and started to persecute the Jews, even passive German bystanders were more likely to accept Nazi ideology, believing that the Jews must have done something to warrant their ill-treatment (Staub, 1989). People want to believe the world is just, so those who suffer are often assumed to have done something to deserve their lot (Lerner & Miller, 1978). The tendency toward such rationalizations may be especially strong among bystanders who have an affiliation with the harm-doers (e.g., shared nationality). Thus the persecution of the Jews, even for those who were not direct perpetrators, was probably important in convincing people of Nazi propaganda concerning the "Jewish threat." A striking example of the strength of these beliefs was recorded by Victor Klemperer (1998) in his diary of life in Nazi Germany; Klemperer witnessed a woman, upon first seeing her severely wounded husband in a military hospital, scream, "It's the Jews' fault! It's the Jews' fault" (p. 128). Ideologies, once they gain sufficient support, create their own social realities and become self-sustaining by doing so.

Did the Nazi leaders believe their own lies? Although the Nazis were cynical and knowing in their use of propaganda, their behavior suggests that most were, on the whole, true believers in their own rhetoric. A strong commitment to ideology seems to be the only viable explanation as to why the Nazis often acted independently of and even in contradiction to their own pragmatic interests. As long as the ideological program was consistent with profiteering, the Nazis did so with ruthless efficiency. In the 1930s, the expulsion of Jews (the main ideological goal at the time) was combined with stripping Jews of their wealth (Arendt, 1964). The death camps extracted all value from the Jews both before they were murdered (slave labor) and afterward (extraction of gold teeth, use of hair for blankets). But when ideology and objective self-interest conflicted, pragmatic concerns were clearly secondary for the Nazi leadership. For example, pressure from business leaders to use Jews for slave labor was accommodated only grudgingly and temporarily. The Nazis clearly intended not to allow a permanent Jewish slave population but only to extract labor from Jews while working them to death. Browning (1998) notes:

> Himmler had been plagued with complaints from industrial and military authorities about the removal of Jewish workers essential to the war effort. In response to such complaints, which he viewed as pure pretense, he agreed to spare some Jewish workers on the condition that they were lodged in camps and ghettos entirely under SS control. This allowed Himmler to parry pragmatic arguments based on the necessities of the war economy while insuring his ultimate control over the fate of all Jews. For in the end, the sanctuary of the labor camps and work ghettos was only temporary. As Himmler said, "There too the Jews shall likewise one day disappear in accordance with the wish of the Führer." (p. 136)

Other populations might be occupied and exploited, but the Nazis believed that Jews were too dangerous to domesticate. The Nazi commitment to accelerating and expanding the extermination of Jews when the war was being lost (and they could ill afford the manpower and resources devoted to the Final Solution), is consistent with their avowed beliefs that the Jews were, ultimately, the root of all evil. Losing the war against the Allies was secondary to losing the war against the Jews.

CONCLUSION

Scapegoating need not be the product of psychodynamic conflict, and the link between frustration and aggression is not automatic. Rather, the ideological model suggests that scapegoating occurs under a more specific set of conditions—when the causes of widespread economic or social frustrations (not separate, idiosyncratic difficulties) can plausibly, in the minds of those affected, be blamed on a particular social group (Billig, 1976; Tajfel, 1981). Plausibility is determined by prior beliefs and stereotypes that cast the targeted group as both powerful and ill intentioned, which can create fertile grounds for the acceptance of scapegoat ideologies. The acceptance of such ideologies is further determined by their ability to fulfill other needs heightened during periods of social and economic disorganization (Staub, 1989). A history of envious prejudice toward the Jews, which stereotyped them as powerful enemies, made them a socially plausible target of blame in post–World War I Germany. In addition, Nazi ideology attracted many adherents because of its ability to meet heightened needs for belonging, hope, and a sense of group superiority.

The ideological model not only helps to illuminate why the Jews were targeted by the Nazis but also should help predict which groups are similarly at risk in countries currently experiencing social and economic problems. The analysis presented here suggests that minority groups perceived to be socioeconomically successful or culturally influential (i.e., targets of envious prejudice) are more likely to be targets of genocidal intent than are disadvantaged groups, which (though they may also be blamed for social problems, be targets of discriminatory policies, and even sometimes be victims of genocide) are less likely to be seen as capable of intentionally causing grievous economic and social harm. The ideological scapegoating pattern fits the genocidal attack of the Turks against the Armenians (who were stereotyped in strikingly similar ways to the Jews), the more recent Rwandan genocide (in which Hutu perpetrators targeted the Tutsis, a successful minority that had been favored by European colonizers and were therefore targets of resentment), anti-Chinese violence in Indonesia (where the Chinese minority is economically powerful), and Serbian aggression in Bosnia and Kosovo (as Serbian ideology casts the Serbs as historic victims of the Muslims).

Perpetrators of such violence typically see themselves as the victims and their aggression as a form of self-defense. Murder seems morally justified to perpetrators who are convinced they are in a life-or-death struggle against an implacable foe. The destruction of the Jews was, in Nazi eyes, "'the battle of destiny for the German people' . . . a matter of life and death for the Germans, who must annihilate their enemies or be annihilated" (Arendt, 1964, p. 52). The ideological model of scapegoating can help explain how and why sacrificial lambs are perceived by perpetrators as predatory wolves.

139

NOTES

1. It is important to note that a comprehensive social-psychological approach to the Holocaust must take account of both popular attraction to Nazi ideology in Germany during the 1930s and 1940s and the role of conformity and obedience. Far from being mutually exclusive explanations, the combination of the two seems necessary for any understanding of the social psychology of the Holocaust. Without significant support for the Nazis, Hitler could never have attained the position of authority that he occupied, and conformity pressures upon any would-be dissidents were no doubt increased by Hitler's popular support. Nevertheless, the relative role of the "pull" of Nazi anti-Semitism and the "push" of obedience and conformity pressures is at the center of debates about the origins of the Holocaust—currently embodied by the contrast between Goldhagen's (1997) "willing executioners" and Browning's (1998) "ordinary men."

2. Consistent with the current theoretical milieu, the new version of authoritarianism eschews Freudian theory and focuses on authoritarianism as a right-wing political ideology.

3. Frijda (1993) suggests that although there may be some short-term catharsis-like effects (e.g., reducing excitement, feeling of relief), these effects are temporary and overwhelmed by the long-term self-reinforcing qualities of violent behavior.

REFERENCES

Adorno, T. W., Frenkel-Brunswik, E., Levinson, D. J., & Sanford, R. N. (1950). *The authoritarian personality*. New York: Harper.

Allport, G. W. (1954). *The nature of prejudice*. Reading, MA: Addison-Wesley.

Altemeyer, B. (1981). *Right-wing authoritarianism*. Winnipeg: University of Manitoba Press.

Arendt, H. (1964). *Eichmann in Jerusalem: A report on the banality of evil*. New York: Penguin.

Asch, S. E. (1955). Opinions and social pressure. *Scientific American, 19,* 31–35.

Baumeister, R F., Dale, K., & Sommer, K. L. (1998). Freudian defense mechanisms and empirical findings in modern social psychology: Reaction formation, projection, displacement, undoing, isolation, sublimation, and denial. *Journal of Personality, 66,* 1081–1124.

Bem, D. (1967). Self-perception: An alternative interpretation of cognitive dissonance phenomena. *Psychological Review, 74,* 183–200.

Berkowitz, L. (1989). Frustration-aggression hypothesis: Examination and reformulation. *Psychological Bulletin, 106,* 59–73.

Berkowitz, L., & Green, J. A. (1962). The stimulus qualities of the scapegoat. *Journal of Abnormal and Social Psychology, 64,* 293–301.

Bettelheim, B., & Janowitz, M. (1950). *Dynamics of prejudice*. New York: Harper.

Billig, M. (1976). *Social psychology and intergroup relations*. London: Academic Press.

Browning, C. R. (1998). *Ordinary men: Reserve Police Battalion 101 and the Final Solution in Poland*. New York: HarperCollins.

Davis, J. A. (1959). A formal interpretation of the theory of relative deprivation. *Sociometry, 22,* 280–296.

Dollard, J., Doob, L. W., Miller, N. E., Mowrer, O. H., & Sears, R. R. (1939). *Frustration and aggression*. New Haven, CT: Yale University Press.

Festinger, L. (1957). *A theory of cognitive dissonance.* Stanford, CA: Stanford University Press.

Fiske, S. T. (1998). Stereotyping, prejudice, and discrimination. In D. T. Gilbert, S. T. Fiske, & G. Lindzey (Eds.), *The handbook of social psychology* (4th ed., pp. 357–411). New York: McGraw-Hill.

Fiske, S. T., Cuddy, A. C., Glick, P., & Xu, J. (in press). A model of (often mixed) stereotype content: Competence and warmth respectively follow from perceived status and competition. *Journal of Personality and Social Psychology.*

Fiske, S. T., & Taylor, S. E. (1991). *Social cognition.* New York: McGraw-Hill.

Fiske, S. T., Xu, J., Cuddy, A. C., & Glick, P. (1999). (Dis)respecting versus (dis)liking: Status and interdependence predict ambivalent stereotypes of competence and warmth. *Journal of Social Issues.*

Freud, S. (1961). *Civilization and its discontents* (J. Strachey, Trans.). New York: Norton. (Original work published 1930)

Friedlander, H. (1995). *The origins of Nazi genocide: From euthanasia to the Final Solution.* Chapel Hill: University of North Carolina Press.

Friedländer, S. (1997). *Nazi Germany and the Jews: The years of persecution, 1933–39* (vol. 1). New York: HarperCollins.

Frijda, N. (1993). *The emotions: Studies in emotion and social interaction.* Paris: Cambridge University Press.

Geen, R. G. (1998). Aggression and antisocial behavior. In D. T. Gilbert, S. T. Fiske, & G. Lindzey (Eds.), *The handbook of social psychology* (4th ed., pp. 357–411). New York: McGraw-Hill.

Glick, P., & Fiske, S. T. (1999). Sexism and other "isms": Interdependence, status, and the ambivalent content of stereotypes. In W. B. Swann Jr., L. A. Gilbert, & J. Langlois (Eds.), *Sexism and stereotypes in modern society: The gender science of Janet Taylor Spence* (pp. 193–221). Washington, DC: American Psychological Association.

Glick, P., & Fiske, S. T. (2001). Ambivalent stereotypes as legitimizing ideologies: Differentiating paternalistic and envious prejudice. In J. T. Jost and B. Major (Eds.), *The psychology of legitimacy: Emerging perspectives on ideology, justice, and intergroup relations* (pp. 278–306). Cambridge: Cambridge University Press.

Goldhagen, D. J. (1996). *Hitler's willing executioners: Ordinary Germans and the Holocaust.* New York: Random House.

Green, D. P., Glaser, J., & Rich, A. (1998). From lynching to gay bashing: The elusive connection between economic conditions and hate crimes. *Journal of Personality and Social Psychology, 75,* 82–92.

Heider, F. (1958). *The psychology of interpersonal relations.* New York: Wiley.

Jackman, M. R. (1994). *The velvet glove: Paternalism and conflict in gender, class, and race relations,* Berkeley: University of California Press.

Klemperer, V. (1998, April 27, May 4). The Klemperer diaries. *The New Yorker,* pp. 120–135

Lerner, M. J., & Miller, D. T. (1978). Just world research and the attribution process: Looking back and ahead. *Psychological Bulletin, 85,* 1030–1051.

Lorge, I., & Solomon, H. (1995). Two models of group behavior in the solution of eureka-type problems. *Psychometrica, 20,* 139–148.

Mandler, G. (1975). *Mind and emotion.* New York: Wiley.

Milgram, S. (1974). *Obedience to authority.* New York: Harper and Row.

Newman, L. S., Duff, K. J., & Baumeister, R. F. (1997). A new look at defensive projection: Thought suppression, accessibility, and biased person perception. *Journal of Personality and Social Psychology, 72*, 980–1001.

Nisbett, R., & Ross, L. (1980). *Human inference: Strategies and shortcomings of social judgment.* Englewood Cliffs, NJ: Prentice-Hall.

Olson, J. M. (1986). Resentment about deprivation: Entitlement and hopefulness as mediators of the effects of qualifications. In J. M. Olson, C. P. Herman, & M. P. Zanna (Eds.), *Relative deprivation and social comparison: The Ontario Symposium* (vol. 4, pp. 57–77). Hillsdale, NJ: Erlbaum.

Pettigrew, T. F. (1979). The ultimate attribution error: Extending Allport's cognitive analysis of prejudice. *Personality and Social Psychology Bulletin, 5*, 461–476.

Rubenstein, R. L. (1966). *After Auschwitz: Radical theology and contemporary Judaism.* Indianapolis: Bobbs-Merrill.

Runciman, W. G. (1966). *Relative deprivation and social justice: A study of attitudes to social inequality in twentieth-century England.* Berkeley: University of California Press.

Staub, E. (1989). *The roots of evil: The origins of genocide and other group violence.* Cambridge: Cambridge University Press.

Tajfel, H. (1981). *Human groups and social categories: Studies in social psychology.* Cambridge: Cambridge University Press.

Vallacher, R. R., & Nowak, A. (1994). *Dynamical systems in social psychology.* San Diego, CA: Academic Press.

Volpato, C., & Capozza, D. (1998). La rappresentazione delle razze umane nel *Mein Kampf* di Adolf Hitler [The representation of the human races in *Mein Kampf* by Adolf Hitler]. *Psicologia Contemporanea, 149*, 4–11.

Zawadzki, B. (1948). Limitations of the scapegoat theory of prejudice. *Journal of Abnormal and Social Psychology, 43*, 127–141.

6

Group Processes and the Holocaust

R. Scott Tindale, Catherine Munier,
Michelle Wasserman, and Christine M. Smith

The Holocaust is arguably one of the most significant (albeit horrifying) social events of the twentieth century. Thus, it is not surprising that
social scientists from many disciplines have attempted to explain how a civilized European country could adopt a mandate, and then take significant
strides toward carrying it out, to eradicate a group of people whose sole "crime"
was that they shared a specific ethnic heritage. Social psychology has not been
negligent in this regard. A number of the classic early findings in this field
were generated, at least in part, in an attempt to understand or explain the
events pertaining to the Holocaust: Obedience to authority (Milgram, 1963),
conformity (Asch, 1956), and the authoritarian personality (Adorno, Frenkel-
Brunswik, Levinson, & Sanford, 1950) are just a few of the main examples.

Given the prominence of these early works in the field, it is not surprising
that the roots of many recent empirical studies and theories in social psychology can be traced to these earlier attempts to explain the events surrounding
World War II and the Holocaust. Thus, many social psychologists found it somewhat distressing to learn that a prominent and highly acclaimed recent addition to the Holocaust literature proposed as one of its primary tenets that the
Holocaust could not be attributed to "social psychological pressures" (Goldhagen,
1996, p. 11).[1] Goldhagen's central claim is that "Germans' anti-Semitic beliefs
about Jews were the central causal agent of the Holocaust" (p. 11). Thus, he
asserts that obedience, social pressure, conformity, and personality characteristics were not the forces driving the "perpetrators'" behavior, but rather their
anti-Semitic beliefs and attitudes were. Although one could argue with the assertion that none of the perpetrators were influenced by such factors as conformity, obedience, and so forth, for the purposes of this chapter we will grant
Goldhagen his central claim—the Germans' anti-Semitic attitudes and beliefs
played a major role in the Holocaust. (Not being economists or political theo-

rists, we will not comment directly on the other causes that Goldhagen rules out.) However, we assert that attitudes and beliefs—particularly those associated with or about groups—are inherently *social* in nature and are largely a function of basic social-psychological processes. Thus, we will attempt to show that social-psychological theory in general, especially theory and research on groups, is essential to our understanding of the Holocaust.

We feel that part of the reason Goldhagen (1996) assumes that "social psychological pressures" cannot help to explain the Holocaust is that he is defining such pressures too narrowly, relying on somewhat dated conceptual frameworks within the field. However, recent trends in social psychology, stemming partly from European perspectives (Hogg & Abrams, 1988; Moscovici, 1984; Tajfel & Turner, 1979), have begun to view individual-level constructs as more socially derived.[2] Rather than seeing social forces (conformity, obedience, etc.) as causing individuals to act differently than they would have if left to their own devices, many social-psychological theories now view individual attitudes, beliefs, cognitions, and identities as being derived from and defined by the social environment. Central to many of these more recent ideas is the social group. Individual cognitions, identities, and so forth depend to a large degree on the groups within which people affiliate and are determined by which group memberships are currently salient. In other words, individual attitudes, beliefs, and so on are social phenomena; they exist in and are produced by social groups. Thus, we will try to show that the beliefs and attitudes held by many Germans at the time of the Holocaust were a direct manifestation of what "being German" (and, by contrast, "being Jewish") meant to Germans at the time.

Our presentation draws on a number of recent theoretical orientations in the field of social psychology. The most central of these in our discussion is social identity theory and its extension, self-categorization theory (Hogg & Abrams, 1988; Tajfel & Tuner, 1979; Turner, 1985). Recent writings on socially shared cognitions and social representations (Moscovici, 1984; Thompson & Fine, 1999; Tindale, Meisenhelder, Dykema-Engblade, & Hogg, 2001) and dynamic social impact theory (Latane & Bourgeois, 2001) also underlie many of the points raised in this chapter. In addition, theory and research on minority influence (Nemeth, 1986), shared representations in groups, and "social sharedness" more generally (Tindale & Kameda, 2000; Tindale, Smith, Thomas, Filkins, & Sheffey, 1996) are used to demonstrate how ideas in a group, regardless of how prevalent, can influence the thoughts and behaviors of group members in both direct and indirect ways.

For each of the aforementioned theoretical orientations, we first outline the key aspects of the theory and its empirical support to lay the groundwork for demonstrating its relevance to the Holocaust. Then, based on the writings of a number of Holocaust scholars (e.g., Browning, 1992; Dawidowicz, 1975, 1976; Goldhagen, 1996; Shirer, 1960), we attempt to show how the situation in Germany during the nineteenth and early twentieth centuries was consistent with expectations drawn from the theory. In our final section we tie the various theories and events together in an attempt to demonstrate the overall importance of social-psychological theories to our understanding of the Holocaust.

Before we begin, two caveats are in order. First, we do not argue that the social-psychological processes discussed here are the only relevant factors leading to the Holocaust. Indeed, a variety of scholars have demonstrated the important role that political, economic, and institutional variables played in the Holocaust. For example, Shirer (1960) provides a particularly interesting description of the political intrigue that helped bring Hitler to power. Our purpose is simply to point out the relevance of the literature on the social psychology of groups and to demonstrate how it can be employed usefully toward a better understanding of the Holocaust. Second, arguing that the Holocaust can be understood, in part, as a function of basic social and group processes does not in any way imply a lack of culpability for the "perpetrators." Just because negative aspects of human behavior can be understood in terms of natural social-psychological processes does not imply that such behaviors are any less reprehensible. The comprehensibility of an event is independent of its justification (or lack thereof).

SOCIAL IDENTITY AND SELF-CATEGORIZATION THEORY

Description

Although Tajfel (1970) laid out the main tenets of social identity theory almost 30 years ago, its impact on the field has increased dramatically in the past decade. With stereotyping and prejudice being dominant topics in social psychology, the idea that people represent themselves and others at multiple levels has helped to explain a number of heretofore perplexing behavior patterns. Social identity theory and its more recent derivative, self-categorization theory (Turner, 1985), argue that people represent themselves and others on multiple levels based on the notion of group membership. Social identity theory argues that people have multiple identities, ranging from the unique individual to the number of groups in which a person can be a member. Turner took this idea and formalized it in terms of categorization. Much as we categorize objects, so, too, do we categorize people, including ourselves. The groups in which we are members form the bases for the categorizations that we use to identify others and ourselves.

Although the motivations behind such categorizations are still not completely understood, two candidates that have achieved at least some empirical support are self-esteem enhancement (Tajfel & Turner, 1979) and uncertainty reduction (Hogg & Mullin, 1999). For example, being a member of a winning team makes one a winner. Thus, positive aspects of a group can be used to increase one's feelings of worth. Additionally, in situations where we are uncertain of our worth or the appropriateness of our behavior, group identity can help to decrease the uncertainty. Group definitions and norms can be used to help guide perceptions and behavior when situational cues are absent or ambiguous. Brewer (1991) has argued that we have motives both for belonging and for distinctiveness, and it is the dialectic exchange of these motives that guides when we will see ourselves as members of a group or as unique individuals.

An additional aspect of this theoretical orientation is that group comparisons serve to both activate group identities and clarify them. In order to know what (or who) our group actually is, it is helpful to know what (or who) it is not. Having an out-group with which to compare one's in-group helps to clarify the categorization process. Thus, group-level categorizations become more prevalent in intergroup situations, and once group-level categories are activated, members try to differentiate their group from the comparison group. Again, perhaps motivated by the need to enhance self-esteem, most intergroup comparisons tend to favor the in-group, placing the out-group at the more negative end of the comparative dimension. Self-categorization theory also argues that members try to position themselves close to the most "prototypical" member of the group. Since the most prototypical member of the group tends to be the member most different from the out-group, this leads to more extreme positions or attitudes by the in-group members when the intergroup context is made salient.

Relevance to the Holocaust

According to Dawidowicz (1975), "Modern German anti-Semitism was the bastard child of Christian anti-Semitism with German nationalism" (p. 23). Anti-Semitism certainly did not begin with the Nazi regime, nor did it end with its defeat. Anti-Semitic beliefs and attitudes have been prevalent in Europe (and the United States) throughout most of modern history. For Christians, Jews were seen as a natural out-group when the dimension of religion was made salient, just as social identity and self-categorization theory would predict. This is partly due to the similarity between the two belief structures. Since the Jewish faith provides the framework within which Christianity was born, there are only a few dimensions along which the two religions can be distinguished—the main one being the acceptance (or not) of Jesus as the promised savior. The Catholic Church often preached that the Jews were agents of the Devil and were not to be trusted because if the Jews were right, the main tenets of the Catholic Church had to be wrong (Dawidowicz, 1975). Even though Martin Luther fought vigorously against Catholic theology, he adopted and intensified the Catholic anti-Semitic position for many of the same reasons. Thus, the move from Catholicism to Protestantism did nothing to change the position of Jews as a salient out-group—and probably intensified the perception.

Such anti-Jewish sentiments were prevalent throughout Europe—they were not unique to Germany. However, Dawidowicz (1975), Goldhagen (1996), and others argue that German nationalism (identification with the in-group) intensified Germans' anti-Jewish sentiments. Dawidowicz (1975) argues that intense German nationalism arose during the French occupation early in the nineteenth century. Although Germany had not been a unified entity prior to the French invasion, the French demolished the ecclesiastical states left over from the Holy Roman Empire and reorganized the land into a manageable number of middle-sized states under French protection. The French had demolished the German military and brought the ideals of the Enlightenment (e.g., inalienable human rights) by force into their society. In fact, while the French ruled over Germany, Jews in some areas were given many basic human and political rights, which in the eyes of the Germans aligned the Jews with the hated French. Although the ideals of the Enlightenment were embraced in some parts of Germany (e.g., Prussia), many of the German people found them at odds with their former, simpler, more understandable lifestyles. Even after the French were driven back into France by the other European powers, the Congress at Vienna divided Germany into a number of small fiefdoms, and the German military and economy were still very weak. At this point, the German people had no nation, no military, no wealth, and no identity. Their collective self-esteem was extremely low, and their future was quite uncertain.

The combined state of low self-esteem and high uncertainty is associated with the use of group identity and intergroup thinking (Hogg & Abrams, 1988; Hogg & Mullin, 1999). This is quite likely what began to happen in Germany. During the French occupation, the German philosopher Johann Gottlieb Fichte (1808, cited in Dawidowicz, 1975) admonished Germans to have character and to be German. Being German during this time meant to be "not French" and "not Jewish." According to Turner (1985), group identity is defined as being least like the out-group. Thus, to be prototypically German was to be least like the Jews (the internal enemy) and the French (the external enemy). Later German philosophers (Arndt, and later Jahn, cited in Dawidowicz, 1975) defined the concept of *Volk*, meaning a group of people with common traditions, culture, values, and so forth. But *Volk* also meant more than this. It came to mean a people with a transcendental essence—a natural grouping of people who were meant to be together. Jahn later argued that *Volk* and state were both essential in order to form a Reich—which is grounded in *Volkstum*. Thus, a German state grounded in the culture and traditions of the German people (largely prior to the French invasion) was necessary in order for Germany to emerge as a great nation. Such a state would encompass the natural order of the *Volk*—"simplicity, naturalness, homespunness, unspoiled by education and civilization" (Dawidowicz, 1975, p. 29). Thus, to be "truly German" was to be anti-Enlightenment, anti-French, and anti-Jewish. It should be noted that the main followers of the Nazi Party—the *Mittelstand* (Dawidowicz, 1975; Shirer, 1960)—were those farmers, artisans, and lower-level white-collar workers who did not fare well under the industrialization that stemmed from the Enlightenment. Thus, the "true German identity" was most salient for those portions of the German population that faced the greatest uncertainty and threats to self-esteem.

It is of no small significance that at the same time the "science of racial differences" was developing and Jews were thought to be a different race— Semites versus Aryans. Racial thinking blurred the distinctions between the Germans, French, and British but enhanced the distinction between Germans and Jews. Again, much of intergroup categorization into in-groups and out-groups depends on being able to define clear dimensions along which the groups differ (Hogg & Abrams, 1988). German scholars at the time were beginning to define races and subraces in terms of their characteristics. Although both Aryans and Semites were seen as Caucasians, and both were seen as developing civilization, the Aryans were defined as harmonious, while the Semites were defined as selfish and exclusive (aspects of the Jewish stereotype that remain even today). In addition, a number of scholars espoused the notion that race intermingling was wrong and could be used to explain declines in former civilizations (Dawidowicz, 1975). Thus, a pseudoscientific justification emerged for the isolation and expulsion of the Jews from Germany.

During the rest of the nineteenth century and up until World War I, anti-Semitism and violence against Jews in Germany waxed and waned largely as a function of different political movements gaining and then losing strength. Most of the violence came from extremist groups responding to government policies granting expanded rights to the Jews, which was in line with the ideals of the Enlightenment dominant in the rest of Europe. Germany was not immune to such ideas, but its extreme nationalism (defined in part by anti-Semitic sentiments) made it difficult for them to take hold for very long. During periods of economic stability and peace, anti-Jewish sentiment tended to wane. Unfortunately, the end of World War I once again brought economic uncertainty and low self-perceptions to the German people. It was during this time that the Nazi Party had its beginnings and anti-Jewish sentiments once again ran high. Jews were blamed, in part, for Germany's defeat and the extreme economic hardships that followed. As economic and political stability began to emerge in the mid-1920s, both anti-Semitism and the popularity of the Nazi Party diminished somewhat. However, the depression of 1929 brought both back very quickly

Goldhagen (1996) argues that German anti-Semitism was different than other types of hostile intergroup prejudices: "It cannot be stressed too much that the hostility towards Jews was not of the sort that we all know so well, consisting of unflattering stereotypes and prejudices of one group towards another (which can be quite powerful) that buttress the self-esteem of the prejudiced" (p. 51). However, when viewed from the theoretical vantage point of social identity theory, the factors identified in the theory that supposedly drive intergroup thinking in any context seemed to influence the degree and prevalence of anti-Semitic feelings and behaviors in Germany as well. One could argue that the level and intensity of intergroup hostility were well beyond the norm, but there is little, if any, evidence to support the idea that it was of a different "sort."

SHARED COGNITIONS AND SOCIAL REPRESENTATIONS

Description

Since the beginnings of the cognitive revolution in psychology, the notion of cognition or mental representation has played a major role in theorizing. Until recently, mental representations were seen as individual entities, formulated and stored within the minds of single individuals. However, recent trends from a number of theoretical orientations have begun to conceptualize cognition as a social phenomenon (Moscovici, 1984; Thompson & Fine, 1999; Tindale et al., 2001).

As far back as the early 1950s, Festinger (1954) used the notion of "social reality" to help explain how and why people compared themselves with others. Much of this was conceptualized as after the fact—one would assess the beliefs and behaviors of others to evaluate the validity or appropriateness of one's current positions. More recent theoretical work makes explicit the social nature of cognitions by positing that beliefs and mental representations are *formulated* in the social realm. Much of what we know, we learn from our social environment, since we often have limited contact with things we know something about. Often we believe certain things to be true simply because most, if not all, of the people around us believe and/or assert them to be true. Without any direct means to assess the validity of such beliefs, we infer their validity based on consensus. Once we have these beliefs, and find that they are shared quite liberally within our social networks, we take them for granted and rarely think about them as needing validation. Moscovici (1984) has referred to such generally shared beliefs as "social representations." Such shared beliefs form the basis of a social aggregate's shared reality and are often used to justify or substantiate other related beliefs or opinions. Moreover, some evidence suggests that the perceived validity of a belief is increased simply by communicating it to someone (Hardin & Higgins, 1996). Thus, social representations are believed because they are shared, not because they are inherently valid outside of our social reality.

149

Moscovici (1984) also argues that social representations form the basis of the shared understandings that allow for communication via language. Such shared cognitions need not be believed by all involved, but simply known to exist. For example, Devine (1989) has demonstrated that virtually all people in the United States know the basic elements of the African American or black stereotype. Even people who do not show prejudicial behavior or negative attitudes toward African Americans are aware of the contents of such stereotypes. Thus, when a communicator makes a racial slur or draws an inference based on a stereotype, the recipient of the communication understands the remark even if she or he does not agree with it or finds it distasteful. A wide variety of research findings have now shown that a person's available and salient knowledge, regardless of its perceived validity, affects her or his processing of information (Wegner & Bargh, 1998). Thus, social representations can have both direct and indirect effects on how people think and the beliefs and attitudes they hold.

Relevance for the Holocaust

By the late 1800s, both the notion of *Volk* and the anti-Semitic stereotypes had become widely shared social representations in Germany. The intergroup processes that had led to the development of these representations had changed— Germany was a unified nation and had gained prominence once more in Europe. Although they were no longer necessary for bolstering self-esteem and reducing uncertainty (their original function), they had become part of the social reality of German culture. As a matter of fact, the strength of Germany as a nation probably helped bolster the ideas of *Volk* and the importance of staying true to the German identity. The ideas of the early *Volkist* philosophers had, in essence, come to pass. The period of Bismarck's reign was considered the Second Reich (Shirer, 1960)—the combination of *Volk* and state.

The social nature of anti-Semitic beliefs is substantiated by the fact that during the late nineteenth century, most Germans had little, if any, contact with Jews. Jews made up only about 1% of the total German population (Goldhagen, 1996). Because of the general anti-Semitic social representation associated with *Volkstum*, many Jews had left Germany for safer havens elsewhere. Thus, most of what people knew (or thought they knew) about Jews was based on social consensus, not actual experience. As Festinger's (1954) social comparison theory argues, social reality becomes paramount when physical reality provides few, if any, cues upon which one can base an opinion.

Another social representation prominent in Germany at the time also (probably) played a role in the ability of Hitler and the Nazis to gain power among the people. This concerned the role of a strong, autocratic leader for the health and destiny of a nation. Much of this representation was derived from the writings of (among others) Frederick Nietzsche (Shirer, 1960). Nietzsche's writings, particularly his later ones, were extremely antidemocratic. He foretold of the "super race" that would produce the "superman" to lead them to victory so they could become "lords of the earth" (cited in Shirer, 1960, p. 101). Nietzsche's ideas were consistent with the supposedly scientific writings on race at the time, and the Aryan race (of which Germans were a part, if not the sole heirs) was seen as the "super race." (It is quite likely that Hitler saw himself as Nietzsche's superman [Shirer, 1960]). Nietzsche's ideas were fairly well accepted by many Germans. They saw Bismarck and Frederick the Great before him as strong, warlike leaders who produced a strong, unified nation. Such ideas played well to the *Mittelstand* and probably contributed to Hitler's ability to convince the nation to follow him after his rise to power.

DYNAMIC SOCIAL IMPACT THEORY, SOCIAL SHAREDNESS, AND MINORITY INFLUENCE

Description

Dynamic Social Impact Theory

Dynamic social impact theory (Latane, 1996; Latane & Bourgeois, 2001) extends social impact theory (Latane, 1981) through the use of a dynamical systems approach (Vallacher & Nowak, 1994). According to this theory, the impact that others have on a person's attitudes, beliefs, preferences, and so on is determined by the strength (e.g., status, expertise), immediacy (closeness in terms of physical or social distance), and number of influence sources. The dynamic version allows for reciprocal influence in a social aggregate over time. A full expression of the theory is beyond our present scope, but the basic findings from both empirical and computer simulations using the model shed light on the natural tendency for certain beliefs, attitudes, and so forth to become shared within a given social space (e.g., society).

The basic idea behind the theory is that beliefs, preferences, attitudes, and so on spread throughout a population in nonlinear and dynamic ways. This leads people who are closer to each other in a social space (which could be defined by physical proximity but also can be defined by ease of communication and contact—phone, Internet, etc.) to be more similar to one another than they are to those who are farther away. This is because people closest to each other in a social space have the most impact on each other. Such similarities can be seen in architecture (houses and buildings in one area or city are more similar to each other than they are to buildings in other regions), food preferences (Chicago-style pizza is easy to find in the Midwest but less so elsewhere), and even car buying (pickup trucks are much more prevalent in the southern and southwestern United States than in other areas of the country). Part of this similarity, according to the theory, develops because people cannot be influenced by ideas to which they are not exposed. However, there is also a social component in that the exposure has more impact

151

to the degree that it comes from a larger number of people within a person's social environment. Thus, a single person espousing an idea is less influential than are many people espousing the same idea.

The most consistent finding from both experimental and computer simulation work with dynamic social impact theory is that, over time, beliefs initially held by a majority of the people tend to spread and become more prominent throughout the aggregate. However, belief clusters also form, thus preventing the majority opinion from totally eradicating the minority. Thus, minority positions, even those that are fairly unpopular, rarely disappear. Also, minorities with particularly influential (i.e., strong) arguments can, over time, become the majority position and subsequently spread to larger segments of the population. Another fairly consistent outcome is that people within belief clusters also tend to become more similar to each other on other issues as well—what Latane (1996) refers to as "correlation." Therefore, people within belief clusters become more similar to each other on many dimensions over time, and thus more immediate in terms of social distance. The most interesting aspect of the model, and its implications, stems from the fact that there are no guiding principles—no authority figures, no assumptions about intentional attempts at influence, and so on. Shared belief structures evolve naturally, and people end up believing many of the same things as their neighbors within a social aggregate.

Social Sharedness, Shared Representations, and Minority Influence

Recent reviews of the small-group performance literature (Hinsz, Tindale, & Vollrath, 1997; Tindale & Kameda, 2000) have shown that groups attempting to reach consensus on decision-making and problem-solving tasks tend to be heavily influenced by things that are shared among the group members. Tindale and Kameda (2000) have referred to this as "social sharedness" and argue that the effects of things that are shared among group members operate on a number of levels. First, one of the most well substantiated findings in the small-group decision-making literature is that majorities tend to win. In other words, shared preferences are a powerful force on group decision making. One of the implications of majorities tending to win is that group decisions tend to be more polarized or extreme than the average initial positions of the individual members. However, polarization can occur even without a group consensus requirement—particularly if a significant out-group is made salient (Hogg, 1996). Thus, interaction among like-minded individuals tends to lead members to have even more extreme positions after interaction or discussion.

Preferences are not the only things that are more powerful when shared. In a now famous study by Stasser and Titus (1985), information about political candidates was distributed among group members such that some items were shared by all three members, while other items were given to only one member. When the group members were presented with all the information, one of the candidates appeared clearly superior to the other two. However, Stasser and Titus distributed the positive information about the superior candidate such that most of it was unshared (given to only one member), while the positive information about the other candidates was shared among all members. Stasser and Titus found that unshared information was much less likely than shared information to be brought up during discussion; consequently, few groups chose the superior candidate. Gigone and Hastie (1993, 1996) replicated this finding in a multicue decision task and found that unshared information played little, if any, role in the groups' judgments. Thus, when a group comes together to make a decision or discuss an issue, information that is already shared by everyone in the group dominates the discussion and tends to guide the group toward decisions consistent with the shared information.

The dominant role of shared information was explained in part by a simple sampling model (Stasser & Titus, 1987). Since each piece of shared information had three times as many chances of being mentioned as each piece of unshared information, even randomly sampling the information across group members gives a heavy advantage to the shared information. In addition, Stasser (1999) argues that shared information is also perceived as more valid than unshared information. Stewart and Stasser (1995) had groups write up reports describing the information that had affected their final decisions. Shared information that was mentioned tended to end up in the report, whereas unshared information, even if mentioned, was less likely to be included. Unshared information was included in the report only when someone considered to be an expert on some aspect of the task brought it up. Stasser (1999) concluded that shared information has social validation, whereas unshared information does not.

In a similar line of research, Kameda, Ohtsubo, and Takezawa (1997) studied the effects of information sharedness across group members. Using both correlational and experimental methods, Kameda et al. looked at the degree to which group members were influential based on how much information they shared with other group members. In both cases they found evidence to support the notion that cognitively central group members (members who share more information with other members) are more influential. Even when the most central member held the minority opinion, more often than not, groups would go with the alternative preferred by that member. When the most central member was in the majority, the majority won virtually all the time. Kameda et al. argued that sharing more information with other group members conveys the perception of expertise to the other members.

Although majorities tend to win in group settings, in some instances minorities can be influential. A recent chapter by Tindale et al. (1996) argued that if minorities can frame or validate their preference within the context of a task-relevant representation that is shared by most or all the members of a group, they can be influential in changing the majority's preference. Both early and more recent work on group problem solving has shown that minorities with a correct solution to the problem can persuade incorrect majorities to switch preferences (Laughlin, 1980). Laughlin and Ellis (1986) have argued that minorities win in such circumstances because group members share the background knowledge necessary to solve the problem, even if a majority of the members could not use this knowledge in an appropriate way to obtain the correct solution. But it is the shared background knowledge (similar to the idea of a social representation discussed earlier) that allows the correct minority to demonstrate the correctness of their position.

More recent work by Tindale et al. (1996) has found similar results for tasks where members share task representations that lead to incorrect solutions. Using tasks where individuals were likely to use simplifying heuristics or strategies that lead to incorrect (or nonnormative) responses, Tindale et al. showed that minorities who favored heuristic-consistent but normatively incorrect responses could persuade correct majorities to agree with the incorrect response. For example, it is incorrect to average probabilities from component events (e.g., having a flat tire, running out of gas) when estimating the probability of both events occurring at once (e.g., both having a flat tire and running out of gas at the exact same time). However, since averaging is a common (i.e., shared) strategy in many situations, a minority who suggested averaging in this estimation task may win out even though its strategy and its suggested answer are incorrect.

Another study by Smith, Dykema-Engblade, Walker, Niven, and McGough (2000) also showed how a shared belief system could be used by a minority to influence a majority. In the sample of students used by Smith et al., between 80% and 85% were in favor of the death penalty. However, the population of students at the university also had rather strong religious (Christian) convictions. In group discussions concerning the death penalty, Smith et al. found that minorities who argued against the death penalty were effective in moving majority members toward their position if they used religious arguments to substantiate them. Minorities had little, if any, influence if they did not rely on the shared religious convictions of the majority. Other minority influence research has also shown that if a local minority (a minority within the current discussion group) argues in favor of positions that are shared by the larger population (the Zeitgeist), it is more effective than local minorities who argue for positions that are less prevalent or popular in the population (Clark, 1990). Thus, framing one's preferred position or solution in terms of a shared belief system (i.e., social representation) can be quite a powerful tool for having influence, even when the majority disagrees with your position initially.

Two additional findings from the minority influence literature will be useful for our later arguments. First, Nemeth (1986) has shown that, although minorities often have little, if any, direct influence, they do lead majority members to think more divergently (both more broadly and more intensely) about the particular issue or task at hand. In some circumstances, the more thorough and active cognitive processing can lead to position changes on related issues, or even delayed changes on the target issue. Majority influence, on the other hand, leads to more focused or convergent thought processes. Thus, when majorities change the positions of minorities, the minority members typically define the issue more narrowly than they had before. In addition, some research has shown that in-group members who advocate minority positions can sometimes produce delayed changes in the majority—or changes on related issues, due, in part, to their in-group status (Crano & Alvaro, 1998; Crano & Chen, 1998). In-group minorities are more likely to be tolerated because they are seen as similar to the majority members on other issues and characteristics. This tolerance will attenuate the amount of counterargumentation that occurs. Thus, at later points in time, or on related issues, majority members may be influenced by the arguments presented earlier by the in-group minority source.

Relevance to the Holocaust

Dynamic social impact theory (Latane & Bourgeois, 2001) can help to explain how both the ideas of *Volk* and anti-Semitic sentiments spread throughout the German population. During times of a weak German identity and high uncertainty, such ideas were easy to entertain for much of the population, and they eventually spread throughout much of the culture. The fact that learned philosophers and religious leaders also espoused these anti-Semitic beliefs most likely enhanced their persuasive strength. Latane and Bourgeois (2001) argue that one of the uses of the model is to show how social representations come about. But we feel much of the theory and research discussed in the previous section can best be used to explain how the Nazis gained popularity during the 1920s.

The Nazi Party formed after World War I from mainly disenfranchised members of society. The Nazi Party garnered only 2% of the popular vote in the first election in which it participated as a party (Dawidowicz, 1975). However, its message was consistent with the social representations previously discussed. It opposed the Weimar Republic (the government that formed at the end of World War I), was against Jews and other "non-Germans," and argued for a strong, powerful leader. The party also espoused other popular ideas for the disenfranchised, such as a redistribution of wealth, that it (perhaps never intending to) never carried out. Despite its lack of popularity at the time, it was a legitimate political party and thus could be considered part of the in-group. A number of authors have argued that in its early existence,

155

the Nazi Party was not taken very seriously (Goldhagen, 1996; Shirer, 1960), and that after its failed attempt at a military coup, most of the powers in Germany felt that it was insignificant. However, as demonstrated by dynamic social impact theory, minority clusters can remain intact even in the face of substantial majorities. Thus, the party remained a political presence, albeit a weakened one.

Research on shared cognitions and minority influence, particularly those of in-group minorities, would suggest that the situation was well suited for both direct and indirect minority influence (Crano & Alvaro, 1998; Nemeth, 1986; Smith et al., 2000). Research has shown that in-group minorities tend to be tolerated and can lead to indirect influence over time (Crano & Alvaro, 1998; Nemeth, 1986). As an in-group (German and/or Aryan) source, the Nazis were politely tolerated, and little effort was made to counterargue against their positions. In addition, their positions, though more extreme than those of the general population, were consistent with and derived from the social representations of nationalism (*Volk*) and anti-Semitism. As Smith et al. (2000) have demonstrated, religion (which, in this case, supported anti-Semitism) can be a fairly powerful shared representation and can allow minorities influence beyond that typically predicted by their numbers. Although it never captured a large percentage of the popular vote until Germany's economic collapse in 1929, the small party from Bavaria slowly gained in popularity. The Nazis also used the Communists as an additional out-group to gain at least some support from the right-leaning wealthy business owners. This allowed them to gain both notoriety in a population segment outside the *Mittelstand* and much-needed funds to run the party.

Hitler was also perceived as a strong leader figure, which again fit with the German social representation of what a nation needs. In addition to having a war record and persuasive oratory skills, he espoused positions that helped make him appear leader-like. Recent research by Hains, Hogg, and Duck (1997) has shown that in-group prototypicality plays a significant role in perceptions of leadership. Thus, members of a group who are seen as prototypical of the in-group are more likely to be perceived as leaders, and leaders who are seen as prototypical are seen as stronger or better leaders. One of the ways to appear prototypical of the in-group is to take strong, opposing positions concerning salient out-groups. Thus, Hitler's strong anti-Semitic stand enhanced his appearance as a leader. His strong adherence to the ideas of *Volk* and the need to return the state to the true German people also made him appear the prototypical German.

In 1929, the collapse of the economy and the uncertainty and loss of self-esteem that engulfed the people in Germany (and elsewhere) once again made intergroup thinking salient. This played well into the hands of the Nazis, who were by then known as the anti-Jew, anti-Communist, antirepublic, and pro–"True German Spirit" (*Volk*) party. Although the depression hurt different people for different reasons, the shared hatred of the Jews and the government that lost World War I, and the longing for German supremacy were, to a large extent, shared among the German people. These were the central positions of the Nazi Party, and the "social sharedness" of these positions among the population allowed the party to become, first, a major player and, later, the largest single political party in Germany—though it never obtained a majority until after Hitler was named chancellor.

CONCLUSION

The specific events that actually led to Hitler's appointment as chancellor, which subsequently gave him and the Nazi Party dictatorial powers over the whole of Germany, involved a combination of factors, including greed, political backstabbing, and general ineptitude (see Shirer, 1960, for an interesting discussion of these events). Obviously, social psychology can provide only a partial explanation for certain aspects of the Holocaust. The group-level social-psychological processes discussed here helped put Hitler in the position necessary for him to take advantage of the situation created by these other factors. In addition, these same processes enabled him to make the extreme political moves (outlaw other political parties, declare himself supreme ruler of Germany, etc.) and to later carry out the horrific atrocities against the Jews and other "nonGermans" that followed.

We do not disagree with Goldhagen (1996) that many of Hitler's executioners were willing. We do disagree with him in that we argue that social-psychological, group-level processes played a central role in their willingness. Beliefs, attitudes, and the behaviors they engender arise out of and help to shape the social environment. German anti-Semitism arose not purely from Christianity but rather as part of a social-psychological process concerning the role of group identity in the definition of the self. These processes then gave rise to social influence processes that allowed German nationalism and anti-Semitism to become social representations in Germany—shared cognitions that form the basis of social reality. Such social representations then allowed for types of social influence that could not have occurred without them. The social representations of *Volk* and anti-Semitism provided the platform from which an extremist minority party could gain enough support in the general population to become an important player in forming the government of Germany in the early 1930s. The same social representations and intergroup thinking also provided the "rationale" behind the horrendous deeds that followed.

Goldhagen's focus on "the perpetrators" was in ways both enlightening and blinding at the same time. It was, in fact, the Nazis and the German people that orchestrated and carried out the Holocaust. Their shared beliefs and attitudes formed the social environment in which the Holocaust occurred. Fur-

157

thermore, it is critical to recognize that the social and group forces that produced the type of ethnic hatred in Germany and allowed people in the extreme tail of the hatred distribution to gain power are ever present, as evidenced by the many recent examples of ethnic cleansing in Eastern Europe and Africa. In fact, they are present to some degree in any intergroup setting, particularly when national or ethnic heritage and religion form the group boundaries. By focusing on the "perpetrators" as if *they* were somehow unique in history, Goldhagen diverts attention from the social forces that defined who the perpetrators were. These forces are becoming better understood by social psychology, but there is much left to be learned. We feel it is toward these social forces, rather than the specific people who are affected by them, that attention must be focused in order to prevent future examples of the horror exemplified by the Holocaust.

NOTES

Preparation of this chapter was funded in part by National Science Foundation grant SBR-9730822 to R. Scott Tindale and Christine M. Smith, and by the Graduate School of Loyola University Chicago. We would like to thank Janice Nadler and the editors for comments on an earlier version of the chapter. Correspondence should be directed to R. Scott Tindale, Department of Psychology, Loyola University Chicago, 6525 N. Sheridan Rd., Chicago, IL 60626, or rtindal@luc.edu.

1. Later, in his discussion of method in Appendix I, Goldhagen (1996) appears to appreciate at least some role for social psychology, in that he argues he chose to study specific institutions rather than sampling from many because "studying some scientific sample of individuals from many units would efface the institutional, material, and social psychological circumstances of the Holocaust perpetration" (p. 466).

2. Although defining beliefs, attitudes, and so forth as social constructs is not really new to social psychology (see Bartlett, 1932; James, 1890; and Sherif & Sherif, 1969), the idea has not played a major role in mainstream theorizing until recently.

REFERENCES

Adorno, T. W., Frenkel-Brunswik, E., Levinson, D. J., & Sanford, R. N. (1950). *The authoritarian personality*. New York: Harper.

Asch, S. E. (1956). Studies of independence and conformity: A minority of one against a unanimous majority. *Psychological Monographs, 70* (9, Whole No. 416).

Bartlett, F. C. (1932). *Remembering: A study in experimental and social psychology*. New York: Cambridge University Press.

Brewer, M. B. (1991). The social self: On being the same and different at the same time. *Personality and Social Psychological Bulletin, 17,* 475–482.

Browning, C. R. (1992). *The path to genocide: Essays on launching the Final Solution*. Cambridge: Cambridge University Press.

Clark, R. D., III. (1990). Minority influence: The role of argument refutation of the majority position and social support for the minority. *European Journal of Social Psychology, 20,* 489–497.

Crano, W. D., & Alvaro, E. M. (1998). Indirect minority influence: The leniency contract revisited. *Group Processes and Intergroup Relations, 1,* 99–116.

Crano, W. D., & Chen, X. (1998). The leniency contract and persistence of majority and minority influence. *Journal of Personality and Social Psychology, 74,* 1437–1450.

Dawidowicz, L. S. (1975). *The war against the Jews, 1933–1945.* New York: Bantam.

Dawidowicz, L. S. (1976). *A Holocaust reader.* New York: Behrman House.

Devine, P. G. (1989). Stereotypes and prejudice: Their automatic and controlled components. *Journal of Personality and Social Psychology, 56,* 680–690.

Festinger, L. (1954). A theory of social comparison processes. *Human Relations, 7,* 117–140.

Gigone, D., & Hastie, R. (1993). The common knowledge effect: Information sharing and group judgment. *Journal of Personality and Social Psychology, 65,* 959–974.

Gigone, D., & Hastie, R. (1996). The impact of information on group judgment: A model and computer simulation. In E. Witte & J. H. Davis (Eds.), *Understanding group behavior: Consensual action by small groups* (Vol. 1, pp. 221–251). Mahwah, NJ: Erlbaum.

Goldhagen, D. J. (1996). *Hitler's willing executioners: Ordinary Germans and the Holocaust.* New York: Knopf.

Hains, S. C., Hogg, M. A., & Duck, J. M. (1997). Self-categorization and leadership: Effects of group prototypicality and leader stereotypicality. *Personality and Social Psychology Bulletin, 23,* 1087–1100.

Hardin, C., & Higgins, E. T. (1996). Shared reality: How social verification makes the subjective objective. In R. M. Sorrentino & E. T. Higgins (Eds.), *Handbook of motivation and cognition: Foundations of social behavior* (3rd ed., pp. 28–42). New York: Guilford.

Hinsz, V. B., Tindale, R. S., & Vollrath, D. A. (1997). The emerging conceptualization of groups as information processors. *Psychological Bulletin, 121,* 43–64.

Hogg, M. A. (1996). Social identity, self-categorization, and the small group. In E. Witte & J. H. Davis (Eds.), *Understanding group behavior: Small group processes and interpersonal relations* (Vol. 2, pp. 227–254). Mahwah, NJ: Erlbaum.

Hogg, M. A., & Abrams, D. (1988). *Social identifications: A social psychology of intergroup relations and group processes.* London: Routledge.

Hogg, M. A., & Mullin, B. A. (1999). Joining groups to reduce uncertainty: Subjective uncertainty reduction and group identification. In D. Abrams & M. A. Hogg (Eds.), *Social identity and social cognition* (pp. 249–279). Oxford: Blackwell.

James, W. (1890). *The principles of psychology.* New York: Holt, Rinehart, and Winston.

Kameda, T., Ohtsubo, Y., & Takezawa, M. (1997). Centrality in socio-cognitive network and social influence: An illustration in a group decision making context. *Journal of Personality and Social Psychology, 73,* 296–309.

Latane, B. (1981). The psychology of social impact. *American Psychologist, 36,* 343–355.

Latane, B. (1996). Strength from weakness: The fate of opinion minorities in spatially distributed groups. In E. Witte & J. H. Davis (Eds.), *Understanding group behavior: Consensual action by small groups* (Vol. 1, pp. 193–219). Mahwah, NJ: Erlbaum.

Latane, B., & Bourgeois, M. J. (2001). Dynamic social impact and the consolidation, clustering, correlation, and continuing diversity of culture. In M. A. Hogg & R. S. Tindale (Eds.), *Blackwell handbook of social psychology: Group processes* (pp. 235–258) Oxford: Blackwell.

Laughlin, P. R. (1980). Social combination processes of cooperative, problem-solving groups on verbal intellective tasks. In M. Fishbein (Ed.), *Progress in social psychology* (Vol. 1, pp. 127–155). Hillsdale, NJ: Erlbaum.

Laughlin, P. R., & Ellis, A. L. (1986). Demonstrability and social combination processes on mathematical intellective tasks. *Journal of Experimental Social Psychology, 22,* 177–189.

Milgram, S. (1963). The behavioral study of obedience. *Journal of Abnormal and Social Psychology, 67,* 371–378.

Moscovici, S. (1984). The phenomenon of social representations. In R. M. Farr & S. Moscovici (Eds.), *Social representations* (pp. 3–69). Cambridge: Cambridge University Press.

Nemeth, C. J. (1986). Differential contributions of majority and minority influence. *Psychological Review, 93,* 23–32.

Sherif, M., & Sherif, C. W. (1969). *Social psychology.* New York: Harper and Row.

Shirer, W. L. (1960). *The rise and fall of the Third Reich.* New York: Simon and Schuster.

Smith, C. M., Dykema-Engblade, A., Walker, A., Niven, T. S., & McGrough, T. (2000). Asymmetrical social influence in freely interacting groups discussing the death penalty: A shared representation interpretation. *Group Processes and Intergroup Relations, 3,* 387–402.

Stasser, G. (1999). The uncertain role of unshared information in collective choice. In L. L. Thompson, J. M. Levine, & D. M. Messick (Eds.), *Shared cognition in organizations: The management of knowledge* (pp. 49–70). Mahwah, NJ: Erlbaum.

Stasser, G., & Titus, W. (1985). Pooling of unshared information in group decision making: Biased information sampling during discussion. *Journal of Personality and Social Psychology, 48,* 1467–1478.

Stasser, G., & Titus, W. (1987). Effects of information load and percentage of shared information on the dissemination of unshared information during group discussion. *Journal of Personality and Social Psychology, 53,* 81–93.

Stewart, D. D., & Stasser, G. (1995). Expert role assignment and information sampling during collective recall and decision making. *Journal of Personality and Social Psychology, 69,* 619–628.

Tajfel, H. (1970). Experiments in intergroup discrimination. *Scientific American, 223,* 96–102.

Tajfel, H., & Turner, J. C. (1979). An integrative theory of intergroup conflict. In W. G. Austin & S. Worchel (Eds.), *The social psychology of intergroup relations* (pp. 33–47). Monterey, CA: Brooks/Cole.

Thompson, L., & Fine, G. A. (1999). Socially shared cognition, affect, and behavior: A review and integration. *Personality and Social Psychology Review, 3,* 278–302.

Tindale, R. S., & Kameda, T. (2000). "Social sharedness" as a unifying theme for information processing in groups. *Group Processes and Intergroup Relations, 3,* 123–140.

Tindale, R. S., Meisenhelder, H. M., Dykema-Engblade, A. A., & Hogg, M. A. (2001). Shared cognitions in small groups. In M. A. Hogg & R. S. Tindale (Eds.), *Blackwell handbook of social psychology: Group processes* (pp. 1–30). Oxford: Blackwell Publishers.

Tindale, R. S., Smith, C. M., Thomas, L. S., Filkins, J., & Sheffey, S. (1996). Shared representations and asymmetric social influence processes in small groups. In E. Witte & J. H. Davis (Eds.), *Understanding group behavior: Consensual action by small groups* (Vol. 1, pp. 81–103). Mahwah, NJ: Erlbaum.

Turner, J. C. (1985). Social categorization and the self-concept: A social cognitive theory of group behavior. In E. J. Lawler (Ed.), *Advances in group processes: Theory and research* (Vol. 2, pp. 518–538). Greenwich, CT: JAI Press.

Vallacher, R. R., & Nowak, A. (Eds.). (1994). *Dynamical systems in social psychology.* San Diego: Academic.

Wegner, D. M., & Bargh, J. A. (1998). Control and automaticity in social life. In D. T. Gilbert, S. T. Fiske, & G. Lindzey (Eds.), *The handbook of social psychology* (4th ed., Vol. 1, pp. 446–496). New York: Oxford University Press.

7

Examining the Implications of Cultural Frames on Social Movements and Group Action

Daphna Oyserman and Armand Lauffer

We are all members of groups, as well as separate individuals. Being a member of a group means sharing something with other members of the group. Durkheim's (1899/1947) classic analysis of societies highlights differences between simple groups, in which everyone does the same thing, and complex groups, in which members take on different roles to sustain the group but share some common beliefs. Modern societies can be thought of as complex groups, yet even in modern societies, Durkheim noted, members must have some "similarities of beliefs" if the group is to function. Another way to describe these 'similarities of beliefs' is to discuss common values or value frames, perspectives, or worldviews. For example, a core value frame for American society is individualism—the pursuit of individual goals, individual advancement, individual happiness, and individual freedom is a core similarity of belief that unites Americans. This core value influences our laws, institutions, and social practices, and explicit rejection of individualism is seen as un-American. By sharing this "similarity of belief" or value frame, Americans have a common perspective; indeed, following Durkheim, it is reasonable to assume that every group develops some group-specific values, norms, and values. Of greater interest for this chapter are the similarities between groups within a society and systematic differences across societies in the extent that individualism is valued and the extent that groups or collectives are valued. Valuation of individual versus group interests is a key to understanding cultures (Hofstede, 1980).

A brief look at recent world history highlights a link between salient cultural worldviews and organized violence against out-groups. During the past century, murders of more than a million civilians were essentially the province of nondemocratic regimes (Fein, 1993). Similarly, in this century, states lacking democratic traditions, such as former colonies and former Soviet states, are the nexus of attempts to ethnically cleanse and eradicate civic and ethnic rivals (Brubaker & Laitin, 1998; Giugni, 1998). This suggests some link between individually based democratic values and reduced risk of intergroup violence and between group-based values and worldviews focused on ethnicity and increased risk of such violence. What is the connection between individual-democratic and group-ethnic worldviews and the risk of organized bloodshed? In the current chapter, we propose that at least part of the answer lies in the ways social movements capitalize on existing cultural frames to create local meanings conducive to organized violence against out-groups.

Our perspective builds on an emerging cultural focus within social psychology and draws attention to the ways a society's codes and values become part of the very fabric of an individual's perceptual frame (Kagitcibasi, 1996; Kuehen & Oyserman, 2000). As cultural beings, we see what it makes sense to see in our local worlds; we make sense of things using a culture-specific scaffolding. Using this social-psychological approach to understanding genocide focuses attention on the role of cultural frame in shaping meaning—through norms, values, and the sense made of actions—as it relates to intergroup relations. Without taking into account cultural framing, our attempts to make sense of bloody ethnic rivalries yield little. How could ordinary citizens carry out inhuman slaughter in Rwanda, for example? Yet when we use a cultural frame to make sense of these conflicts, it becomes clear how perception of the out-group can become so fraught with negative emotion and how deeply meaningful, even intrinsic to in-group definition, conflict with the out-group becomes (Oyserman, 1993).

In particular, we propose that bloody ethnic rivalries and organized violence can be understood by taking into account how the out-group is perceived in a collectivistic cultural worldview. In a collectivistic cultural frame, out-groups, groups one does not belong to, are viewed with suspicion, and their members are seen as very different, even alien, from oneself. The out-group is a source of threat, and in-group members believe that only in-group members can be trusted. By taking a "collectivistic" worldview, it becomes clear why group members perceive interethnic conflicts as tenacious and unsolvable, even when overt expression of conflict is submerged (Brubaker & Laitin, 1998; Roberts, Spencer, & Uyangoda, 1998; Rouhana & Bar-Tal, 1998; Smith, 1998).

Daniel Goldhagen (1996) takes this perspective in thinking about Nazi Germany. He suggests that the national policy of extermination emerged from deep-seated anti-Semitism that predated Nazism. Germans, socialized to automatically think of Jews as the other, as non-German, as the mortal enemy of the German people, and as not quite human, could easily assent to gradually increasing measures of systematic oppression, control, and finally extermination because the Jews were labeled as apart, different, and clearly outsiders. Thus, to understand why individuals in groups believe in conflict with a particular out-group and believe that this conflict cannot be resolved without killing, displacing, and controlling the out-group, we must understand the local reality within which these groups take on meaning.

We suggest that part of the answer to the question of when social movements become violent lies in cultural framing. In the current chapter, we will distinguish between *collectivistic* and *individualistic* cultural frames and argue that (a) social movements such as Nazism gain and maintain membership by evoking and sustaining a collective focus; (b) when social movements are able to operate in the absence of countervailing individualistic values, social movements are more likely to sustain member involvement; and (c) when collectivistic values are evoked without countervailing individualistic values, social movements are also more likely to create an atmosphere in which organized violence or even genocide against out-groups is possible. In this way, we will utilize a cultural social-psychological framework to make sense of how people become involved in social movements and the likely course of their involvement in these movements.

CULTURAL FRAMES AND SOCIAL MOVEMENTS

A critical issue for social movements is how to mobilize and maintain involvement in the movement. We propose a general framework to make sense of involvement in social movement groups, both ones that remain nonviolent and ones that become violent, whether they are public interest lobbies, civil rights movements, Tamil or Irish separatists, even Nazis. All social movement leaders attempt to make individuals feel, first, that group membership is central to personal identity; second, that group goals are indistinguishable from individual goals; and, third, that connections with in-group members are of intrinsic value. To shore up their claim on individual resources, all social movements seek linkages with preexisting belief and value systems, such as the linkage made between Nazism and anti-Semitism. In particular, social movements seek to link beliefs about the nature of the in-group and the existence of out-groups. Thus, Nazi rhetoric depended on Germans' willingness to link Christian anti-Semitism with German mythology about Aryans (Mandel, this volume). It is not that social movement leaders in individualistic societies do not try to evoke these same processes. Rather, social movements within societies with strong individualistic values are less likely to produce violence than are social movements within societies with strong collectivistic values because within individualistic value systems, individuals are more commonly viewed as separate from, rather than a part of, groups.

Cultural Frames

Cultural Frames Scaffold Common Reality

What is more important—being true to yourself and achieving personal goals or being a good group member and sacrificing for the needs of the group? Cultures provide a frame within which to answer these value priority questions. Cultures provide social representations of value systems, telling us what is good or bad, worth committing time, energy, and resources to. In this way, the lexicon we use to make sense of the world is culture-tied. The lexicon or vocabulary we use is a transparent yet omnipresent structure that shapes meaning (Earley, 1995; Oyserman & Markus, 1993). Cultural frames are at the root of our most basic understanding of what it means to be human, what "counts" or is noteworthy in a particular situation (Oyserman & Markus, 1993; Oyserman, Sakamoto, & Lauffer, 1998). To in-group members sharing a common script of normative guidelines, culture-appropriate responses feel normal, obvious, natural, mature, and that which does not need explanation. To out-group members using a different cultural script, these same responses may appear immature, contrived, disingenuous, or even wrong and dangerous (Fiske, 1994; Triandis, 1995).

Cultural Frames Create Individual Realities

At any point in history, cultures differ in the extent to which values are seen as core versus peripheral (Schwartz, 1994). Core values are the ones seen as always important, always relevant. For Americans, freedom of choice is such a core value. It influences all aspects of everyday life, from advertising (e.g., Apple's "think different" slogan) to schooling to personal relationships; we not only expect to be able to choose, we also expect to be able to change our minds and choose again. Even young children are offered choices, with "free play" being scheduled into preschool curriculums. Core values are likely to be used when attempting to influence others. For example, abortion rights and school vouchers are both framed in the language of choice (a woman's right to choose, schools of choice). Core values are thus more commonly evoked than are less core values (Fiske, 1991). In addition to differences in which values are core versus peripheral, societies also differ in how many situations elicit particular values (Hofstede, 1980). Highly individualistic societies such as America or New Zealand present people with many situations that evoke personal freedom and choice as a value. Western European societies may equally value personal freedom when it is evoked and differ primarily in the number of situations that evoke these individualistic values versus other more collective ones.

When a value is rarely evoked, it is less likely to influence behavior than when it is continuously evoked. Thus, one advantage of the increasingly intrusive Nazi laws restricting interactions with Jews was to make more salient to Germans, across more and more everyday situations, the contrasts between being Jewish and being a member of the emerging Aryan German group. By expelling Jews from everyday life and making salient group boundaries by having Jews live separately and wear the distinguishing Star of David, these laws made salient to Germans the value of belonging to a group while simultaneously reducing the salience of individual rights, duties, and responsibilities.

By structuring the public and collective reality, groups thus color one's personal reality as well, differentially highlighting the normative role of individual difference, individual pleasures, and personal achievement versus social embeddedness, care and concern for in-group members, and conformity to group norms (e.g., Hofstede, 1991; Markus & Kitayama, 1991, 1994; Triandis, 1989). When the collective reality focuses on the group, social embeddedness, and living up to social norms and roles, individual everyday reality is different than when the collective reality focuses on individual uniqueness, personal happiness, and individual goals and responsibilities (Kitayama & Markus, 1997; Oyserman & Markus, 1993; Shweder & Sullivan, 1990). A common way to assess these differences is through value or attitude checklists such as the one found in the Appendix. To assess cultural frame, researchers ask samples of individuals to rate the extent to which they agree with each statement, with higher collectivistic scores occurring when individuals more strongly agree that family, relationships with in-group members, and common fate with their in-group are meaningful. Similarly, higher individualistic scores mean that individuals agreed more strongly that being unique and different from others, having personal freedoms and the chance to attain personal goals are important to who they are. Reading through the items in the Appendix also makes clear that while people may differ in how much they agree with each statement, answers clearly depend on the situation. In some situations, almost everyone would agree that loyalty to group leaders is important; in other situations, almost everyone will agree that personal choice is important. A key to understanding how some social movements become violent while others do not is to understand cross-cultural differences in how people usually make sense of these value choices.

Cultural Frames Differ in Chronic Focus

Rather than thinking about societies and the individuals living within them as valuing either individual or group goals, it is more accurate to describe cultures in terms of the relative frequency with which values pertaining to group versus individual good are evoked (e.g., obedience and loyalty vs. personal pleasure and self-direction; Schwartz, 1994). This means that individuals can make sense of the world in terms of both individual and group-focused values and are able to shift between these competing value clusters, depending on what is salient at the moment. A wealth of research on migrants and minorities confirms that individuals can learn new cultures and can switch from one emphasizing groups to one emphasizing personal welfare (e.g., Cameron & Lalonde, 1994; Gurin, Hurtado, & Peng, 1994; Kowalski & Wolfe, 1994; Mays, Bullock, Rosenzweig, & Wessells, 1998; Oyserman, 1993; Oyserman et al., 1998). We are all able to think about what the group needs or how we can be good members of the group when the situation calls for it. One of the important questions raised by the Holocaust asks how it was that so many Germans were focused on the needs of the "Aryan" group and able to stay focused on themselves as simply members of this group rather than as individuals.

Collectivism and Individualism

While there are many possible ways to explore this issue, in this chapter our focus is on the way in which societies can focus members' attention on group versus individual frames of reference. Current cultural research and theorizing distinguish between cultures and societies that tend to focus more on the individual and those that focus more on the group as the basic social unit of analysis (e.g., Triandis, 1995). These cultural frames are termed *individualistic* and *collectivistic*, respectively (e.g., Hofstede, 1980; Schwartz, 1990).

Collectivism

Values central to collectivism are obedience, tradition, safety, and order. Given these values, societies develop specific social norms for how to maintain social harmony, fit in, and do the right thing as a group member. Moreover, when these values are salient, groups also tend to think of themselves in territorial terms (e.g., Triandis, 1996). For Germans, this took the form of belief in the sanctity of German soil and belief in a blood-based "Germanity." In this way, collectivist cultural frames focus attention on the interdependence between individuals, the centrality of family, and the importance of social unity and harmony within in-groups (Chan, 1991; Daniels, 1988; Fugita & O'Brien, 1991; Lee, 1994; Markus & Kitayama, 1991; Rosenberger, 1992; Takaki, 1994). Within a collectivistic frame, relationships involve obligation and generosity toward the in-group (Leung, 1997), along with conflict and competition with out-groups (Oyserman, 1993; Triandis, 1995). Boundaries of the in-group are not permeable. In-groups may be the family, clan, ethnic group, or nation, but membership is ascribed at birth and is not achievable through common interests or other means (Triandis, 1995). Further, since only groups based in these imagined blood ties have legitimacy, to be legitimate and create a sense of loyalty, all groups must present themselves in terms of these "legitimate" groups—bolstering a sense of common ancestry, roots, and family or clan bonds.

From a collectivistic perspective, individuals are permanently located in networks of "blood tie" groups—tribal group, ethnic group, kin, and family (Oyserman, 1993; Triandis, 1995). Even nationality is understood as stemming from membership in an imagined primordial community of blood-related others so that true citizenship will be seen as a birthright, not a choice (Calhoun, 1993). German nationality, especially in the period before and during Nazism, provides an example of this perspective. German nationalists emphasized ethnic rather than civic or political criteria for being German and in that way saw "Germanness" as a blood connection, a natural human identity rather than a chosen group membership (Calhoun, 1993). From a collective perspective, these groups are *entitative*, that is, understood as entities with indivisible meaning as units (Hamilton & Sherman, 1996), whereas individuals are components of groups, in some ways interchangeable (Brewer & Miller, 1996). This belief in the entitativity of groups means that groups are viewed as causing events and as being responsible for the actions of group members (Morris, 1998), while individual actors are less likely to be viewed as causing outcomes (Morris & Peng, 1994).

Thus, within a collectivistic frame, group membership is a central and defining characteristic of the self (e.g., Phinney & Cobb, 1996). Positive self-evaluation and life satisfaction comes from skillfully meeting obligations to one's group members (Ames, Dissanayake, & Kasulis, 1994; Markus & Kitayama, 1991; Oyserman & Markus; 1993; 1998; Singelis, 1994; Triandis, 1995). When one thinks about the self and others in terms of groups, the individuality of out-group members, even their humanity, becomes suspect (Triandis, 1995). As a result, in-group members will have strong ties with and trust in only in-group members; out-group members will not be trusted and will be seen as threatening. Violent response to this perceived threat is more likely in societies and cultures that lack democratic roots, since citizens who lack strongly internalized norms and values of democracy are more likely to be intolerant of out-groups seen as behaving in ways antithetical to in-group norms (Sullivan & Transue, 1999).

Take, for example, Germany in 1932. It lacked a strong democratic tradition, and the Nazi Party successfully connected hate and loathing for Jews with a desire to take part in a "regeneration" of Germany. Traditional Christian and nineteenth-century pseudoscientific anti-Semitism were each interwoven with voters' desires to see themselves as part of a superior Aryan group, regenerate the German nation, and return to a mythic past. Nazi anti-Semitism became a corollary of German belief in the superiority of the Aryan race (Bauer, 1982; Friedlander, 1997a, 1997b; Marris, 1987). Anti-Semitism supported the growth of German consciousness through the promotion of fear of the "other."

For Germans, the Jew was the eternal other, the stranger, dirty, thieving, morally and physically inferior, not fit to be associated with or to be considered a member of the *Volk* but rather a conniving member of an international conspiracy to harm Germans. The Nuremberg Laws of 1935 legally excluded Jews from German society by forbidding marriage and extramarital relationships between Jews and Germans and even the employment of German females under age 45 in Jewish households. Being a Jew, according to these laws, was not a matter of belief, behavior, or self-identification with a group but rather a matter of blood. In 1938 an SS journal further defined Jews as a race of murderers and criminals, mortal enemies of the German people (Bauer, 1982; Friedlander, 1997a, 1997b). Gradually, public descriptions of Jews invoked their common humanity less and less and increasingly used non-human terms such as *fodder* and *excrement*.

Because collectivism provides a ready explanation for intergroup conflict and its consequences, maintaining a collectivist frame provides coherence and reduces stress when organized violence occurs. To the extent that one believes that "blood" groups are important and that individuals are defined by this type of group membership, prejudice, racism, and reduced life chances due to group membership become understandable (Oyserman & Sakamoto, 1998). At the same time, the level of intergroup conflict is perceived as more intense (Oyserman, 1993). In this way, a collectivist focus can reduce negative sequelae of violence. A more recent example of this dynamic comes from our field research with Muslim Bosnian women in the aftermath of dislocation due to Balkan civil wars. Muslim Bosnian women who endorsed more collectivist values and viewed their ethnic and religious identities as defining them more centrally reported less stress, depression, and anxiety overall than did women who endorsed more individualistic values (Mesquita & Oyserman, 1996). Moreover, family members' negative wartime experiences had greater impact on women who endorsed collectivist values. For these women, the correlation between their own symptoms of posttraumatic stress disorder and the negative wartime experiences of their families was stronger.

Individualism

While collectivistic cultural frames focus attention on groups, individualistic cultural frames focus attention on the individual. Three core belief systems constitute the value basis of individualism: valuation of personal independence and freedom of choice, personal uniqueness, and personal achievement (Hsu, 1983; Markus & Kitayama, 1991; Triandis, 1995). Given these core values, individualism promotes the importance of knowing one's beliefs and values and behaving in accordance with these no matter what the context. Individualism as a worldview suggests that what is permanent and stable is the individual himself or herself, not his or her relationships. Further, given the focus on individual freedom and independence, personal goals and feelings weigh heavily in decision making. Individualists are interested in whether they are happy and feeling good about themselves (Bellah, Sullivan, & Swidler, 1988; Wilkinson, 1992; Markus, Mullally, & Kitayama, 1997).

Whereas a collective frame presents groups as organic entities, and individuals as simply parts of groups, an individualistic frame conceives of individuals as organic entities. That is, individuals are meaningful entities in themselves, and will or agency is located within individuals (Shweder, 1991).

By focusing on the individual, this cultural frame highlights the common humanity in all individuals (Hsu, 1983). It sets up a mechanism of basic willingness to be sociable with strangers, who may, after all, be helpful in attaining one's personal goals, since many tasks require cooperative effort. Individualism then puts a premium on a willingness to be flexible and to compromise and negotiate with diverse others in pursuit of one's personal goals (see Oyserman, Coon, & Kemmelmeier, 2002, for a review).

On the other hand, groups themselves are assumed to be temporary. Individuals join with other individuals who have common interests; as goals and interests change, group membership is also assumed to change (Singelis et al., 1995). Thus, within an individualistic worldview, groups are by nature unstable and continue only as long as they are personally worthwhile; even membership in family groups is considered a choice, since one could always choose not to associate with one's family (Fiske, 1991; Sampson, 1988; Triandis, 1995; for a review see Oyserman et al., 2002).

The "relational schema" (e.g., Baldwin, 1992) or relationship prototype that makes sense within an individualistic frame is the relationship as a personal, temporary collaboration or competition between the self and specific other individuals. Individuals are free to form relationships and alliances with any other individual. If a relationship is not equitable or personally satisfying, it fades away, with new relationships established to take its place. Individuals can choose with whom to associate and can determine the degree of association. Intergroup competition and suspicion are not integral to an individualistic perspective. From an individualistic perspective, one is free to choose whether to have friends or enemies (Adams, 1998). Social obligation is not central to individualism. Instead, individuals are assumed to make temporary connections in service of a personal goal or need. Individualism promotes a focus on equity in relationships and short-term cost-benefit analyses of obligations to others.

Individualism, Collectivism, and the Meaning of Groups

As noted in the previous sections, individualistic and collectivistic frames differ in the centrality of group membership to self-definition, in the permanence assumed with regard to groups, and in whether between-group conflict is assumed to be a permanent or natural state of affairs. In this section, we outline a final and crucial way that individualistic and collectivistic frames differ in their fundamental and basic evaluation of groups. While valued and seen as the basis of being human within a collectivistic worldview, groups are suspect and seen as having the potential to influence or subvert individual judgment, reasoning, and perspective taking from an individualistic worldview (for an overview, see Aronson, Wilson, & Akert, 1994).

Within an individualistic frame, one's true opinions and best judgment arise when one thinks for oneself and acts alone. Within a collectivistic frame, obedience to the group, following group norms, and acting to maintain group

harmony are valued. These same behaviors—that is, conformity and obedience to the group or social norms—are described as "mindlessness" and "de-
personalization" within an individualistic frame and seen as the negative
consequences of groups and social situations. In an individualistic frame,
groups are detrimental to individual initiative; they are "crowds," potentially
dangerous "masses," subject to fads, crazes, and hysteria (Lofand, 1992). Thus,
while social conformity is normative and appropriate within a collective frame,
within an individualistic frame, conformity to group norms is inappropriate
and is often considered a failure to act on personal conviction. Consequently,
individuals who follow group norms are seen as being mindless, depersonalized, and deindividuated.

Implications of Cultural Frames for Understanding Social Movements

Social Movements

Social movements challenge a society's status quo in the name of a group
perceived to be disadvantaged within the society, with the goal of benefiting
this subgroup (Giugni, 1998). In order to serve as the impetus for social action, there is no need for the claim of disadvantage to be empirically verifi-
able, as long as it convinces others to join and mobilize for action. Thus, Hitler
described the German people as victimized by world Jewry (see Mandel, this
volume). While social scientists have studied the emergence of social movements from a variety of perspectives (e.g., Giugni, 1998; McAdam, McCarthy,
& Zald, 1988), the influence of cultural frame and the ways individuals can
move between these frames have not received attention. Yet taking into account culture appears necessary if we are to understand the dynamics of
movement involvement and participation and the likelihood that social movements will promote organized out-group violence. In particular, we propose
that social movements attempt to shift the cultural focus of potential participants toward a collective worldview. We will speculate about likely mechanisms of frame shifting and use examples from the social movement and
intergroup conflict literature to support the notion that cultural frames are
central to whether a movement focuses on nonviolent change within a society or violent change of the society (e.g., revolutionary movements or genocidal movements).

Social Movements' Chances for Success Depend on Framing

By focusing attention on group needs rather than individual needs, collective
cultural frames are advantageous to social movement organizers. If group
membership is central to identity and impermeable, acting for the good of the
group and following group norms can more easily replace personal goals and

171

more universalistic norms. Conversely, if individual initiative is made central, individuals will be suspicious of groups, seeing them as mindless, irrational, and corrosive of personal responsibility.

Juxtaposing individualistic and collectivistic cultural frames clarifies the process of joining, remaining in, and leaving social movements. When cultures focus on individuals as the central, defining social unit, then groups of choice are the basis of social structures, with individuals viewed as choosing to become citizens and choosing to become members of a variety of other voluntary associations. As a result, in-group members are likely to have weak ties with multiple groups, to have a general sense of trust in their fellow man, and to perceive others not as threats but as future potential interaction partners (see Oyserman et al., 2002). These ideas of fluid group membership and a belief that others share a common humanity with basic rights have also been termed basic values of democracy (Sullivan & Transue, 1999). When a permeable sense of group membership and valuation of the individual is associated with cultural valuation of democratic norms, violent response to threatening out-group members is less likely (for a review, see Calhoun, 1993). This may help to explain what some perceived as a contrast in both rhetoric and behaviors between ordinary Israelis and Palestinians during the violent confrontations of 2000. The available data suggest that Jewish Israelis are, on average, lower in collectivism than Palestinian Arabs (Oyserman, 1993).

Individualism and Social Movements

By making individuals central, an individualistic cultural frame highlights the ways groups bind, constrain, and limit individual freedom, taking away from the basic requirement of each individual to be responsible for his or her own actions (Zurcher & Snow, 1992). Individualism's negative valuation of groups carries over to a negative valuation of people who join social movements. From this perspective, those who join social movements are deficient in some way, that is, as authoritarian, dependent, in search of personal identity, refusing to take personal responsibility for their actions. Those who act alone are seen as both more independent and more humanistic and caring toward others (McAdam, McCarthy, & Zald, 1988; Zurcher & Snow, 1992). This negative perspective on groups combines with the assumption that groups are of value only as long as they are useful to the individual—that is, that they provide relevant resources.

To be successful in recruiting and maintaining members in a social movement framed in terms of individualistic values, a movement must offer members a way to feel free and independent of constraints, attain personal pleasure or happiness, or work toward other personal goals. Group members will ask themselves if they can have their own personal style while being a group member, if being a group member contributes to personal happiness, and so on. Moreover, participants in individualistically focused movements will engage in ongoing cost-benefit analyses of involvement as compared with other self-defining options. Membership has to provide ongoing benefits that outweigh its costs. Members must feel that groups help them to achieve personal goals that would otherwise remain unmet. To elicit involvement, a movement would need to successfully promote membership as an efficient way to feel good about oneself, reduce constraints on personal freedoms, and attain personal growth experiences.

Examples of individualistic framing of group membership come from promotional messages used as part of the U.S. Navy's advertising campaign— videos show young men and women driving sport utility vehicles and enjoying leisure. Naval service is portrayed as a way to better oneself and attain personal goals—learn skills useful in the job market, earn money toward college, and have a better standard of living and more leisure activities. On the clip, young sailors report that joining the navy gives them a financial edge over their peers. Clearly, the focus is on individual, not group-oriented, appeals. Similarly, the U.S. Army advertises enlistment as a way to "be all you can be," and the U.S. Marines advertise enlistment as a way to attain personal uniqueness—to be one of "the few, the proud, the Marines." While appropriately targeting the individualistic values of the intended audience, this way of presenting social group involvement means that such involvement is likely to be both *temporary*, with members leaving whenever the cost-benefit ratio shifts, and *contingent*, with members feeling free to choose which group goals and tasks to work on.

Collectivism and Social Movements

Clearly, social movements framed by individualism will have a tough time convincing potential participants to sacrifice for the group. Social movements that successfully frame involvement in terms of collectivism do not need to describe membership as a way to be happy, feel unique, and attain personal goals. As can be seen by referring to the Appendix, collectivist social movements need only remind participants of the importance of collective values, obligation to the in-group, common fate with the in-group, and that the self is defined via the in-group and family ties. Certainly it is easier to keep members involved in social movements when honor, tradition, and social obligation are the primary and salient values than when personal happiness, pleasure, and goal attainment are. To elicit a sense of duty or obligation to the social movement in a collectivistic society, a new movement or group would simply need to be framed in terms of existing "blood tie" in-groups.

Recall that the groups that are important to collectivists are seen as permanent, so linking participation in a movement to such a preexisting group would set up conditions for permanent involvement. Thus, if Nazism were simply presented as an economic plan that Germans could choose to be involved in if they felt it would help them attain personal economic security, it

173

is harder to imagine Germans feeling permanently linked to Nazism. Instead, being a member of the Nazi social movement was framed as part of being a member of the "Aryan race," a preexisting ascriptive group; in this way, being Nazi and being German were linked, making social movement involvement more permanent.

Clearly, involvement in the Nazi movement was facilitated by linking the movement with preexisting notions about a mythic blood-based "nation" of Aryans. This facilitated the shift to a collective frame in which "German Aryan" in-group needs were made salient. By focusing on the centrality of the group, needed contributions from individual members could be represented as part of being in the group. Therefore, fulfilling these obligations could be linked with collectivist values without the need to resort to individualistic motives to carry them out. Explicit use of Jews as the enemy facilitated a sense of in-group common fate. Because the social movement involvement is linked with membership in other in-groups, involvement is reinforcing to participants as a way of contributing to group goals. In the case of Nazism, the connection was made between being Nazi and being truly German, between being truly German and being a member of the Aryan race, thus turning participants into an imagined community based in blood ties. Together these crystallized attention to the collectivistic values of respect for group leaders and the desire to serve them.

While individualism promotes the idea that one could join with an array of heterogeneous others for some personal purpose or goal, collectivism promotes the idea that it is only the homogeneous in-group to which one is obligated and connected. Whereas group membership is temporary by nature within an individualistic frame, it is permanent within a collectivistic frame. When framed by individualism, a social movement would have temporary, shifting, and evolving memberships. Individuals join to attain a goal or because they need or want something membership provides. Within such a frame, compromise, flexibility, and alternative routes to goal attainment are sensible. Conversely, in contexts where collectivism is chronic, social movement involvement may be seen as a way to express oneself through membership, and social movements could become more all-encompassing, permanent, and demanding of individual time, energy, and investment. Clearly, salient cultural framing matters in how groups are perceived, willingness to become involved, the perceived costs and benefits of involvement, and the potential of these movements to engage in organized violence or even genocidal attacks on out-groups. These differences are summarized in Table 7.1.

Cultural Frame as Impetus for Individual Action

Until now we have focused on the ways that cultural frames shift the meaning of group membership and the things social groups must do to have and sustain member involvement. We now turn to the ways by which cultural

Table 7.1

Implications of Individualism and Collectivism Relevant to Social Movements

INDIVIDUALISM	COLLECTIVISM
The individual is the focus of analysis and basic meaning unit	The social unit is the focus of analysis and the basic meaning unit
Individuals form, join, and dissolve groups; groups exist for the good of individuals and are means for achieving individual ends; individuals do not owe any particular allegiance to the group as an institution	Group membership shapes and completes individuals; it is as members of groups that individuals make sense of themselves and others; groups are fixed, central, and important and lay a claim to one's time and energy
Individuals are motivated to achieve, be happy, and be unique	Individuals are motivated to be competent, appropriate group members
Conflict is interindividual. Individual needs and personal conflicts are the basis for group formation and dissolution	Conflict is intergroup; groups are permanent and have an existence beyond the individual; groups are imagined communities of others with shared blood ties and history
Today's enemy may be tomorrow's ally; compromise and flexibility are hallmarks of intergroup behavior	Today's enemy is tomorrow's enemy; intransience and refusal to compromise are hallmarks of intergroup behavior

frames shift the salience of aspects of self-concept, making different answers to the basic "Who am I?" question seem appropriate. As noted previously, individualistic and collectivistic cultural frames make salient personal (idiocentric) and social (allocentric) identity elements of self-concept, respectively (e.g., Markus & Kitayama, 1991; Oyserman, 1993; Trafimow, Triandis, & Goto, 1991; Triandis, 1989). Identity includes both personal and social aspects, and both are implicated in basic functions of identity such as maintaining well-being (e.g., Crocker, Voelkl, Testa, & Major, 1991; Haslam, Oakes, Turner, & McGarty, 1996) and behavior control (Hughes & Demo, 1989; Haslam et al., 1996; Taylor & Dube, 1986; Turner, Hogg, Oakes, Reicher, & Wetherell, 1987).

Social identities motivate social action by making group membership norms and obligations salient and personally relevant, encouraging group members to see themselves as prototypical group members, and validating perseverance in working toward group goals. Conversely, personal identities motivate personal action by making personal goals, desires, concerns, and feelings sa-

175

lient; encouraging perception of oneself as unique and valued; and validating the quest for autonomy, independence, and personal happiness.

Shifting Cultural Frames: Implications for Social Movement Involvement

If, in some societies, individualistic frames are almost always used and collectivistic frames rarely used, and, in other societies, the reverse is the case, then these societies should also differ in the nature of the identities that are habitually reinforced. In societies where most contexts make individualism salient, the chronically accessible way of thinking about oneself and others is likely to be in terms of individualism and personal identities. The reverse will be the case in societies where most contexts make collectivism salient, where the chronically accessible way of thinking about oneself and others is likely to be in terms of collectivism and social identities. In individualism-dominant societies, the extent of collective focus should be amenable to contextual manipulation, but the level of individual focus should remain relatively constant; the reverse should be the case for collectivism-dominant cultural contexts. A series of field studies in Northern Ireland and Mexico found some evidence to support this notion of a "cultural working self" (Sanchez-Burks, Oyserman, & Kemmelmeier, 1998). Thus, we were able to prime collectivism in Northern Ireland among college students by making thoughts about friendships salient. This prime did not influence level of individualism, which would likely be chronically salient in this individualistic society (Hofstede, 1980). Similarly, we were able to prime individualism in Mexico among college students by making salient unique characteristics about the self. This prime did not influence level of collectivism, which is likely to be chronically salient in this collectivistic society (Hofstede, 1980).

The working cultural self-concept made salient in a given situation is likely to have consequences for involvement in a social movement. A collective frame may increase perceived salience of social identities, increase obligation to the in-group, highlight boundaries between in-groups and out-groups and personalize conflict between in-groups and out-groups. These aspects of collectivism may be beneficial to increased involvement and to maintenance of membership over time. In addition, the kind of short-term, individually focused cost-benefit analysis of involvement likely in an individualistic frame is unlikely in a collectivist one. A social movement can count on a longer-term and more extensive commitment to the extent that it can align itself with the kind of permanent groups that are part of the collectivistic focus—family or kin groups and "blood ties" with others who share a presumed common ancestry.

In Nazi Germany, efforts to link Nazism with being German, and being Jewish with all that was opposed to Germanness were supported by the regime's propaganda machinery and even by purportedly scientific institutes

176

and universities. Some of the latter focused on Aryan superiority. Others—like the huge library on Jewish affairs at Frankfurt University and the Eisenach Institute—focused on the scientific understanding of Jewish matters or the relationships of Jews to Christians. By turning Jews and the Jewish people into the objects of study, this further supported the process of dehumanization while simultaneously elevating those commissioning and doing the research on Jews.

The reason it was important to keep Germans focused on collective values is that individualistic value frames increase salience of personal identities, highlight boundaries between the self and others, and reduce relevance of issues focused on the group rather than personal goals and desires. When individualistic value frames are chronically accessible, a social movement will need to expend effort to create contexts that cue collectivism and make collectivistic values relevant. Chronic salience of an individualistic lens will mean that involvement must be framed in terms of personal benefits to the individual. Within an individualistic frame, activism makes sense only as a way to attain personal resources and support not otherwise available, or as a way of attaining more abstract personal justice and fairness goals. Once established, these groups are less likely to focus on intergroup conflict and more likely to be pragmatic and focused on compromise. However, if such a group cannot meet members' individualistic goals, it is likely to quickly lose membership.

Stable and long-term groups, whether revolutionary or religious, require that members define membership as central to, overshadowing, or coloring their sense of self. Within a collectivistic frame, remaining true to the group's beliefs and values is important. Negotiation, flexibility, and compromise are likely to be viewed as irresponsible to the group, and "collaborators" are likely to be punished (Mays et al., 1998; Roberts, Spencer, & Uyangoda, 1998). Thus, when unrestrained by individualism, collectivism may result in resistance to compromise and more violent interchanges with the out-group, including attempts to wrest all social power from the out-group. This has been true of other twentieth-century genocides, including the Turkish massacres of millions of Armenians, the excesses of the Pol Pot regime during the Vietnam-Cambodian War, Stalin's purges, and the more recent incidents of ethnic cleansing in the Balkans. However, none of these seem to equal the Holocaust for its systematic and widespread cruelty or for its apparent disconnect from territorial and political gain (Wehler, 1998).

CAN PRIMING COLLECTIVISM PRIME SOCIAL OBLIGATION?

Until now, we have described the risky potential of collectivism to create conditions conducive to organized intergroup violence. In this last section, we would like to speculate about the possibility that collectivism can also increase social obligation not only to in-group members but also to individuals more generally and in this way reduce the risk of organized intergroup violence. Given that both individual- and collective-focused values are in evidence in all societies (Schwartz, 1990), our interest is in the possibility that by melding individualism and collectivism, individuals may feel obligated not only to their smaller in-group but also to society and to humankind at large. That is, they will both feel connected to others and also value individual differences and endorse flexibility and compromise. In a series of studies with Jewish and Asian American college students, we found evidence for the positive effect of such a melded cultural frame (Oyserman et al., 1998).

Students in these studies were asked to read a series of scenarios in which personal goals and social obligation goals were presented as conflicting. For example, in one scenario, students chose between going out on a beautiful spring day or carrying out a commitment. Commitments were framed as either personal commitments to another student, social commitments to help the in-group, or social commitments to help larger society—for example, canvassing voters or volunteering for Martin Luther King Day events. We proposed that the propensity to simply do one's own thing would be dampened when collectivistic values were made salient. In fact, students who first brought to mind values by filling out attitude scales differed systematically in their responses based on the values they endorsed. Participants who endorsed only individualistic values felt obligated only to individuals. These responses parallel the literature suggesting that individualistic frames make group participation suspect and dampen any sense of obligation to groups. Participants who endorsed only collectivistic values felt obligated to the in-group, not the larger society. These responses parallel the concerns we have raised about the potential of collectivism to carry with it intransigent intergroup conflict. However, another group of respondents endorsed both individualistic and collectivistic values. These participants felt particularly obligated to help groups whose membership was inclusive of all American society and whose goals focused on general social issues. These findings provide empirical support for the claim that collectivism primes social obligation. Unlike previous work, they also suggest that a positive aspect of collectivism can carry over to larger society.

CONCLUSION

We have suggested that a collective cultural focus carries with it the tendency to define the self in terms of social identities, to see others in terms of stable group membership, to perceive out-groups as threats, and to be wary of compromise with out-group members. We have suggested that this stance carries with it heightened risk of intergroup conflict and the possibility of organized violence, ethnic cleansing, and other genocidal acts. Further, we have proposed that democratic values and individualism reduce the risk that social movements will develop this type of collective identity. Social institutions in all societies must be capable of evoking some collectivism. A society cannot long survive if its members never develop a sense of collective identity and never feel obligated or committed to it. Similarly, if a social movement cannot evoke a sense of social obligation, a sense of self as bound up with the group and connected to the group's fate, the movement is unlikely to survive over time. The implied social contract between individual and group or society is that each benefits from the other, and societies must develop a way of creating and sustaining such a contract (e.g., Etzioni, 1993; Hewitt, 1989; Schwartz, 1996). Yet, as is clear from the sectarian violence in many parts of the world, a sense of social obligation to the in-group may be quite detrimental to the out-group, especially when both live within the same country (e.g., Fiske, 1991).

A collective orientation toward a family or "blood tie" in-group may paradoxically promote extreme self-sacrifice for the benefit of social obligation yet result in ongoing intergroup conflict because any compromise with the out-group would be seen as abandonment of the in-group. Thus, some analyses of the Republican Sinn Fein in Northern Ireland would suggest that members in this social movement cannot accept a political negotiation or compromise solution because for them the identity of being Republican Sinn Fein requires that there be no compromise with the British (cf. White & Frasier, 2000). Collectivism at its core does not promote negotiation and compromise; flexibility is viewed as abandonment of the group's needs or cooperation with the enemy. Perhaps paradoxically, collectivistic tendencies toward social obligation may promote long-standing and violent ethnically focused conflict. In certain circumstances, a collectivist perspective results in a decreased sense of overarching community and focus only on the in-group, as well as loss of focus on individual rights and responsibilities and a shift to focus on group rights (e.g., Ben-Dor, 1988). Some researchers have argued that democracy depends on the existence of a stable overarching identity, such as "we are all Americans," within the context of fluid allegiances to interest groups (e.g., Oyserman, 1992; Sears, 1987). Such a sense of commitment to the larger national societal community has been described as a hallmark of individualism because collectivism requires a sense of "blood ties" or familial relationship to evoke sustained social obligation (e.g., Triandis, 1995; Wilkinson, 1992).

Individualism and collectivism provide very different perspectives on the meaning of social movements and the costs and benefits of being a group member. Involvement in a social movement is a way to create a certain self-image (Pinel & Swann, 2000), to band together with others to feel good about oneself (Kaplan & Liu, 2000), and to maintain a positive sense of one's uniqueness while also feeling close and connected to similar others (Brewer & Silver, 2000). Yet, when framed collectively, social movements can readily create the context for organized violence. It is imperative that we develop ways to harness the positive power of collective impulses in ways that do not set the stage for violence.

APPENDIX: A MEASURE OF INDIVIDUALISM AND COLLECTIVISM (FROM OYSERMAN ET AL., 2002)

I. *Individualism (valuing personal uniqueness, personal achievement, and personal freedom)*

UNIQUENESS

1. It is important to me to develop my own personal style.
2. I may have some things in common with others, but my personal attributes are what make me who I am.
3. I prefer being able to be different from others.
4. I am different from everyone else, unique.
5. I enjoy being unique and different from others in many respects.
6. It is important for me to be myself.

ACHIEVEMENT

1. For me, hard work and personal determination are the keys to success in life.
2. To know who I really am, you must examine my achievements and accomplishments.
3. A person of character focuses on achieving his/her own goals.
4. I enjoy looking back on my personal achievements and setting new goals for myself.
5. My personal achievements and accomplishments are very important to who I am.
6. It is important for me to remember that my personal goals have top priority.

FREEDOM

1. It is better for me to follow my own ideas than to follow those of anyone else.
2. My personal happiness is more important to me than almost anything else.
3. Individual happiness and the freedom to attain it are central to who I am.
4. If I make my own choices, I will be happier than if I listen to others.
5. I often have personal preferences.

II. *Collectivism (valuing family, relationships with others, and belief in common fate)*

FAMILY

1. I often turn to my family for social and emotional support.
2. Learning about the traditions, customs, values, and beliefs of my family is important to me.
3. My family is central to who I am.
4. I know I can always count on my family to help me.
5. It is important to me to respect decisions made by my family.
6. Family is more important to me than almost anything else.
7. Whenever my family needs something, I try to help.

RELATIONSHIPS WITH OTHERS

1. If you know what groups I belong to, you know who I am.
2. To know who I really am, you must see me with members of my group.
3. My relationships with others are a very important part of who I am.
4. My happiness depends on the happiness of those around me.
5. In some ways, my relationships with others make me who I am.
6. I will sacrifice my self-interest for the benefit of the group I am in.

COMMON FATE

1. The history and heritage of my religious, national, or ethnic group are a large part of who I am.
2. A person of character helps his/her religious, national, or ethnic group before all else.
3. I have respect for the leaders of my religious, national, or ethnic group.
4. It is important to me to think of myself as a member of my religious, national, or ethnic group.
5. In the end, a person feels closest to members of his/her own religious, national, or ethnic group.
6. When I hear about an event, I automatically wonder whether it will be good or bad for my religious, national, or ethnic group.

REFERENCES

Adams, G. (1998, August). *The cultural construction of friends and enemies in West Africa and the USA: Implications for theories of culture.* Paper presented at the Stanford Mini-Conference on Cultural Psychology, Stanford University, Palo Alto, CA.

Ames, R., Dissanayake, W., & Kasulis, T. (1994). *Self as person in Asian theory and practice*. Albany: State University of New York Press.

Aronson, E., Wilson, T., & Akert, R. (1994). *Social psychology: The heart and the mind*. New York: HarperCollins.

Asch, S. (1952). *Social psychology*. New York: Oxford University Press.

Baldwin, M. (1992). Relational schemas and the processing of social information. *Psychological Bulletin, 112*, 461–484.

Bauer, Y. (1982). *A history of the Holocaust*, New York: Franklin Watts.

Bellah, R., Sullivan, W., & Swidler, T. S. (Eds.). (1988). *Individualism and commitment in American life: Readings on the themes of habits of the heart*. New York: Harper.

Ben-Dor, G. (1988). Ethnopolitics and the Middle Eastern State. In M. Esman & I. Rabinovich (Eds.), *Ethnicity, pluralism, and the state in the Middle East* (pp. 71–94). Ithaca, NY: Cornell University Press.

Berry, J. W. (1989). Psychology of acculturation. *Nebraska Symposium on Motivation, 37*, 201–234.

Brewer, M., & Miller, N. (1996) *Intergroup relations*. Belmont, CA: Brooks/Cole.

Brewer, M., & Silver, M. (2000). Group distinctiveness, social identification and collective mobilization. In S. Stryker, T. Owens, & R. White (Eds.), *Self, Identity, and social movements* (pp. 153–171). Minneapolis: University of Minnesota Press.

Brubaker, R., & Laitin, D. (1998). Ethnic and nationalistic violence. *Annual Review of Sociology, 24*, 291–311.

Burnstein, E., Crandall, C., & Kitayama, S. (1994) Some neo-Darwinian decision rules for altruism: Weighing cues for inclusive fitness as a function of the biological importance of the decision. *Journal of Personality and Social Psychology, 67*, 773–789.

Calhoun, C. (1993). Nationalism and ethnicity. *Annual Review of Sociology, 19*, 211–239.

Callero, P. (1986). Putting the social in prosocial behavior: An interactionist approach to altruism. *Humboldt Journal of Social Relations, 13*, 15–32.

Cameron, J., & Lalonde, R. (1994). Self, ethnicity, and social group memberships in two generations of Italian Canadians. *Personality and Social Psychology Bulletin, 20*, 514–520.

Chan, S. (1991). *Asian Americans: An interpretive history*. New York: Twayne.

Crocker, J., & Major, B. (1989). Social stigma and self esteem: The self-protective properties of stigma. *Psychological Review, 96*, 608–630.

Crocker, J., Voelkl, K., Testa, M., & Major, B. (1991). Social stigma: The affective consequences of attributional ambiguity. *Journal of Personality and Social Psychology, 60*, 218–228.

Daniels, R. (1988). *Asian American: Chinese and Japanese in the United States since 1850*. Seattle: University of Washington Press.

Durkheim, E. (1947). *The division of labor in society* (George Simpson, Trans.). Glencoe, IL: Free Press. (Originally published 1899)

Earley, P. C. (1995). *The faces of culture: Workshop on culture and conflicts*. Palo Alto, CA: Graduate School of Business, Stanford University.

Etzioni, A. (1993). *Spirit of community: Rights, responsibilities and the communitarian agenda*. New York: Crown.

Fein, H. (1993). Accounting for genocide after 1945: Theories and some findings. *International Journal on Group Rights, 1*, 79–106.

Fiske, A. (1991). *Structures of social life: The four elementary forms of human relations: Communal sharing, authority ranking, equality matching, market pricing*. New York: The Free Press.

Fowers, B., & Robertson, F. (1996). Why is multiculturalism good? *American Psychologist, 51*, 609–621.

Friedlander, S. (1997a). The extermination of European Jews in historiography: Fifty years later. In A. H. Rosenfeld (Ed.), *Thinking about the Holocaust after half a century*. Bloomington: Indiana University Press.

Friedlander, S. (1997b). *Nazi Germany and the Jews: Vol. 1, The years of persecution, 1933–1939*. New York: HarperCollins.

Fugita, S., & O'Brien, D. (1991). *Japanese American ethnicity: The persistence of community*. Seattle: University of Washington Press.

Gaines, S., Jr., Marelich, W., Bledsoe, K., Steers, W., et al. (1997). Links between race/ethnicity and cultural values as mediated by racial/ethnic identity and moderated by gender. *Journal of Personality and Social Psychology, 72*, 1460–1475.

Garcia, J. A. (1982). Ethnicity and Chicanos: Measurement of ethnic identification, identity, and consciousness. *Hispanic Journal of Behavioral Sciences, 4*, 295–314.

Garcia, M., & Lega, L. (1979). Development of a Cuban ethnic identity questionnaire. *Hispanic Journal of Behavioral Sciences, 1*, 247–261.

Giugni, M. (1998). Was it worth the effort? The outcomes and consequences of social movements. *Annual Review of Sociology, 24*, 371–393.

Goldhagen, D. J. (1996). *Hitler's willing executioners: Ordinary Germans and the Holocaust*. New York: Vintage.

Gurin, P., Hurtado, A., & Peng, T. (1994). Group contacts and ethnicity in the social identities of Mexicanos and Chicanos. *Personality and Social Psychology Bulletin, 20*, 521–532.

Hamilton, D. & Sherman, S. (1996). Perceiving persons and groups. *Psychological Review, 103*, 336–355.

Haslam, S., Oakes, P., Turner, J., & McGarty, C. (1996). Social identity, self-categorization, and the perceived homogeneity of ingroups and outgroups: The interaction between social motivation and cognition. In R. Sorrentino & E. T. Higgins (Eds.), *Handbook of motivation and cognition: The interpersonal context*, pp. 182–222. New York: Guilford.

Hewitt, J. (1989). *Dilemmas of the American self*. Philadelphia: Temple University Press.

Hofstede, G. (1980). *Culture's consequences: International differences in work-related values*. Beverly Hills, CA: Sage.

Hofstede, G. (1991). Empirical models of cultural differences. In N. Bleichrodt & P. Drenth (Eds.), *Contemporary issues in cross-cultural psychology* (pp. 4–33). Berwyn, PA: Swets and Zeitlinger.

Hsu, F. (1983). *Rugged individualism reconsidered*. Knoxville: University of Tennessee Press.

Hughes, M., & Demo, D. (1989). Self-perceptions of Black Americans: Self-esteem and personal efficacy. *American Journal of Sociology, 95*, 132–159.

Kagitcibasi, C. (1996). *Family and human development across cultures*. Mahwah, NJ: Erlbaum.

Kaplan, H., & Liu, X. (2000). Social movements as collective coping with spoiled personal identities: Implications from a panel study of changes in the life course between adolescence and adulthood. In S. Stryker, T. Owens, & R. White (Eds.), *Self, identity, and social movements* (pp. 215–238). Minneapolis: University of Minnesota Press.

Katz, I., & Hass, R. (1988). Racial ambivalence and American value conflict. *Journal of Personality and Social Psychology, 55,* 893–905.

Kitayama, S., Markus, H., Matsumoto, H., & Norasakkunkit, V. (1997). Individual and collective proccesses in the construction of the self: Self-enhancement in the United States and self-criticism in Japan. *Journal of Personality and Social Psychology, 72,* 1245–1267.

Kowalski, R. M., & Wolfe, R. (1994). Collective identity orientation, patriotism and reactions to national outcomes. *Personality and Social Psychology Bulletin, 20,* 533–540.

Kuehen, U., & Oyserman, D. (in press). Does the interdependent self have a better memory than the independent self? Influences of salient self-focus on cognitive processes. *Journal of Experimental Social Psychology.*

LaFromboise, T., Coleman, H., & Gerton, J. (1993). Psychological impact of biculturalism: Evidence and theory. *Psychological Bulletin, 114,* 395–412.

Latanâe, B., & Darley, J. (1970). *The unresponsive bystander: Why doesn't he help?* New York: Appleton-Century-Crofts.

Lee, S. J. (1994). Behind the model-minority stereotype: Voices of high- and low-achieving Asian American students. *Anthropology and Education Quarterly, 25,* 413–429.

Leung, K. (1997). Negotiation and reward allocations across cultures. In P. C. Earley & M. Erez (Eds.), *New perspectives on international industrial/organizational psychology.* San Francisco: Jossey-Bass.

Lewin, K. (1935). *A dynamic theory of personality.* New York: McGraw-Hill.

Liberman, K. (1986). The Tibetan cultural praxis: Brodhicitta thought training. *Humboldt Journal of Social Relations, 13,* 113–126.

Light, I. (1994). Ethnic enterprise in America: Japanese, Chinese, and Blacks. In R. Takaki (Ed.), *From different shores: Perspectives on race and ethnicity in America* (2nd ed., pp. 82–92). New York: Oxford University Press.

Lofand, J. (1992). Collective behavior: The elementary forms. In M. Rosenberg & R. Turner (Eds.), *Social psychology: Sociological perspectives* (pp. 411–446). New Brunswick, NJ: Transaction.

Markus, H., & Kitayama, S. (1991). Culture and the self: Implications for cognition, emotion and motivation. *Psychological Review, 98,* 224–253.

Markus, H., & Kitayama, S. (1994). The cultural construction of self and emotion: Implications for social behavior. In S. Kitayama & H. Markus (Eds.), *Emotion and culture: Empirical studies of mutual influence* (pp 89–130). Washington, DC: American Psychological Association.

Markus, H., Mullally, P., & Kitayama, S. (1997). Selfways: Diversity in modes of cultural participation. In U. Neisser & D. Jopling (Eds.), *The conceptual self in context,* pp. 13–61. New York: Cambridge University Press.

Marris, M. R. (1987). *The Holocaust in history.* New York: Meridian.

Mays, V., Bullock, M., Rosenzweig, M., & Wessells, M. (1998) Ethnic conflict: Global challenges and psychological perspectives. *American Psychologist, 53,* 737–742.

McAdam, D., McCarthy, J., & Zald, M. (1988). Social movements. In N. Smelser (Ed.), *Handbook of sociology* (pp. 695–737). Newbury Park, CA: Sage.

Mead, G. H. (1934). *Mind, self and society.* New York: Free Press.

Mesquita B., & Oyserman, D. (1996). Bosnian women: Coping with the war. *International Journal of Psychology, 31,* 2784–2784.

Morris, M. (1998, August). Untitled presentation. Stanford Conference on Culture and Cognition. Stanford, CA.

Morris, M., & Peng, K. (1994). Culture and cause: American and Chinese attributions for social and physical events. *Journal of Personality and Social Psychology, 67,* 949–971.

Nisbett, R. E., & Ross, L. (1980). *Human inference: Strategies and shortcomings of social judgment.* Englewood Cliffs, NJ: Prentice-Hall.

Oyserman, D. (1992). Conflict and democracy in action. *Small Group Research, 23,* 259–277.

Oyserman, D. (1993). The lens of personhood: Viewing the self, others and conflict in a multicultural society. *Journal of Personality and Social Psychology, 65,* 993–1009.

Oyserman, D., Coon, H., & Kemmelmeier, M. (2002). Rethinking individualism and collectivism: Evaluation of theoretical assumptions and meta-analysis. *Psychological Bulletin, 128,* 3–73.

Oyserman, D., Gant, L., & Ager, J. (1995). A socially contextualized model of African American identity: School persistence and possible selves. *Journal of Personality and Social Psychology, 69,* 1216–1232.

Oyserman, D., & Markus, H. (1993). The sociocultural self. In J. Suls & A. Pratkanis (Eds.), *Psychological perspectives on the self* (Vol. 4, pp. 187–220). Hillsdale, NJ: Erlbaum.

Oyserman, D., & Markus, H. (1998). The self as social representation. In U. Flick (Ed.), *The psychology of the social,* pp. 107–125. New York: Cambridge University Press.

Oyserman, D., & Sakamoto, I. (1998). Being Asian American: Identity, cultural constructs, and stereotype perception. *Journal of Applied Behavioral Science, 33,* 433–451.

Oyserman, D., Sakamoto, I., & Lauffer, A. (1998). Cultural accommodation: Hybridity and the framing of social obligation. *Journal of Personality and Social Psychology, 74,* 1606–1618.

Phinney, J. (1996) When we talk about American ethnic groups, what do we mean? *American Psychologist, 51,* 918–927.

Phinney, J., & Cobb, N. (1996). Reasoning about intergroup relations among Hispanic and Euro-American Adolescents. *Journal of Adolescent Research, 11,* 306–324.

Piliavin, J., & Libby, D. (1986). Personal norms, perceived social norms, and blood donation. *Humboldt Journal of Social Relations, 13,* 159–194.

Pinel, E., & Swann, W. (2000). Finding the self through others: Self-verification and social movement participation. In S. Stryker, T. Owens, & R. White (Eds.), *Self, identity and social movements* (pp. 132–152). Minneapolis: University of Minnesota Press.

Roberts, J., Spencer, J., & Uyangoda, J. (1998). Sri Lanka: Political violence and ethnic conflict. *American Psychologist, 53,* 778–792.

Rosenberger, N. (1992). *Japanese sense of self.* New York: Cambridge University Press.

Rosenberger, N. (Ed.). (1994). *Japanese sense of self.* New York: Cambridge University Press

Rouhana, N., & Bar-Tal, D. (1998). Psychological dynamics of intractable ethnonational conflicts: The Israeli-Palestinian case. *American Psychologist, 53,* 761–770.

Rummel, R. J. (1994). Democide in totalitarian states: Mortacracies and mega-murderers. In I. W. Charney (Ed.), *Widening circle of genocide* (pp. 3–39). New Brunswick, NJ: Translation.

Sampson, E. (1988). The debate on individualism: Indigenous psychologies of the individual and their role in personal and societal functions. *American Psychologist, 43,* 15–22.

Sanchez-Burkes, J., Oyserman, D., & Kemmelmeier, M. (1998). *The working cultural self.* Unpublished manuscript. Ann Arbor, MI: The University of Michigan.

Schwartz, S. (1990). Individualism collectivism: Critique and proposed refinements. *Journal of Cross-Cultural Psychology, 21,* 139–157.

Schwartz, S. (1992). Universals in the content and structure of values: Theoretical advances and empirical tests in 20 countries. *Advances in Experimental Social Psychology, 25,* 1–66.

Schwartz, S. (1994). Beyond individualism/collectivism: New cultural dimensions of values. In H. Triandis (Ed.), *Individualism and collectivism: Theory, method and application,* pp. 85–119. Thousand Oaks, CA: Sage.

Schwartz, S. (1996). Value priorities and behavior: Applying a theory of integrated value systems. *The psychology of values: The Ontario symposium* (Vol. 8, pp. 1–24). Hillsdale, NJ: Erlbaum.

Sears, D. (1987). Political psychology. *Annual Review of Psychology, 38,* 229–255.

Shweder, R. (1991). *Thinking through cultures.* Cambridge, MA.: Harvard University Press.

Shweder, R., & Bourne, E. (1984). Does the concept of the person vary cross-culturally? In R. Shweder & R. LaVine (Eds.), *Culture theory: Essays on mind, self, and emotion* (pp. 158–199). New York: Cambridge University Press.

Shweder, R. A., & Sullivan, M. A. (1990). The seminotic subject of cultural psychology. In L. Pervin (Ed.), *Handbook of personality theory and research* (pp. 399–418). New York: Guilford.

Singelis, T. (1994). The measurement of independent and interdependent self-construals. *Personality and Social Psychology Bulletin, 20,* 580–591.

Smith, D. (1998). The psychocultural roots of genocide: Legitimacy and crisis in Rwanda. *American Psychologist, 53,* 743–753.

Sullivan, J., & Transue, J. (1999). The psychological underpinnings of democracy. *Annual Review of Psychology, 50,* 625–650.

Takaki, R. (Ed.). (1994). *From different shores: Perspectives on race and ethnicity in America* (2nd ed.). New York: Oxford University Press.

Taylor, D., & Dube, L. (1986). Two faces of identity: The "I" and the "we." *Journal of Social Issues, 42,* 81–98.

Trafimow, D., Triandis, H., & Goto, S. (1991). Some tests of the distinction between the private self and the collective self. *Journal of Personality and Social Psychology, 60,* 649–655.

Triandis, H. C. (1989). The self and social behavior in differing cultural contexts. *Psychological Review, 93,* 506–520.

Triandis, H. C. (1995). *Individualism and collectivism.* Boulder, CO: Westview.

Triandis, H. (1996, August). *Consequences of individualism and collectivism.* Paper presented at the Consequences of Cultures Consequences Symposium, 26th International Psychology Congress, Montreal.

Tropman, J. E. (1988). *American values and social welfare: Cultural contradictions in the welfare state.* Englewood Cliffs, NJ: Prentice Hall.

Turner, J. C., Hogg, M. A., Oakes, P. J., Reicher, S. D., & Wetherell, S. M. (1987). *Rediscovering the social group: A self-categorization theory*. Oxford: Blackwell.

Wehler, H. U. (1998). Like a thorn in the flesh. In R. R. Shandley (Ed.), *Unwilling Germans? The Goldhagen debate*, pp. 93–104. Minneapolis: University of Minnesota Press.

White, R., & Frasier, M. (2000). Personal and collective identities and long-term social movement activism: Republican Sinn Fein. In S. Stryker, T. Owens, & R. White (Eds.), *Self, identity, and social movements*. Minneapolis: University of Minnesota Press.

Wilkinson, R. (Ed.). (1992). *American social character*. New York: HarperCollins.

Zurcher, L., & Snow, D. (1992). Collective behavior: Social movements. In M. Rosenberg & R. Turner (Eds.), *Social psychology: Sociological perspectives* (pp. 447–482). New Brunswick, NJ: Transaction.

8

Population and Perpetrators

Preconditions for the Holocaust From a
Control-Theoretical Perspective

Dieter Frey and Helmut Rez

The Holocaust did not begin in the gas chambers of Belzec, Sobibór,
Auschwitz, Maidanek, Chelmno, or Treblinka. The foundations for this genocide were laid years before by a successful political movement eager to implement its anti-Semitic program and by a population that, for a number of
reasons, widely accepted and approved of the regime. Consequently, the
question "How could the Holocaust have happened?" needs to be preceded
by the questions, Why Hitler? Why in Germany? and Why did he find supporters and helpers?

In this chapter we want to explain these preconditions, the basis for the
Holocaust, in a systematic framework by applying the social-psychological
model of *cognitive control*, which appears to be highly suitable for analyzing
the psychological conditions that authoritarian regimes need in order to assume power in general (see also Arendt, 1951). Moreover, we believe that
this theory presents essential insights into the causes of the Nazi movement,
as well as the motivational structure of the Holocaust perpetrators.

One fundamental methodological question remains: whether social psychology can explain complex historical events. Are theories based on intraindividual and inter-individual processes applicable to social groups and
nations as a whole?

Of course historical phenomena are never repeated in identical patterns.
But social and thus historical events do display certain regularities; we can
specify conditions that make the occurrence of riots, uprisings, revolutions,
and so forth more or less likely. Moreover, theories that are inferred from the
behavior of individuals can be transferred to a group or national level insofar
as the individuals face similar external stimuli or historical events and, in

addition, share common patterns of perceiving the outside world, as well as a common system of values. We will demonstrate that these conditions for aggregation were fulfilled in the context of the Third Reich by analyzing different social groups, their principal needs and values, their susceptibility to a loss of control, and the similar ways in which they generally reacted to a loss of control, dealing with this threat. Finally, we will identify various types of immediate perpetrators and briefly apply the control theoretical framework.

THEORETICAL FRAMEWORK FOR EXPLAINING THE CAUSES OF THE NAZI MOVEMENT: COGNITIVE CONTROL THEORY

As Skinner (1996) emphasizes, there is genuine confusion over the concept of control. And there are more than 100 different interpretations and concepts of control (see Frey, Stahlberg, Schulz-Hardt, & Jonas, 2002; Osnarügge, Stahlberg, & Frey, 1985; Seligman, 1975; Skinner, 1996; Wortman & Brehm, 1975). "In general, control refers to the extent to which an agent can intentionally produce desired outcomes and prevent undesired ones. When individuals believe they can do this, they are said to have personal control, perceived control, or a sense of control" (Skinner, 1996, p. 554).

Osnabrügge et al. (1985) and Frey et al. (2002) have formulated a broader concept of control theory than that given by Skinner (1996). According to this definition of control, the concepts of explainability, predictabilty, and influenceability play an important role. Moreover, this control model describes the conditions that are necessary for control and its benefits and emphasizes the dynamic aspect of striving for control, the consequences of losing control, and the motivation for regaining control. The theoretical assumptions underlying this model are as follows (see Fig. 8.1).

The Key Concept of Cognitive Control

People have a need to attain positive and to avoid or reduce negative outcomes (end-states).[1] To achieve this, as our theory proposes, they strive for explainability, predictability, and influenceability whenever possible and when doing so has an *adaptive function*. For example, when the probability of being able to avoid or reduce negative events and thus aversive stressors such as noise, illness, or unemployment (see Glass & Singer, 1972) is low, the striving for influenceability decreases. Also, as regards predictability, people do not want to predict their own death if they are unable to influence and change it. Finally, explainability may be avoided when the results are seen as too threatening.

Influenceability also means that one has the option of choosing between certain actions and behavioral alternatives, as, for example, reactance theory implies (Wortman & Brehm, 1975). The ability to explain cause-effect relationships, as well as to predict the further course of positive and negative events, is a prerequisite for having an experience of control in terms of influenceability.

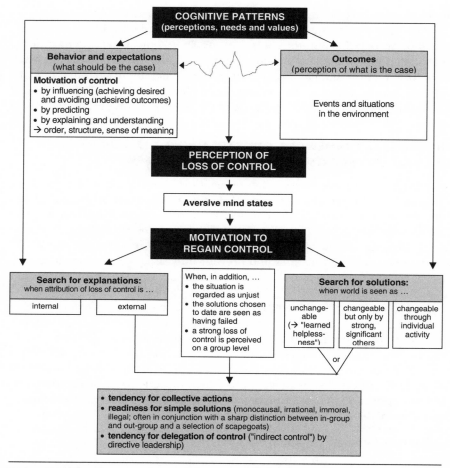

Figure 8.1 The theory of cognitive control: losing and regaining control.

"In other words, a sense of control includes a view of the self as competent and efficacious and a view of the world as structured and responsive (Bandura, 1977; Gurin & Brim, 1984; Weisz, 1986)" (Skinner, 1996, p. 559).

The Positive Consequences of Control

Research by Glass and Singer (1972) shows that when subjects are exposed to aversive stimulation with noise, those who can either predict or influence this noise display better aftereffects, that is, higher frustration tolerance and better performance in achievement tests than subjects who can neither predict nor influence the noise. Objective stressors are comparatively irrelevant when they can be predicted and influenced. Taylor's research on breast cancer shows that the reaction to this type of cancer, which can be viewed as a loss of health, is influenced by three dimensions, which Taylor calls "control categories," namely, meaning, challenge, and self-esteem. The more a woman with breast cancer has a meaning for this illness, the more she regards the illness as a challenge for survival, and the greater her self-esteem, the better her physical well-being, and the stronger her immune system (Taylor, 1983; Taylor, Buunk, Collins, & Reed, 1992; Taylor, Lichtman, & Wood, 1984). This research shows that coping processes are more effective when control cognitions exist or when there is an illusion of being in control of or coping with a negative event. Also Skinner (1996) emphasizes that

> both experimental and correlational studies have shown that across the life span, from earliest infancy to oldest age, individual differences in perceived control are related to a variety of positive outcomes, including health, achievement, optimism, persistence, motivation, coping, self-esteem, personal adjustment, and success and failure in a variety of life domains. So, the research documents that control is important to psychological functioning, and that it is a robust predictor of physical and mental well-being. (p. 549)

The fundamental human motivation to engage in effective interactions with the environment has been referred to as *effectance motivation* (White, 1959), *mastery motivation* (Harter, 1978), or *the need for competence* (Connell & Wellborn, 1991; Deci & Ryan, 1985; Skinner, 1991, 1995).

Individual Versus Collective Control

Most of the approaches to control emphasize that they are modeling individuals and that they want to explain and predict individual behavior. However, both Skinner and Bandura argue that "the control concept can also be applied on the collective level": "Because research has so often focused on personal control, some writers have mistakenly assumed that constructs of control are necessarily individualistic in nature (Schooler, 1990). However, researchers have also studied perceptions of the effectiveness of groups of people, for example, in collective efficacy (Bandura, 1993)" (Skinner, 1996, p. 554).

A central point about our formulation is that the control aspect can be applied on the individual as well as on the group or even national level. The necessary conditions for this are the following: the single individuals (a) live in the same situation, (b) have the same experiences, and (c) interpret the situation in the same way.[2]

Loss of Control

A loss of control occurs when people (a) cannot achieve expected positive end states, or (b) cannot avoid negative end states, or (c) cannot reduce the adverse consequences of such negative events. This implies a lack of contingency between behavior and outcomes; whatever a person does, it has no predictable effect. Seligman (1975) describes this state as one of learned helplessness. Loss of control also exists when important past events cannot be explained and interpreted in a meaningful way.

A loss of control is seen as an aversive state having motivational properties, and consequently people try to regain control. Very often, severe losses in terms of outcomes—such as the loss of a partner, loss of money, loss of body parts, illness, or dramatic experiences—are also connected with a loss of control (because of a lack of explainability, predictability, and influenceability, or behavior/outcomes noncontingency). The aversive state produced by an actual loss (which only indirectly has something to do with a loss of control) increases the aversive state because it is added to the loss of control. This means that there are two sources of aversive stimulation: the noncontingency and the actual loss of outcomes.

The Importance of Perceptions, Needs, and Values (Cognitive Patterns)

The intensity of control and of a loss of control depends on the specific system of perceptions, needs, and values (cognitive patterns). This system reflects the habitual patterns with which an individual or a group approaches and structures the "world." Examples are the importance of security, law, order, employment, peace, nature, God, and so on. The degree of importance differs from era to era, from nation to nation, and from culture to culture. These patterns predispose an individual—and under the conditions described here also collective entities—to perceive his or her world in a certain way, as well as to act upon his or her environment. For example, especially in a nation where order and stability are prevalent needs and values, political instability, social disorder, and chaos resulting from terrorism, economic depression, and downward mobility will result in a loss of control on the level of most individuals and thus on a societal level.

Reactions to a Loss of Control

Loss of control is seen as aversive, producing a motivation to regain control and thereby triggering a number of reactions: attempts to find (subjectively) plausible interpretations and causes and strategies for regaining control. The reactions are closely related to the perceptions, values, and needs of the individual or group in question and depend (a) on the intensity of the perceived loss, (b) on the causes as seen by the individual or the group (internal or external), and (c) on the consequences of this state, that is, whether or not the future consequences are seen as being changeable.

In line with the integration of the theory of reactance and the theory of learned helplessness (Wortman and Brehm, 1975), we argue that when people have *repeatedly* experienced noncontingency between behavior and outcomes, they resign and do not fight anymore. There is a feeling of helplessness, and they withdraw, escape, or otherwise become passive. This type of reaction as the result of prolonged exposure to noncontingency has been referred to as *learned helplessness* (Abramson, Seligman, & Teasdale, 1978).

When loss of control is *attributed internally* (lack of effort, talent, etc.), individual strategies for regaining control can be expected. People will either increase their effort, try to increase their talent, or, when they fail again, begin self-punitive behavior such as alcohol or drug abuse or even suicide. When, on the other hand, loss of control is *attributed externally* (lack of competence on the part of the government, the ineffectiveness of the political or economic system, and so on), collective rather than individual actions can be expected. This will be the case especially when the loss of control is perceived as being completely unjust and when no solutions are seen to overcome the loss of control. There is a great deal of evidence suggesting that when the causes are interpreted as being internal, this has stronger consequences for self-esteem (Abramson et al., 1978), whereas when they are attributed externally, there is a greater likelihood of anger directed at the person or persons to whom they are attributed.

Tendency for Collective Action

Collective action with a motivation for social change can be found under specific conditions (see Frey & Jonas, 1999): (a) when there is a perception of a loss of control (relatively strong deprivation), at least on the group level, (b) when the loss of control is attributed externally, (c) when the situation is seen as being unjust and when the loss of control can be overcome only by means of collective action, and (d) when other solutions chosen to date have failed.

To change the status quo (of one's loss of control), it is necessary for the existing order to be challenged by a new program or a new party or a new leader, and for these aspects to be better than the status quo.[3]

Readiness for Simple Solutions to Regain Control

The greater the loss of control and the greater the pessimism that strategies applied in the past will not be successful in regaining control, the greater the willingness of groups and individuals to agree with new, simple, monocausal, irrational, and emotional explanations for the causes of the loss of control. Simultaneously, immoral and illegal strategies and/or violent modes of action are increasingly accepted as means for regaining control. Staub (1989) argues that aversive and threatening conditions—when people are threatened concerning basic human needs, such as the need for security, for control, for positive identity—often generate a yearning for simple solutions and for ideologies that provide easy recipes and methods for ending the aversive stress situation (and, thereby, strengthening people's self-esteem).

Also, the more a group or nation perceives a loss of control, the lower its tolerance toward out-groups becomes, and the more out-groups are seen as being threatening (Staub, 1989). A sharp distinction between in-groups ("us") and out-groups ("them") arises, in order to strengthen psychological and social identity. The likelihood increases that scapegoats will be chosen and blamed for the loss of control. The aim of regaining control becomes a higher priority than the aim of behaving in accordance with moral values (the end justifies the means).

According to Staub (1989), the Nazi propaganda incriminated the Jewish population and claimed it was to blame for the economic depression in Germany after World War I. Consequently, this ethnic minority was segregated from the "German" population and gradually perceived as being some kind of "subhuman."

Dehumanization and segregation of the victims prepare the ground for a change in moral attitudes: The moral judgment constantly approaches different, less rigorous norms and rules (cf. Opotow, 1990, who debates the issue of "moral exclusion"; and Bandura, 1999, who focuses on the effects of "moral disengagement").

Delegation of Control

Regaining control can be achieved not only through personal activity but also by delegation to strong, significant others. There is a tendency to delegate regaining control to a strong leader who can restore control—a strategy of indirect control (see Glass & Singer, 1972). Because the problem is too complex and unstructured, directive leadership is preferred. The greater the loss of control and the more the loss of control is attributed externally, the more likely it is that political leaders will be elected who have the simplest, most emotional, and probably most radical strategies for a solution.

APPLICATION OF THE THEORY TO THE NAZI MOVEMENT

Control theory as applied to the Nazi movement identifies three components leading to the rise and endorsement of the Third Reich as a precondition for the Holocaust (see Fig. 8.2). First, a substantial *loss of control* was perceived by large sections of the German population during the Weimar Republic because of a number of *crises* in key areas. These areas range from national identity (defeat in World War I, the "disgraceful" Treaty of Versailles), the economic system (hyperinflation, economic depression, unemployment), and the political system (unstable governments, a widely despised constitutional system)

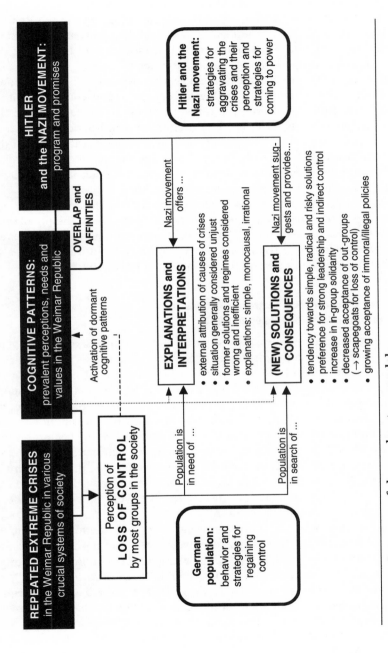

Figure 8.2 Structure of the explanatory model.

to the general social, legal, and cultural system (continuous social unrest, political crimes, "chaos," and a loss of traditional values during the Roaring Twenties). While crises like these would have produced instability in many countries, the situation in Germany was even more severe because of the specific predominant perceptions, values, and needs.

Second, these culture-specific *cognitive patterns*—such as extreme national pride, a deep-rooted preference for hierarchical structures combined with a longing for discipline and order, antimodernism—severely aggravated the widespread *perception* of loss of control. Other values—anti-Semitism and anti-Communism—contributed to a specific *attribution* as far as the causes of the crises were concerned. Not only certain individuals or representatives felt a loss of control, but many people who were in the situation interpreted the situation similarly and had contact with one another.

Third, the Nazi movement presented "explanations" of the crises and promised "solutions" that were accepted by increasing portions of the population as *the* way to *regain control*. After Hitler's legal "assumption of power," he not only occupied vital positions in the country but, by using the mass media, also succeeded in conveying the impression of actually reestablishing control in key areas.

Loss of Control: The Extreme Crises in the Weimar Republic (1919–1933)

The Weimar Republic—especially during the first and the last four years of its existence—can be described from the perspective of many social groups as a period of instability and disorder in various crucial systems of society (see Fig. 8.3). Germany had lost World War I; and in 1919, the Treaty of Versailles forced it to pay high reparations, to give up nearly a quarter of its former territory, and to take the blame for having instigated the war. In addition to this national humiliation, there were severe economic crises at the beginning and especially toward the end of the Weimar Republic: high national debts; extreme inflation; economic depression and high unemployment; poverty; hunger; and the downward mobility of soldiers, aristocrats, industrialists and the bourgeoisie, owners of small businesses, and the working class. All social groups suffered economic losses in the years after 1929.

Moreover, the Weimar Republic was characterized by permanent political instability. Because the Reichschancellor very often had no majority in the Reichstag and numerous elections did not change the situation, many groups in society felt that there was much less stability than in former times. The parliamentary system as a whole was not viewed by the majority of citizens as being a German institution but rather as having been forced upon them by foreign countries. There was no identification with the Weimar Republic and its political constitution, causing Germany's national identity to suffer in many sections of the population.

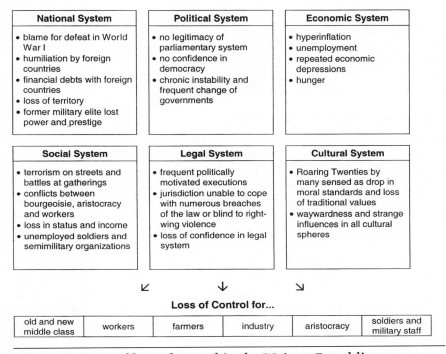

National System	Political System	Economic System
• blame for defeat in World War I • humiliation by foreign countries • financial debts with foreign countries • loss of territory • former military elite lost power and prestige	• no legitimacy of parliamentary system • no confidence in democracy • chronic instability and frequent change of governments	• hyperinflation • unemployment • repeated economic depressions • hunger

Social System	Legal System	Cultural System
• terrorism on streets and battles at gatherings • conflicts between bourgeoisie, aristocracy and workers • loss in status and income • unemployed soldiers and semimilitary organizations	• frequent politically motivated executions • jurisdiction unable to cope with numerous breaches of the law or blind to right-wing violence • loss of confidence in legal system	• Roaring Twenties by many sensed as drop in moral standards and loss of traditional values • waywardness and strange influences in all cultural spheres

Loss of Control for...

old and new middle class	workers	farmers	industry	aristocracy	soldiers and military staff

Figure 8.3 Areas of loss of control in the Weimar Republic.

In addition to all of this, there was a great deal of social disorder, especially before 1924 and after 1929: terrorism and street battles between Communists and Nazis, as well as the assassination of politicians and economists. The social system suffered from relative social deprivation, that is, loss in status and income and increasing impoverishment.

Frequent, politically motivated executions and a jurisdiction that was unable to cope adequately with the enormous number of breaches of the law or, often, that was blind to acts of violence committed by right-wing followers caused a loss of confidence in the legal system. Finally the cultural system: Berlin was perhaps the world capital of cultural renewal in the 1920s. But in Germany these Roaring Twenties and the policy of openness were appreciated only by a minority (see Gay, 1968); the majority, instead, sensed a drop in moral standards and a cultural waywardness (so "obvious" in the cultural sphere, in literature, in the fine arts, in theater, in the entertainment industry). Consequently, large sections of the population suffered a sense of a loss of control, as they felt their old system of values to be going downhill.

And even more important, the experience after 1929 marked a *repetition* of loss of control. Following the first chain of crises up until 1923, extreme economic, social, and political breakdowns were now occurring all over again. The repetition thoroughly and definitely destroyed the thin cushion of mental stability and confidence that might have been established in the brief period of recovery during the mid-1920s.

The Underlying Cognitive Patterns

Certainly, the Weimar Republic produced a loss of control in almost all groups of society on account of its chaos and unpredictability; however, this alone was not enough to make possible the Nazis' rise to power. It could be argued that other European countries also experienced a similar kind of objective loss of control as a result of political, social, and economic instability. What is important, though, is the fact that the crises and the chaos of Weimar were perceived more aversively by the German population than in other European countries because of the *specific cognitive patterns*. We call this a syndrome of existing cognitive patterns. Like each person, each group or nation also has its past, its collective memory. Some of these patterns may be dormant; others are aroused. In Moscovici's (1981) terms, these are social representations, that is, definitions of the situation (including what is necessary, desirable, etc.). Each cognitive pattern is associated with clear perceptions, beliefs, expectations, aspirations, and behavioral dispositions.

In this sense, most social and political groups in Germany shared a number of cognitive patterns. The following principal and widespread cognitive patterns may be identified (see Craig, 1982; Dahrendorf, 1971; Fromm, 1983; Gay, 1968; Kershaw, 1980; Mosse, 1987; Sontheimer, 1978; Strauss & Kampe, 1984):

1. ethnic nationalism, as well as antimodernism (the concept of a national superiority; the concept of an ethnic public feeling; efforts at "restoration," for example, concerning the role of women);
2. racial-biological anti-Semitism;
3. the unpolitical and undemocratic character of large segments of the German population (e.g., antiliberal orientation, a certain political apathy, law-and-order style of thinking, a weak understanding of democracy);
4. obedience and subordination as central values of the German establishment and the German educational system;
5. order, rules, perfection, and technocratic efficiency as central values of German culture;
6. comparatively high readiness to accept acts of violence as a means of solving conflicts (brutalization during World War I).

A central hypothesis is that specific situations arouse specific needs and values, that is, they make specific cognitive patterns salient. In addition, the salient patterns determine how aversive a certain situation is interpreted. For example, when there are no street fights, the values of law and order may be dormant. However, when chronic street battles take place between social groups, such values become salient, and with them the desire for a strong leadership to suppress all forms of street fighting.

Regaining Control: Hitler and the Nazi Movement as a Program That Matched the Prevalent Cognitive Patterns

Even today, Hitler's rise, World War II, and the Holocaust are often reduced to either the phenomenon of Hitler and his Nazi Party or, alternatively, to a "special German way" (*Sonderweg*), that is, to a historical process that established absolutely "unique" German perceptions, values, and needs. This is a profound misunderstanding. One of the most important hypotheses of this chapter is that only the interplay of (a) extreme and repeated crises faced by a population with (b) a particular constellation of prevalent cognitive patterns (which together leads to a loss of control) and (c) a political movement with corresponding promises, strategies, and policies could bring about these effects.

Of course, Hitler was not aware of control theory and its implications, and, of course, he and the Nazi movement did not consciously apply strategies in order to reestablish control for the large sections of the German population. However, the Nazi promises, strategies, and policies, in many regards, had the actual effect of reestablishing control because they corresponded to the prevalent cognitive patterns in Germany and to the needs arising from the loss of control.

This loss of control had produced human helplessness and hopelessness, and people felt that it was difficult to regain control by means of individual or collective efforts. Hitler was seen by many as being an exception: Many people and groups felt that he was capable of regaining control and giving hope. His program presented a clear interpretation of the causes, as well as the solutions, to the loss of control; and this interpretation fitted the already existing perceptions and values better than any of the other programs (see Fig. 8.4).

The communicator (Hitler), his communication (ideology), and his media (mass communication by radio, uniform press media) are only one side. On the other side are the receptors of the communication. To be successful, a communication must fit the existing needs and values already present in the receptors, or at least in a majority of them. The communication must meet with a "latitude of acceptance." And this was the most creative act of Hitler's party and propaganda: to define their message in such a way as to fit the value systems, the human needs of the citizens and the relevant sectors in the society (industry, workers, church, science, military, aristocracy, etc.).

Prevalent Cognitive Patterns in the Weimar Republic		Hitler's Program and Promises
German obedience and preference for hierarchical structures	⇔	Weimar has no authority; Nazis will bring back respect for authority
Discipline and preference for law and order	⇔	Nazis will bring back order and discipline
Antimodernism and respect for traditional values	⇔	Weimar has lost and destroyed traditional values; Nazis will restore them
(Racial-biological) anti-Semitism	⇔	Jews are responsible for the crises and do not belong to the German people; Nazis will punish and remove them
Widespread xenophobia	⇔	Foreign countries and "elements" try to suppress Germany; Nazis will fight them
German nationalism and superiority (*Herrenrasse*)	⇔	Nazis will bring Germany back where it deserves to be: a superpower in Europe
Antiliberalism	⇔	Parliamentary democracy is not able to solve the problems; a strong leader is needed
Anti-Marxism	⇔	Nazis will be a buffer against communism
Rejection of "exploitative" capitalism	⇔	Nazis are a "workers' party" and will fight for the interests of the lower classes
Tendency for technocratic efficiency and modern technologies	⇔	Nazis favor and apply modern technologies

Some of the above cognitive patterns were special to Germany. Some of these patterns were activated by the various crises and so increased the *perceived* loss of control	Hitler's eclectic program fitted the already existing cognitive patterns

Figure 8.4 The match between prevalent cognitive patterns in the Weimar Republic and Hitler's program and promises.

People had different motivations for being favorably disposed toward Hitler. There was not one single, universal motive because the areas of loss of control were heterogeneous. The aristocracy and industry had quite different motives for supporting him than did owners of small businesses or workers. The Nazis' program displayed a great deal of eclecticism. Actually, there was no closed program at all; instead, the Nazi Party represented a dynamic movement, steadily changing its structure. Hitler's eclectic program made it possible for somewhat heterogeneous isolated groups and individuals to back the movement. However, behind all this heterogeneity stood the common perception of a loss of control and the hope that Hitler—and only Hitler—would be able to regain this control for each individual group.

Hitler's program, with all its peculiarities and contradictions, did match the existing needs and longings of the German population very well because these needs and longings reflected the extreme disunity, inner conflict, and disorientation of the people. For example, the program included both restoration *and* revolution (this amalgam being called "conservative revolution"), both old *and* new items on the agenda, both continuity *and* a break, both anticapitalist *and* anti-Communist trends, both official legal orientation (at least from 1929 onward) *and* the assassination of opponents, both a leveling down to a national body and character *and* an extremely hierarchic and authoritarian system, both extreme antimodernism *and*, at the same time, technological enthusiasm, both the Nazi Party as a political party *and*, at the same time, something different (a "movement"), and so on. By mixing such diverse, old and new elements, the Nazi program achieved identification and trust, on the one hand (generated by the well-known elements), and hope, euphoria, and activism, on the other (aroused by the promising new elements).

Regaining Control: Hitler's Promises and Actions

Until 1933, and especially in the 1920s, Hitler acted as the "speaker and pitchman" of the Nazi movement; he and his supporters aggravated the crises and their perception and offered specific interpretations:

- In his speeches, Hitler endlessly dwelled upon the subjects of crisis, turmoil, and impoverishment.
- At the same time, the Nazis deliberately intensified the existing crises and chaos; for example, the most extreme supporters of the Nazi movement, the *Sturmabteilung* (SA, "Stormtroopers"), initiated battles on streets and at gatherings and committed numerous crimes.
- Hitler and his supporters increased the gap between in-group and out-groups by agitating the concept of a racial national group identity and, correspondingly, of *Volksfeinde* (enemies of the German people) such as Jews, Bolsheviks, and the "November criminals" (politicians who had allegedly betrayed the German people in November 1918).
- The causes of the crises were sought outside (external attribution); the *Volksfeinde* and foreign countries were blamed for the misery and chaos.
- Certain (ethnic) minorities, especially Jews, were scapegoated; this monocausal attribution led to a considerable relief in the population because the "solution" seemed to be so simple and easy to attain.

201

After coming to power legally, Hitler embarked upon different strategies that had the effect of reestablishing control in the eyes of most people: (a) Hitler optimized the already existing organization of the Nazi movement and its appeal to many people; simultaneously, the power groups in the country were dissolved or "adapted," and real and potential opposition to these actions and the Nazi government was systematically oppressed; (b) in the various systems that had suffered a loss of control, his actions left the impression that control was soon regained; and (c) he intensified the concept of scapegoats and increasingly attributed present and future threats to Jews, Bolsheviks, and so on.

Institutionalization of Power

THE ORGANIZATION OF THE NAZI MOVEMENT. The organization of the Nazi movement was made increasingly efficient. The main elements were the person (Hitler as the charismatic leader), the organization (the National Socialist German Workers' Party [NSDAP]), the message (the program of this party), and the means to bring this message across (mass propaganda, symbols, mass demonstrations).

Before the Nazis came to power, Hitler and his party, founded in 1919, had suffered numerous failures and setbacks. Their eventual success is understandable in terms of Moscovici's (1980) theory of minority influence. According to Moscovici (1976), a minority—such as the Nazis in their early years—can be successful only when it actively attempts to persuade others of the correctness of its own position, standing firm, committed, self-confident, and unwavering. A minority has to present a clear position on the issue at hand and adhere to it firmly throughout, withstanding the pressures exerted by the majority. The most important component of this style of behavior is the consistency with which the minority defends and advocates its position. This is exactly what the Nazi Party did. Moreover, the party program emphasized a social identity, a promise of personal and national prosperity manifesting Germanic superiority as well as Jewish inferiority.

The mass media contained the necessary technical facilities for disseminating the ideas of the program, and the Nazis made systematic use of the media. Simultaneously, Hitler was able to create a "corporate identity" for his movement, often by borrowing ideas from religion, by means of uniforms, flags, songs, torches, special music, and, of course, the swastika. Finally, he managed to organize his members and sympathizers in mass demonstrations. Here they came into direct contact with the leader, the symbols, the music, and so on. Such situations of togetherness with like-minded others produce a strong sense of solidarity with the organization and in-group, and something like a mental contagion occurs.[4]

THE REORGANIZATION OF PRINCIPAL INSTITUTIONS ("GLEICHSCHAL-TUNG"). Hitler quickly institutionalized his power by replacing the top leaders of important social groups and by changing their politics to come in line with the new regime. Nearly every organization in society was connected with and subordinated to the new movement. Together with the symbols and the ideology of the Nazi movement, a sense of community and solidarity was created, along with a strong identification with the new semiromantic movement, which gave everybody (except for outsiders) a place in the country. The identification with the Nazi regime was so strong that very often young children informed the Nazis about their parents' "wrong" system of beliefs.

At the same time, all real and potential resistance toward the regime was soon suppressed. Members of the political opposition, as well as members within the Nazi Party itself who were skeptical of Hitler's politics, were eliminated. At an early point, a full protest by the legal system or a full-scale social uprising by the population could have stood in Hitler's way. However, this did not happen, not only because of people's fears about the consequences of such actions but also because most Germans were not motivated, since they were too enthusiastic about Hitler's success and blind toward some of the negative aspects of his politics. The combination of terror and intimidation, on the one hand, and the "beautiful make-belief of the Third Reich," on the other (see Reichel, 1993), led them to a willing adaptation and acceptance.

Regaining Control in the Various Social Spheres

After 1933, Hitler was increasingly viewed by numerous countrymen as "Germany's rescuer": the man who had reestablished order, national pride, and the prospect of prosperity. In other words, the population perceived Hitler as actually capable of regaining control in virtually all the fields where it had appeared to be lost before.

Hitler tried from the start to improve Germany's economic situation. This strategy allowed him to give people a sense of material security while at the same time permitting him to begin preparing for war. Industry felt satisfied because the threat of a Communist revolution and the abolition of private property had been thwarted, and production was almost back to what it had been in the old days—especially in cars and weapons. So all the production for the potential war was giving rise to a flourishing economy. Workers also profited by Hitler's economic success in the early years.

From the point of view of most Germans, Hitler also succeeded in regaining national identity and pride through a foot-in-the-door strategy: From the beginning, he tested limits by violating every aspect of the Treaty of Versailles, step by step. Since there was no clear resistance—in contrast to political action taken during the Weimar Republic, when the French had occupied the Ruhr Valley— Hitler felt invited to increase his efforts. He let the public know from an early stage that he was not prepared to be a pawn for other countries. On the contrary, he declared that Germany deserved to be a respected nation, and through his speeches and political actions he incited a feeling of national superiority. Very early on he began—partly in secret—to rebuild the army. The military, that is,

203

former soldiers, and also the aristocracy were therefore quite happy because they regained the prestige that had been lost during the Weimar Republic.

In the other spheres, he quickly regained control with his law-and-order campaigns and the restoration of traditional cultural values. Demonstrations and protests were forbidden, there was no fighting in parliament, no chronic change of chancellors, no terrorism in the streets, no strange cultural influences. All these actions fit the cognitive patterns of discipline, order, anti-Marxism, and antiliberalism.

The strategies for regaining control impressed the majority of Germans: Many people felt better off than they had previously in the chaotic Weimar Republic. The population was very proud of Hitler's successes: the reintegration of the Saar region, the introduction of universal military service, the occupation of the Rhineland, the summer Olympic Games in Berlin, the *Anschluss* of Austria, the Munich Agreement, and so on. For many Germans these "successes" seemed like a miracle of regaining control: Hitler gave them back a feeling of progress, of political stability, of economic prosperity, of national superiority, of community and togetherness, a perspective for the future and a vision, especially for the silent majority. Most Germans attributed the regaining of control to the strength of Hitler's leadership and to their own strength—including the economic recovery (as a worldwide phenomenon) and the successes in foreign policy (which also depended on other countries). In other words, it was a clear case of a "fundamental attribution error," meaning there was a clear tendency to overemphasize these dispositions and to underemphasize the situational influences. It was of course also a self-serving and group-serving bias; people were more likely to attribute their success to internal dispositions such as their own abilities (Cialdini et al., 1976; Osnabrügge et al., 1985; Ross & Fletcher, 1985;).

Because of the positive changes, the threshold within the population for accepting immoral or unjust behavior was lowered.[5] If Hitler had the right strategies for bringing back economic success and national pride, his other politics would probably not be as bad as they looked. The latitude of acceptance increased—also among those who until then had been very skeptical of him. Above all, Hitler's success discredited the constitutional, parliamentary, and liberal system of government, Weimar democracy itself. People enjoyed less personal freedom in individual spheres of life, but in general they believed themselves to be better off than before. In their mind, Hitler had managed to regain control on their behalf.

The Selection of a Scapegoat as a Strategy for Regaining Control

The selection of a scapegoat played a significant role when the illusion of regaining control was created. First, we will discuss some functions of the scapegoat and then ask why Hitler chose the Jews as scapegoats.

THE FUNCTIONS OF SCAPEGOATS. Scapegoats fulfill three functions for a person, a group, or a nation: social explanation, social justification, and positive distinctiveness (see also Tajfel, 1978).

The function of social explanation is fulfilled when there is a socially shared interpretation that a scapegoat is responsible for certain negative events. According to the theory of cognitive control (Frey et al., 2002; Osnabrügge et al., 1985), people dislike diffuse and chance attributions as opposed to concrete attributions of negative events, as well as internal instead of external attributions of such events. Instead of chance attributions (everything appears to be unpredictable, unexplainable, and uncontrollable) or internal attributions (which can be very self-threatening), this theory holds (and is supported in this by research) that they prefer clear, concrete, external attributions for negative events.[6] With the external attribution of negative events to scapegoats, it is possible to find an outlet for frustration and hate and very often a displacement of hate, especially because retaliation is not expected. Many observers seek a single efficient and salient explanation for behavior, and causal attributions are often shaped by highly salient stimuli (Taylor & Fiske, 1978). Altogether, scapegoating can sustain a feeling of control, as well as a feeling of high self-esteem.

Second, scapegoats serve the function of social justification. The in-group justifies its behavior because the scapegoat has (allegedly) initiated or at least aggravated the problem and therefore deserves discrimination or punishment. Social justification can also explain how different standards of morality get applied to the scapegoat, who does not deserve the same high moral standards one is obliged to apply to the in-group.

Finally, the third function is positive distinctiveness. By finding a scapegoat, the in-group can feel superior and have a positive sense of social identity. According to Tajfel (1978), trivial categorization is enough to produce in-group favoritism ("we") and out-group discrimination ("they"). The in-group is associated with positive traits (we are better and superior), and the out-group is associated with negative traits (they are worse). There is a tendency to see the attributes of the out-group in an undifferentiated way and to overgeneralize where the out-group is concerned (see Kruglanski, 1987; Moscovici, 1987).

Intergroup relations may even form the basis of ideologies that ascribe group differences to genetic characteristics (Pettigrew, 1986) or attribute societal problems to a conspiracy by a small but easily identifiable out-group such as witches, Jews, Jesuits, Freemasons, or Marxists.

WHICH PERSONS OR GROUPS ARE CHOSEN AS SCAPEGOATS? Any out-group can potentially serve as a scapegoat. Nearly every group (or nation) has its own scapegoat, which can be a group within the group or a group outside the group. The existence of a scapegoat will increase the cohesiveness and solidarity of the in-group. The more the in-group can be convinced by its leaders that the scapegoat is a threat for the whole group, the higher the group cohesion.

A facilitating condition for establishing a scapegoat is that there already be existing cognitive patterns in people's minds such that the scapegoats are seen as an out-group, for example, when these patterns are embedded in present or earlier value systems such as the religious system, as was the case historically with the Jews. These latent cognitive patterns may remain dormant as long as there is no conflict of interest, political instability, economic depression, or similar problem (see Pruitt, 1987).

The scapegoat must not be too strong so that no dangerous retaliation to discrimination is expected. Also, the in-group must not feel guilty toward the scapegoat or feel any empathy for him. "Feeling guilty" and "fearing retaliation" are the best predictors for aggression toward scapegoats. Both aspects must be low before discrimination or cruelty can be displayed toward scapegoats. Also, it helps when the scapegoat can be distinguished easily from other people (see Taylor & Fiske, 1978). The more visible a minority is, the better it can be identified as an odd group.

The Jews fulfilled these criteria: They made up less than 1% of the population in Germany and were traditionally viewed as a negative out-group. Since only orthodox Jews could be identified easily, other Jewish groups were forced to become visible (e.g., by the Star of David, additional first names). This visibility paved the way for further stages of the Holocaust: identification, concentration, and liquidation.

Hitler's Appeal

Especially the early founding members and supporters of the Nazi Party were mostly persons whose existential expectations had been frustrated or who had suffered a loss in status or income (Gerth, 1952). In the years that followed until 1933, the *Nationalsozialistische Deutsche Arbeiterpartei* (NSDAP) gained a broad basis in German society. More than any other party in the Weimar Republic, Hitler and the Nazi Party had a strong appeal to virtually all societal groups, with a special focus on the old and new middle classes (particularly officials, clerks, shopkeepers, farmers, businessmen), sections of the upper class, young males, university students, industrialists, Protestants, and former soldiers (Broszat, 1969; Childers, 1983; Falter, 1991). In this sense and with regard to both voters and members, the NSDAP had become a mass integration party. As the "people's protest party" (Falter, 1991), it radically represented the widespread rejection of and opposition to the "Weimar System" and appeared to show radical new ways out of the crises. In our terms, it was the party that expressed both the feeling of loss of control and the prospect for regaining control.

This basis of support was further broadened after Hitler had come into governmental power. Theodor Abel gave evidence of the background of

Hitler's supporters at that time, which underlines the elements of control theory as described here. In 1934, he announced a prize contest in Germany and induced 600 National Socialists to submit their autobiographies. He concluded that

> four general factors had a bearing on the ultimate success of
> National Socialism:
>
> 1. the prevalence of discontent with the existing order;
> 2. the peculiar ideology and program for social
>   transformation;
> 3. the National Socialist organizational and promotional
>   technique;
> 4. the presence of a charismatic leadership. . . .
>
> The four factors were dependent upon and supported each other in
> such fashion that the absence or deficiency of any one factor would
> have fatally disabled the movement. . . . The movement must be
> viewed as . . . a pattern in which none of the component parts was
> more significant than the others. (Abel, 1938/1982, pp. 166, 185)

In a way, Hitler himself embodied both the origins and the aspirations of numerous Germans because he was not only the leader of the Nazi movement but also its typical exponent. As Kettenacker (1983) points out, Hitler was both a representative of the petty bourgeois coming from the midst of the masses and the new "overlord" now reigning absolutely over these masses. This synthesis made him appealing to the majority of Germans, and in this sense the German people found the Führer they were longing for in order to reestablish the control they had lost.

LINKAGES: GERMAN POPULATION AND
HOLOCAUST PERPETRATORS

In which ways does control theory (and its complementary elements such as attribution theory) translate into an explanatory basis for the mass crimes of the Third Reich? First, it presents a necessary *precondition* for the escalation of terror culminating in the Holocaust. As we have shown, control theory explains the rise and widespread support or at least acceptance of the Nazi regime by various groups of German society due to an interaction of (general) situational forces and (more or less specific) perceptions, values, and needs. Only the combination of these elements—the experience of repeated crises, the prevalent set of cognitive patterns, and an adequate set of "explanations" and "solutions" offered by Hitler—made it possible for the Nazis to erode and permanently replace the German political, legal, and social institutions in an

207

extremely short period of time without encountering decisive resistance. Thus an institutional guarantee for democracy and human rights was abolished, and the population, including the later (and potential) perpetrators, lived in a political and societal environment of increasing indifference, inner hardening, and acceptance of violence.

Second, control theory as presented here also appears to be directly applicable to the psychosocial background of perpetrators. In the following we will briefly identify various types of perpetrators, their prevalent cognitive patterns, and the social and cultural conditions and circumstances to which they had been exposed mainly in the years before they were involved in the crimes. Since these circumstances would not be of decisive importance if perpetrators displayed pathologically deviant traits, the question arises of whether perpetrators had sadistic dispositions or instead were essentially "normal," ordinary men.

Personalities: Sadistic Traits of Perpetrators?

Estimates of the number of perpetrators involved in the Nazi murder crimes range from many tens of thousands to half a million (for an overview see Schoeps, 1996). The *Schutzstaffel* (SS, "Protection Detachment")—the core group of these perpetrators—had reached almost 200,000 members when Hitler came to power; during World War II, this number came close to 1 million. However, only a minority of SS members belonged to the "Death's Head Units" (*Totenkopfverbände*), which were in charge of guarding concentration and death camps: In January 1945 these comprised fewer than 38,000 men and about 3,500 women, and throughout all the 12 years of the Third Reich, 55,000 persons at the very least (Sofsky, 1997). Thousands of other men (including many persons who belonged to neither the NSDAP nor the SS) participated in group and mass executions in task forces in eastern Europe. How did they—and many others—become perpetrators?

Early studies on the motivational structure of particular perpetrators focused on psychiatric deviations and presupposed sadistic traits in their personalities. In some instances psychiatrists contended emotional deficiencies, which, for example, made some commanders of concentration camps act like robots, maintaining that at most 10% of the guards in these camps were "abnormal" in terms of clinical criteria (Gilbert, 1950; Kren & Rappoport, 1980). The vast majority of expert opinions hold that Nazi perpetrators in various areas and in both high- and low-ranking positions were not exceptional by psychiatric standards (see, e.g., Dicks, 1972; Harrower, 1976; Lifton, 1986; Miale & Selzer, 1975; Ritzler, 1978). Moreover, after 1945 the former SS men did not show any significant recurrence of roles or activities that would indicate a continuation of previous modes of behavior (Steiner, 1980). All in all, it appears that the personality of Nazi perpetrators does not involve utterly evil and sadistic traits. As one psychiatrist concluded with regard to Adolf

Eichmann, "He is normal—at least more normal than I am after having examined him" (quoted by Arendt, 1986, p. 99, translation by the authors). The "banality of evil," as Hannah Arendt views the Holocaust, is not a banality of the crimes, for the crimes were monstrous; but obviously it is a banality of the criminals involved.

However, not being abnormal does not necessarily imply that Nazi perpetrators were ordinary people like us. The authors are convinced that the study of Nazi perpetrators (and likewise the study of perpetrators of other totalitarian regimes) cannot be accomplished without an adequate understanding of their historical, political, and societal context. And this psychosocial background, as shown by our application of control theory, *was* significantly different from what we face today. The question is, Were the needs and values of actual (or potential) perpetrators, their perception of crises, and thus the loss of control experienced by them similar to those of average Germans of that time? Or, in short, were Nazi perpetrators typical Germans, and thus (most) Germans at least potential Nazi perpetrators?

Needs, Values, and Circumstances: Types of Perpetrators and Their Psychosocial Background

Raul Hilberg (1992), one of the most profound experts on the files and biographies of Nazi perpetrators, observes that the executioners of the extermination process differed with respect to both their position in society and their psychological profiles. As other studies for different groups of perpetrators confirm, they encompassed all segments of society and all educational levels (Browning, 1992; Herbert, 1998; Orth, 2000; Tuchel, 1994a, 1994b). Perpetrators were not social outsiders but stemmed from the midst of Weimar society. Also, their perceptions and values basically reflected German society at that time (only with a few aspects being more pronounced, as we will show later).

Analyses of their personal data from files, interrogations, interviews, and so forth underline that during the Weimar Republic they had experienced a loss of control that was at least as severe as that of the German population in general. For instance, the 46 commanders and the more than 270 departmental chiefs in concentration camps mainly came from lower or medium middle-class families, which had been heavily hit by the economic, political, and social crises and felt threatened by social decline; almost 39% of the key departmental chiefs had lost their jobs in the early 1930s (Orth, 2000). Many later commanders joined the SS during this period of personal or family crises (Segev, 1977).

"If men define situations as real, they are real in their consequences." John M. Steiner (1980) quotes this statement by W. I. Thomas in his study based on interviews with about 300 former members of the SS and 50 biographical accounts, and he concludes that during the Weimar Republic "members of the SS tended to see an immense historical threat to existing institutions and to the very existence of Germany as a sovereign nation state. Their experi-

209

ence of personal misery, existential insecurity, and anxiety due to the lost war lent force to this putative threat and helped make it very real indeed in its consequences" (p. 434).

Hitler and the Nazi movement offered highly acceptable explanations and simple solutions for the individual and social crises, and the SS, in particular, promised to provide a new psychosocial identity fitting the perceptions, needs, and preferences of many. As Ralph H. Turner (1969) maintains, one of the main reasons that individuals are attracted by sociopolitical movements is a strong desire for a new, more acceptable psychosocial identity. These movements promise to meet such desires through a symbolic construction and dissemination of new personal and collective identity models. The SS had a strong appeal for many Germans as they attempted to overcome their existential crisis and disorientation by shedding their unwanted selves and acquiring new and more satisfying psychosocial identities—a means of regaining lost control. The prospect of SS fellowship implied that similarly situated persons sharing commonly held perceptions and values banded together under an ideologically persuasive leadership with a strong sense of esprit de corps.

The military-style esprit de corps was the most essential element of their new identity in the SS. Based on their own experiences in World War I and on the widespread glorification of the military before and after this war, the German military was more than just a job; to them, it was a way of living. For instance, as SS guards in concentration camps, they conceived of themselves as "political soldiers" on a special "inner front." Tom Segev (1992, p. 90) summarizes their aspirations: To them, the SS was a new and, more important, an undefeated army. Its members could attain even the highest officers' ranks regardless of their family background and their education (whereas in the regular army, higher education was a prerequisite for a career). In our terms, the SS gave the members a new feeling of cognitive control.

Despite these shared attitudes and values, SS perpetrators differed significantly. Their specific psychosocial identity was considerably linked to their age and level of education, and consequently to their motives for joining the SS and their functions afterward. In the following we will identify, five types of SS men and other Germans who are intended to represent the most important groups of Holocaust perpetrators.

Volunteer-Activists

Typical members of this group were the so-called old fighters who had already become members of the NSDAP and the SS before Hitler's assumption of power. Most of them came from the lower middle class, but there were also aristocrats, former officers of the old German army, political criminals, and others (Höhne, 1997; Koehl, 1983). For our analysis, it is mainly the small proportion of them who shaped the concentration camps in the early years of the Third Reich who are relevant. They were significantly older than the officers and guards in the years that followed. Almost all of them had participated voluntarily in World War I, among them about two thirds of the (later) commanders of concentration camps (Orth, 2000). After the war many had joined semimilitary organizations, the so-called Freikorps. The military gave their lives a meaning, and so, in a sense, the SS offered what they were longing for. Structured like a military organization, the SS provided—or at least promised—a feeling of security: hierarchy, obedience, uniforms, order, drills, the esprit de corps among comrades in an elitist military-religious order. Most of them had extreme problems adjusting to the new and unstable situation in the 1920s. Even more than average Germans, they were radically opposed to the Weimar political system from the beginning; in many instances, they killed its representatives and supporters. The "old fighters" laid the blame for their personal hardships and for the decline of Germany in general on their political, social, or "racial" enemies and turned them into scapegoats. And now, they met them again as inmates in concentration camps and wanted to take "revenge" (Drobisch & Wieland, 1993; Segev, 1992).

These early "volunteer-activists," as Steiner (1980) calls them, scored significantly higher on the original American fascism scale (conformity and pronounced authoritarian, antidemocratic attitude) than members of the German armed forces, as a study by Steiner and Fahrenberg (1970) indicates. Many of them are typical examples of a process of self-selection. The SS offered them the opportunity to pursue their interests and inclinations, and, after years of personal downfall, it served as a vehicle for overcoming their loss of control.

A representative of this group is Theodor Eicke, one of the first commanders of the Dachau concentration camp. Up until 1939, as "inspector" of all such camps, he was decisive in shaping the camp organization and the "spirit" of the training program for new SS guards (Drobisch, 1983; Sydnor, 1977). His psychohistory of losing and regaining control, along with that of many others, is neither an excuse for nor a full explanation of the crimes committed; however, it represents a vital precondition.

Intellectual Functionalists

The key organizers and commanders of the genocide in the 1940s were, in some respects, antipodes to the group just described. Born between 1900 and the first years of World War I, they were exponents of the remarkably homogeneous "generation style" of the so-called war youth generation (Stambolis, 1984). About three quarters of the several hundred men in leading positions in the Security Police (Sipo, which encompassed the Secret State Police [Gestapo]) and in the Security Service of the SS (SD, the intelligence organization of the NSDAP) were born between 1903 and 1915. Two thirds held university degrees, almost one third a Ph.D. in jurisprudence (Herbert, 1998; see also Banach, 1999; Wegner, 1997). Prior to 1933 they had experienced a political socialization that combined an elitist self-awareness as a new and different generation with political radicalism, which led them to construct a new ideological and mental framework.

Thus they had more in common than age, education, and an upper-middle-class descent: in many cases, early political activities in extreme right-wing circles as student representatives; lasting close personal contacts among the alumni; a rejection of both the new Weimar Republic and traditional patriotism; strong "elitist anti-Semitism" (which despised the "primitive rowdy anti-Semitism" of the early volunteer-activists) coupled with a biological-racial concept of a "pure" German "people's community" (*Volksgemeinschaft*); a high esteem for modern technology and engineering; and an appreciation of efficiency and "rationalist" and functionalist solutions (instead of personal sentiments and emotional struggles; Herbert, 1996; Welzer 1993).

Attitudes of this type of explicitly nonhumanist rationality, functionalism, and efficiency can also be found especially among numerous physicians in the Third Reich. Forty-five percent of them were members of the NSDAP—more than any other occupational group—and a comparatively high percentage joined the SS. Their emphasis on a "biological-medical vision of national health" often led them to perform the "cleansing of the people's body" (*Reinigung des Volkskörpers*): eugenics as a form of "racial hygiene" (i.e., racial selection and breeding) and the Nazi-type "euthanasia" implying the murdering of, among others, mentally disabled children (Frei, 1991; Kater, 1989; Proctor, 1988; Weingart, 1985).

Well-known examples of this intellectual functionalist group are Reinhard Heydrich, chief of the SS Security Service and the Security Police; his deputy Werner Best; and Josef Mengele, SS doctor in Auschwitz. Their dangerousness did not result from ordinary sadistic orientations but from a combination of inner hardness and a "functionalist" Weltanschauung. Wolfgang Sofsky (1997) points out that "if bloodthirstiness and lust for murder had been the motive powers for the Nazi barbarity, the atrocities would have never been as inventive as they actually were. A perpetrator merely driven by blind hatred, an instinctive impulse to destroy or pure sadism loses control over the situation and over himself. He would hardly have been able to commit the atrocious crimes that were actually committed" (p. 256, translation by the authors).

Efficient Conformists

Another very large group emerged from the "war youth generation." However, their political socialization did not occur at universities, and their middle-class families were exposed more than others to the economic crises of the Weimar Republic. Basically, though, they shared the attitudes and values just described, perhaps on a less "elaborate" ideological level. Typically, they occupied medium ranks in the execution squads in eastern Europe and in the system of concentration and death camps. For instance, two thirds of all commanders and departmental chiefs in the camps belonged to the "war youth generation" born after 1900 (Orth, 2000).

Their time came especially in the early 1940s, when top priority was given to high productivity and "efficiency," both with regard to the exploitation of labor for the arms industry and the systematic industrial-style extermination of human beings. To this end, new "talents," particularly with organizational skills, were in high demand—and found in the shape of "efficient conformists" such as Rudolf Höss, the first commander of Auschwitz. To Heinrich Himmler, chief of the SS, Höss represented the "ideal commander": obeying any order, disciplined, effective, and, despite his assignment, a "decent" person. In an autobiography written by Höss (1992) while he was waiting for his death sentence to be carried out, he portrayed himself as an idealist who believed that gassing millions of Jews was a service to his country. His main concern had been to find the most efficient and "hygienic" method for killing. Like a detached observer of his own behavior, he described what he "had" to do and how he had tried to fight personal "weakness" and feelings of mercy, as well as "unnecessary" arbitrary torment by his inferiors. This form of "moral disengagement" (Bandura, 1999) allowed Höss and others to conceive of themselves as morally "right": The violence may be deplorable, but "it is in a good cause," "the lesser evil" in the long run.

Adapted Pupils

The Nazi movement was a youth movement, and the SS, too, increasingly became an organization of minors. By December 1938, the average age of the SS "Death's Head Units" guarding the concentration camps was a mere 20.7 years, with 37% between 15 and 18 years of age (cf. Drobisch & Wieland, 1993). This generation born after World War I was confronted with family hardship, social disorder, and mental disorientation in childhood. The generation preceding them had already set the course for a political break and for new radical values, which were now absorbed enthusiastically by many teenagers. Himmler deliberately tried to attract and recruit them for the SS.

Those who became guards in concentration camps were soon confronted with an adjustment and training process that compared with a loss of control in its own right. Their drilling demanded extreme willingness to endure danger and submission to superiors, and it included fighting and occasionally killing. It was "a constant learning by participation," as Staub (1989, p. 134) maintains. During the Auschwitz trial in Frankfurt in 1964 the historian Hans Buchheim (1967, p. 255) described drilling methods of humiliation that "essentially did not differ from those faced by the inmates in concentration camps." The adaptation of the young SS men was further precipitated by ideological indoctrination and pressure to sever still-existing bonds, for example, to leave their Protestant or Catholic denomination (by 1938, 69% of the members of the "Death's Head Units" had joined the new SS "religion" established by Heinrich Himmler; cf. Steiner, 1983). The goal of all these methods was described by Theodor Eicke in a 1937 publication for the "Death's Head Units": "We have to teach the men to forget their own 'self' in a self-sacrificing manner so that they can, whenever necessary, do their utmost and fulfill their duty doggedly" (quoted by Buchheim, 1967, p. 244, translation by the authors)

Under these circumstances, the adjustment of perceptions, values, and modes of behavior and the integration in a network of strong group ties represented means for the young SS men to regain control or at least not to lose further control.

Ordinary Compliants

A last type of perpetrator demonstrates that the mass crimes in the Third Reich were not only brought about by SS men acting upon convictions, opportunism, or adaptation in concentration camps. A considerable number of Holocaust perpetrators neither belonged to the SS nor were enthusiastic believers in Nazi ideals or mentally adjusted by means of a coercive training or violent pressures. Against the background of a general loss of control, these "ordinary compliants" acted in the broad context of the "War of Extermination" (*Vernichtungskrieg*) against the Soviet Union; the goal was no longer a simple victory but, in addition, the systematic extermination of men (cf. Herbert, 1998).

Staub (1989, 1990) points out that genocide does not result directly but usually as a progression of actions along a "continuum of destruction": The starting point is what we call an extreme loss of control on a societal level; what usually follows is scapegoating of subgroups, their devaluation, and more and more intense maltreatment coupled with an increasing acceptance of violence. At first, certain acts of violence against the subgroups prepare the ground; in a gradual escalation, further, more extreme violent acts follow. Individuals as well as groups change on the basis of these actions. Extreme war situations may accelerate this dynamic of disinhibition.

An example of "ordinary compliants" is the German police units who shot thousands of men in Poland and Russia during the second half of World War II. Christopher R. Browning (1992) presented the first in-depth analysis of the roughly 500 members of one of these units, the Reserve Police Battalion 101. All but a dozen of them participated in the executions of Jewish men and women, elderly persons, and children. Most murderers were policemen and reservists from Hamburg, between the ages of 37 and 42, and, in 1942, considered not young enough to serve in the German armed forces. Almost two thirds of the ordinary ranks came from workers' families. On average, their background was not Nazi-prone. As policemen they might have been more disposed toward obedience to government and other authorities. All in all, however, they appear to be typical for the German society of the time.

For an explanation of their actions, Browning (1992, 1998) hints at a number of social-psychological processes and situative factors against the background of an escalation of violence during the "War of Extermination." Such processes and forces—for example, conformity to groups and authorities, bureaucratic segregation and diffusion of responsibility, in-group/out-group differentiation, dehumanization of victims—also had an aggravating impact on the other types of perpetrators identified here, of course. Were all of them, in the end, "ordinary men," as Browning argues, specifically with regard to the members of the Reserve Police Battalion 101?

PERPETRATORS: "ORDINARY MEN" OR "ORDINARY GERMANS"?

None of the five types of perpetrators presented was exceptional for the German society of that time. However, we believe that German society itself was exceptional. Yet the explanation of the Holocaust is not "Germanness" or some similar monocausal construction such as Daniel J. Goldhagen's (1996) assertion of a unique German type of anti-Semitism. Such notions of a "national character" of "ordinary Germans" not only oversimplify reality; they also carry a dangerous message: Only uniquely extreme prejudices held by the vast majority of a people can lead to genocide—so there's no need to worry today.

Control theory is not an ahistorical concept that disregards cultural characteristics. Its universal assumptions about "ordinary men" (such as their need for control, modes of attributing a loss of control, and general strategies for regaining control) are "filled" with specific elements such as the cognitive patterns and crises in a particular society and during a particular period in time. Only the interaction of prevailing cognitive perceptions, values, and needs in Germany with the crises in the aftermath of World War I led to the widespread and extreme loss of control on an individual and societal level and made the Nazi movement highly attractive as a means of regaining control. The distinctive "German" psychosocial background of Holocaust perpetrators evolved from this interaction, and in this sense they were "ordinary Germans." Such a background does not directly explain the mass crimes, but it does represent an essential precondition on the way to the Holocaust.

NOTES

We would like to thank the following persons for their constructive feedback: Elisabeth Frank, Stefan Hormuth, Eva Jonas, Monika Kraemer, Renate Neumann, Albrecht Schnabel, and Stefan Schulz-Hardt.

1. We could, of course, have arrived at the same dynamic coming from other social-psychological theories or concepts, such as stress theory or frustration-aggression theory. However, we feel that these display more weaknesses than the control concept.

2. In his work on economic psychology, Katona (1975) argues that individual behavior multiplies on a collective level. He demonstrates that singular events in economics or in politics have huge effects not only on individuals but also on a collective level, for example, on consumer and savings behavior or on investment behavior. The stock market, too, is a good example of collective behavior in response to singular economic data.

3. Tajfel and Turner (1986) have proposed that the perception of instability and illegitimacy of the status quo is necessary for such a cognitive alternative. Experimental studies support this notion. Where laboratory groups coexist in stable and justifiable status relations, subordinate groups show little sign of throwing off their inferiority. If, however, the status hierarchy is implied to be flexible or unfair, the subordinate groups respond by displaying strong in-group favoritism and hostility toward the dominant group (Brown & Ross, 1982; Caddick, 1982).

4. *Mental contagion* was also a key term in Le Bon's influential crowd psychology (Le Bon, 1895). The term *contagion* and its connotative meaning have survived (see also Milgram & Toch, 1969).

5. It should be noted that the theory of cognitive control postulates that the acceptability of immoral methods increases in the phase of loss of control but also in the phase of regaining control.

6. This aspect of having control is even more pronounced the more negative certain events are. It would be very threatening for a person to be confronted with extremely negative events and not to have a good explanation.

REFERENCES

Abel, T. F. (1982). *Why Hitler came into power*. New York: AMS Press. (Original work published 1938)

Abramson, L. Y., Seligman, M. E. P., & Teasdale, J. D. (1978). Learned helplessness in humans: Critique and reformulation. *Journal of Abnormal Psychology, 8*, 49–74.

Arendt, H. (1951). *The origins of totalitarianism*. New York: Harcourt Brace Jovanovich.

Arendt, H. (1986). *Eichmann in Jerusalem: Ein Bericht von der Banalität des Bösen*. Munich: Piper. English edition: Arendt, H. (1963). Eichmann in Jerusalem. A report on the banality of evil. New York: Viking.

Banach, J. (1999). *Heydrichs Elite: Das Führerkorps der Sicherheitspolizei und des SD 1936–1945*. Paderborn, Germany: Schöningh.

Bandura, A. (1977). Self-efficacy: Toward a unified theory of behavioral change. *Psychological Review, 84*, 191–215.

Bandura, A. (1993). Perceived efficacy in cognitive development and functionining. *Educational Psychologist, 28*, 117–148.

Bandura, A. (1999). Moral disengagement in the perpetration of inhumanities. *Personality and Social Psychology Review, 3*, 193–209.

Baumann, Z. (1992). *Dialektik der Ordnung: Die Moderne und der Holocaust*. Frankfurt am Main: Europäische Verlags-Anstalt.

Broszat, M. (1969). *Der Staat Hitlers: Grundlagen und Entwicklung seiner inneren Verfassung*. Munich: Deutscher Taschenbuch Verlag.

Brown, R. J., & Ross, G. R. (1982). The battle for acceptance: An exploration into the dynamics of intergroup behavior. In H. Tajfel (Ed.), *Social identity and intergroup relations* (pp. 155–178). Cambridge: Cambridge University Press.

Browning, C. R. (1992). *Ordinary men: Reserve Police Battalion 101 and the Final Solution in Poland.* New York: HarperCollins.

Browning, C. R. (1998). Die Debatte über die Täter des Holocaust. In U. Herbert (Ed.), *Nationalsozialistische Vernichtungspolitik 1939–1945: Neue Forschungen und Kontroversen* (pp. 148–169). Frankfurt a. M., Germany: Fischer.

Buchheim, H. (1967). Befehl und Gehorsam. In H. Buchheim, M. Broszat, H.-A. Jacobsen & H. Krausnick (Eds.), *Anatomie des SS-Staates* (Vol. 1, pp. 215–318). Munich: Deutscher Taschenbuch Verlag.

Caddick, B. (1982). Perceived illegitimacy and intergroup relations. In H. Tajfel (Ed.), *Social identity and intergroup relations* (pp. 137–154). Cambridge: Cambridge University Press.

Childers, T. (1983). *The Nazi voter: The social foundations of fascism in Germany, 1919–1933.* Chapel Hill: University of North Carolina Press.

Cialdini, R. B., Borden, R. J., Thorne, A., Walker, M. R., Freeman, S., & Sloan, L. R. (1976). Basking in reflected glory: Three (football) field studies. *Journal of Personality and Social Psychology, 34,* 366–374.

Connell, J. P., & Wellborn, J. G. (1991). Competence, autonomy and relatedness: A motivational analysis of self-system processes. In M. Gunnar & L. A. Sroufe (Eds.), *Minnesota Symposium on Child Psychology* (Vol. 23, pp. 43–77). Chicago: University of Chicago Press.

Craig, G. A. (1982). *The Germans.* New York: Putnam.

Dahrendorf, R. (1971). *Gesellschaft und Demokratie in Deutschland.* Munich: Deutscher Taschenbuch Verlag.

Deci, E. L., & Ryan, R. M. (1985). *Intrinsic motivation and self-determination in human behavior.* New York: Plenum.

Dicks, H. V. (1972). *Licensed mass murder: A socio-psychological study of some SS killers.* New York: Basic Books.

Drobisch, K. (1983). Theodor Eicke: Verkörperung des KZ-Systems. In H. Bock, W. Ruge, & M. Thomas (Eds.), *Sturz ins Dritte Reich: Historische Miniaturen und Porträts 1933/35* (pp. 283–289). Leipzig: Urania.

Drobisch, K., & Wieland, G. (1993). *System der NS-Konzentrationslager 1933–1939.* Berlin: Akademie Verlag.

Falter, J. W. (1991). *Hitlers Wähler.* Munich: C. H. Beck.

Frei, N. (Ed.). (1991). *Medizin und Gesundheitspolitik in der NS-Zeit.* Munich: Oldenburg.

Frey, D., & Jonas, E. (1999). Anmerkungen zur Gerechtigkeit anläßlich der deutschen Wiedervereinigung: Theorie und Empirie. In M. Schmitt & L. Montada (Eds.), *Gerechtigkeitserleben im wiedervereinigten Deutschland* (pp. 331–349). Opladen: Leske & Budrich.

Frey, D., Stahlberg, D., Schulz-Hardt, S., & Jonas, E. (2002). Theorie der kognizierten Kontrolle. In D. Frey & M. Irle (Eds.), *Theorien der Sozialpsychologie* (Vol. 3). Bern, Switzerland: Huber.

Fromm, E. (1983). *Arbeiter und Angestellte am Vorabend des Dritten Reiches: Eine sozialpsychologische Untersuchung.* Munich: Deutscher Taschenbuch Verlag.

Gay, P. (1968). *Weimar culture: The outsider as insider.* New York: Harper and Row.

Gerth, H. H. (1952). The Nazi Party: Its leadership and composition. In R. K. Merton, A. P. Gray, B. Hockey, & H. C. Selvin (Eds.), *Reader in bureaucracy* (pp. 100–113). New York: Free Press.

Gilbert, G. M. (1950). *The psychology of dictatorship: Based on an examination of the leaders of Nazi Germany.* New York: Ronald Press.

Glass, D. C., & Singer, J. (1972). *Urban stress.* New York: Academic Press.

Goldhagen, D. J. (1996). *Hitler's willing executioners: Ordinary Germans and the Holocaust.* New York: Knopf.

Gurin, P., & Brim, O. G. (1984). Change in self in adulthood: The example of sense of control. In P. B. Baltes & O. G. Brim (Eds.), *Life-span development and behavior* (pp. 282–334). San Diego, CA: Academic Press.

Harrower, M. (1976). Were Hitler's henchmen mad? *Psychology Today, 10,* 76–80.

Harter, S. (1978). Effectance motivation reconsidered: Toward a developmental model. *Human Development, 21,* 36–64.

Herbert, U. (1996). *Best: Biographische Studien über Radikalismus, Weltanschauung und Vernunft 1903–1989.* Bonn: Dietz.

Herbert, U. (1998). Vernichtungspolitik: Neue Antworten und Fragen zur Geschichte des Holocaust. In U. Herbert (Ed.), *Nationalsozialistische Vernichtungspolitik 1939–1945: Neue Forschungen und Kontroversen* (pp. 9–66). Frankfurt am Main: Fischer.

Hilberg, R. (1961). *The destruction of the European Jews.* Chicago: Quadrangle Books.

Hilberg, R. (1992): *Täter, Opfer, Zuschauer: Die Vernichtung der Juden 1933–1945.* Frankfurt am Main: Fischer.

Höhne, H. (1997). *Der Orden unter dem Totenkopf: Die Geschichte der SS.* Augsburg: Weltbild.

Höss, R. (1992). *Death dealer: The memoirs of the SS Kommandant at Auschwitz* (S. Paskuly, Ed.). Buffalo, NY: Prometheus Books.

Jaide, W. (1988). *Generationen eines Jahrhunderts: Wechsel der Jugendgenerationen im Jahrhunderttrend. Zur Sozialgeschichte der Jugend in Deutschland 1871–1985.* Opladen, Germany: Leske + Budrich.

Kater, M. (1989). *Doctors under Hitler.* Chapel Hill: University of North Carolina Press.

Katona, G. (1975). *Psychological economics.* New York: Elsevier.

Kershaw, I. (1980). *Der Hitler-Mythos: Volksmeinung und Propaganda im Dritten Reich.* Stuttgart: Deutsche Verlags-Anstalt.

Kettenacker, L. (1983). Sozialpsychologische Aspekte der Führer-Herrschaft. In K.-D. Bracher, M. Funke, & H.-A. Jacobsen (Eds.), *Nationalsozialistische Diktatur 1933–1945: Eine Bilanz* (pp. 97–131). Bonn: Bundeszentrale für politische Bildungsarbeit.

Koehl, R. L. (1983). *The Black Corps.* Madison: University of Wisconsin Press.

Kren, G. M., & Rappoport, L. (1980). *The Holocaust and the crisis of human behavior.* New York: Holmes and Meier.

Kruglanski, A. W. (1987). Blame-placing schemata and attributional research. In C. F. Graumann & S. Moscovici (Eds.), *Changing conceptions of conspiracy* (pp. 219–229). New York: Springer.

Le Bon, G. (1895). *Psychologie des foules.* Paris: Alcon.

Lifton, R. J. (1986). *The Nazi doctors: Medical killing and the psychology of genocide.* New York: Basic Books.

Miale, F. R., & Selzer, M. (1975). *The Nuremberg mind: The psychology of Nazi leaders.* New York: Quadrangle.

Milgram, S., & Toch, H. (1969). Collective bahavior: Crowds and social movements. In G. Lindzey & A. Aronson (Eds.), *The handbook of social psychology* (2nd ed., Vol. 4, pp. 507–610). Reading, MA: Addison-Wesley.

Moscovici, S. (1976). *Social influence and social change*. London: Academic Press.

Moscovici, S. (1980). Towards a theory of conversion behavior. In L. Berkowitz (Ed.), *Advances in experimental social psychology* (Vol. 13, pp. 208–239). New York: Academic Press.

Moscovici, S. (1981). On social representation. In J. P. Forgas (Ed.), *Social cognition: Perspectives and everyday understanding* (pp. 181–209). London: Academic Press.

Moscovici, S. (1987). The conspiracy mentality. In C. F. Graumann & S. Moscovici (Eds.), *Changing conceptions of conspiracy* (pp. 151–169). New York: Springer.

Mosse, G. L. (1987): Der Erste Weltkrieg und die Brutalisierung der Politik: Betrachtungen über die politische Rechte, den Rassismus und den deutschen Sonderweg. In M. Funke, H.-A. Jacobsen, H.-H. Knütter & H.-P. Schwarz (Eds.), *Demokratie und Diktatur: Geist und Gestalt politischer Herrschaft in Deutschland und Europa* (pp. 127–139). Bonn: Bundeszentrale für politische Bildungsarbeit.

Opotow, S. (1990). Moral exclusion and injustice: An introduction. *Journal of Social Issues, 46,* 1–20.

Orth, K. (2000). *Die Konzentrationslager-SS: Sozialstrukturelle Analysen und biographische Studien.* Göttingen: Wallstein.

Osnabrügge, G., Stahlberg, D., & Frey, D. (1985). Die Theorie der kognizierten Kontrolle. In D. Frey & M. Irle (Eds.), *Theorien der Sozialpsychologie: Vol. 3, Motivations- und Informationsverarbeitungstheorien* (pp. 127–172). Munich: Urban & Schwarzenberg.

Pettigrew, T. F. (1986). The ingroup contact hypothesis reconsidered. In M. Hewstone & R. Brown (Eds.), *Contact and conflict in intergroup encounters* (pp. 169–195). Oxford: Basil Blackwell.

Proctor, R. (1988). *Racial hygiene: Medicine under the Nazis.* Cambridge, MA: Harvard University Press.

Pruitt, D. G. (1987). Conspiracy theory in conflict escalation. In C. F. Graumann & S. Moscovici (Eds.), *Changing conceptions of conspiracy* (pp. 191–202). New York: Springer.

Reichel, P. (1993). *Der schöne Schein des Dritten Reiches: Faszination und Gewalt des Faschismus.* Frankfurt am Main: Fischer.

Ritzler, B. A. (1978). The Nuremberg mind revisted: A quantity approach to Nazi Rorschachs. *Journal of Personal Assessment, 42,* 344–353.

Ross, M., & Fletcher, G. J. O. (1985). Attribution and social perception. In G. Lindzey & E. Aronson (Eds.), *Handboock of social psychology* (3rd ed., Vol. 2, pp. 73–122). New York: Random House.

Schoeps, J. (Ed.). (1996). *Ein Volk von Mördern? Die Dokumentation zur Goldhagen-Kontroverse um die Rolle der Deutschen im Holocaust.* Hamburg: Hoffmann & Campe.

Schooler, C. (1990). Individualism and the historical and social-structural determinants of people's concerns over self-directedness and efficacy. In J. Rodin, C. Schooler, & K. W. Schaie (Eds.), *Self-directedness: Cause and effects throughout the life course* (pp. 19–49). Hillsdale, NJ: Erlbaum.

Segev, T. (1977). Commanders of Nazi concentration camps. (University Microfilms No. DAI-A 38/04, p. 2293).

Segev, T. (1992). *Die Soldaten des Bösen: Zur Geschichte der KZ-Kommandaten.* Reinbek bei Hamburg: Rowohlt. English edition: Segev, T. (1988). Soldiers of evil. The commandants of the Nazi concentration camps. New York: McGraw-Hill.

Seligman, M. E. P. (1975). *Helplessness: On depression, development, and death.* San Francisco: Freeman.

Skinner, E. A. (1991). Development and perceived control: A dynamic model of action in context. In M. Gunnar & L. A. Sroufe (Eds.), *Minnesota Symposium on Child Psychology* (Vol. 23, pp. 167–216). Chicago: University of Chicago Press.

Skinner, E. A. (1995). *Perceived control, motivation, and coping*. Thousand Oaks, CA: Sage.

Skinner, E. A., (1996). A guide to constructs of control. *Journal of Personality and Social Psychology, 71,* 549–570.

Sofsky, W. (1997). *Die Ordnung des Terrors: Das Konzentrationslager*. Frankfurt am Main: Fischer.

Sontheimer, K. (1978). *Antidemokratisches Denken in der Weimarer Republik: Die politischen Ideen des deutschen Nationalismus zwischen 1918 und 1933*. Munich: Deutscher Taschenbuch Verlag.

Stachura, P. D. (1975). *Nazi youth in the Weimar Republic*. Santa Barbara, CA: Clio Books.

Stambolis, B. (1984). *Der Mythos der jungen Generation: Ein Beitrag zur politischen Kultur der Weimarer Republik*. Unpublished doctoral dissertation, University of Bochum, Germany.

Staub, E. (1989). *The roots of evil: The origins of genocide and other group violence*. Cambridge: Cambridge University Press.

Staub, E. (1990). The psychology and culture of torture and torturers. In P. Suedfeld (Ed.), *Psychology and torture* (pp. 49–76). Washington, DC: Hemisphere.

Steiner, J. M. (1980). The SS yesterday and today: A sociopsychological view. In J. E. Dimsdale (Ed.), *Survivors, victims, and perpetrators: Essays on the Nazi Holocaust* (pp. 405–456). Washington, DC: Hemisphere.

Steiner, J. M. (1983). Über das Glaubensbekenntnis der SS. In K.-D. Bracher, M. Funke, & H.-A. Jacobsen (Eds.), *Nationalsozialistische Diktatur 1933–1945: Eine Bilanz* (pp. 206–223). Bonn: Bundeszentrale für politische Bildungsarbeit.

Steiner, J. M., & Fahrenberg, J. (1970). Die Ausprägung autoritärer Einstellung bei ehemaligen Angehörigen der SS und der Wehrmacht. *Kölner Zeitschrift für Soziologie und Sozialpsychologie, 22,* 552–566.

Strauss, H. A., & Kampe, N. (Eds.). (1984). *Antisemitismus: Von der Judenfeindschaft zum Holocaust*. Frankfurt am Main: Campus.

Sydnor, C. W., Jr. (1977). *Soldiers of destruction: The SS Death's Head Division, 1933–1945*. Princeton, NJ: Princeton University Press.

Tajfel, H. (Ed.). (1978). *Differentiation between social groups: Studies in the social psychology of intergroup relations*. London: Academic Press.

Tajfel, H., & Turner, J. C. (1986). An integrative theory of intergroup conflict. In W. C. Austin & S. Worchel (Eds.), *The social psychology of intergroup relations* (2nd ed., pp. 7–24). Monterey, CA: Brooks/Cole.

Taylor, S. E. (1983). Adjustment to threating events: A theory of cognitive adaptation. *American Psychologist, 38,* 1161–1173.

Taylor, S. E., Buunk, B. P., Collins, R. L., & Reed, G. M. (1992). Social comparison and affiliation under threat. In L. Montada, S.-H. Filipp, & M. J. Lerner (Eds.), *Life crises and experiences of loss in adulthood* (pp. 213–227). Hillsdale, NJ: Erlbaum.

Taylor, S. E., & Fiske, S. T. (1978). Salience, attention, and attribution: Top of the head phenomena. In L. Berkowitz (Ed.), *Advances in experimental social psychology* (Vol. 11, pp. 250–289). New York: Academic Press.

Taylor, S. E., Lichtman, R. R., & Wood, J. V. (1984). Attributions, beliefs about control, and adjustment to breast cancer. *Journal of Personality and Social Psychology*, *46*, 489–502.

Tuchel, J. (1994a). Die Kommandanten des Konzentrationslagers Dachau. *Dachauer Hefte*, *10*, 69–90.

Tuchel, J. (1994b). Die Kommandanten des Konzentrationslagers Flossenbürg: Eine Studie zur Personalpolitik in der SS. In H. Grabitz, K. Bästlein, & J. Tuchel (Eds.), *Die Normalität des Verbrechens: Bilanz und Perspektiven der Forschung zu den nationalsozialistischen Gewaltverbrechen* (pp. 201–219). Berlin: Edition Hentrich.

Turner, R. H. (1969). The theme of contemporary social movements. *British Journal of Sociology*, *20*, 586–599.

Wegner, B. (1997). *Hitlers Politische Soldaten: Die Waffen-SS 1933–1945. Leitbild, Struktur und Funktion einer nationalsozialistischen Elite* (5th, enlarged ed.). Paderborn, Germany: Schöningh.

Weingart, P. (1985). Eugenik eine angewandte Wissenschaft: Utopien der Menschenzüchtung zwischen Wissenschaftsentwicklung und Politik. In P. Lundgreen (Ed.), *Wissenschaft im Dritten Reich* (pp. 314–349). Frankfurt am Main: Suhrkamp.

Weisz, J. R. (1986). Understanding the development of the understanding of control. In M. Perlmutteer (Ed.), *Minnesota Symposium on Child Psychology* (Vol. 18, pp. 219–278). San Diego, CA: Academic Press.

Welzer, H. (1993). Männer der Praxis: Zur Sozialpsychologie des Verwaltungsmassenmordes. In H. Welzer (Ed.), *Nationalsozialismus und Moderne* (pp. 105–127). Tübingen: edition diskord.

White, R. W. (1959). Motivation reconsidered: The concept of competence. *Psychological Review*, *66*, 297–333.

Wortman, C. B., & Brehm, J. W. (1975). Response to uncontrollable outcomes: An integration of reactance and the learned helplessness model. In L. Berkowitz (Ed.), *Advances in experimental social psychology* (Vol. 8, pp. 277–336). New York: Academic Press.

9

The Zoomorphism of Human Collective Violence

R. B. Zajonc

Sociobiology must be counted as one of the *big* ideas of our times. New understanding of some fundamental aspects of social behavior, such as cooperation, altruism, or dominance, came from the premises of sociobiology. These complex social phenomena are explained by invoking the concept of inclusive fitness, a force of nature that promotes the perpetuation of our genes—our own and that of our own species. Broad and profound scientific, philosophical, and pragmatic consequences were drawn from sociobiology. Its notions were absorbed not only by physiologists, geneticists, and molecular biologists but also by anthropologists, historians, political scientists, and, of course, psychologists. In fact, the fields of evolutionary psychology and evolutionary social psychology were spawned by the intellectual ferment created by the principles of inclusive fitness and reproductive success.

Based on these ideas, a number of bold implications deriving from the concepts of sociobiology and evolutionary psychology have been drawn in the scholarly domain—implications that were very rapidly echoed in the popular press and other media, most often in a simplified and vulgarized form. Thus, the Columbine High School shooting was explained in *Newsweek* by the genetically fixed urge to eliminate competitors for offspring, citing as culprit the cingulate gyrus, a brain structure that is apparently active in juvenile aggression (Begley, 1999). And in a recent book, Thornhill and Palmer (2000) treat rape as a *natural* phenomenon, merely an expression of the innate tendency to disperse the rapists' genes. Even genocide has become subject to sociobiological explanation. This chapter questions the widespread and often uncritical applications of sociobiological principles to the explanation of collective violence, which in the twentieth century alone produced by some estimates, over 100 million civilian deaths. It argues that the enthusiasm is at best premature and the evidence scant.

Wrangham and Peterson (1996) draw a direct parallel between aggression in the chimpanzee and genocide, in particular, the Burundi genocide. These authors address the problem of aggression among males, which, of course, is virtually all of human aggression, from the following perspective:

> Aggression among males within a chimpanzee community happens most obviously at "election time" . . . when suddenly the old hierarchy is being challenged. Such times occur particularly when a young, low-ranking male whose physical and political power is growing develops a disrespectful attitude toward established authority. (p. 186)

The authors then go on to claim that the social dynamics in the chimpanzee community promise to help us understand what happened in Burundi 30 years ago:

> Burundi was not at peace. . . . In one month in 1972, Tutsi killed nearly every Hutu leader and any other Hutu who appeared literate. . . . The June elections produced Burundi's first Hutu president . . . Melchior Ndadaye. But . . . an army tank rammed a hole in the white stucco wall of the presidential palace and radical Tutsi soldiers stabbed President Ndadaye to death. . . . They also assassinated a half dozen high officials. (p. 2)

"Elections" in both cases! The parallel seems irresistible. We read the following account, offered as a corresponding specimen of chimpanzee violence:

> On January 7, 1974, in Gombe National Park, Tanzania, a group of eight chimpanzees traveled purposefully . . . toward the border of their range. . . . Godi [an ordinary male] ate peacefully, alone in a tree. . . . By the time he saw the eight intruders they were already at his tree. Humphrey got to him first. Godi toppled at once. The other adult males pummeled his shoulder blades and back. After ten minutes Humphrey let go. The others stopped hitting him. (pp. 5–6)

In contrast to the chimpanzee raids at Gombe, which resemble what we observe during a high school or middle school recess, I cite a report by Iris Chang (1997) of what has become known as the Rape of Nanking. In 1931, the Japanese army occupied Manchuria. In 1937, Beijing, Tiensin, and Shanghai were taken. On December 13, 1937, Japanese troops entered Nanking (now Nanjing), at that time capital of Nationalist China. According to Iris Chang, the Japanese troops

223

began an orgy of cruelty seldom if ever matched in world history. Tens of thousands of young men were . . . mowed down by machine guns, used for bayonet practice, or soaked with gasoline and burned alive. For months the streets of the city were heaped with corpses. . . . Chinese men were used for decapitation contests. An estimated 20,000 to 80,000 Chinese women were raped. . . .

Not only did live burials, castration, carving of organs, and the roasting of people become routine, but more diabolical tortures were practiced, such as hanging people by their tongues on iron hooks or burying people to their waists and watching them get torn apart by German shepherds. (p. 6)

One estimate counts as many as 300,000 noncombatants killed by the Japanese in just a few weeks. This figure is greater than four years of World War II military casualties of Great Britain (61,000), France (108,000), and Belgium (101,000) put together. Is it simply stretching the imagination to equate a chimpanzee beating with a massacre of 300,000 innocent civilians?

Sociobiological accounts of behavior have become much more strident, fueled by the recent discovery that we share as much as 98.5% of DNA with the chimpanzee (Gibbons, 1998). At the biological level, therefore, we humans are simply another ape. According to the views of the sociobiologists Dawkins (1989) Wilson (1975) and their followers (Barash, 1982) and predecessors (Morris, 1967), human social phenomena, such as cooperation and competition, aggression and affiliation, cruelty and kindness, monogamy and polygamy, heterosexuality and homosexuality, conformity and deviance, dominance and submission, and morality and decadence are all hardwired and can be explained by an appeal to the revised theory of evolution. There is at the same time a widening conviction that brain structures controlling these social processes will soon be identified.

The argument is that evolution worked for millions of years, whereas civilization had only a few thousand to overcome its influences (Morris, 1967). Hence, the analysis of animal behavior should give us clues, if not answers, to our own behavioral tendencies. The prototypical evolutionary position on aggression, which in sociobiology readily generalizes to phenomena of aggression among humans, is best represented by the Nobel laureate Konrad Lorenz (1966). It holds that these millions of years have endowed humans with the instinct (or whatever nativist term one wishes to substitute) for aggression, as they have endowed other species. Normally aggression remains dormant. Occasionally, however, under some specifiable circumstances, the inhibitions break down, and it is then that our "true" nature—our bestiality—emerges. We then descend to the level of our animal ancestors. We owe this view to Gustave LeBon (1995):

By the mere fact that he forms part of an organized crowd, a man descends several rungs in the ladder of civilization. Isolated he may be a cultivated individual; in a crowd, he is a barbarian—that is, a creature acting by instinct.

Impulsiveness, irritability, incapacity to reason, the absence of judgment . . . , the exaggeration of the sentiments, . . . which are almost always observed in beings belonging to inferior forms of evolution. (pp. 52, 55–56)

Lorenz offered the concept of the *innate releasing mechanism*, a sort of hydraulic model (shown in Fig. 9.1), to represent aggression, which some could not resist calling the "flush toilet model." Two opposing forces describe the aggression process: the accumulation of aggression energy that seeks expression represented in the figure by the reservoir (ER) and inhibitions of natural and cultural origin represented by the restraining valve. The spring, which represents fears of punishment or guilt, makes the valve press against the

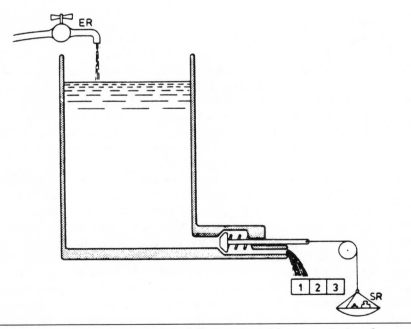

Figure 9.1 Lorenz's hydraulic model. Reprinted by permission from Karl Lorenz, *The Foundations of Ethology*, p. 81. Translated by K. Z. Lorenz and R. W. Kickert. Copyright © 1981 by Springer.

225

reservoir opening. When appropriate stimulus conditions arise, depending on their intensity (shown in kilogram weights), the valve is pulled back against the spring, and aggression (SR) is released.[1]

Note that the model features aggression as a compelling urge that accumulates constantly, putting an ever-increasing pressure on the inhibitory valve. Opposed to the building up of aggressive energy, the spring of restraints seems weak and inconsequential. One has the impression that the release of the aggressive urge is a matter of minimal force. And, in fact, the theory holds that the more intense, salient, and conspicuous the instigating stimulus (represented in the model by the counterweights), the more rapid and more complete is the release of the aggressive tendencies. This disinhibition model of aggression has been the pervasive, unquestioned view of aggression for centuries (Ardrey, 1961; Lorenz, 1966; Moyer, 1969; Storr, 1968). It is firmly imprinted on the intellectual discourse not only in science but also in the humanities. It is readily found in the literature. The Nobel laureate novelist Ivo Andric, in his epic about the Ottoman history in the Balkans (1959), affirms unambiguously the disinhibition theory of aggression in his description of the outbreak of World War I:

> That wild beast, which lives in man and does not dare to show itself until the barriers of law and custom have been removed, was now set free. The signal was given, the barriers were down. As so often happens in the history of man, permission was tacitly granted for acts of violence and plunder, even for murder. . . . It is true that there had always been concealed enmities and jealousies and religious intolerance, coarseness and cruelty, but there had also been courage and fellowship and a feeling for measure of order, which restrained all these instincts. (pp. 282–283)

This theory of human violence is part of our common understanding, transmitted from one generation to the next in increasingly simplified form. We are exposed to it over and over again. It is uncontested, and it looms "true," "obvious," and "natural." The unprecedented rush to the fMRI laboratory is reminiscent of the early 1999 stock market rush to the technology shares that Allan Greenspan termed "irrational exuberance." Thus, for example, Hammer and Copeland (1998) write: "The emerging science of molecular biology has made startling discoveries that show beyond a doubt that genes are the single most important factor that distinguishes one person from another. We come in large part ready-made from the factory. We accept that we *look* like our parents and other blood relatives. We have a harder time with the idea we *act* like them" (p. 11). Yet, more recently, voices of constraint have been heard. Paul Ehrlich (2000) firmly argued that genetic identity "does not necessarily produce identical natures, even when combined with substantially identical environments" (p. 10), and that variation in behavior goes well beyond the mathematical limits of genetic variation (p. 4).

More specifically, there are good reasons why the current theory of aggression, that is merely a superficial modification of the original version, cannot begin to explain the 100 million casualties inflicted on unarmed civilians in the twentieth century alone.

1. Given the theory is true that human aggression is nothing but animal aggression, released when inhibitions are removed, we would expect the behavioral form of our own massacres to resemble those of lower animals. But the level of unspeakable atrocity seen in human massacres surpasses any animal aggression by many orders of magnitude, and its forms of brutality find no counterpart among any conspecific violence among the lower animals, even those closest to us.
2. Some massacres contradict the very principles of kin selection and reproductive success. Other cultural developments, for instance, contraception, also contradict the principle of reproductive success.
3. No animal kills on principle.

INNATE RELEASERS AND FIXED ACTION PATTERNS

Not only is the zoomorphic generalization a wild exaggeration, but the sociobiological theory of aggression is unsupported by empirical data, and in many instances it is contradicted by them. The sociobiology that formerly was practiced under the label of "ethology" held that the aggressive responses are evoked only if the individual confronts an appropriate stimulus in the environment, the "innate releaser." Thus the red cape is an innate releaser for a bull, for example, that elicits charging behavior. The innate releaser theory was challenged on a number of grounds, although its main tenets remain today intact. The innate releaser theory suffered because it featured a most inefficient dynamic system. It had to assume a continuous accumulation of energy for the aggressive response. The response had to be assumed sitting in readiness to be released when the restraining "valve" was removed. At the same time, the system required an equal amount of energy for the inhibition of the release, a most wasteful arrangement. Eventually, the term *innate releaser* was replaced by the *fixed action pattern* (Hinde, 1974), changing the original formulation so as not to require a continuous energy deployment, half for the incipient aggressive response and the other half for its restraint. But the notion that fixed action patterns are recruited by appropriate specific stimuli remained intact.

These ideas are perpetuated in textbooks, which ignore the fact that they are false. Note that both innate releaser and fixed action pattern theories are

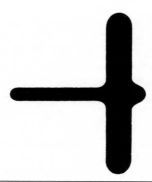

Figure 9.2 Schematic shape said to evoke flight behavior in goslings.

very cumbersome in requiring very constraining assumptions. First, the organism must be capable of fairly precise identification of just the right eliciting stimuli. Second, the stimuli releasing the behavior are limited to a very specific type. For example, the schematic shape in Figure 9.2 is said to evoke flight behavior in the young gosling when moving overhead in one direction but not in the opposite direction because, ostensibly, the short-neck direction resembles a hawk, whereas the long-neck direction resembles a goose. Third, the theory holds that the more energy has accumulated to release the response, the less stimulus intensity is required for its release. Fourth, because the behavioral tendency is instinctive, it should not extinguish, even in the presence of negative reinforcement. Fifth, it should not habituate spontaneously. Sixth, it is a tendency that does not need to be learned, for it is given at birth. All of these presuppositions were contradicted by experimental data first reported by Hirsch, Lindley, and Tolman (1955) and confirmed in many subsequent experimental studies. Yet the original claim is cited frequently, whereas the contradictions are known by only a handful of scholars.

The classical documentation of the innate releaser (and fixed action pattern) theory is due to Tinbergen, with whom Lorenz shared the Nobel Prize. Tinbergen (1952) quite explicitly offered the releaser theory as explaining human behavior:

> To get light on the behavior of man, particularly his innate drives
> and conflicts, it is often helpful to study the elements of behavior
> in a simple animal. Here is a little fish that exhibits a complicated
> pattern of activities, all dependent on simple stimuli and drives. We
> have studied and analyzed its behavior by a large number of
> experiments, and have learned a good deal about why the

> stickleback behaves as it does. . . . Let us begin with the stimulus
> that causes one stickleback to attack another. Early in our work we
> noticed that a male patrolling its territory would attack a red-
> colored intruder much more aggressively than a fish of some other
> color. Even a red mail van passing our windows at a distance of
> 1200 yards could make the males in the tank charge its glass side
> in that direction. (p. 23)

The stickleback lives in the shallow waters of muddy streams. In early spring the male leaves its school and seeks to stake out a territory. He does so by digging a nest in the form of a mound in the bottom of the stream, on which he piles up algae and coats it with a sticky secretion from his kidneys. He then bores a tunnel in the mound and is ready to mate. As soon as the nest is ready, he changes the color of his belly from inconspicuous gray to pink and then to brilliant scarlet. His back and eyes turn turquoise. Having achieved the conspicuous appearance, he attracts gravid females by zigzagging around them and guiding them to the nest. The gravid females are easy to spot, for they carry 50 to 100 large eggs. Once in the nest, the female lays eggs, with the male prodding her tail in a series of rhythmic thrusts. Once the eggs are laid, the male fertilizes them. When the first female leaves the nest, the male starts looking for another gravid female. Three to five gravid females are thus seduced into the male's nest. He then loses interest in females and also loses his bright coloring. Yet he guards the nest and fans the water to supply more oxygen to the hatching eggs. In the course of guarding his nest, he attacks other conspecifics, both males and females.

The sticklebacks' coloring is treated by Tinbergen as an innate releaser, and the aggression among sticklebacks is regarded as a reproductive fixed action pattern, for its function is to space out individuals so as to exploit the habitat most efficiently. Because the story has been perpetuated in psychology and biology textbooks and in the popular science press, few know that subsequent experimentation failed to confirm the theory. For instance, in thorough experiments by Peeke and his colleagues (Peeke, 1969; Peeke, Wyers, & Herz, 1969), models of fish that were colored totally red did not invite any more aggression than those that were colored less than 10%. In fact, no difference was found between colored models and models without any coloring at all. Ten out of 37 subjects did not display any aggressive responses. Moreover, when aggressive responses did occur, there was rapid habitation—a reaction that one would not expect from instinctive behavior. But not only models of fish, but a live stickleback as well, elicited responses that habituated very quickly.

The most damaging research, however, was carried out in France by Berthe Muckensturm (1965, 1969), and because it was published in a French journal, it is largely unknown in the United States. Muckensturm used models colored not only red but also violet, gray, and yellow. Her results are striking because she tested her animals twice in individual trials and obtained consistent results over the repeated tests. Vast individual differences characterized the sticklebacks observed. The number of attacks at the models ranged from 1 to 141, similar over the repeated tests. We would not expect such extensive variability of instinctive behavior. The models colored red were not the most frequent targets. On the second test, 7 out of 15 did not attack the red target at all, and only 2 out of 15 fish attacked the red target most frequently. The most frequently attacked target, however, was the violet one. And, quite important, when the aquarium was illuminated by light that suppressed color, aggression did not stop.

Muckensturm noted that the males' coloring was reflective of the dominance structure—the leader being most brilliant. She also noted that the coloring changes only *after* the male acquires a nest. Before he acquires a nest, he must physically compete for his territory, and he does so by engaging in considerable combative behavior. Only *after* succeeding does he change his coloring, and then aggression wanes, both in the target and in his competitors. Since Tinbergen considered stickleback coloring and the aggression it elicited to be serving optimal distribution of the habitat's resources for healthy population growth, we would expect the coloring to appear *before*, not *after*, the stickleback has successfully set up a nest. Yet Muckensturm observed a great number of attacks before there was any coloring at all. In fact, it appeared that the coloring was the outcome of aggression rather than its cause or antecedent. The leader, which was the most brilliant fish, however, was seldom attacked. The main generalization that could be made from Muckensturm's data was that the sticklebacks attacked the unfamiliar targets. There is no yellow or violet in the sticklebacks' streams; these were the models most often attacked.

PRINCIPLES OF KIN SELECTION AND INCLUSIVE FITNESS CONTRADICTED

According to the principles of inclusive fitness and kin selection, we are more likely to risk our lives trying to save our son or daughter than to save a cousin. Clearly, if we are interested in the propagation of our genes, the last thing we want to do is to kill our own. But we do kill our own. Large numbers of close relatives and neighbors were denounced to the Gestapo between 1933 and 1945. In Saarbrücken, a woman reported her own husband to the Gestapo for listening to the "enemy radio." In the former Yugoslavia, numerous instances of murder of members of one's own family were reported. And the following horrible account was published by Wole Soyinka (1998), the Nigerian dissident:

> A Hutu, a leading citizen of a small Rwandan town, . . . felt
> personally indicted [when] an official accused the citizenry of being
> lax in the task of "bush clearing"—one of the many euphemisms
> for the task of eliminating the Tutsi. A day after his departure, the
> notable called a meeting of the villagers. . . . He began his address
> by revealing that, having taken to heart the rebuke . . . , he had
> decided to set an example, and thus slaughtered his Tutsi wife.
>
> But that was only the first step. . . . they must eliminate every
> vestige of Tutsi blood . . . And in one stroke of his machete, he
> lopped off the head of his oldest son. One by one, his three sons
> were led out of the hut . . . and slaughtered. (p. 11)

The principle that by force of nature all species seek to perpetuate their
genes makes aggression against virtual competitors a plausible derivation—a
derivation also attractive to economists who assume behavior to be dominated
by self-interest. But when applied to human aggression, where victims are
counted in six- and seven-digit numbers, the concept of a "selfish" gene is
not compelling, theoretically or empirically. We find in nature in profusion
not only parasitic, antagonistic, and exploitative relations among and within
species but also symbiotic. Given some specifiable constraints, parasitism *and*
symbiosis follow equally from the premise of inclusive fitness. In fact, it was
the difficulty that standard evolutionary theory had in explaining altruistic
and communal behavior that brought about the theory of inclusive fitness
(Hamilton, 1964). And the political theorist Francis Fukuyama (1992), rejecting the notion of the "selfish gene," does not hesitate to argue for affiliation,
cohesion, and communal order as the basic forces of human nature.

RAPE IN SERVICE OF INCLUSIVE FITNESS

Another false application of the principle of inclusive fitness is a recent attempt by Thornhill and Palmer (2000) to feature rape as a natural phenomenon whereby the male simply increases the likelihood that his genes will be
more extensively seeded. Their work has been widely cited in the popular
media. The intent of rape, they say, is not just lust. Since the victims are mostly
females of childbearing age, the main goal of rape is to impregnate. What
Thornhill and Palmer do not acknowledge, however, is that the rapist very
seldom stays around for 9 months to give protection to his offspring and to
make sure that it thrives. In fact, in one out of five cases there is quite severe
violence to the victim. Such violence does nothing but harm the carrier of
the rapist's genes and thus, as Barbara Ehrenreich (2000) aptly said, "It's a
pretty dumb Darwinian specimen who can't plant his seed without breaking
the 'vessel' in the process" (p. 88). And a substantial proportion of rape victims were prepubescent children, some less than 8 years old.

An example of rape that could not possibly serve the reproductive ambitions of its perpetrator is one that accompanied other atrocities when the Soviet army entered Germany in 1945. The following, of which there are many parallels, is an eyewitness testimony of one Hermann Sommer:

> The victims had been beaten and stabbed. . . . A large number of bodies had . . . the genitals stabbed through and were disemboweled. . . . A corporal told me of a church where a girl and two soldiers had been found. The girl had been actually crucified on the altar cross, the two soldiers strung up on either side. . . . [T]he women were completely naked, raped and then killed . . . with stab wounds or rifle butt blows to the head. (De Zayas, 1993, pp. 40–41)

Similarly, the Japanese soldiers entering Nanking in 1937 engaged in rape that was far from having a reproductive potential. Chang (1997) writes: "Many soldiers went beyond rape to disembowel women, slice off their breasts, nail them alive to walls. Fathers were forced to rape their daughters, and sons their mothers, as other family members watched" (p. 6).

Of course, the significance of biological factors cannot be denied. We do know quite well that the hypothalamus is involved in suppression of violence, or that testosterone levels are important. But there is a gaping derivational chasm between these facts and the Rape of Nanking. During the last decade, neuroscience has celebrated many discoveries of brain regions that are associated with fairly specific functions. But we should not be prompted by these facts to apply this new knowledge to the massacre in Littleton, as was unabashedly done in a recent issue of *Newsweek*, proclaiming the birth of the new "science of teen violence." These are gross oversimplifications. A host of features occur in tandem with human collective violence that are not present among animals. These features give human massacres an entirely distinct character that calls for an analysis focusing on these unique features.

ANIMALS DON'T, BUT HUMANS DO KILL ON PRINCIPLE

It is true that we share 98.5% of our genetic variance with the chimpanzee. But the meager 1.5% of our unshared variance makes for an enormous chasm. The 98.5% of shared DNA allows the chimp to produce a grunt, even several different grunts. But the 1.5% of unshared DNA allowed Mozart to write *The Magic Flute*. Our capacities for benign achievements, invention, and creation surpass those of the chimpanzee by many orders of magnitude. But our capacities for malign achievements are also enormous. We have shown extraordinary creativity, originality, and ingenuity in killing and torturing our own conspecifics. There is no animal species that has committed atrocities on our scale. In the measure of evil we stand alone. And the scale of atrocities in itself implies that there has to be elaborate organization, risk assessment, extensive planning, and preparation.

The attempt to construct an animal model of human collective violence faces so many discontinuities that only very superficial generalizations can be drawn. Of course, there is aggression among animals. Of course, animals protect their territory. Of course, we can locate brain structures in higher animals that correspond to ours and are activated in agonistic behavior. Of course, we can find collective animal aggression, such as among wolves. But human massacres are directed at our *conspecifics*. Animal aggression on the scale that would even remotely approximate any of the known massacres is never against conspecifics. And the scale of collective violence observed among humans surpasses that among animals by many orders of magnitude. Two million, which amounts to two out of every seven, Cambodians were killed between 1975 and 1978. During World War II, 6 million Jews, 3 million Poles, and millions of innocent civilians belonging to other ethnic groups lost their lives. Stalin's purges reach to nearly 15 million victims. In the Cultural Revolution in China, 43 million civilians lost their lives, many by starvation and disease, according to some estimates. And, as we have seen earlier, the ingenuity of mass murder and the level of atrocity accompanying some programs of genocide are never to be found among any animal species.

Above all, it is a deplorable but undeniable fact that most of the carnage of humans by other humans was the outcome of a deliberate, planned, and highly organized enterprise. In their work on violence, Wrangham and Peterson (1996) report a violent incident, cited previously, that started when "a group of eight chimpanzees traveled *purposefully* . . . toward the border of their range" (p. 5; italics mine) and attacked a lone male. How would one know that the actions of these eight chimpanzees were driven by a *purpose*, that there was a plan to deliberately inflict harm on a particular individual or just any individual? There was nothing in the behavior of the group of eight that would indicate such a circumstance. Most conspecific aggression of the form that is reported in the animal literature is spontaneous and arises when there are disputes over access to resources such as nesting, prey, or mating priorities. And aggression so motivated is immediately preceded by a threat to these scarce resources—a threat that is patently conspicuous. There is no parallel to Wannsee Conference that decided on the Final Solution in 1942 and laid out plans, organization, and logistics for the extermination of millions of innocent conspecifics. To assume that these cataclysmic events belong to a common category with the beating that eight chimpanzees inflicted on one of theirs nears on obscenity. The term *bestiality* when characterizing human violence is an offense to the nonhuman species.

There is abundant evidence that human massacres are highly organized and previously planned. The Rwanda massacre of 1994, according to Gérard

Prunier (1995), was meticulously planned for years. Involved in the planning was the president's wife, Mme Agathe Habyarimana, and the circle of her loyal supporters known as the Clan de Madame. The major plans were developed in 1993 by Colonel Théoneste Bagosora. And only half an hour after the plane carrying President Habyarimana was shot down on April 6, 1994, atrocities began in a most methodical way. There was a clear order of targeting victims that started with the liberal members of the government, the president of the Constitutional Court, civil rights activists, priests, journalists, and others for whom deliberate lists with addresses arranged by priority and precedence were prepared. And 2 million machetes, bought from China, were freely distributed among the Hutu population. In 100 days, 800,000 Tutsi were killed.

We are tempted to believe that pogroms taking place in eastern Europe at the turn of the nineteenth century and later were spontaneous events, or that Kristallnacht was an impromptu outburst of violence. Yet both were planned and organized. As late as 1945, when only a handful of Jews remained in the Polish town of Kielce, violence erupted that was originally reported as a spontaneous riot. Yet, according to a recent historical account (Wiacek, 1992), the pogrom was well organized and well prepared. Wiacek cites the fact that the violence started when groups of perpetrators gathered in the town square, and each group was deployed to a separate section of town, known to be housing Jews. More important, on the previous day, Christian stores were boarded up and had crosses painted on their entrances.

But if human massacres are carefully and deliberately planned and highly organized campaigns, it is important to inquire what forces drive hundreds of thousands of ordinary men to commit extraordinary acts—acts of murder, mutilation, rape, expulsion, and total extermination. I have suggested elsewhere (Zajonc, under review) that, bizarre as it may seem, human collective violence is driven and justified on moral grounds. In all instances of extraordinary mass violence, the acts are endowed with the high purpose of a moral imperative. The doctrine of Manifest Destiny was invoked to justify the Philippine-American war of 1898, in which a quarter of a million were killed or died of disease or hunger. The bombings of Dresden, Hiroshima, and Nagasaki were justified on a moral principle. And so were the Holocaust, the Rwanda and Burundi genocides, China's Cultural Revolution, the slaughter of Native Americans, and the slaughter of the Herrero in 1904 by General Von Trotha. I was unable to find *any* accounts of massacres that were not viewed by their perpetrators as right and necessary.

It is true, however, that the subsequent generations sometimes accept the guilt of their forefathers, but it is also true that in only exceptional cases is there any punishment of the perpetrators. The standard outcome is nearly complete impunity. There is also a great deal of denial and distortion (App, 1973; Butz, 1976; Irving, 1977; Seidel, 1986; Stern, 1994; Vidal-Naquet, 1992). Shintaro Ishihara, the governor of Tokyo, denied the occurrence of the Nanjing massacre altogether (French, 2000). Because of the wide diffusion of responsibility, it is difficult to assign guilt to particular individuals. Thus, even though the International Convention Against Genocide was signed in December 1948, the first trial for genocide took place not less than half a century later, against Dr. Milan Kovacevic.

SCIENTIFIC OBJECTIVITY AND THE STUDY OF MASSACRES

Massacres are extremely complex phenomena that will not be explained by a single factor, and no one discipline alone can explain the hundreds of massacres all over the globe. The task is novel and quite difficult. One important source of difficulty is our commitment to objectivity. Confronted with the scope and scale of atrocities that the twentieth century bestowed on our collective conscience, psychologists find themselves in a totally new setting of research. True: Pure and full objectivity is not to be found in *any* conventional research. After all, we *want* some research outcomes and not others. And we do hope for them. True: Empirical scientists introduce safeguards and control groups, counterbalance their experimental conditions, carry out independent replications, and invite opportunities for disconfirmation of their hypotheses. But, at the bottom, there lingers a wish, an expectation, a hope that things will turn out in a preferred way.

When we commit ourselves to the study of massacres, the criterion of objectivity becomes even more vulnerable. Two aspects of bias visit even the most impartial researcher. One is the revulsion against the unspeakable evil of the atrocities themselves. No one who has read historical accounts of the recent massacres and who has an ambition to understand these phenomena can formulate the problem without introducing one's own moral element into the study. In fact, Claude Lanzmann, the maker of the film *Shoah*, is adamant about the "obscenity of the very project of understanding [the Holocaust]" (Rosenbaum, 1998, p. 250). The analysis of massacres cannot be value-free. The point cannot be put more convincingly than in Langer's (1999) book on the Holocaust:

> Recently I was watching the testimony of a survivor of the Kovno ghetto. He spoke of the so-called *Kinderaktion*, when the Germans rounded up all the children (and many elderly) and took them to nearby Ninth Fort for execution. The witness was present in the room when an SS man entered and demanded from a mother the one-year-old infant she was holding in her arms. She refused to surrender it, so he seized the baby by its ankles and tore the body in two before the mother's eyes. . . . I ask myself what we can do with such information, how we can inscribe it in the . . . narratives that later will try to reduce to some semblance of order or pattern

the spontaneous defilement implicit in such deeds? How can we enroll such atrocities in the human community and identify them as universal tendencies toward evil inherent in all humankind? . . . Well, we can't. (p. 3)

The other source of bias is our own ethnic, national, or racial identity. A Chinese scholar will look at the Rape of Nanking (Chang, 1997) differently than a Japanese scholar, and Germans and Jews will be predisposed to study the Holocaust from different perspectives. Because in each case there is a clearly identifiable group of perpetrators and a clearly identifiable group of victims, the researcher has little chance of giving equally impartial attention to both. This difficulty is exacerbated by the fact that scholars engaged in massacre research have more often than not some personal connection with the victims or the perpetrators. Can survivors' anger be put aside and an impartial, dispassionate analysis be put in place? Can descendants overcome their bewilderment upon learning that their parents or grandparents were killers or countenanced killing, rape, and plunder? Can those who were not witnesses or bystanders of past brutalities have legitimate insights into these horrid events? The revulsion bias and the engagement bias are both sources of partiality to which the researcher must be sensitive.

NOTE

1. Lorenz, who died in 1989, wrote the earliest version of the innate releasing mechanism (*angeborener Auslösemechanismus*) theory between 1944 and 1948, when he was a prisoner of war in Yerevan, Armenia. The material was edited by his daughter, Agnes von Cranach, and published in German in 1978 (Lorenz, 1978) and in English in 1981 (Lorenz, 1981). The exact statement reads as follows: "This phenomenon of *lowering of the threshold of releasing stimuli in proportion to the time elapsed since the last discharge of a motor pattern suggests the existence of some form of response-specific arousal energy. This would have to be continuously produced by the organism but used up by performance of the motor pattern specific to that response*" (Lorenz, 1981, p. 283 italics in the original). The 1981 publication features a modified version of the "old psycho-hydraulic" model, which he acknowledged was "much ridiculed" (p. 180). The new model, however, retains all the energy hydraulics that the old model required. It differs only in the variety of sources for that energy.

REFERENCES

Andric, I. (1959). *The bridge over the Drina*. London: Harvill.

App, A. J. (1973). *The six-million swindle: Blackmailing the German people for hard marks with fabricated corpses*. Tacoma Park, MD: St. Boniface Press.

Ardrey, R. (1961). *African genesis: A personal investigation into the animal origins and nature of man*. New York: Atheneum.

Barash, D. P. (1982). *Sociobiology and behavior* (2nd ed.). New York: Elsevier.

Begley, S. (1999, May 3). Why the young kill. *Newsweek*.

Butz, A. R. (1976). *The hoax of the twentieth century: The case against the presumed extermination of European Jewry.* Torrance, CA: Institute for Historical Review.

Chang, I. (1997). *The rape of Nanking.* New York: Basic Books.

Dawkins, R. (1989). *The selfish gene.* Oxford: Oxford University Press.

De Zayas, A. M. (1983). *Zeugnisse der Vertreibung.* Krefeld, Germany: Sinus Verlag.

Ehrenreich, B. (2000, January 21). How "natural" is rape? *Time,* p. 88.

Ehrlich, P. R. (2000). *Human natures: Genes, cultures, and the human prospect.* Washington, DC: Island Press.

French, H. W. (2000, January 23). Japanese call '37 massacre a war myth, stirring storm. *New York Times,* p. A5.

Fukuyama. F. (1992). *The end of history and the last man.* New York: Free Press.

Gibbons, A. (1998). Which of our genes make us human: Comparison of primate DNA. *Science, 281,* 1432.

Hamilton, W. D. (1964). The genetical evolution of social behaviour. *Journal of Theoretical Biology, 7,* 1–52.

Hammer, D., & Copeland, P. (1998). *Living with our genes: Why they matter more than you think.* New York: Doubleday

Hinde, R. A. (1974). *Biological bases of human social behavior.* New York: McGraw-Hill.

Hirsch, J. U., Lindley, R. H., & Tolman, E. C. (1955). An experimental test of an alleged innate sign stimulus. *Journal of Comparative and Physiological Psychology, 48,* 278–280.

Irving, D. (1977). *Hitler's war.* New York: Avon.

Langer, L. L. (1999). *Preempting the Holocaust.* New Haven, CT: Yale University Press.

LeBon, G. (1995), *The crowd.* New Brunswick, NJ: Transaction.

Lorenz, K. Z. (1966). *On aggression.* London: Methuen.

Lorenz, K. Z. (1978). *Vergleichende Verhaltensforschung: Grundlagen der Etholgie* [Comparative study of behavior: The foundations of ethology]. Vienna: Springer.

Lorenz, K. Z. (1981). *The foundations of ethology* (K. Z. Lorenz & R. W. Kickert, Trans.). New York: Springer.

Morris, D. (1967). *The naked ape: A zoologist's study of the human animal.* New York: McGraw-Hill.

Moyer, K. E. (1969). Internal impulses to aggression. *Transactions of the New York Academy of Science, 31,* 104–114.

Muckensturm, B. (1965). Let nid et le territoire chez l'Epinoche *Gasterosteus aculeatus. Comptes Rendues d'Acedemie des Sciences, 260,* 4825.

Muckensturm, B. (1969). La signification de la livrée nuptiale de l'Epinoche. *Revue du Comportement Animal, 3,* 39–65.

Peeke, H. V. (1969). Habituation of conspecific aggression in the three-spined stickleback (*Gasterosteus aculeatus L.*). *Behaviour, 35,* 137–156.

Peeke, H. V., Wyers, E. J., & Herz, M. J. (1969). Waning of the aggressive response to male models in the three-spined stickleback (*Gasterosteus aculeatus L.*). *Animal Behaviour, 17,* 224–228.

Prunier, G. (1995). *The Rwanda crisis: History of genocide.* New York: Columbia University Press.

Rosenbaum, R. (1998). *Explaining Hitler: The search for the origins of his evil.* New York: Random House.

Seidel, G. (1986). *The Holocaust denial: Antisemitism, racism and the New Right.* Leeds, Yorkshire: Beyond the Pale.

Soyinka, W. (1998, Oct. 4). Hearts of darkness. *New York Times Book Review.*

Stern, K. (1994). *Holocaust denial.* New York: American Jewish Committee.

Storr, A. (1968). *Human aggression.* New York: Atheneum.

Thornhill, R., & Palmer, C. T. (2000). *A natural history of rape: Biological bases of sexual coercion.* Cambridge, MA: MIT Press.

Tinbergen, N. (1952). The curious behavior of the stickleback. *Scientific American, 187,* 22–26.

Vidal-Naquet, P. (1992). *Assassins of memory: Essays on the denial of the Holocaust.* New York: Columbia University Press.

Wiacek, T. (1992). Zabic zyda! Kulisy i tajemnice pogromu kieleckiego 1946. Kraków: Temax.

Wilson, E. O. (1975). *Sociobiology.* Cambridge, MA: Belknap Press of Harvard University Press.

Worchel, S. (1999). *Written in blood: Ethnic identity and the struggle for human harmony.* New York: Worth.

Wrangham, R., & Peterson, D. (1996). *Demonic males: Apes and the origins of human violence.* Boston: Houghton Mifflin.

Zajonc, R. B. (under review). *Massacres: Mass murder in the name of moral imperatives.*

Part III

DEALING WITH EVIL

10

The Holocaust and the Four Roots of Evil

Roy F. Baumeister

The Holocaust was one of the most shocking and disgraceful events of the twentieth century. A nation renowned for science, music, and philosophy, in the forefront of modernity, followed a fascist leader and his gangster cronies in a downward spiral that began with dictatorship and police state and led to mass murder and world war. It is widely estimated that the brutally efficient system brought death to 11 million civilian victims, including 6 million Jews and large numbers of Roma (Gypsies), homosexuals, Communists, and others. This tally of victims does not even include the civilian victims of bombing and other military operations, which were on an unprecedented scale (even World War I had directed its violence almost exclusively against military targets and forces), nor does it include the millions of soldiers killed in action.

Nazi Germany's mass executions of millions of defenseless civilians who had not been convicted of any crime and who for the most part were guilty of nothing more than belonging to a disfavored ethnic category has captured the imagination as an extreme example of human evil. Above all, it has challenged many assumptions about human nature, especially insofar as the cooperative effort of perhaps hundreds of thousands of seemingly ordinary, decent citizens was required to achieve the grisly toll. Many Germans continued to regard themselves as decent, upright, moral individuals despite having played some role in bringing other civilians to their deaths. To be sure, this challenge was not readily taken up, and many people (including many psychologists) were slow to accept the implication that human nature was widely capable of such atrocities. Some preferred to regard Nazi Germany as an anomaly that could not be repeated in other countries. The psychological researcher Stanley Milgram (1963) famously surveyed his colleagues and students in psychology as to what proportion of American students would follow orders to give dangerous and potentially lethal electric shocks to another participant, and the forecasts typically extended to only a handful of unscrupulous or sadistic individuals—whereas when he actually conducted the experiment, the majority complied right up to the extreme end. That study, perhaps compounded by reports of American atrocities in Vietnam, finally produced a recognition that psychologists needed to face up to the enormous potential for cruelty and violence that lies not far beneath the surface of the modern Western individual.

Some scholars have protested the application of psychology to the Holocaust. With some justification, they say that treating the Holocaust as an instance of general psychological principles undermines its status as a unique (and uniquely immoral) episode. They worry, also with some justification, that providing a psychological explanation of the perpetrators' actions will make them seem less heinous and even closer to something that could be considered understandable and forgivable. I am sympathetic to those views up to a point because it seems essential to maintain our collective moral outrage at the mass killing.

There are, however, two crucial arguments in favor of applying psychology to the Holocaust. One is that any hope of avoiding a repetition of those murders—and mass killings became more common in the decades after World War II, suggesting that the moral lesson of the Holocaust was not effectively learned—involves understanding their causes. As with medicine, engineering, and natural disasters, the best way to prevent misfortunes is to know what causes them and to apply that knowledge effectively.

The other argument is that psychology itself cannot afford to ignore the lessons of the Holocaust. To treat the Holocaust as a unique event outside the realm of psychology is in an important sense to marginalize and even dismiss it. Idealistic, otherwise virtuous, seemingly normal and decent people have cooperated in mass killings in the Soviet Union, China, Cambodia, Rwanda, Yugoslavia, and other places, and these events undermine the case that the Holocaust was somehow outside the realm of psychological principles. If psychology is ever to furnish an adequate account of human nature, it cannot afford to ignore the dark side of human nature that showed its face repeatedly in many parts of the globe during these recent decades. For example, some psychological theorists have recently embraced the view that human beings, as products of evolution, are essentially similar to other animal species, but such reductionist views are severely challenged by evidence that human beings are apparently the only species whose culture and socialization can bring them to murder conspecifics on a massive scale.

In that connection, it seems essential not only to use psychological theories to examine the Holocaust but also to seek parallels with other mass killings, such as the ones just mentioned. Psychology is not interested (at least not primarily) in the Holocaust as an end in itself or a separate phenomenon; rather, the goal is to discover generalizable knowledge about human behavior, and generality can only be confirmed by finding parallels in other cases.

The methodological difficulties of applying psychology to the Holocaust are formidable. Some are typical, such as the inevitable ambiguity and uncertainty that must attend any effort to use psychology to analyze events that are long past and whose participants are now mostly dead. Others are specific to such episodes of enormous repugnance. A particular difficulty of this sort is our natural human tendency and the associated moral obligation to have empathy and sympathy with the victims. It is our concern for past and future victims that motivates us to want to study such horrors as the Holocaust—and yet that very concern becomes a serious obstacle to understanding the psychological motivations and cognitions of the perpetratrors (see Miller, Gordon, & Buddie, 1999). Many writers on evil and violence have insisted that to understand is not to forgive, but I fear that such claims are often facile attempts to gloss over a profound difficulty.

The difficulty is rooted in the pervasive differences between perpetrator and victim perspectives. Many of these boil down to the fact that nasty events, both great and small, typically seem much worse to the victim than to the perpetrator. Baumeister, Stillwell, and Wotman (1990) obtained people's firsthand accounts of interpersonal conflicts, and the victims' accounts depicted the events as worse than the perpetrators' accounts, even though the same people furnished both sets of accounts. For example, the victims described the episode as more unjustified and causing more lasting harm than the perpetrators, and their stories were less likely to have happy endings, to cite mitigating circumstances, or to refer to conciliatory acts.

A researcher therefore cannot understand the perpetrator's perspective without at least briefly adopting a view of the episode that makes it far less bad than it seems to the victim—and that entails relinquishing some of our empathic sympathy for the victim. It is therefore necessary to recognize a genuine moral danger in the study of perpetrators of evil and violence. My view is that danger must be accepted, because the cost of not understanding the psychology of perpetrators is even greater. Still, it is perhaps vital to recognize that requirement. To understand perpetrators, it is necessary to suspend one's sympathy for the victims and to make a serious, honest effort to look at events from the perpetrator's point of view. When one has finished one's study, however, it is important to remember that one has done this and to resume both one's sympathy with the victims and one's moral condemnation of evil actions.

My approach in this chapter is based on my broader work on the psychology of evil (Baumeister, 1997). I concluded from an extensive survey that the causes of human evil can be sorted into four major categories. This chapter will take those four roots of evil and apply them to the Holocaust. These are idealism, threatened egotism, instrumental pursuit of selfish gain, and sadism.

IDEALISM

The Nazis have become one of the most widely recognized images of modern evil. Throughout most of the world today, the concept of evil can readily be evoked by displaying almost any cue reminiscent of Nazism, such as the swastika, the name of any of the principal Nazis, or their garb or affectations (e.g., the goose-stepping march or Hitler salute). In children's cartoons, evil creatures from outer space are made to speak with German accents. Germany's efforts to atone for its Nazi atrocities have been extensive but fall far short of being able to wipe away the moral stain, and indeed it is often suggested that modern Germany's widespread enthusiasm for pan-European union (such as the common currency) derives from the inability of its citizens to take pride in their disgraced nation.

Although Nazism has become a symbol for evil, it is not safe to conclude that the Nazis and their German contemporaries regarded it as evil during its heyday. On the contrary, one conclusion from my survey of human cruelty and violence is that perpetrators of evil do not generally regard themselves as evil.

How, then, did the perpetrators of the Holocaust regard themselves? One important answer is that many of them regarded themselves as idealistic patriots who were doing difficult, unpleasant work that was justified by its contribution to a higher cause. This pattern appears to be common to many of the large-scale evil acts of the twentieth century (and other eras as well): Perpetrators do not regard themselves as evil but rather see their violent acts as necessary means toward high ideals and positive, valued ends. Thus, the greatest body counts of all time were the roughly 20 million victims (each) of the Stalinist purges of the Soviet Union and the Maoist Cultural Revolution in China (see Conquest, 1990; Thurston, 1987). Yet the people who carried out those extensive killings believed, by and large, that they were acting in the service of noble goals and helping bring about the paradise on earth that would result from the full actualization of socialist principles.

Although the Nazis, like the Russian and Chinese Communists, included the term *socialist* in their title, in fact they held a somewhat different vision of the paradise on earth they wanted to create. Their fascist dream did not extend to the abolition of private property or hierarchical authority. Still, their ideals included many that we would recognize and even embrace today. The Nazis advocated much of what we today call "family values," including stable marriages that permit the raising of healthy, well-adjusted children in safety. They supported small businesses, law and order, and economic stability leading to prosperity. They restored national pride and patriotism to a nation that had been deeply humiliated (see later discussion). They advocated progress and modernity, including the application of scientific doctrines to social engineering (such as in their programs to improve the gene pool by preventing mentally retarded and other genetically suspect individuals from procreating).

They insisted on high standards of personal honor and expected that honorable individuals would make altruistic sacrifices in order to serve the greater good of all.

Like the Communists and many others, the Nazis had an overarching vision of an ideal society in which good people would live together in peace and harmony. Indeed, in that respect it is not so different from the social visions of countless other idealists and utopians, including the Founding Fathers of the United States, the leaders of the French Revolution, and many more. With the exception of the United States, most of those dreams have come to grief, degenerating into violence and social chaos. Were it not for the United States, one would be tempted to conclude that the ideal is somehow inherently flawed or at least profoundly impractical if not impossible to realize. And even the American dream was only realized at some considerable cost of victims' blood, most notably that of the indigenous North Americans who were killed or exiled to make room for the expanding young nation.

How do such seemingly fine and noble ideals produce such horrific bloodshed? One crucial part of the answer lies in the perennial temptation to believe that the ends justify the means. Although in today's United States it has become commonplace to assert that ends do not justify means, I am convinced that that is a historically exceptional position, and it has been far more common to believe the opposite. The very structure of moral discourse goes against the American view. Specifically, moral discourse typically seeks justification by appealing to some higher value or broader principle. By definition, ends are higher values than means, and so ends do tend to lend justification to means. In the extreme, people who believe they have been instructed by God to perform certain acts are often fairly certain that they are doing the right thing, because God's authority is sufficiently high as to override any other considerations. The biblical example of Abraham is relevant: God told him to kill his son, and he obeyed (although God rescinded the command at the last minute). This parable is still read and discussed today, typically with a positive message that the man was doing the right thing by obeying God's law without question, but it is a classic statement of the view that the end justifies the means and that one should submit to higher moral authorities even when the specific commands seem very questionable. (Imagine, for example, a modern-day Abraham appearing on the *Jerry Springer Show* to explain to a skeptical audience that God had told him to cut his child's throat.)

Because ends justified means, the Nazis set about erecting their ideal society by first getting rid of all the people whom they regarded as unsuitable for membership. Some scholars believe that the Nazis had intended from the start to kill all Jews, but the evidence for this assertion is quite weak. Thus, an influential statement of this view was presented by Dawidowicz (1975), who argued that murderous hatred of Jews was Hitler's first priority all his life and was regarded as more important to the Nazi regime than all other goals, including winning the war. Her evidence, however, is little more than some selected rantings from Hitler's various speeches and writings, the observation that in the 1940s some trains were used to transport Jews to concentration camps when those same trains might have been used instead for military purposes, and the fact that killing certain Jews disrupted some corners of the war economy (such as by the loss of skilled workers in arms factories).

To me, it seems more likely that the overriding factor was simply to get rid of the Jews from the Aryan utopia the Nazis envisioned. Emigration was long permitted and even encouraged, and forcible deportations were carried out as long as they were practical. But other countries were largely unwilling to accept the people whom the Germans seemed to regard as not good enough to live in Germany, and when the loopy schemes such as resettlement of Jews on Madagascar proved impractical, killing emerged as seemingly the only practical way to get rid of the unwanted unfortunates.

Zygmunt Bauman (1991) has offered a profound assessment of Nazi Germany's attitude toward the Jews, and it is one that seems to explain the Holocaust far better than the simple assertion of anti-Semitic hatred that is offered by such facile and simplistic thinkers as Goldhagen (1996). Bauman's analysis is that the mentality that directed the Holocaust was a gardener's mentality. As he explains, the gardener has in mind an ideal notion of what his beautiful garden will look like, and to achieve that, he believes he has to get rid of the weeds (who do not belong in his ideal garden). Some gardeners may in fact hate the weeds. Others may regard the weeds as an irritating impediment. Some may have no particular feelings about the weeds. Others may even feel sorry for the weeds or admire their tenacious efforts to survive and thrive where they are not wanted. But all agree that the weeds must go, if only because the imagined ideal of the garden has no place for weeds. Whether the gardener hates the weeds or not is largely irrelevant—his feelings are merely a matter of his subjective experience while he carries out his task of getting rid of them.

The very irrelevance of the gardener's feelings is itself a tragic, even heartbreaking, aspect of Bauman's analysis, and it may help explain why people have been reluctant to accept it. In a way, it lowers the status of the victim, because one does not regard the weeds as "victims" of the gardener and his plan. Probably most people would prefer to be killed by someone who hated them passionately, because that contains a degree of respect, as opposed to being killed by someone who regarded them as an inconvenient obstacle to his plan. They very zeal with which scholars such as Goldhagen have sought to attribute deeply passionate hatred to all Germans, using flimsy evidence and generalizing wildly from isolated anecdotes, may well be a reflection of this wish for more dignity than the gardener analogy allows.

Conspiracy theories are popular among victims, perhaps precisely for the reason that they construe the perpetrators' intentions in a suitably grand and evil manner to match the suffering of the victims. In recent decades in the

United States, for example, many African Americans have subscribed to the theory that crack cocaine and AIDS are part of a systematic plot by the government and white establishment to annihilate the black community, and some have even asserted that black-on-black violence is in fact a result of manipulation by the white-controlled government (e.g., Shakur, 1993). In a similar vein, Brownmiller (1975) has asserted that the acts of rape scattered all over the country (and probably the world) are linked as part of a conscious, deliberate conspiracy by all men to intimidate and subjugate all women. It may be easy to dismiss such theories as preposterous rantings or paranoid fantasies, but in my view they have a psychologically important foundation in the victims' wish for dignity. There is far more self-esteem and importance in being the target of a huge, demonic conspiracy that will take a large, evil satisfaction in your death—as opposed to believing that you suffered because other, more powerful people were getting what they wanted and did not care one way or another what happened to you along the way. And perhaps it is worse yet to think that the people who torment and kill you believe they are pursuing some grand, positive ideal, so that your suffering is not only trivial and irrelevant but an inconvenience to them in the realization of their better world. They would prefer that you had never been born.

A further complication of the moral aspect of participating in genocide is that disobedience is often regarded as immoral, and the hierarchy of moral authority in fascist Germany probably encouraged unquestioning obedience. It is likely that many individuals had serious moral qualms about playing a part in the oppression of Jews. (How much they realized that Jews were being not just deported but actually killed remains in dispute, but they had to recognize that many of their fellow citizens were being oppressed to a significant degree.) Today, Americans believe that those individuals should have acted on their individual principles and defied the moral authorities of those who gave orders for these oppressive acts. Yet this defiance is difficult to achieve even in a society dedicated to freedom and equality, and it must have been considerably more difficult in a society such as Nazi Germany. For a low-ranking individual to dispute the moral judgment of superiors would constitute unthinkable arrogance, especially in a society where respect for superiors is deeply embedded in centuries of tradition.

Moreover, an essential feature of fascism is the elevation of the collective above the individual, and so individuals are supposed to do their duty without question. German culture probably more resembled the kind of culture one has usually found in military organizations rather than modern America with its autonomous individuals. In the military, soldiers have generally been strictly socialized to obey orders without question in order to serve the greater good. The American military establishment has recently (after the My Lai massacres came to light) changed to embrace the doctrine to begin asserting that low-ranking soldiers have the right and perhaps the duty to disobey immoral orders, so that in principle each soldier becomes the moral arbiter who can pass judgment on what superior officers decide. What will happen if this doctrine is ever put to the test—and it is doubtful that American soldiers will ever face such moral tests on the scale that the German functionaries did under the Nazi killing program—remains to be seen, but I suspect we would be disappointed in the outcome.

There is even some indication that the Nazis used the hierarchy of moral authority to facilitate their brutal policies. Lifton's (1986) research into the Nazi medical personnel was aimed at learning how these idealistic young men became involved in helping to kill. Many claimed that when they began work they were paired with a highly respected, senior physician, and they naturally deferred to his (perhaps occasionally her) moral authority. The first killings involved seriously ill or handicapped individuals who were regarded as hopeless cases. The older man would determine that the case was hopeless and would assign the younger one to terminate the life. That helped remove the older man from the actual killing. The younger man performed the deed, but he could rest assured that the decision had been made by someone whom everyone respected and whom he would not deign to question. Once in a while one of the younger physicians would question such a decision and would find himself quietly transferred to another position, but most of them were willing to believe that they should simply carry out the decisions of their betters.

THREATENED EGOTISM

A second root cause of violence and evil is *threatened egotism*, a term that refers to favorable views of self that have been disputed or impugned by others. Both groups and individuals have a tendency to attack others who insult or humiliate them.

The theory that violence results from threatened egotism goes against the long-standing view that low self-esteem is a major cause of violence. For many years it was treated as common knowledge that low self-esteem was the decisive factor, although this theory lacked both a corpus of empirical support and even a definitive theoretical statement. In retrospect, it is unclear exactly why low self-esteem was supposed to lead to aggression. Most plausibly, perhaps, it was presumed that people with low self-esteem were desperate to raise their self-esteem (i.e., engage in self-enhancement) and regarded attacking others as a potentially effective way of accomplishing that. It has also been suggested that they tend to blame their failures on others and therefore might attack people out of frustration when things go bad (Long, 1990).

But the characterization of people with low self-esteem as aggressive self-enhancers is contrary to most accumulated knowledge about low self-esteem. People with low self-esteem are generally oriented toward protecting them-

248

selves against failure and humiliation rather than boosting their self-esteem—in fact, self-enhancement is far more typical of people with high rather than low self-esteem (see Baumeister, Tice, & Hutton, 1989, for review). Attacking another person involves risk, but people with low self-esteem tend to prefer to avoid risks. Contrary to Long's (1990) assertion that people with low self-esteem blame their failures on others, they in fact tend to blame themselves and accept responsibility for failure to a much greater extent than people who are high in self-esteem (Blaine & Crocker, 1993; Fitch, 1970). More generally, people with low self-esteem typically are shy, modest, and insecure. They doubt their ability to know what is best and readily defer to the advice and influence of others (e.g., Baumeister, 1993; Brockner, 1984; Campbell, 1990). Such a person is unlikely to become a violent aggressor.

One could more plausibly suggest that the person with high self-esteem would tend to become aggressive. People with high self-esteem are often oriented toward self-enhancement, are willing to take chances to seek out victories, and tend to blame others for failures and setbacks. Yet many people with high self-esteem are buoyed by an easygoing confidence and stock of positive, optimistic feelings that could deter them from aggression. Not all of them, however.

Kernis, Grannemann, and Barclay (1989) used a simple questionnaire procedure to investigate how self-esteem might be related to aggression. They measured not only each person's level of self-esteem but also how stable it was across repeated measurements at different times. Then they sought to correlate these measures with self-reported hostile tendencies. They concluded that the most hostile people were a subset of people with high self-esteem. More precisely, people with high but unstable self-esteem were the most hostile. Meanwhile, people with high but stable self-esteem were the least hostile. To some extent these two groups canceled each other out, and so measuring self-esteem without assessing stability produced no result.

The important conclusion was that aggression is most common among a subgroup of people with favorable opinions of themselves. This conclusion was supported and extended by a literature review by Baumeister, Smart, and Boden (1996), who also concluded that violent people tend to have very favorable opinions of themselves, but not all people who think well of themselves are violent. Moreover, members of the violent subgroup are violent not simply because they think well of themselves but because their exalted and inflated self-views are undermined when others criticize, humiliate, or otherwise show disrespect to them. The violence is a response to the (perceived) attack on their favorable views of themselves.

Laboratory studies by Bushman and Baumeister (1998) confirmed the importance of threatened egotism in aggression. They included both a simple measure of self-esteem and a measure of narcissism (which, not incidentally, is significantly correlated with unstable high self-esteem; see Rhodewalt, Madrian, & Cheney, 1998). They measured how much people chose to deliver aversive stimulation (in the form of blasts of unpleasant loud noise) to people who, by random assignment, had either insulted or praised them. Self-esteem had no direct relationship to aggression, either alone or in combination with other factors. Aggression was highest among narcissists who had received insulting criticism. In particular, they were highly aggressive toward the person who had humiliated them.

The humiliated narcissist is thus the leading candidate for violent action. Does this image fit the perpetrators of the Holocaust? To be sure, it is risky to generalize psychological principles based on individuals to groups, and so one should not easily speak of collective narcissism. Then again, many studies have found that groups act just like more extreme versions of individuals, so some tentative generalizations can be warranted. Baumeister et al. (1996) did review evidence to suggest that threatened groups sometimes react with defensive violence, just like threatened individuals.

Let us consider the two factors (humiliation and narcissism) separately. Narcissism is defined by a series of factors (American Psychiatric Association, 1994). These begin with favorable, even grandiose self-regard, including a strong sense of superiority over others, arrogance, fantasies of greatness, and a belief that oneself is unique. The German Nazis fancied themselves a "master race" superior to all others, and they clearly regarded their dream of Continental, if not world, domination to be an achievable goal. Their self-declared Third Reich signified a pretentious claim to be the successor to the Holy Roman Empire that had once dominated the civilized world. (They also were fond of calling it the thousand-year empire, which in comparison with their actual twelve-year reign was another bit of grandiose fantasy.) Their legendary arrogance was perhaps their undoing, insofar as trying to make war against Russia, England, and the United States simultaneously looks in retrospect to have been an absurd and doomed project. Napoleon's invasion of Russia irreparably ruined his army, and Hitler repeated that megalomaniac mistake, with similar results.

Narcissism is also marked by an inflated sense of entitlement. This, too, seems to have been a fair description of the Nazis. The invasions of France and Poland seem to have been based at least in part on the sense that the Nazis had a right to claim those lands. With Poland in particular, the Nazis seem to have believed that it was appropriate to expel the inhabitants simply to make room for the Germans. (These attitudes may sound absurd, but perhaps they are not entirely different from the way early Americans regarded their continent as uninhabited despite the millions of natives already living there—and who were killed or herded off to make room for the expanding nation of white immigrants.) Meanwhile, the attack on the Jews was accompanied by policies under which the German authorities helped themselves to the considerable wealth of the victims, beginning with charging extortionate fees for emigration, and ending with the expropriation of the last valuables and other possessions of the death camp victims.

Two last defining features of narcissism are also easily apparent in Nazi behavior. First, narcissists tend to take an exploitative attitude toward others. Nazi Germany exploited its victims to a degree scarcely imagined even by the most brutal of the other killing campaigns of the century. Not only were wealth and property confiscated, but slave labor was extorted from the hapless victims in between their imprisonment and their death, and at the end even their body parts were exploited as raw material for consumer goods (e.g., hair shorn from concentration camp inmates was used to stuff pillows).

Second, narcissists are now regarded as capable of empathizing with others, but they often neglect to use this capacity toward others around them. Clearly the Nazi regime wasted little effort trying to empathize with its victims, and indeed the extensive dehumanization and casual cruelty with which the Nazis treated their victims would be scarcely imaginable if they had been empathically connected with them.

Thus, it is not difficult to discern the essential features of narcissism in the attitudes of the Nazis. To be sure, this analysis is retrospective, and the danger of confirmation bias must be recognized in all such approaches. To dismiss that analysis as mere confirmation bias would, however, require that one could just as easily find evidence of the opposite features, and I think it would be very difficult to make such a case. To characterize the Nazis as essentially marked by humility, a deep belief in their own inferiority and unworthiness, a sense of being ordinary or common, a feeling of low deservingness, deeply respectful treatment of other groups, and high empathy toward outsiders would seem ridiculous. Hence it does seem reasonable to accept the characterization of them as narcissistic.

The other element in the threatened egotism formula is the experience of humiliation (or other blows to pride). There again it would seem beyond doubt or contradiction that Germany between the two world wars fit the pattern. The late eighteenth and nineteenth centuries saw Germany rise from a chaotic collection of quarreling localities to one of the world's greatest countries. Its achievements in philosophy, music, literature, science, and technology put it in the forefront of nations. These triumphs were capped by a series of small but very successful wars. The Germans' crushing defeat of mighty France in 1871 was immediately followed by national unification, whereupon they became one of the foremost military powers in the world. They eagerly began World War I with the expectation that it would allow them to prove themselves better than their rivals. Although the war dragged on longer than expected, it was fought on foreign soil (including land the Germans had conquered in France and Russia). The propaganda in the government-controlled news probably kept the population believing that Germany was winning the

251

war right up to the end, and that belief could have only been encouraged by Russia's surrender to Germany in 1917.

The abrupt series of collapses that followed must have seemed shocking and even inexplicable to the Germans. Their army, which supposedly was winning the war, suddenly surrendered. Their proud emperor abdicated. The expectation of honorable treatment in the peace settlement was cruelly disappointed by the humiliating, exploitative treatment in the Treaty of Versailles. The victorious enemy installed a new form of government that was plainly inept at dealing with the escalating social problems. The bill for war reparations bankrupted the government, and the economy collapsed to a degree that had never been seen before. In short, within a few years Germany was transformed from a proud leader of nations into a helpless and pitiful failure. It is hardly surprising that the Germans hungrily embraced Hitler's message that theirs was still a great nation, especially when his early policies met with such extraordinary success (politically, economically, and militarily).

There is one apparent gap in this analysis. Bushman and Baumeister (1998) found that narcissists were mainly aggressive toward the people who had delivered the blow to their pride. Why did the Nazis direct such animosity toward Jews, homosexuals, Gypsies, and others who seemingly had done them little harm? There are two answers to this question. First, Nazi Germany had ample animosity toward the Allies who had humbled it at the end of World War I, especially France and England. Second, there was a widespread belief that the Jews had contributed in decisive ways to the catastrophic defeat. The seeming inexplicability of the defeat in that war fostered belief that the Germans had been betrayed from within or stabbed in the back (in the popular phrase). The Jews, as outsiders living in their midst, had for centuries been perennial targets of such conspiracy theories, and they came into play once again here. Moreover, the Jews had also been heavily involved in financial dealings, and the astonishing collapse of the German money system—which must have been especially unbelievable in the era prior to modern economic theory—would have fueled suspicions of Jewish machinations. In other words, it does seem plausible that by oppressing and killing Jews, the Germans did believe, even if wrongly, that they were getting revenge on the people who had caused them their great national humiliation.

INSTRUMENTAL

A third root of evil is that people will sometimes perform violent or oppressive acts as a means toward achieving personal or collective gain. They may want much the same things that other people want, such as money, power, sex, or status, and they try to reach these goals by ways that involve harm to others.

In my view, such factors played an important but secondary role in the Holocaust. To be sure, some have asserted them as primary. The journalist

Gitta Sereny (1983) published a lengthy interview with Franz Stangl, who was commandant of the death camps at Sobibor and Treblinka. She asked him what he had believed to be the Nazis' reason for killing the Jews. "They wanted their money," he replied immediately, adding that he thought "fantastic sums" of money were involved (p. 101). In his view, the Holocaust was conducted primarily for the sake of enriching the Nazi Party and the German war effort by extorting money from its Jewish (and other) victims.

Still, most scholars do not find this explanation satisfactory, and neither do I. (Nor did Sereny.) Certainly, the executions themselves were not necessary if the goal was simply to get the victims' money, and by the time the victims arrived at the concentration camps, they retained only a relatively small amount of their property. The overhead cost of transporting and killing them and then making use of their personal effects was probably substantial and unlikely to be offset by the value gained from those effects. If money were the main goal, it would have been enough to strip the Jews of homes and savings. (To be sure, before the concentration camp phase, the Nazi regime simply pressured Jews to emigrate, and it charged increasingly high fees for the privilege of leaving, which suggests that the Nazis were attuned to the prospects of financial gain early in the campaign.)

As a secondary purpose, though, it is likely that the money was a significant factor. The Jews were killed to get rid of them for the sake of creating a fascist utopia and to gain revenge (however misdirected) for the humiliations Germany had suffered. But along the way the state and many individuals discovered they could gain material advantage in the process. The state confiscated the main wealth. Individuals could bring down persons against whom they held personal grudges. Guards could gain money or sex by taking bribes from desperate prisoners. Undoubtedly this process fueled the momentum of the system and helped it continue to operate. Few large operations can continue indefinitely if everyone involved suffers ongoing material losses, and if the Holocaust had been costly to the Nazi state and the individual Germans involved, it is likely it would have stopped much sooner.

A useful parallel can be found in Roth's (1964) account of the Spanish Inquisition. It, too, began with persecution of Jews, in that case sparked mainly by religious zeal and idealism. Spain passed a law requiring that only Christians remain in the country, and the Jews faced a rough choice of leaving at once or converting. As elsewhere, many Jews were active in commerce and finance and had accumulated some degree of wealth despite being held back by official discrimination. Those who converted were suddenly freed of those restrictions and became much more wealthy and successful, thereby arousing the envy of the Christian population, who began to complain that the Jews were reaping the benefits of Christianization without being proper Christians. The church establishment then began to conduct investigations to see how thoroughly and properly Christian these individuals were. Although it seems undeniable that the Inquisition was carried out and guided by high-minded religious motives and ideals, it was also undoubtedly sustained by material self-seeking. The Vatican did not have a budget to give to the Spanish clerics conducting the Inquisition, and so it stipulated that the latter could confiscate the property of those convicted of heresy. This may have seemed like a fair and reasonable way to finance the procedures, but it created a heavy bias toward conviction among the Inquisitors. Although the riches were supposed to go exclusively to the authorities, it seems likely that many individuals took advantage of the opportunities to enrich themselves. Likewise, many locals could eliminate business rivals by denouncing them to the Inquisition, and others could use it to carry out grudges. Whether the Inquisition was also used to extort sex is not well documented—the inquisitors being, after all, bound by vows of celibacy—but there are records that inquisitions of young females included stripping them naked, which suggests that sexual interests played a role as well as monetary greed.

In short, material gain almost certainly became involved as a secondary motive for the Holocaust, but it does not seem plausible as a primary cause.

SADISM

The fourth and final root of evil identified by Baumeister (1997) was sadism, which is to say the derivation of pleasure from inflicting harm. In that work I concluded that sadism is almost always a secondary factor (when it appears at all, which is not often). That is, perpetrators undertake acts of violence and oppression initially for other reasons, but some learn to enjoy the activities and so may continue or escalate them in an almost addiction-like quest for pleasure. In various groups of perpetrators, the sadists are typically a fairly small number, such as 5 or 6%.

The theoretical model I offered for the emergence of sadistic pleasure was based on opponent-process theory (Solomon, 1980; Solomon & Corbit, 1974; see also Baumeister & Campbell, 1999). This theory is based on the body's homeostatic mechanisms and holds that departures from the resting state set off processes that function to restore the resting state. For example, physical exertion brings an increase in heart rate and breathing, but eventually other processes bring these back to their normal baseline rates. With repetition, the secondary (restorative) processes become more powerful and efficient and can take precedence. This is why people may learn to enjoy seemingly dangerous activities such as falling (as in hang gliding or bungee jumping): Although the initial fear is highly aversive, the body creates euphoria to offset it, and with repeated trials the euphoric opponent process comes to dominate the experience.

Applied to sadism, opponent-process theory would begin by recognizing that most people experience sharp distress the first time they inflict suffering on another. Various accounts of Holocaust perpetrators, such as Browning's (1992) work on reserve policemen abruptly assigned to conduct killing operations, suggest that anxiety, nightmares, gastrointestinal distress, and other negative reactions were common at first. The opponent process initially is slow and inefficient, but with repetition it gains in strength. Sadists are thus made, not born. To the question of why does not everyone turn into a sadist eventually, my answer is that most people would refuse to allow themselves to recognize that they enjoy inflicting harm, because of guilt. People with a weak sense of guilt may, however, be willing to recognize the rising sense of pleasure in harming others. I suspect that hunters would go through a similar process in their feelings about the animals they kill, with initial remorse and disgust gradually giving way to pleasure and satisfaction.

The Holocaust has certainly furnished an ample stock of anecdotes that indicate gratuitous cruelty, and so it seems likely that sadism became a factor. Goldhagen's (1996) anecdotes illustrate such patterns. (Goldhagen sought to claim that the anecdotes he reports were typical, but it seems far more likely that he selected extreme examples.)

Another instructive example was furnished by Browning (1992). A group of soldiers was guarding a contingent of Jewish men who were to be shot. During the wait, one of the soldiers organized a sort of game in which the victims were forced to crawl on hands and knees while the soldiers beat them with sticks. This resulted in bruises and broken bones. There would seem to be little explanation for this other than sadistic enjoyment: The victims were destined to be killed anyway, and breaking their bones prior to killing them served no purpose but to increase their suffering and entertain their tormentors.

As a parallel, one might readily point to the Stanford Prison Experiment, conducted by Phil Zimbardo and colleagues in the late 1960s (Zimbardo, 1972). College students were randomly assigned to play the roles of either guards or prisoners. The guards were at first hesitant and uncertain, but fairly soon they evolved into three types, one of which involved sadistic and dominant guards who inflicted gratuitous punishments on the prisoners and seemed to derive pleasure from exercising power. (The other two were the tough but fair guards, and the lenient ones who sought to befriend the prisoners.)

A cautious social scientist must of course consider alternative explanations, and it is probably unsafe to rely on victim judgments of sadism. Victims probably seek to regard their tormentors as supremely evil, and in assimilating their tormentors to the dominant images of evil they are likely to overinterpret ambiguous behaviors as reflecting enjoyment (because the dominant mythic image of evil includes enjoyment of cruelty; see Baumeister, 1997). For example, Milgram (1963) noted that the students in his study who were assigned to deliver electric shocks to an accomplice exhibited patterns of nervous laughter, sometimes in seemingly uncontrollable fits. Milgram considered these outbursts of laughter to be a sign of inner struggle to cope with a difficult, awkward situation, but victims might well simply remember that the perpetrators were laughing and would interpret the laughter as a sign of sadistic pleasure.

Gratuitous cruelty itself can have a function. Katz (1988) has said that perpetrators often feel it is crucially important to maintain control over the situation, and toward this end they may seek to intimidate victims with displays of seemingly random or unnecessary violence. He reported, for example, that the rate of injury to victims of armed robbery is actually higher when the perpetrators are female than when they are male, which he interpreted as indicating that women find it harder to intimidate victims so as to maintain control and must therefore actually use their weapons more frequently than male perpetrators. Browning's (1992) account of German reserve policemen in the Polish Holocaust suggests that they became most brutal on occasions when they found it most difficult to maintain control over the situation, such as when they were understaffed and far outnumbered by their captives, or when they were moving the group through a setting that presented many opportunities for escape.

Although some instances of cruelty can be understood as serving instrumental functions, that explanation is plainly inadequate to cover all the instances. It therefore seems reasonable to conclude that sadism played a role in the Holocaust. The extent of that role is difficult to ascertain, but the best guess is that it probably aggravated the suffering of many victims without changing the outcome in a major way. It does not seem plausible that 11 million people were murdered for the fun of it. Furthermore, most of the victims of sadistic treatment were probably destined for death anyway, and so had they escaped the sadistic treatment, they still would have ended up dead. But being killed can be made considerably worse when administered by a sadist, and moreover the final weeks or months of many lives were probably made much worse than they already were. Sadism cannot explain the Holocaust, but it almost certainly contributed to making it much more ugly and cruel than it already was.

CONCLUSION

The four main root causes of evil can all be identified as having contributed to the Holocaust, although not in equal measure. The primary factors were probably idealism and threatened egotism. That is, victims were killed because the Nazis embraced an ideal vision for a German utopia that held no place for the victims, and killing them gradually emerged as the only way to get rid of these unwanted individuals. The end was seen as justifying the means. Additionally, Nazi Germany held a narcissistically inflated view of itself and considered the events of previous decades to have been a shocking humiliation that required aggressive revenge.

The other two root causes of evil were probably not decisive in bringing about the mass murders but almost surely contributed to sustaining the campaign and making it considerably worse than it already was. Oppressing and eventually killing the Jews was a means for both the Nazi state and many individual Germans to gain personal advantage, such as by extorting money from the victims, and these material benefits probably fueled the momentum of the killing campaign. Last, any large-scale pattern of violent oppression affords an opportunity for sadism to emerge, as certain individuals discover in themselves the unexpected pleasures of inflicting harm, and the Holocaust certainly produced an ample crop of brutal sadists among the oppressors.

One might hope that the lessons from the Holocaust would help the human race avoid any repetition of such atrocities. The record is not encouraging, however, and a cynic might suggest that the main lesson learned from the Holocaust is how to conduct mass murder even more effectively. My own view is more optimistic, however, and I hope that advances in psychological understanding of the perpetrators of such horrors will eventually help the world to recognize and prevent such calamities, or at least to stop them before the toll of cruelty and death reaches the shocking extent visited by the Nazis on central Europe during their decade of grisly power.

REFERENCES

American Psychiatric Association. (1994). *Diagnostic and statistical manual of mental disorders* (4th ed.). Washington, DC: Author.

Bauman, Z. (1991). *Modernity and the Holocaust*. Ithaca, NY: Cornell University Press.

Baumeister, R. F. (1993). Understanding the inner nature of low self-esteem: Uncertain, fragile, protective, and conflicted. In R. Baumeister (Ed.), *Self-esteem: The puzzle of low self-regard* (pp. 201–218). New York: Plenum.

Baumeister, R. F. (1997). *Evil: Inside human violence and cruelty*. New York: Freeman.

Baumeister, R. F., & Campbell, W. K. (1999). The intrinsic appeal of evil: Sadism, sensational thrills, and threatened egotism. *Personality and Social Psychology Bulletin, 3,* 210–221.

Baumeister, R. F., Smart, L., & Boden, J. M. (1996). Relation of threatened egotism to violence and aggression: The dark side of high self-esteem. *Psychological Review, 103,* 5–33.

Baumeister, R. F., Stillwell, A., & Wotman, S. R. (1990). Victim and perpetrator accounts of interpersonal conflict: Autobiographical narratives about anger. *Journal of Personality and Social Psychology, 59,* 994–1005.

Baumeister, R. F., Tice, D. M., & Hutton, D. G. (1989). Self-presentational motivations and personality differences in self-esteem. *Journal of Personality, 57,* 547–579.

Blaine, B., & Crocker, J. (1993). Self-esteem and self-serving biases in reactions to positive and negative events: An integrative review. In R. Baumeister (Ed.), *Self-esteem: The puzzle of low self-regard* (pp. 55–85). New York: Plenum.

Brockner, J. (1984). Low self-esteem and behavioral plasticity: Some implications for personality and social psychology. In L. Wheeler (Ed.), *Review of personality and social psychology* (Vol. 4, pp. 237–271). Beverly Hills, CA: Sage.

Browning, C. R. (1992). *Ordinary men: Reserve Police Battalion 101 and the Final Solution in Poland.* New York: HarperCollins.

Brownmiller, S. (1975). *Against our will: Men, women, and rape.* New York: Simon and Schuster.

Bushman, B. J., & Baumeister, R. F. (1998). Threatened egotism, narcissism, self-esteem, and direct and displaced aggression: Does self-love or self-hate lead to violence? *Journal of Personality and Social Psychology, 75,* 219–229.

Campbell, J. D. (1990). Self-esteem and clarity of the self-concept. *Journal of Personality and Social Psychology, 59,* 538–549.

Conquest, R. (1990). *The Great Terror: A reassessment.* New York: Oxford University Press.

Dawidowicz, L. S. (1975). *The war against the Jews: 1933–1945.* New York: Bantam.

Fitch, G. (1970). Effects of self-esteem, perceived performance, and choice on causal attributions. *Journal of Personality and Social Psychology, 16,* 311–315.

Goldhagen, D. J. (1996). *Hitler's willing executioners: Ordinary Germans and the Holocaust.* New York: Knopf.

Katz, J. (1988). *Seductions of crime: Moral and sensual attractions in doing evil.* New York: Basic Books.

Kernis, M. H., Grannemann, B. D., & Barclay, L. C. (1989). Stability and level of self-esteem as predictors of anger arousal and hostility. *Journal of Personality and Social Psychology, 56,* 1013–1022.

Lifton, R. J. (1986). *The Nazi doctors: Medical killing and the psychology of genocide.* New York: Basic Books.

Long, D. E. (1990). *The anatomy of terrorism.* New York: Free Press.

Milgram, S. (1963). Behavioral study of obedience. *Journal of Abnormal and Social Psychology, 67,* 371–378.

Miller, A. G., Gordon, A. K., & Buddie, A. M. (1999). Accounting for evil and cruelty: Is to explain to condone? *Personality and Social Psychology Review, 3,* 254–268.

Rhodewalt, F., Madrian, J. C., & Cheney, S. (1998). Narcissism, self-knowledge organization, and emotional reactivity: The effects of daily experiences on self-esteem and affect. *Personality and Social Psychology Bulletin, 24,* 75–86.

Roth, C. (1964). *The Spanish Inquisition.* New York: Norton.

Sereny, G. (1983). *Into that darkness: An examination of conscience.* New York: Vintage/Random House.

Shakur, S. (1993). *Monster: The autobiography of an L.A. gang member.* New York: Atlantic Monthly Press.

Solomon, R. L. (1980). The opponent-process theory of acquired motivations: The costs of pleasure and the benefits of pain. *American Psychologist, 35,* 691–712.

Solomon, R. L., & Corbit, J. D. (1974). An opponent-process theory of motivation: I. Temporal dynamics of affect. *Psychological Review, 81,* 119–145.

Thurston, A. F. (1987). *Enemies of the people: The ordeal of the intellectuals in China's Great Cultural Revolution.* New York: Knopf.

Zimbardo, P. G. (1972). The Stanford Prison Experiment. A slide/tape presentation produced by P. G. Zimbardo, Inc., PO Box 4395, Stanford, CA 94305.

11

Instigators of Genocide

Examining Hitler From a Social-Psychological Perspective

David R. Mandel

The question that this volume poses—What can social psychology tell us about the Holocaust?—is a difficult and complex one to answer. Perhaps it is fair to begin by saying that the Holocaust has influenced our understanding of social psychology more than the other way around. Early work in the field was directly motivated by the devastation and tragedies that took place between 1933 and 1945 (e.g., on the Holocaust, see Hilberg, 1973; on Jewish persecution from 1933–1939, see Friedländer, 1997; on the Third Reich, see Shirer, 1998). Central topics in social psychology such as attribution, social influence, and intergroup processes all have their roots in the works of thinkers who had the events of the 1930s and 1940s seared in their minds, many of whom had to flee their homelands to escape the specter of Nazism.

In the 1960s and early 1970s, seminal work in the field, such as Milgram's (1974) research on obedience to authority and the Stanford Prison Experiment by Zimbardo and his colleagues (Zimbardo, Banks, Haney, & Jaffe, 1973), continued to be motivated by a need to understand the perpetrators of the Holocaust and other acts of collective violence. To this day, these studies represent social psychology's most salient demonstrations of *situationism*—a core tenet of the field that emphasizes the power of the situational forces over human behavior (see Ross & Nisbett, 1991). This research, along with Arendt's (1965) insightful report on the trial of Adolf Eichmann, also provided the basis for the "banality of evil" perspective, which rejects the notion that evil acts are the result of "sadistic monsters" and instead emphasizes that evildoers are usually ordinary people who find themselves in extraordinary circumstances (e.g., Zimbardo, 1995; for recent critiques of the banality of evil perspective, see Berkowitz, 1999; Mandel, 1998).

From the end of World War II to the present day, we have seen the types of social problems and historic tragedies that have motivated much of social psychology's most socially relevant research continue to reappear. Examples of war, genocide, and democide—"the murder of any person or people by a government" (Rummel, 1994, p. 3)—are commonplace. As Global Action International Network (1999) reported, "According to some estimates, up to 35 million people—90% civilians—have been killed in 170 wars since the end of World War II." It is because of this stark reality that we must address the question that this volume poses, with a view to addressing the more general question, What can social psychology tell us about the origins of, and possible solutions to, the many forms of collective violence that plague us today?

INSTIGATORS: THE FOURTH LEG OF COLLECTIVE VIOLENCE

Psychological research and theory geared toward understanding collective violence—sometimes termed the *psychology of evil* (e.g., Baumeister, 1997; Darley, 1992; A. G. Miller, 1999; Staub, 1989)—has tended to focus on three groups: victims, perpetrators, and bystanders (e.g., Hilberg, 1995; Staub, 1989). In this chapter, I have proposed that the second category—perpetrators—needs to be refined or perhaps divided. Specifically, those who instigate collective violence need to be distinguished from those who subsequently carry it out. We may call the former *instigators* and the latter *perpetrators*. The main point is that the instigator is critical for the *origination* of an act of collective violence, whereas the perpetrator—usually one of many—is critical for its *execution*.

In the first few sections of this chapter, I discuss some of the ways in which instigators differ from perpetrators. I have tried to articulate why a psychology of instigation is important and doable and also why it has largely been ignored. In the latter part of this chapter, I examine the most notorious genocidal and democidal instigator of the twentieth century, Adolf Hitler, from a social-psychological perspective. So many have attempted to explain Hitler (for a recent overview, see Rosenbaum, 1998), and scores of books have been written about him, including some notable biographies (e.g., Bullock, 1990; Kershaw, 1998). The present discussion is certainly not a comprehensive account either of Hitler's psychological makeup or of how and why he became the instigator of a series of democides that claimed the lives of close to 21 million innocent victims (Rummel, 1992). Rather, the aim here is to show that *even Hitler* can be examined in terms of the same social-psychological principles used to describe and explain ordinary individuals. In so doing, the chapter offers a situationist message—that instigators, much like their followers, are people who have been molded by the interplay of powerful situational forces and basic psychological needs.

TOWARD A PSYCHOLOGY OF INSTIGATORS

Why Study Them?

Given that it is the goals, plans, and acts of instigators that set in motion a complex, causal chain of events leading to collective violence, the pragmatic importance of understanding what we can of the psychology of instigators should be evident. Nevertheless, the significance of examining instigators has sometimes been downplayed in favor of understanding how ordinary members of society can be led to participate in acts of collective violence. For example, at the end of a chapter on Hitler, Staub (1989) wrote, "There will always be wild ideas and extreme ideologies. For us the question is how the German people came to follow a leader and a party with such ideas, and how they came to participate in their fulfillment" (p. 98).

One reason for this focus is social psychology's aim of formulating accounts that generalize to the mass of ordinary people (Suedfeld, 2000). Instigators of genocide, with their "wild ideas," do not seem to fit this mold. Thus, some theorists share the view that although instigators, like Hitler, are important causal factors, they are nevertheless inexplicable in terms of the psychological processes that are used to describe normal or ordinary individuals. Consider Milgram (1974): "The psychological adjustments of a Wehrmacht General to Adolf Hitler parallel those of the lowest infantryman to his superior, and so forth, throughout the system. *Only the psychology of the ultimate leader demands a different set of explanatory principles*" (p. 130, italics mine).

Another reason for reluctance may be the concern that people will misconstrue explanations as exculpations and condonations. In fact, recent research has shown that explaining a perpetrator's behavior can increase the likelihood of condoning that behavior (A. G. Miller, Gordon, & Buddie, 1999), and, as I have argued elsewhere (see Mandel, 1998), the social dangers of such accounts need to be carefully considered. There are also some attributional reasons why the psychological study of instigators has received little attention. For instance, perpetrators greatly outnumber instigators and may seem more important to understand. Also, perpetrators tend to commit the actual killings, and because murder is a salient, abnormal act, it is especially likely to prompt the question of why (Kahneman & Miller, 1986). However, it is precisely because instigators can lead other people to participate in murder that we need to try to understand them as well as their followers.

Instigators and Perpetrators

The distinction between instigators and perpetrators shares some similarities to that between leaders and followers, but the two distinctions are not synonymous. Leaders and followers represent a much broader social grouping. Many high-ranking Nazis were leaders, but their roles in the ontogene-

261

sis of the Holocaust were nevertheless as perpetrators, not instigators. For instance, although Heinrich Himmler and Reinhardt Heydrich, each in his own way, were architects of the Final Solution of the European Jewish Question[1] (Breitman, 1991), it was Hitler who "commissioned" the plan to annihilate the Jews in the first place (on the timing of the order, see Cesarani, 1994).

Like instigators, perpetrators may include people other than those who directly carry out the killing or torture of victims. Rather, perpetrators are those people who take deliberate actions that contribute to the social production of collective violence and who do so with an understanding that their actions will contribute to such ends. Central planners of genocide, like Himmler, Heydrich, and their underlings like Eichmann, are obvious examples. However, the industrialists who knowingly built crematoria for the burning of corpses that resulted from Nazi atrocities also are perpetrators. Indeed, the division of labor among the perpetrators of the Holocaust represented a microcosm of modern society complete with its bureaucrats, businessmen, lawyers, doctors, scientists, writers and commentators, police and military, each of whom contributed to the production of genocide.

Instigators as Catalysts of Collective Violence

One might describe Hitler as a necessary cause of the Holocaust, and the counterfactual logic is clear: If no Hitler, then no Holocaust (Himmelfarb, 1984). Still, this label fails to convey the fact that Hitler was the person most *responsible* for instigating that catastrophe. Or, as Yehuda Bauer (1994) put it, Hitler was "the radicalizing factor" (p. 308). Bauer's statement is indicative of an important point about instigators. It is characteristic of instigators, but not perpetrators, that they serve a *catalytic* role in the development of collective violence.

Instigators offer hope to their followers, usually in times of social crisis in which many are searching for meaning and a sense of belonging in their lives. This hope is energizing and provides a common vision, but it is often a vision that rests on hatred and distrust, and that relies on scapegoating and violence. Hitler capitalized on Germany's high propensity for violence during a period of dramatic social unrest and consolidated immense power in the process. In exchange, he imparted a new form of coherence to an unstable social system, albeit one that culminated in incalculable misery and destruction and that proved to also be unstable. In so doing, his role was figural against a background of other enabling conditions and transformed those conditions.

The catalytic function served by instigators does not, however, mean that they are initial causes of collective violence. Rather, they dramatically increase the propensity for violence, and they act to accelerate its pace once it has started. For instance, the racial anti-Semitism propagated by the Nazis under

Hitler had as one of its own proximal causes the anti-Semitic German writings of the late 1800s. Consider a few examples: In 1873, Wilhelm Marr published *The Victory of Jewry over Germandom, Considered from a Non-denominational Point of View*. In 1878, Paul Bötticher (under the pseudonym of Paul de Lagarde) published *German Writings*, in which he prophesied a mortal struggle between the Jews and the Germans and called for the extermination of "these bacilli." In 1881, Eugen Dühring, a lecturer in economics and philosophy, published *The Jewish Question as a Question of Race, Morals and Civilization*. In 1899, Houston Stewart Chamberlain, an Englishman by birth but German by choice, published *Foundations of the Nineteenth Century*, a book that, as Cohn (1996) pointed out, "became the Bible of the *völkisch*-racist movement" (p. 190). And, in 1905, Alfred Plötz (1860–1940) founded the German Society for Racial Hygiene, which "was dedicated to the creation of optimal conditions for the maintenance and development of the German 'race' in competition with other peoples" (Stackelberg, 1999, p. 52).

If Hitler had not been exposed to the ideas and acts expressed by these and other anti-Semitic ultranationalists as a teenager and young adult, it is almost certain he would not have turned out to be the world's most notorious democidal instigator. But Hitler was exposed to them, and, significantly, he was more effective than any of his contemporaries at bringing anti-Semitic *völkisch* nationalism to the general public and eventually creating a *mortacracy*— "a type of political system that habitually and systematically murders large numbers of its own citizens" (Rummel, 1994, p. 3)—based on that ideology.

The Noninterchangeability of Instigators

In his recent biography of Hitler, Kershaw (1998) noted that "whatever the external circumstances and impersonal determinants, Hitler was not interchangeable" (p. xxvii). Kershaw's statement, like Bauer's, is indicative of another important difference between perpetrators and instigators: Unlike the former, the latter exhibit *noninterchangeability*. That is, instigators, particularly the most notorious ones like Hitler, seem to be characterized by a sense of singularity that is generally lacking from even their most repugnant bureaucrats and henchmen, from the Himmlers and Hösses who plan and implement democide.

The noninterchangeability of instigators is impossible to demonstrate unequivocally and may in some cases be more apparent than real. In hindsight, it is difficult to imagine how the Holocaust would have happened as it did without Hitler, but we can never know with certainty what would have happened instead if Hitler had not existed. More generally, the counterfactual simulations (see Kahneman & Tversky, 1982) of theorists who attempt to account for acts of collective violence may give rise to perceptions of noninterchangeability. Nevertheless, those perceptions may be legitimately based on an analysis of the disproportionate influence that instigators exert on an emerging system of collective violence. In totalitarian regimes, such as the Third Reich, it is evident that such influence is real.

Instigators as Power Holders

In his analysis of power in contemporary societies, Toffler (1990; cf. Russell, 1992) defined three forms: *Low-grade* power relies on physical force or the threat of violence; *medium-grade* power relies on control of capital wealth; and *high-grade* power relies on access to, and control of, information and knowledge. A critical factor that clearly distinguishes instigators from other perpetrators is the acquisition of power across this power spectrum. Instigators are likely to achieve higher positions of authority than perpetrators (often dictatorial status). Moreover, the roles that even high-ranking perpetrators take on are often shaped and sanctioned by ultimate leaders (Kelman & Hamilton, 1989). This was certainly true of Hitler's totalitarian mortacracy. Unlike most perpetrators, instigators may attain the power to mobilize armies, paramilitary forces, and the police. They can direct capital spending and can change laws. They can influence the attitudes of the masses via propaganda and media control, and they can influence mass behavior more directly through enticements and fear tactics.

For instance, a subtle psychological tactic that may be employed by instigators is to induce *false consensus effects* (Ross, Greene, & House, 1977). False consensus typically refers to situations in which people falsely believe that their attitudes or beliefs are shared by a majority of other people. This definition implies an egocentric focus: Namely, people believe that other people think like *they* do. However, a more general definition of the false consensus effect would be simply to subscribe to a false belief about consensus. Media-controlling instigators may propagate mass false consensus effects by suggesting that the nation (or a large majority of its constituency) subscribes to beliefs and endorses policies that in fact are not widely shared. Thus, the leaders of countries at war will try to instill not only the belief that "the war is necessary" but also the belief that "most citizens agree that the war is necessary." Such consensus beliefs provide social justifications for moral disengagement (Bandura, 1999), thus serving as precursors to collective violence and facilitating the transition of the eventual perpetrators (Staub, 1990).

With power over the media, instigators can also manipulate the perceived credibility of individuals and groups that they view as friends or adversaries. It is well known that Nazi propaganda portrayed Jews as corrupt liars who, because of their ostensibly malign genetic heritage, could do nothing else but threaten the integrity of the German people and their way of life. The belief in the unchangeable nature of "the Jew" allowed Germans to morally justify even such heinous acts as killing Jewish babies. Moreover, derogatory messages about Jews were frequently reiterated to the public, and we know from psychological research that the mere reiteration of a message increases the likelihood that it will be believed—a finding known as the *reiteration effect* (Hertwig, Gigerenzer, & Hoffrage, 1997). In short, instigators not only have the power to authorize individuals to participate directly in collective violence but also have the power to shape bystanders' reactions to these events.

The power of instigators ultimately extends to the victims themselves. According to Fiske and her colleagues, power may be defined as "the disproportionate ability for some people or groups to control others' outcomes" (Goodwin, Operario, & Fiske, 1998, p. 679; see also Fiske, 1993)—an ability they term *fate control*. The power that instigators exercise over their victims is the starkest reminder of fate control. They can strip victims of their human and legal rights, destroy their cultural institutions, instill fear and terror in them, and loot their possessions—even their corpses after they have been tortured and murdered (Strzelecki, 1994).

Instigators also exercise the ability to stigmatize their victims. Goffman (1990) defined *stigma* as "the situation of the individual who is disqualified from full social acceptance" (p. 9). Victims of collective violence may be stigmatized in many ways: through escalations in violence levied against them; through repressive laws that curtail their personal, religious, and economic freedoms, that increase their social burdens, and that identify them as menaces or pariahs of society; through propaganda that depersonalizes and dehumanizes them and ascribes to them a host of negative attributes; and through enticements granted to those who take it upon themselves to worsen the victim's situation.

For instance, the decree on September 1, 1941, that Jews must wear the Star of David on their clothing served to stigmatize Jews by visibly, and legally, setting them apart from the rest of society. The decree was an example of state-organized moral exclusion. The message was clear: Those people are Jews, not Germans, and not people to whom "real Germans" have moral obligations. Significantly, the decree also signaled the start of the planned deportation of the Jews to the death camps (Friedlander, 1995). More generally, once a group is morally excluded from a society, it becomes much easier for others to act violently against its members, to knowingly benefit from their exploitation, or to stand by without feeling empathy upon witnessing their destruction (Staub, 1990).

Instigators as Propagators of Nationalism

As LeBon (1896) emphasized over a century ago, the effective instigator energizes his followers by agitating their emotions and appealing to the sentiments that guide their reason. In modern history, *nationalism* has been one of the most effective political strategies for accomplishing this goal (Berlin, 1991; Hobsbawn, 1992; Smith, 1986), and its success is fundamentally due to its psychological power. On one hand, nationalism creates an egotistic sense of

265

in-group cohesion by emphasizing the shared greatness of a people. On the other hand, it exacerbates feelings of threat by pointing to the nation's precariousness, feelings of hatred by pointing to those deemed responsible for its hardships and failures, and feelings of insult due to the belief that one's nation has not received the respect it deserves. As Isaiah Berlin (1991) noted long ago, nationalism is often motivated by some form of collective humiliation (see also Staub, 1989). Chirot (1994) has documented that, in case after case, twentieth-century tyrannies have been characterized by a combination of perceived national superiority coupled with perceived national threat and/ or a collective sense of insult from the outside world. The Nazi image of a German master race threatened by an international Jewish plague that mocked Germany and her people illustrates the point.

Nationalism plays upon a fundamental aspect of human social cognition, namely, the tendency to categorize individuals into groups. Indeed, it has been shown that people will discriminate in favor of in-group members and against out-group members even when the basis of social categorization is trivial (Tajfel, 1981). Nationalism is particularly effective at creating this sense of *us* versus *them* because nations (unlike states) tend to be defined in terms of features that are of high personal and social importance, such as ethnicity, race, religion, ideology, and language (Azzi, 1998). Consequently, the nation may be perceived, and may in fact behave, not merely as an aggregate but as a cohesive *entity* (Campbell, 1958). For example, German *völkisch* nationalists conceived of their nation as an organic whole whose members were united by blood bonds that went back to the beginning of human history (Stackelberg, 1999).

Hitler, with his charisma as an orator, was able to use nationalist messages to effectively build support for his leadership. Once in power, he used racist nationalistic rhetoric to justify the discriminatory policies that he introduced and, later, the democides that he instigated. As I discuss next, however, Hitler's affinity for nationalism and violence went far beyond any calculated strategy and had much to do with his own threatened sense of greatness.

NORMALIZING HITLER

Threatened Egotism

According to Baumeister, Smart, and Boden (1996), *egotism* refers "both to favorable appraisals of self and to the motivated preference for such favorable appraisals, regardless of whether they are valid or inflated" (p. 6). These authors have reviewed considerable literature indicating that violence is more likely to be carried out by people with high but unstable self-esteem than by people with either high and stable self-esteem or low self-esteem. Their account posits that when people with inflated but uncertain self-esteem encounter negative evaluations from others, they experience a salient ego threat. The threatened egotist may respond by accepting negative feedback and lowering his self-appraisal, or he may reject such feedback and maintain his self-appraisal. In both cases, negative emotions are likely to ensue. However, in the former case they are likely to be self-directed feelings of dejection, whereas in the latter case they are likely to be directed toward the source of ego threat and may provoke aggression or violence against that source.

Baumeister et al.'s (1996) account is eminently applicable to Hitler. Biographies of Hitler (e.g., Bullock, 1990; Kershaw, 1998) reveal time and again that (a) he had a highly inflated sense of self-worth, (b) he received feedback that contradicted his hubristic self-image, (c) he could not accept those negative self-appraisals, and (d) he responded emotionally, directing his negative feelings at those he blamed for his failures. Consider one example from his teenage years. At 18, Hitler left home for Vienna. He was certain that he possessed the artistic ability to enter the Academy of Fine Arts in Vienna and become a great artist, but he was not admitted. Reflecting on his disconfirmed expectancy, Hitler later wrote in *Mein Kampf* (1992), "I was so convinced that I would be successful that when I received my rejection, it struck me as a bolt from the blue" (p. 18). Moreover, at the same time, Hitler's only friend and roommate, August Kubizek, was accepted into the Vienna Conservatoire to pursue his musical ambitions, thus providing Hitler with a constant upward social comparison.

That Hitler could not accept the negative appraisal was revealed by the fact that for some time he lied to Kubizek about his rejection from the academy. As Kershaw (1998) noted:

> For a teenager to fail to pass an extremely tough entrance examination is in itself neither unusual nor shameful. But Adolf could evidently not bear to tell his friend, to whom he had always claimed to be so superior in all matters of artistic judgement, and whose own studies at the Conservatoire had started so promisingly, of his rejection. The blow to his self esteem had been profound. And the bitterness showed. According to Kubizek, he would fly off the handle at the slightest thing. His loss of self confidence could flare up in an instant into boundless anger and violent denunciation of all who he thought were persecuting him. (p. 39)

The preceding description provides a good example in support of Baumeister et al.'s (1996) proposition that "because the angry, hostile response is essentially a means of preventing oneself from having to suffer through a depressing revision of self-appraisal, its function is largely anticipatory. Hence, highly sensitive individuals may react with considerable hostility to seemingly minor ego threats" (p. 11). In short, Hitler was prototypical of exactly the kind of threatened egotist and aggressor that Baumeister et al. (1996) have described.

It is important to note, however, that the threatened egotism that Hitler displayed is not a sign of abnormality; nor is it inexplicable in psychological terms. Indeed, considerable research indicates that ordinary individuals are highly resistant to lowering their self-appraisals in light of negative feedback (e.g., Greenwald, 1980; Swann, 1987). Of course, it is true that Hitler's threatened egotism was extreme. The magnitude of his emotional and behavioral reactions was certainly uncommon. However, there is little to suggest that the underlying psychological processes are somehow fundamentally different from those used to explain the behavior of less notorious figures or even the common man on the street.

As noted earlier, nationalism tends to embody threatened egotism within a collective ideology, and it is no surprise that Hitler gravitated toward nationalism (although his rise to power was certainly unpredictable). Hitler's nationalist identity was very much the result of his need to establish a positive social identity in light of the repeated personal failures and disconfirmed expectations that he had experienced as a teenager and young adult (see Kershaw, 1998). Because he could neither plausibly protect his high self-esteem with personal examples of success nor accept his failures, he bolstered his egotistic sense of self by identifying with what he conceived of as a strong and great nation. When Germany entered into World War I, Hitler was euphoric. Self-affirmation theory (Steele, 1988) predicts that when people receive negative feedback in one domain, they often respond by asserting themselves in another domain. The war provided Hitler with a chance to affirm his positive self-identity in a domain in which he had no track record of failure. Indeed, Hitler was fanatical about his duties as a soldier and was certain that Germany would win the war (Kershaw, 1998).

When Germany lost the war, Hitler's positive self-image was easily destabilized. Indeed, he reacted to the news "of the greatest villainy of the century" (Hitler, 1992, p. 183) with extreme negative emotions. His description in *Mein Kampf* of his reaction indicates his sense of *shock*—"Again everything went black before my eyes; I tottered and groped my way back to the dormitory, threw myself on my bunk, and dug my burning head into my blanket and pillow" (p. 185); *misery*—"Since the day when I stood at my mother's grave, I had not wept. . . . But now I could not help it" (pp. 185–186); *despair* and *hopelessness*—"There followed terrible days and even worse nights—I knew that all was lost" (p. 187); and ultimately *hatred*—"In these nights hatred grew in me, hatred for those responsible for this deed" (p. 187).

Self-Serving Attribution and Motivated Reasoning

Like so many other disillusioned nationalists, who had exhibited euphoric overconfidence in 1914 and were totally unprepared for the brutal disconfirmation of 1918, Hitler desired an external causal attribution for Germany's defeat, one that would quell his own renewed sense of personal failure, frustration, and futility, as well as repair his damaged social identity. Already by the middle of the war, the hard times that Germans faced resulted in a radicalization and polarization of the political scene. *Völkisch* anti-Semitism was on the rise in Germany, fomented by the nationalist Right, which accused Jews of war profiteering, evading military service, and, outlandishly, of secretly arranging for Germany's defeat. In short, Jews had "stabbed Germany in the back." In reality, Jews were a salient scapegoat. Germans and Austrians had long been primed with images of the Jewish threat, and, given the social context, it took no great leap of imagination to make the connection between Jewish conspiracy and the loss of the war.

Hitler's attributional account of Germany's failure is illustrative of the same *self-serving bias* (D. T. Miller & M. Ross, 1975) common among ordinary individuals—namely, the tendency for people to attribute their successes to their own or their in-group's behaviors or characteristics (internal attributions) but to attribute their failures to factors located outside of themselves or their in-group (external attributions). The self-serving bias may occur partly because people *expect* to succeed and tend to attribute expected outcomes to internal factors such as their efforts and abilities (L. Ross, 1977). Just as Hitler had no doubt that he would be admitted to the Academy, he was convinced at the outset that Germany would win World War I.

The self-serving bias may also occur due to directional motivated reasoning (Kunda, 1990) geared toward protecting one's self-esteem (Greenberg, Pyszczynski, & Solomon, 1982). By directional motivated reasoning, I mean reasoning that is carried out with the goal of supporting a particular conclusion that an individual *wants* to believe in. Hitler wanted to believe that Germany had been deceived because he could not accept that it would have lost the war any other way. The Jewish conspiracy account allowed Hitler to deflect blame away from Germany, Germans, and himself personally and redirect it toward *the Jew*: As he stated in *Mein Kampf*, "the better acquainted I became with the Jew, the more forgiving I inevitably became towards the worker" (1992, p. 58).

Hitler's self-serving attributional account also served an important social-cohesion function by uniting him with other like-minded Germans who similarly consoled themselves with hatred and blame of a depersonalized and dehumanized external enemy. Moreover, this account provided Hitler with a viable target for his displaced aggression (see Baumeister et al., 1996). Even though Hitler perceived Jews as cunning, powerful creatures who orchestrated German defeat through international influence, he also viewed them as vulnerable if only Germans realized this "simple fact" and acted on it. Consistent with Weiner's (1986) attributional theory of motivation and emotion, Hitler's account likely helped him substitute feelings of dejection that were behaviorally paralyzing with feelings of anger that motivated violent behavioral intentions against the perceived enemy.

269

The Jewish conspiracy account, and the reprisals it engendered, was also conducive to establishing a renewed sense of order and purpose—hallmarks of psychological well-being (Antonovsky, 1982)—in Hitler's life. Indeed, it provided Hitler with no less than the basis for a messianic mission to save humanity from perdition, a mission that would go a long way toward bolstering his hubris and countering his earlier failures:

> If, with the help of his Marxist creed, the Jew is victorious over the
> other peoples of the world, his crown will be the funeral wreath of
> humanity and this planet will, as it did thousands of years ago,
> move through the ether devoid of men. . . . Hence today I believe
> that I am acting in accordance with the will of the Almighty
> Creator: by defending myself against the Jew, I am fighting for the
> work of the Lord. (Hitler, 1992, p. 60)

Once again, I point out that the tendency to generate self-bolstering accounts of one's personal history is not a sign of abnormality. Indeed, the dispositional account of Jews that Hitler and others came to believe also exemplifies an attributional tendency so common it has been called the *fundamental attribution error* (L. Ross, 1977)—namely, the tendency to attribute the causes of events to the dispositions or traits of individuals or groups rather than to situational forces. Of course, this does not mean that everyone is equally motivated to generate causal attributions, search for information, and evaluate its significance in a biased and self-serving manner. It seems likely that Hitler's threatened egotism would have amplified these attributional tendencies. Nevertheless, the preceding analysis should indicate that Hitler's social cognition is neither incomprehensible nor beyond the scope of what social psychology has revealed about the processes underlying human nature.

Social Influence and the Need for Cognitive Balance

Social psychologists have long realized that individuals and the groups to which they belong are in a state of constant tension. As L. Ross and Nisbett (1991) put it:

> Individuals will have different sources of information about
> important topics and will construe this information in various
> ways. This will produce opinion deviance, which will be met with
> forces toward uniformity by the group. . . . In the event that it does
> not prove possible to move the group toward one's own view *and*
> the group is less than convincing on informational grounds *and*
> one is unwilling to reject the group, there is a powerful kind of
> tension recognized by many theorists of the 1950s, including
> Heider, Newcomb, and Festinger. (pp. 45–46)

That tension stems from the individual's need to seek cognitive balance or consistency among a set of affective relations, such that if A likes B, and B dislikes C, then A should also dislike C.

In the present context, this theoretical perspective indicates that if (a) Hitler was an ardent nationalist (strong positive valence toward German nationalist movements) and (b) nationalist movements were ardently anti-Semitic (strong negative valence toward Jews), then (c) Hitler would also be motivated to feel negatively toward Jews in order to maintain balance or to avoid *cognitive dissonance* (Festinger, 1957)—that negative drive state resulting from an awareness of one's attitudinal and/or behavioral inconsistencies. The exception would be if Hitler also had felt a strong positive connection to Jews, in which case he might have been forced to modify his views of some nationalist movements. But that obviously was not the case. What is most likely, and what in fact coheres with Hitler's own account in *Mein Kampf*, is that he simply did not give much thought to Jews until he began to identify with the Christian Social Party, which was headed by his anti-Semitic role model, Karl Lueger. According to theories of cognitive consistency, it is precisely an ambivalent relation that is most easily changed in order to restore cognitive balance.

Dynamics of Attitudinal Change

The need to restore cognitive balance does not result in an immediate change in one's attitude toward a particular object. Rather, it biases the way individuals seek and interpret information about that object, such that any new "evidence" found tends to confirm the view that would restore balance. Note also that one need not be aware of the directional nature of such reasoning for it to take place. Indeed, it is far more compelling if one does not realize the biases that may have led to the adoption of particular attitudes or beliefs. This allows one to maintain the illusion of objectivity characteristic of what L. Ross and Ward (1996) have called *naive realism*.

According to Ross and Ward, the naive realist subscribes to three basic tenets: First, he believes that his attitudes, beliefs, preferences, and perceptions follow from a relatively dispassionate, objective apprehension of reality. Second, he believes that other social perceivers will share his views provided they have access to the same information and have had adequate time to process that information. Third, he believes that divergent views are the result of ignorance, irrationality, or reasoning biased by self-interest, ideology, or some other distorting factor. For instance, while Hitler believed that his perceptions of Germany's greatness were objective truths, he viewed French nationalism as the result of socially constructed, self-serving attitudes. In *Mein Kampf* (1992), he wrote, "The fact is that the young Frenchman is not brought up to be objective, but is instilled with the most subjective conceivable view, in so far as the importance of the political or cultural greatness of his fatherland is concerned" (p. 29). Hitler's naive realism resulted in an unshakable convic-

271

tion in the truth of his attributions and perceptions, including the "objective" threat posed by Jews.

Hitler's naive realism also revealed itself when he described how his reason, sharpened by Lueger's arguments, had finally come to dominate his sentiments, which he claimed were initially somewhat favorable toward Jews:

> My views with regard to anti-Semitism thus succumbed to the passage of time, and this was my greatest transformation of all. It cost me the greatest inner soul struggles, and only after months of battle between my reason and my sentiments did my reason begin to emerge victorious. Two years later, my sentiment had followed my reason, and from then on became its most loyal guardian and sentinel. (p. 51)

To the contrary, it is quite likely that Hitler's reasoning came to follow his sentiments.

Consider a sketch of the dynamics of restoring balance in Hitler's case: Hitler identifies with German nationalism. He knows that nationalists tend to spend a lot of time talking or writing about the "Jewish question" (i.e., the Jewish *problem*). Initially, he does not perceive a "Jewish problem" and even suspects that his nationalist contemporaries are, as he put it in *Mein Kampf*, "reactionary" (p. 51). Yet, to be sure, he encounters no one who dissents from these views. Despite the apparent oddity of this obsession with Jews, Hitler still feels positive toward members of this movement, and so he is willing to listen to their arguments about Jews. Mingled with praise of Germany and the German people, which makes Hitler feel good, is condemnation of Jewry. The mere frequency of the "debate" of the Jewish problem makes him wonder whether there can be no truth to the arguments, even if the validity of these arguments appears weak.

Slowly, he perceives things on his own that he had previously not seen. For instance, he observes that some articles he reads, which strike him as having anti-German sentiments, are authored by people with Jewish-sounding names. He encounters "trashy" art that he dislikes and discovers that the artist, or director, or producer is Jewish. Perhaps this makes him think back to a recent anti-Semitic argument he heard about how Jews are undermining German culture. As his encounters with nationalists continue, he becomes progressively less inclined to view their anti-Semitic arguments as reactionary. Indeed, he begins to see their point, and this serves to strengthen his bond with them. Intrigued by his new insights, Hitler starts to investigate the Jewish problem more actively. He examines those things he dislikes and searches for evidence that Jews are involved. Sure enough, he finds more and more evidence. He pays no attention, however, to the numbers of non-Jews that are also involved. Nor does he search for evidence of positive contributions of Jews to society. To him, these questions are irrelevant to his investigation, since he is examining the Jewish *problem*. At any rate, the important truth has already been revealed: *The Jewish problem is real.*

To the social psychologist, the preceding (and admittedly oversimplified) sketch will be recognizable as an informal instantiation of several well-known and generalizable psychological principles: Individuals have a need to identify with groups whose members share with them similar attitudes, beliefs, or interests. This provides them with a sense of belongingness, stability, and meaning, allowing them to coordinate their personal and social identities. When group cohesiveness is high, as in Newcomb's (1943) Bennington study or in Sherif, Harvey, White, Hood, and Sherif's (1961) Robber's Cave experiment—and certainly as it was in the *völkisch* movement of the late 1900s—pressures toward uniformity of thought, emotion, and action also run high.

Conformity to a group norm can occur for several reasons. An individual may conform because of a fear of rejection or a desire to manage others' impressions of oneself or simply because the thought of doing otherwise can evoke feelings of anxiety or embarrassment, particularly when no other group member has openly done so (Asch, 1956). Conformity, however, may also reflect one's genuine personal convictions or a genuine change in one's convictions. When group norms are internalized, they can have long-lasting effects on individuals' attitudes and beliefs (Newcomb, Koenig, Flacks, & Warwick, 1967). Particularly when people do not have objective information on which to base their attitudes, they may rely on social information as a basis for these evaluations (Sherif, 1937). The vagueness of the Jewish question, which Hitler himself noted in *Mein Kampf*, may very well have contributed to a reliance on the social information he accumulated from anti-Semitic peers, role models, and writers.

The internalization of norms can also take place over time due to basic associative processes of conditioned response (Rescorla & Wagner, 1972). The anti-Semitic attitudes expressed in the *völkisch* circles to which Hitler gravitated would almost certainly have become associated with the positive feelings that nationalism instilled in Hitler. With time, the feelings evoked by anti-Semitism might have become akin to those evoked directly by nationalism. Attitude changes resulting from social influence can also be mediated by cognitive processes that influence how social inferences are made. For instance, I have suggested that the mere frequency of the debate of the Jewish problem may have helped to persuade Hitler that the Jewish threat was real. Why else would so many of his like-minded peers and Germanic brethren take this problem so seriously? This is an example of the reiteration effect that I noted earlier (see Hertwig et al., 1997). The frequency with which a belief is expressed, however, is never sufficient proof that the belief is true.

273

As an individual's attitude changes in the direction of a group norm, other reasoning processes can help to reinforce and stabilize it. Previous knowledge may be reinterpreted in line with new attitudes, and attitude-discrepant knowledge may be discounted. Indeed, even balanced media information may come to be seen as hostile toward one's side (Vallone, Ross, & Lepper, 1985), particularly for those who see issues in "black-or-white" terms, as Hitler did (perhaps this partly explains why Hitler was convinced that Jews were maligning Germany's reputation through their influence in the media). The search for new information is also likely to be sought and assimilated in a similarly biased manner (Lord, Lepper, & Ross, 1979). In particular, information that can be construed as supportive of one's attitudes is likely to be easily accepted, while counterattitudinal evidence may be scrutinized so that every attempt is made to minimize its importance or view it as biased.

One only need look as far as Hitler's own account of his "objective inquiry" to see that such processes facilitated his transition to anti-Semitism. For instance, in the second chapter of *Mein Kampf,* Hitler described his first encounter with a Hasidic Jew. Hitler wondered whether this "apparition in a black caftan and black hair locks" (p. 52) could possibly be regarded as a German. How does he attempt to solve this social categorization problem? "As always in such cases, I now began to try to relieve my doubts by books. For a few hellers I bought the first anti-Semitic pamphlets of my life" (p. 52). So, to allay his doubts that Jews might not be Germans, Hitler turned to anti-Semitica! The result: "Wherever I went, I began to see Jews, and the more I saw, the more sharply they became distinguished in my eyes from the rest of humanity" (p. 52).

Hitler began to search directly for confirmatory evidence that Jews were responsible for a variety of things he detested. For instance, concerning his search for Jewish influence in the arts, he wrote in *Mein Kampf:* "I now began to examine carefully the names of all the creators of unclean products in public artistic life. Regardless of how my sentiment might resist, my reason was forced to draw its conclusions" (p. 54). His conclusion: "The fact that nine tenths of all literary filth, artistic trash, and theatrical idiocy can be set to the account of a people, constituting hardly one hundredth of all the country's inhabitants, could simply not be tanked away; it was the plain truth" (p. 54). Hitler applied the same confirmatory search strategy (see Synder, 1981) over and over in different domains with the same basic result.

In each case Hitler asked questions in such a way that, in all probability, would have to be answered in favor of his existing views. For instance, he asked, "Was there any sort of filth or profligacy, particularly in cultural life, without *at least one Jew* involved in it?" (p. 53, italics mine). Of course, it should not be difficult to answer this question in the affirmative; however, that would be the case regardless of the social group that was being scrutinized. As the "objective evidence" accumulated, he was able to reorganize and reinterpret much of what he had already come to know within an anti-Semitic worldview:

"A thousand things which I had hardly seen before now struck my notice, and others, which had previously given me food for thought, I now learned to grasp and understand" (p. 54).

Cognitive Style

Even if the social-psychological processes and socially pervasive anti-Semitic beliefs already noted are taken into consideration, it may still be difficult to see how Hitler could have come to firmly believe in something as outlandish as an international Jewish conspiracy. I believe the adoption of these beliefs was also facilitated by various aspects of Hitler's cognitive style. Specifically, Hitler's thinking revealed an intolerance of ambiguity and a high need for structure and "cognitive closure" (see Kruglanski, 1980) that is characteristic of authoritarians (see Suedfeld & Schaller, this volume). His lengthy description in the second chapter of *Mein Kampf* of how one should read books in order to support the scaffolding of one's established beliefs is indicative of his intolerance of inconsistency and opposing views.

Hitler was also prone to conspiratorial thinking. He firmly believed in the veracity of the "Protocols of the Elders of Zion" (Rauschning, 1939), a conspiratorial account of Jewish world domination (Cohn, 1996). At first glance, the complexities of a conspiracy theory may seem unlikely to attract such a thinker's attention. However, conspiracy theories, complex as they may seem, actually provide causal structures that allow simple, monocausal attributions to a particular scapegoat to appear plausible. For Hitler, belief in an international Jewish enemy provided a means to find the locus of all the numerous perceived threats to Germany and himself.

Ironically, all the inconsistencies—the improbable twists and turns inherent in the "conspiracy"—are willingly accepted by believers because the conspiracy provides the degrees of freedom necessary for many of their deeply held attitudes to cohere and to be consolidated in a single account that has storylike properties (e.g., see Trabasso, Secco, & van den Broek, 1984). Such causal accounts, though based on weak data, are likely to persevere once they are formed even if the initial evidence on which they are based is subsequently discredited (e.g., see Anderson, 1983; Anderson, Lepper, & Ross, 1980).

Hitler was also prone to totalistic "all-or-nothing" thinking. Although there were endless tactical uncertainties that Hitler knowingly faced, in his long-range view everything was reducible to two unambiguous possibilities: *utopia* or *perdition*. According to his utopian vision, Germany was to be the superlative racial state, "the Germanic State of the German Nation," as Hitler described in *Mein Kampf* (1992, p. 299). Through ruthless conquests, Germany would acquire the extensive living space (*Lebensraum*) that the "German folk community" (*Volksgemeinschaft*; see Barkai, 1994) deserved (see Hitler, 1992, chap. 4). In generations to come, the purity of German blood would be reclaimed through the fruits of "racial science" (*Rassenwissenschaft*) and the policies of "racial hygiene" (Proctor, 1988), resulting in a nation of strong, healthy Aryan men, women, and children united by a *völkisch* Weltanschauung. Should he fail, he believed, all would be lost, and the Jew would be crowned with the funeral wreath of humanity. This kind of "ultimate stakes" thinking can engender an incredibly strong motivation to achieve one's goals at any price, particularly for naive realists like Hitler who, as noted earlier, are convinced that their observations are unbiased reflections of reality.

Once again, it is important to point out that a rigid cognitive style is not necessarily a sign of abnormality or inexplicable evil. Indeed, the "authoritarian personality" construct was developed by Adorno, Frenkel-Brunswik, Levinson, and Sanford (1950) in an attempt to explain why so many ordinary Germans allowed themselves to become perpetrators of genocide. The point is that similar cognitive processes may be just as important for explaining why some leaders are willing to pursue policies that are knowingly designed to result in the mass murder of innocent civilians.

Totalistic thinking lends itself to totalitarianism, the ideology of absolute power, and this increases the likelihood of democide. Rummel (1994; see also, Fein, 1993) has shown that, during the twentieth century, 7 of the 11 *megamurders*—namely, "those states killing in cold blood, aside from warfare, 1,000,000 or more men, women, and children" (p. 10)—were totalitarian regimes. These regimes accounted for 90% of the 142,902,000 deaths caused by megamurdering states. In Hitler's case, his totalism motivated him to destroy elements of his social world, as he perceived it, that negated the possibility of his utopia. These perceived threats were organized primarily along racial lines, with Jews representing the greatest menace.

Thinking, Emotion, and Action

Extreme evildoers are often portrayed as monsters devoid of any human emotion. Although this stereotype may help to preserve certain comforting assumptions about humanity, it could not be farther from the truth. A considerable amount of psychological research has shown that negative emotional reactions to personal experiences are likely to trigger attributional thinking geared toward explaining past failures and planning for future success (Schwarz, 1990; Taylor, 1991). As noted earlier, Hitler's contempt for Jews became pronounced at a time when he was experiencing several intense negative emotions following Germany's loss in World War I (Kershaw, 1998). His attributional account of Germany's defeat provided the basic cognitive structure within which those negative feelings could be interpreted. The result was a core cluster of attitudes that Hitler would build on in the months and years that followed the war, attitudes that would fundamentally shape all his subsequent democidal plans. In particular, Hitler's desire for a Jew-free (*Judenrein*)

Europe was fueled by a conjunction of emotional reactions that "the Jew" evoked in him. Primary among these were disgust, hatred, and fear. Each of these emotions in turn can be linked to dominant themes in anti-Semitic propaganda that influenced Hitler. And each can be found replicated in Hitler's own Nazi propaganda. I touch on each briefly next.

Disgust

Evocative of disgust, Jews were portrayed as dirty animals. Analogies to rats and bacilli were common in pre-Nazi and Nazi propaganda. For instance, the Nazi "documentary" film entitled *Der Ewige Jude* (The Eternal Jew) depicted the spread of Jews as a worldwide plague of bacillus-carrying rats (Kershaw, 1987). Hitler's personal disgust with Jews is evident in many passages of *Mein Kampf* (1992):

> By their very exterior you could tell they were no lovers of water, and, to your distress, you often knew it with your eyes closed. Later I often grew sick to my stomach from the smell of these caftan-wearers. Added to this, there was their unclean dress and their generally unheroic appearance. (p. 53)

> Was there any form of filth or profligacy, particularly in cultural life, without at least one Jew involved in it? If you cut even cautiously into such an abscess, you found, like a maggot in a rotting body, often dazzled by the sudden light—a kike! (p. 53)

As these passages illustrate, Hitler was disgusted with Jews in both physical and moral terms, and these were closely intertwined.

Hatred and Revenge

Of all the groups targeted by the Nazis for democide, none was so hated by Hitler as the Jews. This had much to do with the contents of Hitler's attributional thinking toward Jews. Not only had Hitler come to view Jews as a threat to Germany (and, indeed, humanity), he had become convinced that Jews had *intentionally* sought to undermine Germany and the *Volksgemeinschaft* and, moreover, that Jews were mocking Germany in its defeat. His speech to the Reichstag on January 30, 1939, also indicates that Hitler believed that the Jews had mocked *him* personally:

> During the time of my struggle for power it was in the first instance the Jewish race which only received my prophesies with laughter when I said that I would one day take over the leadership of the state, and with it that of the whole nation, and that I would

then among other things settle the Jewish problem. Their laughter was uproarious but for some time now I think they have been laughing on the other side of their face. Today I will once more be a prophet: If the international Jewish financiers in and outside Europe should succeed once more in plunging the nations into a world war, then the result will not be the Bolshevization of the earth, and thus the victory of Jewry, but the annihilation of the Jewish race in Europe. (trans. in Berenbaum, 1997, p. 161)

Jewish annihilation, therefore, was to represent more than a solution to a powerful threat; it was to be the ultimate form of *retribution* for "the diabolical craftiness of these seducers" (Hitler, 1992, p. 58) who had stabbed Germany in the back and who thought that they had gotten away with it without harm. Hitler took great pleasure in overseeing the systematic destruction of European Jewry, in exercising fate control over his mortal enemy, and in having the last laugh.

Fear and Threat

The perception of threat, and its accompanying emotion of fear, was central to most of the democidal operations that Hitler instigated. The extermination of Jews, Gypsies (Kenrick & Puxton, 1972), and the "hereditarily ill" (Friedlander, 1995) all have in common a focus on minimizing further prevention failures (see Higgins, 1987), and all followed from Hitler's belief that history was a long, racial struggle (*Volkstumskampf*). The racial desecration (*Blutschande*) of the German nation that had taken place over centuries had to somehow be undone, for if not, it would eventually succumb to an irreversible effect of genetic entropy. Without an urgent response—a thorough cleansing of the Aryan gene pool—the Aryan race would inevitably witness its final undoing. Hence, on November 23, 1939, Hitler informed his military leaders: "A racial war has broken out and this war shall determine who shall govern Europe and with it, the world" (quoted in Förster, 1994, p. 87).

The threat posed by "the Jew" was the most serious to Hitler. Jews, he perceived, were powerful, numerous, widely distributed throughout the world and highly organized, seductive, and the physical incarnation of pure evil. To Hitler, Jews were at the heart of the sociopolitical forms that he passionately opposed. Jews, he believed, were the originators of Marxist communism, capitalism, and parliamentary democracy. But, to Hitler, these were mere sociopolitical smoke screens that Jews had created to cover up their plans for world domination: "Only in this way is it possible for the real wirepuller to remain carefully in the background and never be called to responsibility" (Hitler, 1992, p. 83). Thus, the Jew was the primary enemy that Hitler perceived Germany to face. It was hence that, at the close of his political life and just before his suicide in Berlin, Hitler ended his political testament, dated April 29, 1945, with the following paragraph: "Above all, I enjoin the government and the people to uphold the race laws to the limit and to resist mercilessly the poisoner of all nations, international Jewry" (trans. in Berenbaum, 1997, p. 165). The war against the Jews, as Dawidowicz (1986) correctly labeled it, remained Hitler's highest priority right to the end of his life.

CONCLUSION

In this chapter, I have indicated the need to develop a psychology of the *instigator* of collective violence. I have also tried to show that our understanding of Hitler—and of the evil that Hitler represents—might be increased by examining him through the lens of social psychology. I have proceeded from the assumption that an examination of Hitler's thinking, emotions, motivations, and behaviors might reveal tendencies similar to those observed in ordinary individuals. The initial observations noted in this chapter suggest that some of those psychological tendencies were not absent but perhaps *exaggerated* in Hitler—a hypothesis that might be profitably pursued in future archival research. A next step might also be to compare the social-cognitive tendencies of different instigators of collective violence, examining as well the background sociopolitical conditions under which they rose to power.

In closing, it is important to note that my attempt to "normalize Hitler" by examining his behavior from a subjectivist and situationist perspective does not imply, as some might wrongly assume, that there is a Hitler in all of us. However, I hope that this chapter may convince the reader that social-psychological accounts of evil do not necessitate a view of people as fundamentally good either. Lay dispositionist accounts of evil may erroneously portray evildoers as monsters, but situationist accounts may also erroneously portray evildoers as good-intentioned souls who are swept along by the power of bad situations. In particular, the banality perspective on evil, which tends to portray evildoers as merely dutiful bureaucrats (e.g., see Milgram, 1974; Zimbardo, 1995), needs dramatic revision because it presently offers an oversimplified situationist account that is especially likely to be misconstrued as exculpatory (Mandel, 1998). In this chapter, I have tried to show that there is a darker side to human nature that is nevertheless consistent with much of what social-psychological research has revealed.

NOTES

Send correspondence to David R. Mandel, Department of Psychology, University of Victoria, P.O. Box 3050 STN CSC, Victoria, British Columbia, Canada V8W 3P5. E-mail: dmandel@uvic.ca.

1. *Endlösung der europäischen Judenfrage* was how the Nazis labeled the murder of all Jews within their jurisdiction from the invasion of the Soviet Union on June 22, 1941, until the defeat of the Third Reich.

REFERENCES

Adorno, T. W., Frenkel-Brunswik, E., Levinson, D. J., & Sanford, R. (1950). *The authoritarian personality.* New York: Harper.

Anderson, C. A. (1983). Abstract and concrete data in the perseverance of social theories: When weak data lead to unshakeable beliefs. *Journal of Experimental Social Psychology, 19*, 93–108.

Anderson, C. A., Lepper, M. R., & Ross, L. (1980). Perseverance of social theories: The role of explanation in the persistence of discredited information. *Journal of Personality and Social Psychology, 39*, 1037–1049.

Antonovsky, A. (1982). *Health, stress, and coping.* San Francisco: Jossey-Bass.

Arendt, H. (1965). *Eichmann in Jerusalem: A report on the banality of evil* (Rev. ed.). New York: Viking Compass.

Asch, S. E. (1956). Studies of independence and conformity: A minority of one against a unanimous majority. *Psychological Monographs, 70* (9, Whole No. 416).

Azzi, A. E. (1998). From competitive interests, perceived injustice, and identity needs to collective action: Psychological mechanisms in ethnic nationalism. In C. Dandeker (Ed.), *Nationalism and violence* (pp. 73–138). New Brunswick, NJ: Transaction.

Bandura, A. (1999). Moral disengagement in the perpetration of inhumanities. *Personality and Social Psychology Review, 3*, 193–209.

Barkai, A. (1994). Volksgemeinschaft, "Aryanization" and the Holocaust. In D. Cesarani (Ed.), *The Final Solution: Origins and implementation* (pp. 33–50). New York: Routledge.

Bauer, Y. (1994). Conclusion: The significance of the Final Solution. In D. Cesarani (Ed.), *The Final Solution: Origins and implementation* (pp. 300–309). New York: Routledge.

Baumeister, R. F. (1997). *Evil: Inside human violence and cruelty.* New York: Freeman.

Baumeister, R. F., Smart, L., & Boden, J. M. (1996). Relation of threatened egotism to violence and aggression: The dark side of high self-esteem. *Psychological Review, 103*, 5–33.

Berenbaum, M. (1997). *Witness to the Holocaust.* New York: HarperCollins.

Berkowitz, L. (1999). Evil is more than banal: Situationism and the concept of evil. *Personality and Social Psychology Bulletin, 3*, 246–253.

Berlin, I. (1991). The bent twig: On the rise of nationalism. In H. Hardy (Ed.), *The crooked timber of humanity: Chapters in the history of ideas* (pp. 238–261). London: Fontana.

Breitman, R. (1991). *The architect of genocide: Himmler and the Final Solution.* New York: Knopf.

Bullock, A. (1990). *Hitler: A study in tyranny* (Rev. ed). London: Penguin.

Campbell, D. T. (1958). Common fate, similarity, and other indices of the status of aggregate of persons as social entities. *Behavioral Science, 3*, 14–25.

Cesarani, D. (1994). Introduction. In D. Cesarani (Ed.), *The Final Solution: Origins and implementation* (pp. 1–29). New York: Routledge.

Chirot, D. (1994). *Modern tyrants: The power and prevalence of evil in our age.* New York: Free Press.

Cohn, N. (1996). *Warrant for genocide: The myth of the Jewish world conspiracy and the Protocols of the Elders of Zion.* London: Serif.

Darley, J. M. (1992). Social organization for the production of evil. *Psychological Inquiry, 3*, 199–218.

Dawidowicz, L. S. (1986). *The war against the Jews, 1933–1945.* New York: Bantam.

Fein, H. (1993). Accounting for genocide after 1945: Theories and some findings. *International Journal on Group Rights, 1,* 79–106.

Festinger, L. (1957). *A theory of cognitive dissonance.* Stanford, CA: Stanford University Press.

Fiske, S. T. (1993). Controlling other people: The impact of power on stereotyping. *American Psychologist, 46,* 621–628.

Förster, J. (1994). The relation between Operation Barbarossa as an ideological war of extermination and the Final Solution. In D. Cesarani (Ed.), *The Final Solution: Origins and implementation* (pp. 85–102). New York: Routledge.

Friedlander, H. (1995). *The origins of Nazi genocide: From euthanasia to the Final Solution.* Chapel Hill: University of North Carolina Press.

Friedländer, S. (1997). *Nazi Germany and the Jews: Vol. 1, The years of persecution, 1933–1939.* New York: HarperCollins.

Global Action International Network. (1999). *Global Action to Prevent War policy proposal and action plan* (10th rev.) [On-line]. Available HTTP: www.globalactionpw.org/

Goffman, E. (1990). *Stigma: Notes on the management of spoiled identity* (reprinted ed.). London: Penguin.

Goodwin, S. A., Operario, D., & Fiske, S. T. (1998). Situational power and interpersonal dominance facilitate bias and inequality. *Journal of Social Issues, 54,* 677–698.

Greenberg, J., Pyszczynski, T., & Solomon, S. (1982). The self-serving attributional bias: Beyond self-presentation. *Journal of Experimental Social Psychology, 18,* 56–67.

Greenwald, A. G. (1980). The totalitarian ego: Fabrication and revision of personal history. *American Psychologist, 35,* 603–618.

Hertwig, R., Gigerenzer, G., & Hoffrage, U. (1997). The reiteration effect in hindsight bias. *Psychological Review, 104,* 194–202.

Higgins, E. T. (1987). Self-discrepancy: A theory relating self and affect. *Psychological Review, 94,* 319–340.

Hilberg, R. (1973). *The destruction of the European Jews* (Rev. ed.). New York: New Viewpoints.

Hilberg, R. (1995). *Perpetrators victims bystanders: The Jewish catastrophe 1933–1945.* London: Secker and Warburg.

Himmelfarb, M. (1984). No Hitler, no Holocaust. *Commentary, 76,* 37–43.

Hitler, A. (1992). *Mein kampf* (R. Manheim, Trans.). London: Pimlico.

Hobsbawn, E. J. (1992). *Nations and nationalism since 1780* (2nd ed.). Cambridge: Cambridge University Press.

Kahneman, D., & Miller, D. T. (1986). Norm theory: Comparing reality to its alternatives. *Psychological Review, 93,* 136–153.

Kahneman, D., & Tversky, A. (1982). The simulation heuristic. In D. Kahneman, P. Slovic, & A. Tversky (Eds.), *Judgment under uncertainty: Heuristics and biases* (pp. 201–208). New York: Cambridge University Press.

Kelman, H. C., & Hamilton, V. L. (1989). *Crimes of obedience: Toward a social psychology of authority and responsibility.* New Haven, CT: Yale University Press.

Kenrick, D., & Puxton, G. (1972). *The destiny of Europe's Gypsies.* New York: Basic Books.

Kershaw, I. (1987). *The "Hitler myth": Image and reality in the Third Reich.* Oxford: Oxford University Press.

Kershaw, I. (1998). *Hitler: 1889–1936: Hubris.* London: Penguin.

Kruglanski, A. (1980). Lay epistemology process and contents. *Psychological Review, 87*, 70–87.

Kunda, Z. (1990). The case for motivated reasoning. *Psychological Bulletin, 108*, 480–498.

LeBon, G. (1896). *The crowd.* London: Unwin. (Translated from *Psychologies des foules.* Paris: Oleon, 1895.)

Lord, C. G., Lepper, M. R., & Ross, L. (1979). Biased assimilation and attitude polarization: The effects of prior theories on subsequently considered evidence. *Journal of Personality and Social Psychology, 37*, 2098–2109.

Mandel, D. R. (1998). The obedience alibi: Milgram's account of the Holocaust reconsidered. *Analyse & Kritik: Zeitschrift für Sozialwissenschaften, 20*, 74–94.

Milgram, S. (1974). *Obedience to authority: An experimental view.* New York: Harper and Row.

Miller, A. G. (Ed.). (1999). Special issue: Perspectives on evil and violence. *Personality and Social Psychology Review, 3*(3).

Miller, A. G., Gordon, A. K., & Buddie, A. M. (1999). Accounting for evil and cruelty: Is to explain to condone? *Personality and Social Psychology Review, 3*, 254–268.

Miller, D. T., & Ross, M. (1975). Self-serving biases in attribution of causality: Fact or fiction? *Psychological Bulletin, 82*, 313–325.

Newcomb, T. M. (1943). *Personality and social change.* New York: Dryden.

Newcomb, T. M., Koenig, K. E., Flacks, R., &Warwick, D. P. (1967). *Persistence and change: Bennington college and its students after twenty-five years.* New York: Wiley.

Proctor, R. (1988). *Racial hygiene: Medicine under the Nazis.* Cambridge, MA: Harvard University Press.

Rauschning, H. (1939). *Hitler speaks: A series of political conversations with Adolf Hitler on his real aims.* London: Thorton Butterworth.

Rescorla, R. A., & Wagner, A. R. (1972). A theory of Pavlovian conditioning: Variations in the effectiveness of reinforcement and nonreinforcement. In A. H. Black & W. F. Prokasy (Eds.), *Classical conditioning II: Current theory and research* (pp. 64–99). New York: Appleton-Century-Crofts.

Rosenbaum, R. (1998). *Explaining Hitler: The search for the origins of his evil.* New York: Random House.

Ross, L. (1977). The intuitive psychologist and his shortcomings. In L. Berkowitz (Ed.), *Advances in experimental social psychology* (Vol. 10, pp. 173–220). New York: Academic Press.

Ross, L., Greene, D., & House, P. (1977). The "false consensus effect": An egocentric bias in social perception and attribution processes. *Journal of Experimental Social Psychology, 13*, 279–301.

Ross, L., & Nisbett, R. E. (1991). *The person and the situation: Perspectives of social psychology.* New York: McGraw-Hill.

Ross, L., & Ward, A. (1996). Naive realism in everyday life: Implications for social conflict and misunderstanding. In T. Brown, E. Reed, & E. Turiel (Eds.), *Values and knowledge* (pp. 103–135). Hillsdale, NJ: Erlbaum.

Rummel, R. J. (1992). *Democide: Nazi genocides and mass murder.* New Brunswick, NJ: Translation.

Rummel, R. J. (1994). Democide in totalitarian states: Mortacracies and mega-murderers. In I. W. Charney (Ed.), *Widening circle of genocide* (pp. 3–39). New Brunswick, NJ: Translation.

Russell, B. (1992). *Power.* London: Routledge. (Original work published 1938)

Schwarz, N. (1990). Feelings as information: Informational and motivational functions of affective states. In E. T. Higgins & R. M. Sorrentino (Eds.), *Handbook of motivation and cognition: Foundations of social behavior* (Vol. 2, pp. 527–561). New York: Guilford.

Sherif, M. (1937). An experimental approach to the study of attitudes. *Sociometry, 1,* 90–98.

Sherif, M., Harvey, O. J., White, J., Hood, W., & Sherif, C. (1961). *Intergroup conflict and cooperation: The Robber's Cave experiment.* Norman: University of Oklahoma, Institute of Intergroup Relations.

Shirer, W. L. (1998). *The rise and fall of the Third Reich* (Rev. ed). London: Arrow. (First edition published 1960 by Secker & Warberg)

Smith, A. (1986). *The ethnic origins of nations.* Oxford: Oxford University Press.

Snyder, M. (1981). Seek and ye shall find: Testing hypotheses about other people. In E. T. Higgins, C. P. Heiman, & M. P. Zanna (Eds.), *Social cognition: The Ontario Symposium on Personality and Social Psychology* (pp. 277–303). Hillsdale, NJ: Erlbaum.

Stackelberg, R. (1999). *Hitler's Germany: Origins, interpretations, legacies.* London: Routledge.

Staub, E. (1989). *The roots of evil: The origins of genocide and other group violence.* New York: Cambridge University Press.

Staub, E. (1990). Moral exclusion, personal goal theory and extreme destructiveness. *Journal of Social Issues, 46,* 47–65.

Steele, C. M. (1988). The psychology of self-affirmation: Sustaining the integrity of the self. In L. Berkowitz (Ed.), *Advances in experimental social psychology* (Vol. 21, pp. 261–302). New York: Academic Press.

Strzelecki, A. (1994). The plunder of victims and their corpses. In Y. Gutman & M. Berenbaum (Eds.), *Anatomy of the Auschwitz death camp* (pp. 246–266). Bloomington: Indiana University Press.

Suedfeld, P. (2000). Reverberations of the Holocaust fifty years later: Psychology's contributions to understanding persecution and genocide. *Canadian Psychology, 41,* 1–9.

Swann, W. B. (1987). Identity negotiation: Where two roads meet. *Journal of Personality and Social Psychology, 53,* 1038–1051.

Tajfel, H. (1981). *Human groups and social categories.* Cambridge: Cambridge University Press.

Taylor, S. E. (1991). Asymmetrical effects of positive and negative events: The mobilization-minimization hypothesis. *Psychological Bulletin, 110,* 67–85.

Toffler, A. (1990). *Power shift: Knowledge, wealth, and violence at the edge of the 21st century.* New York: Bantam.

Trabasso, T., Secco, T., & van den Broek, P. (1984). Causal cohesion and story coherence. In H. Mandl, N. L. Stein, & T. Trabasso (Eds.), *Learning and comprehension of text* (pp. 83–111). Hillsdale, NJ: Erlbaum.

Vallone, R. P., Ross, L., & Lepper, M. R. (1985). The hostile media phenomenon: Biased perception and perceptions of media bias in coverage of the "Beirut Massacre." *Journal of Personality and Social Psychology, 49,* 577–585.

Weiner, B. (1986). *An attributional theory of motivation and emotion.* New York: Springer-Verlag.

Zimbardo, P. G. (1995). The psychology of evil: A situationist perspective on recruiting good people to engage in anti-social acts. *Research in Social Psychology, 11,* 125–133.

Zimbardo, P. G., Banks, W. C., Haney, C., & Jaffe, D. (1973, April 8). The mind is a formidable jailer: A Priandellian prison. *The New York Times Magazine,* pp. 38–60.

12

Perpetrators With a Clear Conscience

Lying Self-Deception and Belief Change

Ralph Erber

With the killing of Jews I had nothing to do. I never
killed a Jew or a non-Jew for that matter—I never killed
any human being.
—Adolf Eichmann

This chapter attempts to add to the literature on the psychological
mechanisms underlying perpetrator behavior by looking at the possibility that
a specific form of self-deception may play an important role. Specifically, adopting lies and communicating them to others may enable perpetrators to carry
out their evil tasks on a daily basis and may even enable them to live out the
remainder of their lives with a clear conscience. I specifically look at what
Arendt (1965) calls "lying self-deception": the effects of telling lies repeatedly
on subsequent belief change. The present analysis focuses heavily on how such
processes may have operated on Adolf Eichmann, one of the main perpetratrors of the Holocaust. In addition, I will offer speculations on how such
an analysis may extend to other perpetrators, bystanders, and, to some extent, victims.

THE BANALITY OF EVIL REVISITED

For many, thinking about perpetrators of genocide brings to mind images of
gun-toting, machete-wielding thugs, motivated by bloodlust and hatred, deriving pleasure from carrying out their grim task. This mental image of the
prototypical perpetrator was forever altered when Adolf Eichmann was
brought to trial for his role in the Final Solution in the District Court of Jerusalem on April 11, 1961. Despite the prosecution's best efforts, it was clear for

the world to see that the man in the cage enclosed by security glass was not a monster but instead a zealous bureaucrat who came to personify the banality of evil (Arendt, 1965).

Nobody could have predicted that Eichmann would someday become the defendant in the most celebrated trial of a Nazi war criminal since the Nuremberg trials, clumsily defending himself by repeatedly denying any involvement in the systematic extermination of 6 million Jews. The oldest of five children, young Adolf did little to distinguish himself. Lacking both intellectual talent and a penchant for hard work, he flunked out of high school and failed to graduate from the vocational school he subsequently attended. He got his first jobs from his father, who initially put him to work as a laborer in the small mining business he had purchased in Austria before securing him a dead-end job in the sales department of a company selling electric construction equipment. Ironically, he got his first break when a relative who was married to the daughter of a Jewish businessman used his connections with the Jewish director of the Vienna Vacuum Oil Company to secure him a job as a sales representative. He held this job until 1932, when he was unceremoniously fired.

That same year, Eichmann first joined the Austrian equivalent of the Nazi Party and then the SS. However, his career as a Nazi stalled when the Austrian government suspended the National Socialist Party as a result of Hitler's rise to power. Out of a job and with no prospects for a career, he returned to Germany, where he enlisted in military training. Having risen to the rank equivalent of corporal, Eichmann found life as a soldier dull. That he lacked talent and was averse to hard work did not mean he was not ambitious. Thus, when he heard that Heinrich Himmler's Security Service (Sicherheitsdienst) had openings, he quickly applied and was hired in 1934. Much to his dismay, he initially found himself doing boring work: filing information about the Freemasons, a group of which the Nazis were deeply suspicious. However, when the Security Service decided to establish an office devoted to "Jewish Affairs" in 1934, Eichmann, by joining it, was on his way to a career that eventually landed him in the Jerusalem courtroom.

Interestingly, he devoted much of his early time in this office to gaining some dubious expertise on Jewish issues. He educated himself by reading a couple of books about Zionism. This may not sound like much, but for someone who never read more than newspapers, it was quite an accomplishment. His experience converted him into an avowed Zionist who believed that Jews should be provided with their own soil under their feet so that they would have a place of their own. Having become an "expert" on Jewish issues, he was sent back to Vienna in 1938 to oversee the forced emigration of Austrian Jews. There he quickly established mostly cordial relationships with leaders of the Jewish communities. He obtained their cooperation to carry out what essentially constituted the expulsion of the Jews from Austria. He devised an assembly line system designed to provide prospective emigrants with the necessary documents in a more efficient manner. He negotiated with representatives of Palestine the illegal immigration of Jews, and he even set up farms and facilities to provide vocational training for prospective immigrants. His efforts were not in vain. Within 8 months of his assignment, well over 40,000 Jews had left Austria. Within 18 months, Eichmann had succeeded in the expulsion of 150,000 people, making Austria 60% *judenrein* (free of Jews).

By Arendt's (1965) account, Eichmann enjoyed his years in Vienna tremendously. He was promoted rapidly, rising to a rank equivalent to lieutenant. More important, he had finally become *somebody*. He felt that his job was important, he found it fulfilling, and he was proud of what he accomplished. In fact, during his trial he frequently pointed to his role in the expulsion of the Austrian Jews as an indication that he had saved hundreds of thousands from certain death. And while this may be true in a technical sense, it is also true that the expulsion plan was no invention of his own. Instead, he had merely implemented orders received from Reinhard Heydrich. A less benign look at his years in Vienna would reveal his primary contribution to be in the increased efficiency with which Jewish emigrants were stripped of their wealth and property.

In March 1939, after Hitler annexed the Sudetenland, which had been a part of Czechoslovakia, Eichmann was transferred to Prague to implement an emigration system similar to the one he had set up in Vienna. However, compared with Vienna, Prague was a bust as avenues for emigrations were beginning to clog up. Partly because of his own efforts, hundreds of thousands had left their homeland, and because Poland and Romania were anxious to follow Germany's example with respect to expelling Jews, millions were waiting to leave. At the same time, the British stepped up their efforts to curb immigration into Palestine, and many countries around the world were unwilling to adjust their policies to accommodate the growing number of potential immigrants. The outbreak of World War II in September 1939 complicated matters further as more and more of Europe came under German control. As a result, the policy of expulsion was suspended, and Eichmann was recalled to Berlin.

Back at his old desk, Eichmann's final transformation was about to occur. A few weeks after Germany attacked the Soviet Union in June 1941, he was summoned to Heydrich's office for what was essentially an interview for a new assignment. Heydrich had been charged by Hermann Göring to come up with a proposal for how the Final Solution could be accomplished. And who would be better suited for this job than the man who had distinguished himself in overseeing the expulsion of the Jews from Austria? At the time Eichmann was recruited, the Nazi killing machine was already in high gear. In order to transform the expert on Jewish emigration into an expert on Jewish extermination, Eichmann was asked to visit several sites that applied various killing methods. He witnessed the aftermath of a mass shooting and a mass killing using mobile gassing units (essentially vans that vented their exhaust into the cargo area), and he was shown a stationary gassing site using the exhaust from a Soviet submarine engine. Nine months after his initial tour, he visited the killing center in Treblinka, which employed cyanide gas as a means for extermination.

By his own account, Eichmann was appalled at what he saw. He could not bear the sights of people being loaded onto the gassing trucks, he went to the back of the line when the commander at Treblinka gave a demonstration of the gas chambers, and he even complained to a local SS commander about having young people bang away at women and children (although his concern was mostly with the effects of mass shootings on the killers rather than victims). Moreover, having developed a system for expulsion, he objected to the crudeness of the whole extermination enterprise, wishing for a political rather than a physical solution to the Jewish question.

All his reservations fell by the wayside, however, during the course of the Wannsee Conference in 1942 in which the undersecretaries of state put their stamp of approval on the Final Solution, thus effectively guaranteeing the full cooperation of the civil service. Eichmann was the lowest-ranking official to attend the conference, which lasted all of 90 minutes. His primary duty had been to send out the invitations. Finding himself among men of much higher rank who quickly reached an agreement on the Final Solution before turning their attention toward technical matters regarding how it should be carried out assured Eichmann that once again he was *somebody*. For the first time since his days in Vienna, he had an important job, and for the next 4 years he coordinated the enterprise that resulted in the death of 6 million men, women, and children with a zeal and efficiency that remain unmatched in history. He once again could install an assembly line, except this time it was an assembly line of death rather than emigration. It is important to note that this was not simply a matter of obeying orders. Toward the end of the war, with certain defeat apparent, Heinrich Himmler, Hitler's second-in-command, attempted to trade 10,000 Jews for trucks from the Allies and even began to contemplate reconciliation with the Nazis' victims. Eichmann defied his orders, insisting that the transports continue.

For those familiar with Arendt's report on the Eichmann trial, this partial curriculum vita provides little in the way of news. However, it is worth repeating for several reasons. First, it is clear that Eichmann was not a sadistic monster who took pleasure in sending millions of people to their deaths. This conclusion is troublesome, however. When we hear of monstrous crimes, it is often soothing to know that they were committed by evil people. We breathe a sigh of relief when we hear that the brutal death of a Black man by dragging him behind a pickup truck was caused by a couple of avowed racists and neo-Nazis on the fringes of society. Because they are so different from us, including those of us whose prejudice is accompanied by a sense of compunction (Devine, Monteith, Zuwerink, & Elliot, 1991), it allows the defensive attribution (Burger, 1981; Thornton, 1984) that *we* neither would nor could ever commit anything remotely like it. However, Eichmann was clearly not a fringe person; he was not one of the beer-drinking, skat-playing dregs of society who, according to Augstein (1998), killed because they failed to imagine alternative assignments. Under other circumstances we would not find fault with someone who wishes to be *somebody*, who wants a job that is important and fulfilling. We could call it ambition. And there is little wrong with having such ambitions in the face of adversity provided by one's limitations. We could call it overcoming the odds. The point is that there are probably many who fit this part of Eichmann's profile.

Complicating matters with respect to explaining Eichmann's participation in the Holocaust is the fact that there is little to indicate that he was particularly anti-Semitic. During his trial he went to extraordinary lengths to explain that he harbored no ill feelings toward his victims. He held the Jewish emissaries with whom he dealt in Vienna in high regard, considering them like-minded idealists. He intervened (unsuccessfully) on behalf of one of them who had been sent to a concentration camp. He helped his distant Jewish relative to leave the country well after emigration had become illegal. Finally, there are indications that during his Vienna days he committed the greatest crime an SS member could commit: carrying on an affair with an "old flame," a Jewish woman from Linz. This lack of any obvious prejudice poses a problem for Goldhagen's (1996) central thesis that the Holocaust was possible because of the massive "eliminationist" anti-Semitism prevalent in Germany at that time. To be sure, there is little doubt that many who participated in the killings did so because they were staunchly anti-Semitic. Others may have done so to satisfy an already existing disposition toward cruelty (Naumann, 1966; see also Blass, this volume). Yet others, like Police Battalion 101's infamous First Lieutenant Gnade, may have started as ordinary men who acquired a predilection for cruelty as they went about their business of shooting mostly women and children (Browning, 1998).

In attempting to understand how the Holocaust could happen, there is little to be gained from analyzing the backgrounds and motives of the eager killers who actively sought opportunities to kill. And social psychology is ill equipped for this type of task. There is far more to be gained by illuminating the processes that can turn ordinary men into killing machines. Browning's (1998) study of Police Battalion 101 is a brilliant attempt to explain such transformations through stalwart social-psychological ideas such as conformity pressures and escalation of commitment. However, we are still left with the task of explaining one of the Holocaust's unique features:

> It is not the angry rioter we must understand but Eichmann, the
> colorless bureaucrat, replicated two million times in those who
> assembled the trains, dispatched the supplies, manufactured the
> poison gas, filed the paper work, sent out the death notices,
> guarded the prisoners, pointed left and right, supervised the
> loading and unloading of the vans, disposed of the ashes, and
> performed countless other tasks that also constituted the
> Holocaust. (Sabini & Silver, 1980, p. 330)

SOOTHING ONE'S CONSCIENCE THROUGH SELF-DECEPTION

Eichmann's example makes it obvious that anti-Semitism was neither necessary nor sufficient for the Holocaust to happen. So what turned him and millions of others into Hitler's willing executioners? Arendt points to Eichmann's
ability to effectively shield himself against the reality of his actions. He was a
master at combining bad faith with lying self-deception and outrageous stu-
pidity (Arendt, 1965). He was the quintessential self-deceiver, who was able
to simultaneously believe that *b* and non-*b* were true (Sackeim & Gur, 1979).
As a consequence, he could simultaneously proclaim that he would die laughing knowing that he had the death of 5 million Jews on his conscience and
that he would gladly hang himself to set an example for all anti-Semites on
this earth. This should not be taken as an indication that his self-deception
was due to a unique disposition that allowed him to maintain *b* and non-*b*
without seeing a contradiction. Instead, he may merely have been very good
at doing what millions of Germans did. As Arendt observed:

> And that German society of eighty million people had been
> shielded against reality and factuality by exactly the same means,
> the same self-deception, lies, and stupidity that had now become
> ingrained in Eichmann's mentality. These lies changed from year
> to year, and they often contradicted each other; moreover, they
> were not necessarily the same for the various branches of the party
> hierarchy or the people at large. But the practice of self-deception
> had become so common, almost a prerequisite for survival, that
> even now, eighteen years after the collapse of the Nazi regime,
> when most of the specific contents of its lies has been forgotten, it
> is sometimes difficult not to believe that mendacity has become an
> integral part of the German national character. During the war, the
> lie most effective with the whole of the German people was the
> slogan of "the battle of destiny for the German people" (*der
> Schicksalskampf des deutschen Volkes*) . . . which made self-deception
> easier on three counts: it suggested, first, that the war was no war;
> second that it was started by destiny and not by Germany; and,

third, that it was a matter of life and death for the Germans, who must annihilate their enemies or be annihilated. (1965, p. 52)

Arendt is silent on how this collective mendacity may have played itself out in the days following the end of World War II. However, growing up in postwar Germany, I encountered many self-deceptive strategies employed by Germans in attempts to reconcile how the land of poets and thinkers (*Dichter und Denker*) became the land of judges and henchmen (*Richter und Henker*). Many of these centered on the notion that Hitler's rise to power was a result of the humiliation suffered in the Treaty of Versailles. This version of history, heard over and over in high school history classes, essentially put the blame for the Holocaust on the shoulders of the World War I Allies. Those who failed to see a direct link to Versailles frequently espoused the belief that the Holocaust was concocted by a small, criminal elite and carried out in semisecrecy by Augstein's dregs of society. Consequently, repeated inquiries of the kind "What did you do during the war?" left the impression that we were growing up in a nation of innocents. If anything, repeated inquiries about the Holocaust were met with a sense of exasperation rather than shame. After all, Hitler had also done a lot of good things, like eliminate the chaos and unemployment of the Weimar Republic, provide a sense of order, and create feelings of belonging among young people. And, of course, he built the autobahns. Even those whose previous membership in the SS was obvious and identified them as possible perpetrators were quick to deflect inquiries about their involvement in any aspect of the Holocaust by pointing to the sense of camaraderie and group spirit in their units (see also Staub, this volume).

From a social-psychological point of view, the question is, Through what processes did Eichmann and perhaps countless other Germans acquire their self-deceptive beliefs regarding the nature of their actions and their innocence? Looking at Eichmann first, there initially were a couple of things that led him down the path to self-deception. First, he had personally overseen the "forced emigration" of Jews from Austria. He had taken a number of concrete actions that produced the end result of saving hundreds of thousands from concentration camps and likely death. Second, his involvement in the Holocaust was never that comprehensive, that is, he was never personally involved in any killings. Instead, he worked primarily at the front end of the lethal assembly line, rounding up Jews and coordinating their transport to the killing centers in the east. He could draw on examples like that to convince himself that he, in fact, had nothing to do with the killing of the Jews. The rigid language rules under which the Holocaust was carried out may have further added to his self-deception. Terms like *liquidation, extermination*, and *killing* were rarely used. Instead, the official lingo revolved around *evacuation, resettlement, labor duty in the East*, and *special treatment* in the service of a *final solution*. Thus, whenever Eichmann may have needed to soothe his conscience, he could remind himself that he was in the business of resettlement rather than extermination.

There is evidence that such a strategy may lead to lasting belief change, especially when done repeatedly. As it happens, most people like to think of themselves in positive ways, and they frequently believe that they are superior to others in terms of their qualities and abilities (e.g., Brown, 1998). Because of this positivity bias, people think and talk about themselves in terms of their positive qualities. Such a lifetime of positive self-descriptions eventually makes the positive self automatic in the sense that we do not need to consciously search our memory for positive qualities. Instead, because we have frequently accessed them in the past, they come to mind with ease. In essence, positive self-views can come about by the force of mere repetition. Thus, when one's positive self-views are under attack, it is possible to maintain or restore positivity by way of repeated positive affirmations (Paulhus, 1993).

Of course, we do not know what Eichmann did after leaving his office every day. But there is reason to believe that perhaps he, too, wished to think of himself as a person with good qualities and abilities superior to those of others. In fact, even though he fully bought into the Nazi ideology, he made no secret of his disdain for the more blatant and vulgar anti-Semites, like *Der Stuermer* editor, Julius Streicher. But even if he never spent as much as a minute lying to *himself*, he repeatedly lied to *others*. Each time he ordered a transport, negotiated supplies, or coordinated train schedules, he essentially told a lie by omitting the fact that all these efforts went into extermination. And he lied to the court in Jerusalem when he repeatedly proclaimed his innocence.

LYING SELF-DECEPTION AND BELIEF CHANGE

Social psychology has studied the idea that lying to others may result in subsequent belief change in the context of self-presentation. In one study (Schlenker & Trudeau, 1990), research participants were asked to fake an interview by presenting themselves as either above or below average in independence. As it turns out, faking the interview led to a corresponding shift in participants' self-perceptions of their independence as long as it was consistent with their prior beliefs. Those who already thought of themselves as somewhat independent rated themselves as more independent as a result of faking it in the interview. Those who previously thought of themselves as somewhat dependent rated themselves as more dependent as a result of faking dependence. Self-ratings of independence of control participants who did not participate in the interview remained stable. Finally, faking independence or dependence on the part of those whose prior beliefs were inconsistent with the task did not result in significant changes. Thus, it appears that lying is most likely to result in corresponding belief change when the lie is small rather than outrageous.

Of course, given the monstrosity of his crimes, Eichmann's lie about his innocence seems rather outrageous. However, in his own mind the gap between his belief and reality may have been small enough to allow for an increase in the conviction he had in his innocence. After all, in his mind he had "saved" the Jews of Austria from extermination, he had personally helped several Jews escape a similar fate, and, lest we forget it, he had overseen the "resettlement" rather than the extermination of Jews from 1942 to the end of the war. His recollections in that regard may have served as the foundation for a partially constructed platform of belief that centered around his innocence. Presenting himself as innocent may thus not have been too terribly inconsistent with his prior beliefs and may have convinced him further that he was, in fact, not guilty.

The Power of Repeating a Lie

Eichmann's trial lasted for well over a year. During that time he repeated his claim of innocence over and over. Could it be that the force of repetition influenced his beliefs in his innocence? Could it be that the lie he repeatedly told in public became the lie he adopted privately? To answer these questions, we devised a series of experiments that on the surface has very little to do with Eichmann and the Holocaust but has everything to do with how repeating a lie can lead to corresponding belief change.

In all the experiments, participants were recruited under the guise of a marketing study. Upon arrival at the lab, they were told that the study was concerned with identifying the specific variables that make pitchmen (and women) successful in advertising. Toward that end, they would be making a videotape to be used in a separate study. The experimenter then showed participants five pairs of sunglasses and asked them to pick the one they felt either enhanced their appearance or detracted from it. Participants were then seated in front of a video camera and, depending on the experimental condition, repeated the statement "These sunglasses make me look better" or "These sunglasses make me look worse" four times or eight times. The need to make the statement repeatedly was justified on the grounds that the experimenter wanted to make sure to get the best take. After completing this task, all participants answered a brief questionnaire that included three crucial measures embedded in a total of 10 questions. The first measure asked participants to indicate the extent to which they believed the sunglasses did, in fact, enhance their appearance or detract from it. The second question asked them to indicate the extent to which they were happy with their appearance in general. And the third question asked them to indicate how attractive they thought others perceived them. Participants in a control condition did not make either of these statements but instead proceeded to answer a questionnaire after an appropriate delay.

The results indicated that the number of repetitions did not influence the extent to which participants perceived the sunglasses to make them look better or worse. This did not come as a complete surprise in light of the fact that participants gave their ratings immediately upon completing the video task, with the sunglasses still in full view. We did find evidence of self-deceptive belief change when we examined participants' responses to the appearance questions. Repeating the statement "These sunglasses make me look better" eight times significantly increased participants' satisfaction with their attractiveness, compared with those who repeated the statement four times or did not repeat it. At the same time, participants who repeated the statement "These sunglasses make me look worse" became more dissatisfied with their appearance. We found a similar pattern of results when we examined participants' beliefs regarding how attractive others perceived them.

Can we conclude from these findings that participants' beliefs changed through the mere force of repetition? Not quite yet. Because they were allowed to choose the pair of sunglasses, one could argue that the results may reflect attempts on the part of our participants to reconcile their private beliefs with their very public behavior by way of dissonance reduction.

According to dissonance theory (Festinger & Carlsmith, 1959), people are compelled to change their attitudes and beliefs in light of inconsistent behavior. As long as the behavior is freely chosen, such inconsistencies produce unpleasant physiological arousal. Because in most instances the behavior cannot be easily undone, people reduce the aversive arousal by bringing their attitudes and beliefs in line with their behavior. Note that this is a very different route to belief change as a result of lying. Because in Study 1 our participants chose the sunglasses themselves, it is possible that our results may be explainable in terms of dissonance theory. There is one qualification, however. In order for dissonance reduction to account for our findings, one would have expected a significant effect on the direct question regarding the appearance-altering qualities of the sunglasses. Nonetheless, to more thoroughly rule out a dissonance-based explanation, we conducted a second experiment that contained one important modification. Rather than letting participants choose, we randomly assigned them to lie about a particular pair of glasses. We obtained the same results.

In light of these findings, it appears that our participants were not simply trying to reconcile discrepancies between their attitudes and their behavior, as dissonance theory would suggest. Yet it is still possible that our failure to observe a difference on the most immediate measure ("These sunglasses make me look better/worse") is due to an aspect of our procedure. As alluded to earlier, the presence of the sunglasses during the ratings task may have served as a highly salient reminder of participants' true beliefs about their appearance-altering qualities, effectively obscuring any change in belief. To look at the veracity of this explanation, we replicated Study 2 with one important modification. Specifically, in Study 3 we modified the procedure to include a delay between the completion of the video task and the ratings. After repeating the statement about the sunglasses to the camera, research participants were led into an adjacent room, where they proofread a 10-page paper on marketing. After 15 minutes, the experimenter returned and once again asked participants to fill out the questionnaire.

As it turns out, the delay did not affect the outcome very much at all. Spending 15 minutes proofreading and filling out the questionnaire without the sunglasses present did not affect participants' beliefs about the extent to which the sunglasses made them look better or worse. However, once again they were happier with their general appearance and believed others considered them more attractive as the number of positive affirmations increased. An increase in the number of negative affirmations had a mirror image effect in that participants became more dissatisfied with their appearance and believed that others found them less attractive.

Of course, our experimental paradigm is a far cry from the horrors of the Holocaust. One could even argue that the findings to date merely scratch the surface of the processes that operate in lying self-deception. Nonetheless, they are at least suggestive of the effects that lies may have on those who generate and spread them. In the short run at least, repeating lies may not convince liars of the truth of the lie they tell. However, liars may convince themselves that a more general variant of the lie is, in fact, true. In the long run, this effect may well be more dramatic. As liars tell the same lies over an extended period of time, they may well forget that they were the source of the lie to begin with (Johnson, Hashtroudi, & Lindsay, 1993). Consequently, what may have begun as an internally generated lie may eventually achieve the status of an externally generated "truth," resulting in the conviction that what we believe about ourselves is derived from what others say about us. Ironically, because of this failure to monitor the source of the lie, it may well be that in many cases liars are the only ones who are convinced that their lie represents the truth.

Eichmann's Lying Self-Deception

It is impossible to tell if Eichmann's lying self-deception convinced him that he was innocent of the murder of millions of Jews. We know for sure that he failed to convince the court in Jerusalem and the vast majority who witnessed the trial in some form. Arendt (1965) reports that Eichmann went to his execution with dignity and even a sense of elation. Had he forgotten that he was going to his own funeral? Probably not. It is more likely that he took his final steps reaffirmed in the belief that he once again was *somebody*. His exile in Argentina had been less than kind to him. Instead of creating assembly lines of death, he had been a manual laborer working on an assembly line that turned out automobiles. His trial once again catapulted him into the limelight. That he had to defend himself against the accusation of having committed the crime of the century mattered relatively little. Walking to the gallows for the murder of 6 million Jews may have been a final, triumphant reaffirmation of his importance. Based on the research presented in this chapter, when he took those final steps, he may not have been entirely convinced of his innocence. But, if nothing else, the lie he repeated so often in Jerusalem along with the lies he told in Berlin may ultimately have convinced him of his own rectitude.

Other Perpetrators

If we accept the conclusion that the man primarily responsible for carrying out the Holocaust came to believe in his rectitude and perhaps even his innocence, it is easily possible to understand why so many more low-level perpetrators ended up with similar convictions. Once fully operative, the Nazi death machine was characterized by a high degree of division of labor. Those in charge of train schedules were not in charge of getting Jews on the trains, and those who were in charge of transports were not in charge of killing. This assembly line system not only was highly efficient but also enabled the vast majority of those involved to convince themselves that they were not killing anyone. In essence, it enabled individuals to identify their actions on a relatively low level of abstraction. According to the theory of action identification (Vallacher & Wegner, 1987), people strive to identify their behavior at an optimal level of abstraction. They generally construe their behavior on relatively high levels of abstraction simply because it adds meaning to their actions. Thus, someone flipping pancakes is likely to think of his actions as "making breakfast" rather than "handling batter" (a suboptimally low level of action identification) or "contributing to end world hunger" (a suboptimally high level of action identification). The generally observed striving toward moderately high levels of action identification is somewhat reversed when it comes to *difficult* tasks. For example, parents who think of child rearing in very concrete and detailed ways enjoy more success than parents who think of the task in relatively abstract terms, such as "fulfilling a duty" (Wegner & Vallacher, 1986).

If we assume that aiding in carrying out mass exterminations of people is a difficult task for most, at least emotionally, the research on action identification has some pretty straightforward implications. Rather than thinking of their work as carrying out part of the Final Solution, perpetrators thought of it as making schedules, filling train cars, running trains, and so forth. Ultimately, this strategy may have aided in the success of the operation, as well as the mental health of those who carried it out. It is entirely possible that repeatedly telling oneself things like "I was just coordinating schedules" increased the subjective belief that this was all one was doing. Moreover, because many of these actions were carried out collectively, it is likely that perpetrators used each other to assure themselves that they were doing less than they were. When they were confronted with their actions after the war, they often repeated the same lies about the nature of one's doings, thus possibly solidifying existing beliefs regarding innocence and rectitude.

Of course, this same avenue for self-deception is not open to perpetrators who directly and actively participated in executions in the infamous special units (*Einsatzgruppen*) and police battalions. The latter were in charge of killing Jewish civilians (primarily women and children) in areas of eastern Europe occupied by Germany. Initially, their duties included everything from rounding up their victims, to escorting them to the execution site, to shooting them at close range (Browning, 1998). This highly personalized way of killing left little opportunity for self-deception via identifying actions at a low level of abstraction. But the example of a 35-year-old policeman who specialized in shooting children only shows that the human capacity for self-deception knows no bounds:

> I made the effort, and it was possible for me, to shoot only children. It so happened that the mothers led the children by the hand. My neighbor then shot the mother and I shot the child that belonged to her, because I reasoned with myself that after all without its mother the child could not live any longer. It was supposed to be, so to speak, soothing to my conscience to release children unable to live without their mothers. (Browning, 1998, p. 73)

As Browning points out, the significance of this statement cannot be fully appreciated unless one considers that the German word for "release" (*erloesen*) also means redeem or save. Thus, it appears that this particular policeman soothed his conscience by identifying the act of killing a child on a higher level of abstraction (redemption) to the point where he seemed to have convinced himself that he was doing good rather than evil. The police battalions operated in relative isolation, and their members were forced to spend nearly all their time in the company of their fellow policemen. Again, it is entirely conceivable that they convinced themselves of their rationalizations and lies by repeating them to each other. The resulting reality of lies they created may have contributed to their ability to carry out their evil tasks day in and out and to return to civilian life with a clear conscience.

Bystanders and Victims

To fully comprehend how the Holocaust could happen requires not only an understanding of the psychological mechanisms that enabled its perpetrators to carry out their tasks but also an understanding of the processes that operated on the bystanders and perhaps even the victims. There is reason to sus-

297

pect that self-deceptive processes amplified by the power of repetition may have determined their respective behavior to some extent.

It seems like a matter of historical record that the Nazis attempted to carry out the Final Solution in relative secrecy. For example, they set aside considerable resources in order to move the systematic killing to Poland, and much of it was done by non-Germans from occupied countries. Nonetheless, the killings were preceded by the deportations of massive numbers of people that could not have gone unnoticed by the larger population. How could these people stand by and watch as their neighbors were forcibly removed from their homes and loaded onto cattle trains? There are probably many reasons, ranging from general bystander apathy (Latane & Darley, 1970) to the effects of a totalitarian regime that punished dissent with force. And there appears to be growing evidence that the proportion of those who agreed with Nazi policies is higher than previously thought (Herbert, 1999). However, in line with the present analysis, it is entirely conceivable that many who may have been appalled by what they saw adopted the view that they witnessed resettlements rather than transports to extermination camps. In addition to considering this lie as an explanation for what was happening, bystanders may have repeatedly communicated it to each other and, in the process, may have acquired the collective conviction that it was true.

Of course, to soothe one's conscience at the sight of people being dragged from their homes by adopting the view that they are "merely" being resettled seems cruel. However, in light of the alternative (death), it may well have seemed like the lesser of two evils. Could it be that the victims were similarly willing to adopt and spread lies about their impending fate? It is impossible to say with any degree of certainty. However, it seems safe to speculate that any group of people forced into living in horrible conditions behind barbed wire might want to adopt a somewhat self-serving outlook regarding their future. The ability to adopt a lie about what the future holds and to communicate it to others while separated from the reality of the outside world may ultimately be a cornerstone of what one could call "ghetto mentality."

CONCLUSION

This chapter has attempted to shed light on the psychological processes that enable perpetrators of genocide to carry out their evil tasks without being troubled by their conscience. It looked at self-deception, with a particular focus on the outcomes of repeatedly telling a lie on subsequent belief change. It further looked at how this process may have lead Adolf Eichmann and other perpetrators of the Holocaust as well into believing that they had done nothing wrong. It is important to note that the present analysis does not attempt to present a single process to explain perpetrator behavior. Nor does it aim to replace previous social-psychological explanations. Rather, it is intended to contribute toward a multicausal understanding of perpetrator behavior.

If Eichmann's case is any indication, the human propensity for self-deception has few, if any, limits. Director Errol Morris, commenting on his movie about Fred Leuchter (author of the infamous Leuchter report, which claims no gassing occurred at Auschwitz), put this very eloquently by claiming that self-deception may be a fundamental part of human behavior (Roiphe, 2000). According to his analysis, after God expelled Adam and Eve from the Garden of Eden, he had second thoughts. Realizing that he was sending them to a truly awful place, he gave them self-deception as a means to cope. It appears that Eichmann and his countless henchmen used a combination of lying and self-deception as one means to *create* a truly awful place for millions of people.

REFERENCES

Arendt, H. (1965). *Eichmann in Jerusalem: A report on the banality of evil* (Rev. and enlarged ed.). New York: Viking.

Augstein, R. (1998). The sociologist as hanging judge. In R. R. Shandley (Ed.), *Unwilling Germans? The Goldhagen debate* (pp. 47–50). Minneapolis: University of Minnesota Press.

Brown, J. D. (1998). *The self.* New York: McGraw-Hill.

Browning, C. R. (1998). *Ordinary men: Reserve Police Battalion 101 and the Final Solution in Poland.* New York: HarperCollins.

Burger, J. M. (1981). Motivational biases in the attribution of responsibility for an accident: A meta-analysis of the defensive-attribution hypothesis. *Psychological Bulletin, 90,* 496–512.

Devine, P. G., Monteith, M. J., Zuwerink, J. R., & Elliot, A. J. (1991). Prejudice with and without compunction. *Journal of Personality and Social Psychology, 60,* 817–830.

Festinger, L., & Carlsmith, J. M. (1959). Cognitive consequences of forced compliance. *Journal of Abnormal and Social Psychology, 58,* 203–210.

Goldhagen, D. J. (1996). *Hitler's willing executioners: Ordinary Germans and the Holocaust.* New York: Knopf.

Herbert, U. (1999). Academic and public discourses on the Holocaust: The Goldhagen debate in Germany. *German Politics and Society, 52,* 35–53.

Johnson, M. K., Hashtroudi, S., & Lindsay, D. S. (1993). Source monitoring. *Psychological Bulletin, 114,* 3–28.

Latane, B., & Darley, J. (1970). *The unresponsive bystander: Why doesn't he help?* Englewood Cliffs, NJ: Prentice-Hall.

Naumann, B. (1966). *Auschwitz.* New York: Praeger.

Paulhus, D. L. (1993). Bypassing the will: The automatization of affirmations. In D. M. Wegner & J. W. Pennebaker (Eds.), *Handbook of mental control* (pp. 573–587). Englewood Cliffs, NJ: Prentice Hall.

Roiphe, K. (2000, December/January). Death becomes him. *George,* p. 60.

Sabini, J. P., & Silver, M. (1980). Destroying the innocent with a clear conscience:

A sociopsychology of the Holocaust. In J. E. Dimsdale (Ed.), *Survivors, victims, and perpetrators: Essays on the Nazi Holocaust*. Washington, DC: Hemisphere.

Sackeim, H. A., & Gur, C. R. (1979). Self-deception, other deception, and self-reported psychopathology. *Journal of Consulting and Clinical Psychology, 47*, 213–215.

Schlenker, B. R., & Trudeau, J. V. (1990). Impact of self-presentations on private self-beliefs: Effects of prior self-beliefs and misattribution. *Journal of Personality and Social Psychology, 58*, 22–32.

Thornton, B. (1984). Defensive attribution of responsibility: Evidence for an arousal-based motivational bias. *Journal of Personality and Social Psychology, 46*, 721–734.

Vallacher, R. R., & Wegner, D. M. (1987). What do people think they are doing? Action identification and human behavior. *Psychological Review, 94*, 3–15.

Wegner, D. M., & Vallacher, R. R. (1986). Action identification. In R. M. Sorrentino & E. T. Higgins (Eds.), *Handbook of motivation and cognition* (pp. 550–582). New York: Guilford.

13

Explaining the Holocaust

Does Social Psychology Exonerate the Perpetrators?

Arthur G. Miller, Amy M. Buddie, and Jeffrey Kretschmar

For the social psychology of this century reveals a major lesson: Often, it is not so much the kind of person a man is as the kind of situation in which he finds himself that determines how he will act.

—Stanley Milgram, *Obedience to Authority*

Claude Lanzman . . . is the most prominent member of a growing faction of intellectuals who believe that any attempt to understand Hitler inevitably degenerates into an exercise in empathy with him. To understand all is to forgive all. . . . even the first steps down the slippery slope to understand are impermissible.

—Ron Rosenbaum, "Explaining Hitler"

In this chapter, we examine the proposition that social-psychological explanations of the Holocaust tend to exonerate perpetrators. Our intent is not to provide a new explanation of the Holocaust nor to assess existing theories. We are also not suggesting that social-psychologists personally condone the actions of perpetrators. Our specific interest is in the impact that social-psychological explanations may have on those who read or study them. Our focus is a comparative one. We will suggest that social-psychological explanations, as contrasted with dispositional or personality-oriented explanations, may be viewed as relatively condoning toward perpetrators. The objectives in this chapter are to consider why social-psychological explanations are likely to be viewed in this manner and to discuss the implications of this effect.

THE DEFINING FEATURE OF SOCIAL-PSYCHOLOGICAL EXPLANATIONS: THE POWER OF THE SITUATION

In our view, the most central, defining feature of social psychology—one that distinguishes social psychology from other disciplines such as personality, developmental, or clinical psychology—is an emphasis on social influence, or what Ross and Nisbett (1991) term the "power of the situation" (p. 27). Consider a well-known study by Darley and Batson (1973), in which helping a stranger in distress was observed to be strongly influenced by the situational context—specifically whether or not research participants (potential helpers) were in a hurry to complete another appointment. Commenting on this study, Ross and Nisbett (1991) noted:

> Social psychology has by now amassed a vast store of such empirical parables. . . . Often the situational variable makes quite a bit of difference. Occasionally, in fact, it makes nearly all of the difference, and information about traits and individual differences that other people thought all-important proves all but trivial. . . . Such empirical parables are important because they illustrate the degree to which ordinary men and woman are apt to be mistaken about the power of the situation (p. 4)

Philip Zimbardo (1995) made a similar observation, specifically addressing Browning's (1992) influential study of the men of Reserve Police Battalion 101 who murdered Jews in Poland: "There is no evidence of any special selection of these men, only that they were as "ordinary" as can be imagined until they were put into a situation in which they had permission and encouragement to act sadistically and brutishly against those labelled as the enemy" (p. 131).

People typically do not acknowledge the pervasive, often subtle, influences of situational pressures, preferring instead to account for behavior—at least of those other than themselves—in terms of dispositional characteristics of the actor. Many social psychologists have contended that this preference for dispositional explanations, even in the face of incontrovertible evidence of situational causation, constitutes a pervasive bias or judgmental error (e.g., Gilbert & Malone, 1995; Jones, 1990; Ross & Nisbett, 1991). In the context of explanations of the Holocaust, it is of crucial importance to consider not only the evidence documenting situational control of harmful behavior but also, for the lay observer, the extraordinary appeal of dispositional accounts of that behavior.

An emphasis upon external or situational influence does not, of course, rule out the importance of internal or dispositional attributes. There may be important differences among individuals in how a particular situational context is construed, and there may be personality differences that determine the specific behavior that is observed. One thinks immediately, for example, of the significant role of gender in the display of aggressive or violent behaviors (Baumeister, 1997). Also, over time, the power of a context to control social behavior may exert changes in the individuals exposed to that situation. For example, in discussing the social organization of evil actions, Darley (1992) has described what he terms the *conversion process*. A German physician might, upon first entering a concentration camp, be quite accurately described as relatively normal, adjusted, and so forth. However, over time, crucial changes may occur: "The person who is induced into participation, and who goes far enough in the conversion process so that he or she autonomously and intelligently initiates evil actions, is an individual who has become evil" (p. 209).

THE CAUSAL IMPLICATIONS OF RANDOM ASSIGNMENT

A prototypical experiment in social psychology—for example, on aggression, helping behavior, prejudice, or conformity—randomly assigns participants to different conditions. The logic of random assignment permits the social psychologist to interpret behavior as caused by the situation or by the participant's definition of the situation into which he or she was placed. Had the same participant been randomly assigned to a different condition of the experiment, his or her behavior would likely have been quite different. Let us consider an illustrative experiment, one concerning the effects of labeling a target on aggression. This experiment is, in our view, very relevant to the Holocaust in capturing the dehumanizing impact of group stereotypes.

The Effect of Labeling the Target on Aggression

Bandura, Underwood, and Fromson (1975) told their research participants that their experiment concerned the effects of punishment on the quality of decision making. Participants were to assume a supervisory role and observe a three-person group engaging in a series of bargaining problems. This group (the target) would select options and receive an "effective" or "ineffective" signal in the form of an amber or red light, respectively. On red-light signals, the subject was instructed to administer a shock on a graded series of shock levers (1 to 10) at any level thought appropriate. (Cover instructions justified aspects of this procedure; no shocks were actually administered.)

A key experimental manipulation was the labeling of the other persons (those receiving the shock). Subjects were led to believe they were overhearing the research assistant tell the experimenter that the students from another school were present to start the study. In one condition (humanized), the target was described "as a perceptive, understanding, and otherwise humanized group" (p. 258); in another condition (dehumanized), the decision makers were described "as an animalistic, rotten bunch" (p. 258). A neutral condition involved no evaluative references made about the target.

The dependent variable of shock intensity clearly indicated the power of the situational manipulation: "Dehumanized performers were treated more than twice as punitively as those invested with human qualities and considerably more severely than the neutral group" (p. 266). Thus, although the target groups behaved identically, the use of a single phrase depicting an idealized or strongly disparaging label influenced subjects to treat the target in a relatively benign or severely harsh manner. Being assigned randomly to the different labeling conditions had extremely powerful effects upon the subjects' subsequent behavior.

Implications of Situational Interpretations of Harmful Behavior: Diminished Intentionality and Responsibility

In a recent commentary on the preceding study, its principal investigator, Albert Bandura (1999), noted:

> The findings from research on the different mechanisms of moral disengagement are in accord with the historical chronicle of human atrocities: It requires conducive social conditions rather than monstrous people to produce atrocious deeds. Given appropriate social conditions, decent, ordinary people can be led to do extraordinarily cruel things. (p. 200)

Bandura's conclusion is similar to the views of Ross and Nisbett (1991) and Zimbardo (1995), cited earlier. The idea that "conducive social conditions" rather than "monstrous people" produce atrocious deeds, in our view, clearly implies a diminished sense of personal responsibility or intentionality on the part of the actors. In this study, research participants assigned to the dehumanized-target condition certainly had no a priori intent or personal motivation to engage in the harmful behaviors they so clearly committed in these studies.

THE EXONERATING IMPLICATIONS OF SCIENTIFIC EXPLANATIONS

Theorists of evil and violence frequently suggest that their explanations will be misconstrued as forgiveness (Miller, Gordon, & Buddie, 1999). Recent analysts of the Holocaust, for example, express the concern that they will be perceived as exonerating the perpetrators:

> Some would argue that rather than studying Nazi evil, it should simply be recognized for what it is and condemned. Any efforts at understanding the causes of the Third Reich only serve to explain

such actions, thus making them seemingly understandable and perhaps even excusable or justifiable. (Zillmer, Harrower, Ritzler, & Archer, 1995. p. 13)

Some went on to make a compelling case for leaving the whole subject alone. Their argument was that Nazi evil should merely be recognized and isolated; rather than make it an object of study, one should simply condemn it. Psychological study in particular, it was feared, ran the risk of replacing condemnation with "insights." (Lifton, 1986, p. xi)

I also fear that some readers may see me as exculpating killers; I have no such intention. . . . Although outrage is easier to feel in the face of uncomprehended evil, to understand is not necessarily to forgive. (Staub, 1989, pp. xiii–xiv)

Not to resist all or any inquiry, not to resist thought, but to resist the misleading exculpatory corollaries of explanation. To resist the way explanation can become evasion or consolation, a way of making Hitler's choice to do what he did less unbearable, less hateful to contemplate, by shifting responsibility from him to faceless abstractions, inexorable forces, or irresistible compulsions that gave him no choice or made his choice irrelevant. To resist making the kind of explanatory excuses for Hitler that permit him to *escape*, that grant him the posthumous victory of a last laugh. (Rosenbaum, 1999, p. 395)

Miller et al. (1999) have suggested that these concerns are well founded in terms of a variety of cognitive and emotional effects of explanations. They note that in contrast to the intuitive reactions of the layperson to the Holocaust—where reactions of anger, sadness, disgust, and perhaps disbelief are virtually automatic—explicit theoretical accounts by social scientists are likely to be more complex, less exclusively reliant upon denigrating the personal moral character of perpetrators, and relatively devoid of personal anger on the part of the theorist. Roy Baumeister (1997) has noted that formal (social science) explanations are also more likely, relative to the accounts of laypersons, to take into account the perspective of perpetrators, a perspective with exonerating implications: "There is ample reason to fear that understanding can promote forgiving. Seeing deeds from the perpetrator's point of view does change things in many ways" (p. 386).

A concern with the exonerating implications of social-psychological explanations is illustrated by Sabini and Silver (1980). After reviewing classic social-psychological experiments that have been interpreted as illuminating vital aspects of the Holocaust—the Milgram obedience experiments, Zimbardo's prison simulation, and Asch's conformity studies—they noted:

> The thrust of this chapter has been to bring the phenomena of the camps closer to home, to see how this horror, this inhumanity could have been the product not only of deranged individuals but of normal people placed in deranged and degrading circumstances. We have attempted to draw links between what we know the artisans of the Holocaust did and what ordinary, American people have done in laboratory settings. . . . There is, however, a danger in this. The task of making something understandable is to make us see how it could have happened by showing how it is akin to something we can already grasp. There is a common tendency to slide from understanding to excusing. We are accustomed to thinking that once we have understood how someone came to do something, we are then compelled to forgive. In this case we cannot allow understanding to lead to excuse or forgiving. (pp. 356–357)

When Staub (1989) states that "to understand is not necessarily to forgive" or when Sabini and Silver assert that "we cannot allow understanding to lead to excuse or forgiving," one can readily appreciate their position. Clearly, it is understandable why those involved in explanations of the Holocaust would not want to be perceived as personally condoning the perpetrators nor as attempting to influence their readers in this direction. Nevertheless, we think that an exonerating perspective is precisely what the outcome of social-psychological explanations—at least those with a strongly situationist focus—is likely to be.

SCIENTIFIC EXPLANATIONS OF SOCIAL BEHAVIOR: AN ATTRIBUTIONAL PERSPECTIVE

Scientific explanations of social behavior present causal analyses of the behavior at issue (Kelley, 1992). Readers (i.e., students, professional colleagues) exposed to a particular explanation are likely to draw inferences regarding the degree of freedom or constraint characterizing the actor. According to various attributional theories (e.g., Gilbert, 1995; Jones & Davis, 1965; Weiner, 1995), these inferences are related to judgments of intentionality, responsibility, and other reactions toward the actor. Inferences regarding the constraint on actors may occur explicitly or implicitly, with varying degrees of awareness on the part of both the theorist (explainer) and the reader.

Weiner, Perry, and Magnusson (1988) have shown that people's emotional (e.g., sympathy, anger) and behavioral reactions toward a deviant or stigmatized target person are strongly mediated by attributions of controllability and responsibility. In conditions involving relatively high perceived responsibility (e.g., obesity, AIDS, child and drug abuse), reactions are extremely and uniformly negative, for example, high attributions for personal blame and anger. However, if the stigmatizing condition evokes a perception of low personal responsibility (e.g., victims of cancer, blindness, or paraplegia), judgments are more favorable. The key issue is the degree of personal responsibility attributed to the target. As we have noted earlier, social-psychological explanations of harm-doing tend to portray the perpetrator as relatively low in personal responsibility for his or her behavior. Thus, based on Weiner's attributional model of stigma, we would expect a relatively condoning image of the perpetrator contained in social-psychological explanations of harm or misconduct. This hypothesis was examined in a recent set of experiments.

THE EXONERATING IMPLICATIONS OF SOCIAL-PSYCHOLOGICAL EXPLANATIONS: EMPIRICAL EVIDENCE

Miller et al. (1999) reported the results of two studies, which tested the hypothesis that a social-psychological explanation of an act of harm will be perceived as more condoning toward the perpetrator than will an explanation focused on dispositions of the perpetrator. In the first study, participants were first given a synopsis of an experiment on cheating, modeled after Diener and Wallbom (1976), who hypothesized and found evidence that people would cheat less if they were in a situation that accentuated self-awareness. Their method involved college students working on an anagram task, described as predictive of scholastic success. Their participants were randomly assigned to work on the anagrams either directly in front of or to the side of a large mirror. Viewing oneself in a mirror is thought to increase self-awareness and thereby curtail antisocial behavior. These participants were instructed to stop working upon the ringing of a bell. Subjects, without their awareness, were observed by the researcher, who noted whether or not cheating occurred by working beyond the allotted time.

Participants in the Miller et al. study were assigned to one of two conditions. In the *social-psychological explanation* condition, results were provided which indicated a powerful situational effect—5% cheating in the mirror condition and 90% cheating in the no-mirror condition (similar to the actual results of this study). The discussion emphasized the power of the situation (mirror present or absent) to influence cheating behavior and the implications of random assignment to conditions. There were no references in the discussion section to inferences on the part of the researcher regarding the subject's intentions, responsibility, or moral blameworthiness for having cheated.

In the *personality-explanation* condition, the results indicated the total absence of any situational effect—50% cheating in both the mirror and no-mirror conditions. The hypothesis concerning the effects of mirror presence was thus not supported. Participants were told that in order to clarify the failure to obtain the expected effect, the researcher administered a follow-up study in which the same participants returned to complete an "honesty test" (e.g., "It is important never to lie," "Cheating is probably more common than most people realize"). A new set of results was then presented, showing that only 5% of those scoring high on the honesty test had cheated in the earlier session, whereas 90% of those scoring low on the honesty test had cheated. The discussion section emphasized the failure of the situational manipulation and the power of the individual participant's level of honesty to predict cheating behavior. Again, no explicit reference was made to issues regarding intent, responsibility, or moral blameworthiness.

After participants read either the social-psychological or the personality results and explanation, they were given two sets of measures. On the "researcher's impressions" form, they were asked to estimate the researcher's views concerning various aspects of the study. The key measures were the degree to which the researcher felt that cheating was *intentional* on the part of the students who had cheated, that the persons who cheated were *personally responsible* for their cheating, and that the participants who had cheated should be *blamed* for their cheating. On the "participant's impressions" form, participants were asked to respond to the identical judgment items, but from their own personal perspective (e.g., how much do you feel that the students who cheated were personally responsible?).

Of particular interest was the fact that *participants who had read a social-psychological explanation of cheating viewed the researcher as more condoning toward the perpetrators than did subjects who had read a dispositional explanation.* This pattern of results confirms our hypothesis regarding the exonerating implications of social-psychological explanations. However, when rendering their personal opinions, participants held cheaters accountable for their behavior regardless of the type of explanation they had read. Thus, subjects essentially ignored the situational implications of the social-psychological explanations when giving their personal judgments about the cheater, a pattern characteristic of the dispositional bias.

To assess the reliability of these findings, a second experiment was conducted that differed only in regard to the particular type of harm being considered. The core script, which all subjects received, described a social-psychological experiment dealing with the effects of high temperature on aggression, modeled after studies by Anderson and his colleagues (Anderson, Benjamin, & Bartholow, 1998). The design of the study and the dependent variables were identical to those used in the first study on cheating. The pattern of results was highly similar to that in the study on cheating. As in the first study, participants' own judgments of the aggressive target were relatively similar in both the social-psychological and the personality explanation condition, whereas their estimates of the researcher's judgments were substantially more condoning in the social-psychological explanation condition.

We have recently extended this line of research to examine whether social-psychological (contrasted with dispositional) explanations of stereotyping and prejudice convey, to readers, an exonerating stance on the part of the theorist. Preliminary results suggest that social-psychological explanations—for example, emphasizing the pervasive, cognitive (automatically activated) aspects of stereotyping—are *not* viewed as exonerating the perpetrators. We suspect, tentatively, that unlike other situational factors influencing behavior (which are more readily viewed as external to the actor), prejudice may be viewed as inherently dispositional and not susceptible to exoneration, regardless of how it is articulated by the theorist.

Although we have not incorporated explanations of genocide, per se, in our research, our findings point to the usefulness of investigating, in an empirical manner, reactions to different types of explanations of the Holocaust. Clearly, the Holocaust is an extraordinarily complex and controversial topic. Virtually any scholarly work on the subject—explanations of Hitler being a classic illustration—is an automatic catalyst for debate, if not acrimony (e.g., Rosenbaum, 1999; Zillmer et al., 1995). We would suggest that one key issue in understanding conflicting explanatory accounts resides in the degree to which the perpetrators are held personally responsible for their actions. Those strongly motivated to hold perpetrators accountable are likely to disagree vehemently with explanations that they construe, accurately or not, as condoning. In this context, we turn now to a consideration of explanations of the Holocaust in the social-psychological literature. Our specific focus is on the manner in which harm-doers are construed on the dimension of personal responsibility.

SOCIAL-PSYCHOLOGICAL EXPLANATIONS OF THE HOLOCAUST

There are numerous behaviors which have been identified as relevant to the Holocaust and for which there exist considerable research literatures. We will consider four selected behaviors: obedience, evil and violence, prosocial behavior, and stereotyping. Our primary interest is the attribution of responsibility to a perpetrator that a reader is likely to make after considering social-psychological explanations of a relevant act of harm-doing.

Obedience to Malevolent Authority: The Milgram Experiments

When one considers the contribution of social psychology to an understanding of the Holocaust, invariably it will be the obedience experiments of Stanley Milgram (1963, 1974) that first come to mind. As is well known, two key findings in Milgram's initial report of his studies (1963) were the unexpectedly high proportion of individuals who obeyed an experimenter's orders to inflict increasingly severe punishment upon a protesting victim, and the extreme emotional stress that characterized many participants in the course of their obedience. Milgram also reported (1974) that the degree to which obedience occurred was very strongly associated with specific aspects of the situation. Obedience was extremely reduced, for example, if participants first had witnessed other (apparent) participants withdrawing from the experiment, or if two experimenters argued among themselves regarding what the participant should do. A willingness to engage in destructive obedience thus was not, in Milgram's view, an inherent characteristic of human nature. Disobedience, in fact, was predominant in certain conditions.

Does Milgram's interpretation exonerate those who obey malevolent authority? In our view, the answer to this question is at least a qualified yes. Consider the quoted passage at the beginning of this chapter. Milgram's idea that it is the situation rather than a person's inner qualities that determines behavior illustrates the exonerating implications of social-psychological explanations. A similar emphasis is Milgram's view that obedience reflects an individual's divesting of personal responsibility. Individuals, receiving orders, may exonerate themselves:

> It is the old story of "just doing one's duty" that was heard time
> and time again in the defense statements of those accused at
> Nuremberg. But it would be wrong to think of it as a thin alibi
> concocted for the occasion. Rather, it is a fundamental mode of
> thinking for a great many people once they are locked into a
> subordinate position in a structure of authority. The disappearance
> of a sense of responsibility is the most far-reaching consequence of
> submission to authority. (1974, p. 8)

In a recent analysis of the diverse interpretive constructions of the Holocaust in American culture, the historian Peter Novick (1999) has commented on the impact of the obedience studies. He notes, initially, the different meaning that "following orders" acquired as a result of Milgram's experiments:

> In the mid-sixties Milgram's work began to reach an audience
> wider than the readership of the *Journal of Abnormal Psychology*. By
> then, Arendt's version of Eichmann had also entered common
> discourse. . . . A kind of synergy developed between the symbol of
> Arendt's Eichmann and the symbol of Milgram's subjects, invoked
> in discussing everything from the Vietnam war to the tobacco
> industry, and, of course, reflecting back on discussions of the
> Holocaust. It was in large part as a result of the acceptance of

> Arendt's portrait of Eichmann (with an assist from Milgram) that
> "just following orders" changed, in the American lexicon, from a
> plea in extenuation to a damning indictment. (p. 137)

Novick is suggesting that "following orders" was, via the dual influence of
Arendt and Milgram, now viewed as an empirically verified, psychological
reason for engaging in destructive behavior. One might be dismayed at the
readiness of individuals in diverse military and bureaucratic contexts to claim
"obeying orders" in defending their actions, but it could no longer be simply
dismissed as a self-serving excuse or rationalization.

Novick's conclusion relates closely to our focus in this chapter. He suggests,
in this context, that despite some resistance among scholars, Daniel Goldhagen's book, *Hitler's Willing Executioners* (1996) has been extremely popular.
The reason is that Goldhagen's explanation, which argues for "eliminationist
antisemitism" in Germans as the key factor in the Holocaust, distances perpetrators from the average reader:

> It is a comforting argument: if such deep and long-standing hatred
> is a necessary precondition for mass murder, we're a lot safer than
> many of us think. But the desire to frame the perpetrators in the
> traditional way remains powerful—which is why Goldhagen's book
> was a runaway bestseller. (p. 137)

Novick's conclusion illustrates our primary concern in this chapter. He is, in
effect, arguing that Goldhagen's explanation indicts rather than exonerates
perpetrators, and thus is telling his readers exactly what they want to hear.

Milgram's Exonerating Position: A Basis for Controversy

If the position advocated in this chapter—that is, the exonerating implications
of social-psychological analyses—is correct, it follows that social-psychological interpretations of harm-doing are likely to be controversial and, for some,
unacceptable. Two recent analyses of the obedience experiments have taken
a particularly critical position, and a brief examination of these criticisms may
be instructive.

The Obedience Alibi

David Mandel's (1998) primary objection is the claim that the major perpetrators of the Holocaust were simply following orders, that they, like Milgram's
subjects, were not personally motivated to harm or kill Jews but did so only
under the extraordinarily harsh and unrelenting pressure of orders from Hitler
and other high-ranking Nazi officials. A key passage is Mandel's commentary
on the "social dangers" of social-psychological explanations of the Holocaust
(epitomized by the Milgram experiments):

> The many oversimplified statements about the Holocaust that have
> been made by Milgram and a number of other social scientists, like
> the claims of most accused Nazis, constitute little more than an
> *obedience alibi*. The term alibi is especially fitting because it connotes
> both an excuse or assurance of innocence and an explanation or
> statement. Holocaust perpetrators have asserted the obedience alibi
> as an assurance of their innocence. Social scientists have asserted
> the obedience alibi as an ostensibly situationist explanation of the
> Holocaust. Though the intent of one group has differed from the
> other, the message conveyed has been strikingly similar. (p. 91)

Mandel has also spoken to what he views as a danger in viewing "following orders" as social psychology's primary contribution to an understanding
of the Holocaust. He is concerned with how certain readers will react to a social-
psychological explanation:

> The "just following orders" claim regarding the Holocaust . . . is . . .
> offensive to survivors . . . who know all too well that there was
> much more behind the way they were viciously brutalized,
> mocked, and tormented than a mere obligation to follow orders.
> This is not to suggest that social scientists should try to construct
> theories that comfort any particular group. Researchers and
> theorists should . . . seek the truth even if it is a terrible truth and
> they should reveal what they find. Nevertheless, care should be
> taken in how explanations are communicated, especially when
> they have a clear potential to cause harm. (p. 91)

Mandel's thoughts regarding "how explanations are communicated" and their
"clear potential to cause harm" are particularly relevant to our thesis. While
it may not be clear how a theorist can consciously attempt to avoid offending
readers while at the same time seeking truthful explanations, even if a "terrible truth," it is precisely this dilemma that lies at the heart of our concerns
in this chapter.

Evil Is More Than Banal

Leonard Berkowitz (1999), in a highly critical analysis, suggests that social
psychology's virtually unqualified endorsement of the Milgram experiments
fails to distinguish between those who authorized the policy of genocide and
those who followed their orders:

> Another factor influencing people's judgments of evil has to do
> with the perceived responsibility for the action. This particular

consideration has been surprisingly neglected by those who talk
of the banality of evil as if it did not at all matter who initiated,
or was primarily responsible for, the behavior being assessed.
(p. 251)

Berkowitz argues that in failing to address the psychology of "genocide initiators"—that is, Eichmann, Heydrich, and Hitler—and, instead, continuously
pointing to obedience in the Milgram paradigm as an example of blameless
harm-doing by subordinates, social psychology has failed to recognize degrees
of evil. This failure, in itself, leads to a dangerously shortsighted and exonerating picture of the Holocaust:

> Social psychology's relative inattention to the great atrocities
> committed during the extermination program reflects the field's
> failure to establish a conception of evil that differentiates among
> categories of wrongdoing. In so doing, there is a danger of
> trivializing terrible actions. (p. 250)

In summary, Mandel and Berkowitz suggest that the Nazi perpetrators were
personally motivated to harm, even kill, Jews. (For a similar argument, see
Fenigstein, 1998; Goldhagen, 1996; Lutsky, 1995.) For these critics, social
psychology has simply glossed over processes far more vital to the Holocaust
than obedience—namely, personally held beliefs about Jews and the resulting perceived legitimacy, even correctness, of exterminating them.

Evil and Violence

Philip Zimbardo has been a major contributor to social-psychological analyses of harmful behaviors, specifically his research on deindividuation (1970)
and the Stanford prison-simulation study (Zimbardo, Haney, Banks, & Jaffe,
1973). He recently articulated his position on social-psychological analyses
of harmful acts:

> It is only through the recognition that no one of us is an island
> unto itself, that we are all part of the human connection, that
> humility takes precedence over unfounded pride in acknowledging
> our vulnerability to situational forces. It seems essential to learn to
> appreciate the extent to which ordinary people can be seduced or
> initiated into engaging in evil deeds if we want to develop
> mechanisms for combating such transformations, mechanisms that
> address causal factors that influence so many people, as in the
> epidemic of violence in the U.S., and indeed taking place in
> countries throughout the globe. (1995, p. 127)

313

It is Zimbardo's use of the phrase "seduced or initiated into engaging in evil deeds" that, in our view, implies a relatively exonerating or condoning stance on harm-doing. Consider the different implications had Zimbardo concluded: "It seems essential to learn to appreciate the extent to which ordinary people freely choose to engage in evil deeds."

Haney and Zimbardo (1998), in a recent analysis of the status of prisons in the United States, took a very critical position. At the center of their discussion is the claim that social-psychological explanations of antisocial behavior—and, specifically, the implications of the Stanford Prison Experiment (SPE)—have been ignored. The SPE (1973) had shown that well-adjusted male volunteers, randomly assigned to play the roles of prisoners or guards in a mock prison, exhibited extremely degrading and distressed behaviors, as if their assigned roles were more real than simulated. The SPE has been interpreted by many social psychologists as an example of a social-psychological experiment with extraordinary relevance to the Holocaust. For example, Sabini and Silver (1980), in observing that Zimbardo's prisoner-subjects were forced to chant songs that degraded themselves, noted:

> This too is a nearly constant theme in the concentration camp literature. . . . These results strongly suggest that perfectly normal people will, in certain circumstances, treat others in a brutal, inhumane way, even though they know that their victims are ordinary people much like themselves, even though they know, literally in this case, that there but for chance would they be. (p. 349)

Perhaps nowhere in society is there a domain to rival criminal behavior in terms of displaying the inclination of both lay and professional observers to dispositionalize the behavior and render harsh judgments regarding how perpetrators should be treated. In Haney and Zimbardo's analysis, one sees the clearly unpopular effect of the condoning implications of a social-psychological perspective:

> The SPE (Stanford Prison Experiment) and related studies also imply that exclusively individual-centered approaches to crime control (like imprisonment) are self-limiting and doomed to failure in the absence of other approaches that simultaneously and systematically address criminogenic situational and contextual factors. Because traditional models of rehabilitation are person-centered and dispositional in nature (focusing entirely on individual change), they typically have ignored the postrelease situational factors that help to account for discouraging rates of recidivism. (p. 720)

The Failure to Help Others in Distress

A major legacy of the Holocaust in terms of stimulating psychological research was the failure of bystanders, both within Germany and in foreign institutions and governments, to intervene on behalf of Jewish victims. Staub (1989) has observed:

> Germans accepted, supported, and participated in the increasing persecution of Jews. Resistance and public attempts to help were rare. Bystanders too were influenced by difficult life conditions, German culture, and the resulting psychological processes and motives. These gave them a shared societal tilt with perpetrators. (p. 151)

The failure to help others in distress may often be construed by observers as aggressive behavior because inevitably there is someone harmed, or even killed, as a result of the nonintervention. Not helping another in need is thus, for many observers, likely to evoke a powerful dispositional causal explanation. It was in this context—specifically the intense societal reaction to the murder of Kitty Genovese in 1964—that Latane and Darley developed the most famous social-psychological analysis of this problem. Kitty Genovese was raped and killed in front of her Queens, New York apartment in the full view of numerous witnesses. The fact that despite her screams of terror and pleas for help no one came to her aid (possibly preventing her murder) became a celebrated occasion for analyses in the media (e.g., Rosenthal, 1964). A prevailing conclusion was that the witnesses to her attack were apathetic, afraid, and generally disinterested in the welfare of their neighbors. However, numerous experimental investigations of what came to be known as the *bystander effect* demonstrated that the failure to intervene was caused by a glaringly simple situational factor—the number of observers witnessing the victim's predicament—rather than dispositional factors. Latane and Darley (1970) concluded:

> As we have seen, individual difference variables account for remarkably little variance in helping behavior. None of the personality tests we have investigated have related to helping, and autobiographical information seems to do little better. These findings suggest that anybody can be led either to help or not to help in a specific situation. Characteristics of the immediate situation may have a more important influence on what the bystander does than his personality or life history. (p. 120)

In our view, this situational interpretation of bystander nonintervention is a relatively exonerating position. It construes the failure to help as a normative response, as something that "anybody" would be expected to do in certain circumstances. Note how different the tone of this account is as compared with an explanation that would explain the failure to help another person as a consequence of a person's undeveloped sense of morality, empathy, compassion, or altruism.

It is, of course, important to acknowledge that bystanders may, on occasion, help victims. There is a significant historical record of non-Jews helping Jews escape Nazi persecution. Because it was hardly a normative response, those who helped victims of Nazi oppression are understandably often portrayed as heroic, as having acted because of their uniquely compassionate dispositional nature. However, our argument in this chapter suggests that a social-psychological analysis of helping behavior would, in its situational emphasis, not focus on heroic or uniquely altruistic traits and motives.

In a recent analysis of rescuers during the Nazi period, specifically the activities of rescuers in the French village of Le Chambon, Rochat and Modigliani (1995) develop a conception of the "ordinariness of goodness." Their argument essentially parallels Arendt's banality of evil thesis and Milgram's position, suggesting that helping as well as harming behaviors are well within the province of many persons:

> Those who refused to obey the orders of authorities, and came to the aid of persecuted people, were neither saints nor heroes. Rather, their goodness was that of ordinary men and women who were responsive to the victims' manifest need for help. The way they acted was part of their everyday life, and they did not perceive it as something extraordinary. They did not feel like heroes at the time, nor do they want to be seen as such in retrospect. (p. 197)

Rochat and Modigliani hasten to add that the "ordinariness of goodness" does not necessarily imply that helping under duress will be commonplace, nor that there are not true acts of uniquely courageous heroism. Their main point is that "goodness—where and when it does happen to exist—can be expressed in quite ordinary ways that are mere extensions of common civility or basic decency" (p. 206). In our view, this is a social-psychological account that supports the general theme of this chapter.

Stereotyping and Prejudice

Anti-Semitic stereotyping and prejudice have long been viewed as key features of the Holocaust, particularly in terms of creating the psychological climate that ultimately produced and accepted the policy of genocide. In an earlier period in the United States, social-psychological treatments of stereotyping and prejudice were primarily characterized by analyses of motives to harm and disparage other groups. Developing measures to assess individual differences in prejudice was a priority, as illustrated in studies of the authoritarian personality (Adorno, Frenkel-Brunswik, Levinson, & Sanford, 1950).

Over the past three decades, however, social-psychological theories of stereotyping and prejudice have taken on a decidedly more cognitive orientation. Reflecting the remarkable foresight of Gordon Allport in his chapter on the "normality of prejudgment" (1954), current social-psychological explanations essentially argue that stereotyping is ubiquitous, pervasive, and a normal characteristic of human cognitive functioning; that it reflects mental representations (schemas) of groups that are acquired in a largely unconscious and automatic manner as a result of socialization. Susan Fiske (1992), in discussing the pragmatic functions of social cognition, noted that "recent work . . . is turning away from the view of stereotypes as a unique and pernicious phenomenon and situating them in the context of goal-directed person perception in a broader social context" (p. 883).

Numerous experiments have recently documented the automatic (noncontrollable) aspect of stereotyping. An entire recent issue of the *American Psychologist* (1999) was devoted to the extraordinary role of involuntary processes in human behavior. In a seminal article in this issue, Bargh and Chartrand provided a review of research in contemporary social cognition, focusing largely on experiments on stereotyping, social perception, and self-regulation processes. In numerous studies, evidence was cited supporting the crucial role of nonconscious processes. For example, in a study by Bargh, Chen, and Burrows (1996), subjects who were subliminally presented with faces of young male African Americans later reacted with greater hostility to a mild provocation than did a control group. Bargh and Chartrand (1999) concluded that "the automatic activation of the African American stereotype caused the participants to behave themselves with greater hostility" (p. 467).

In terms of our focus in this chapter, the central question is, to what degree can individuals be held personally responsible for their stereotyping (and behaviors related to their stereotypes)? More specifically, from the accounts of stereotyping in Bargh and Chartrand's review, how are readers likely to consider issues of responsibility and intent on the part of those engaging in stereotype-driven judgments and behaviors? In our view, individuals would likely be viewed as not responsible. We regard the emphasis upon automaticity and nonconscious processes in current conceptualizations of prejudice and stereotyping as strongly consistent with our thesis that social psychology exonerates harm-doing. This position has been articulated by Banaji and Greenwald (1994) in a recent chapter:

> Empirical discoveries about the implicit nature of social judgments are indeed relevant to discussions about the legal consequences of such acts for the perpetrator as well as the survivor of stereotyping

317

and prejudice. Specifically, if implicit stereotyping arises (a) from knowledge shared by a culture as a whole and is not uniquely possessed by the perpetrator alone, (b) from an accurate understanding of reality and not necessarily from misperception or distortion, and (c) without the conscious awareness of the perpetrator, such data would argue for removing responsibility from individual perpetrators of social crimes of stereotyping and prejudice. Such conditions surrounding discoveries of implicit stereotyping encourage consideration of the notion of *perpetratorless crimes* (as a parallel to the existing notion of victimless crimes). The notion of removing responsibility and blame from individual perpetrators differs vastly from conventional assumptions of most justice systems. Discussion of the implications of this construct for justice systems must be considered at length, without sacrificing attention to the consequences of perpetratorless crimes for the target of prejudice. (pp. 70–71)

It should be noted that two leading theorists on stereotyping and prejudice, Susan Fiske (1987) and Patricia Devine (1989), have suggested that people are responsible for their stereotyping because, at least under certain conditions and in some individuals, stereotyping is controllable. In our view, however, the primary message of the stereotyping literature is that the default response is to stereotype. Although Devine and Fiske point to meaningful exceptions to the rule of stereotyping, in a sense these exceptions might in fact serve to make the operative rule more glaringly evident.

DISPOSITIONAL EXPLANATIONS OF THE HOLOCAUST: INVESTING HARM-DOING WITH RESPONSIBILITY AND INTENTIONALITY

We turn now, briefly, to explanations that focus on dispositions or personality characteristics of perpetrators as primary causes of the Holocaust. Our main contention is that dispositional explanations, relative to social-psychological explanations, are likely to be construed as endowing perpetrators with responsibility and intentionality. Several lines of reasoning support this point of view.

Dispositional explanations are likely to be construed by readers as indicating that the actor behaved intentionally, that his or her behavior has been under "onset control" (Weiner, 1995). Consider, as an example, a hypothetical experiment in which two White observers—A and B—evaluate a qualified African American applicant for a position. Person A is known to have scored high on a measure of racial prejudice, whereas B scored extremely low. Imagine further that the prediction that A will evaluate the target more negatively than B is confirmed. In this prototype of a dispositional explanation, we suggest that readers of this study would view the prejudice displayed by person A as relatively controllable, and that A would be held personally responsible for denigrating the applicant. There are several reasons for this expectation.

First, because person B has not disparaged the applicant, person A's behavior is likely to be construed as freely chosen and intentional. The simple fact of two people behaving very differently in the same external situation makes salient the possibility that each person could have behaved differently, and that the reason why their behavior differed was something *about each person*, some attribute perceived to reside *inside* the person that caused the specific behavior. Devine (1989) makes this argument in her analysis of what she terms the "controlled" component of prejudice.

There is, at least in principle, no obvious reason that dispositional explanations should necessarily be construed as implying strong volition or intentionality on the part of the actor. An individual's personality—for example, a person who is characteristically obedient, aggressive, or conformist—might logically be construed as beyond the individual's control, as a complex of psychological motives reflective of earlier experiences and biological factors that would essentially determine behavioral choices without the person having much freedom to do otherwise. This argument, of course, is frequently made by defense attorneys in arguing that a client's behavior reflects mental illness or insanity. Yet we suspect that it is the simple fact of *individual differences* in behavior that registers particularly strongly in observers, that is viewed as dramatizing the "free will" aspect that is central to attributions of personal causality and responsibility.

Because of the overwhelmingly negative emotions associated with the Holocaust, there is, understandably, a particularly strong motivation to attribute personal responsibility to the perpetrators, to "find them guilty and punish them." Consider, in this regard, the appeal for many readers of Daniel Goldhagen's *Hitler's Willing Executioners* (1996). Goldhagen's thesis is that major perpetrators of the Holocaust were fully responsible for their actions and engaged in murderous behaviors knowingly, intentionally, and without coercion:

> The conclusion of this book is that antisemitism moved many thousands of "ordinary" Germans . . . to slaughter Jews. Not economic hardship, not the coercive means of a totalitarian state, not social psychological pressure, not invariable psychological propensities, but ideas about Jews that were pervasive in Germany, and had been for decades, induced ordinary Germans to kill unarmed, defenseless Jewish men, women, and children by the thousands, systematically and without pity. . . . My explanation . . . is that the perpetrators, "ordinary Germans," were animated by

antisemitism, by a particular *type* of antisemitism that led them to conclude that the Jew *ought* to die. The perpetrators' beliefs, their particular brand of antisemitism . . . were a most significant and indispensable source of the perpetrators' actions and must be at the center of any explanation of them. Simply put, the perpetrators, having consulted their own convictions and morality and having judged the mass annihilation of Jews to be right, did not *want* to say no. (pp. 9, 14)

Notice the powerful theme of intentionality and personal responsibility of perpetrators in Goldhagen's writing. Notice, also, the clear disavowal of external causal factors—in particular, his phrase "not social psychological pressure." Goldhagen's position may be driven, at least in part, by a strong motive to punish the perpetrators. Goldhagen views social-psychological explanations as exonerating perpetrators, and it may well be for this reason (among others) that they are unacceptable to him.

CONCLUSION

We have suggested that social-psychological explanations of the Holocaust are likely to be regarded as taking a relatively exonerating position toward perpetrators. Our main point is that social-psychological explanations, in emphasizing the causal power of situational forces, construe actors committing harmful actions as having relatively low personal responsibility and intentionality for their actions, and, in some instances, a low degree of conscious awareness of the determinants of their behaviors. If this is the case, students (readers) exposed to a strongly situationalist argument are likely to infer that social psychology leans in an exonerating or condoning stance toward harm-doers.

We have emphasized the controversial aspects of the exoneration thesis, that social-psychological explanations of the Holocaust will be resisted by those construing them as absolving perpetrators. However, from a different perspective, the exonerating implications of social-psychological theories could in fact be particularly convincing because one of the effects of casting perpetrators in a less negative light is not simply to excuse their actions or "let them off the hook" but to humanize them and, by extension, to indict ourselves as potential perpetrators.

This line of reasoning is, in our view, a primary reason why the Milgram experiments have achieved, in the annals of social science, an unparalleled acclaim (Miller, 1995). Clearly, it is not the case that people want to excuse or forgive perpetrators and thus endorse social-psychological explanations because these accounts enable them to reach their preferred (condoning) conclusion. Rather, by exonerating perpetrators in terms of advancing a situational causal attribution, social-psychological explanations in fact convey a more skeptical and accusatory posture toward the propensity of most persons—that is, ourselves—for committing harm. Regarding the Holocaust, many social psychologists, and those endorsing their argument, would claim that their most useful and unique contribution has been to "humanize genocide," to recognize that such horrific actions are in fact within the capability of ordinary human beings and not only deviant, pathological monsters or sadists (e.g., Baumeister, 1997; Darley, 1992; Kelman, 1973; Kelman & Hamilton, 1989). Zimbardo, Maslach, and Haney (2000) have recently articulated this position:

> Thus, any deed that any human being has ever done, however horrible, is possible for any of us to do—under the right or wrong situational pressures. That knowledge does not excuse evil; rather it democratizes it, shares its blame among ordinary participants, rather than demonizes it. (p. 206)

This line of reasoning notwithstanding, the exonerating implications of social-psychological explanations are likely to add to the complexity and difficulty involved in advancing theoretical understanding of the Holocaust and other, more mundane instances of harmful behavior. Our review raises the possibility of awkard or controversial situations. Social psychologists discussing prejudice and stereotyping, for example, may find themselves accused of exonerating instead of condemning those who engage in these acts (Banaji & Greenwald, 1994).

We recommend that the exonerating aspect of social-psychological explanations of the Holocaust merits the attention of teachers, researchers, and writers. A more precise awareness of the impact of diverse explanations on the construal of perpetrators may increase our ability to understand the basis for the extraordinarily controversial nature of explanations of the Holocaust (e.g., Rosenbaum, 1999). Andrew Colman (1991) has, in this context, discussed in detail the controversy involved in South African courts, where accepting testimony regarding social-psychological interpretations of obedience, bystander nonintervention, and other phenomena served as extenuating or mitigating factors in murder trials. Colman noted that "anything that helps to explain the behavior of a defendant might reduce the perceived moral blameworthiness of that behavior" (p. 1078). This idea, simply voiced, captures the main premise of our chapter.

REFERENCES

Adorno, T. W., Frenkel-Brunswik, E., Levinson, D. J., & Sanford, R. N. (1950). *The authoritarian personality*. New York: Harper and Row.

Allport, G. W. (1954). *The nature of prejudice*. Reading, MA.: Addison-Wesley.

Anderson, C. A., Benjamin, A. J., Jr., & Bartholow, B. D. (1998). Does the gun pull the trigger? Automatic priming effects of weapon pictures and weapon names. *Psychological Science, 9,* 308–314.

Arendt, H. (1963). *Eichmann in Jerusalem: A report on the banality of evil.* New York: Viking.

Banaji, M. R., & Greenwald, A. G. (1994). Implicit stereotyping and prejudice. In M. P. Zanna & J. M. Olson (Eds.), *The psychology of prejudice: The Ontario symposium* (Vol. 7, pp. 55–76). Hillsdale, NJ: Erlbaum.

Bandura, A. (1999). Moral disengagement in the perpetration of inhumanities. *Personality and Social Psychology Review, 3,* 193–209.

Bandura, A., Underwood, B., & Fromson, M. E. (1975). Disinhibition of aggression through diffusion of responsibility and dehumanization of victims. *Journal of Research in Personality, 9,* 253–269.

Bargh, J. A., & Chartrand, T. L. (1999). The unbearable automaticity of being. *American Psychologist, 54,* 462–479.

Bargh, J. A., Chen, M., & Burrows, L. (1996). Automaticity of social behavior: Direct effects of trait construct and stereotype activation on action. *Journal of Personality and Social Psychology, 71,* 230–244.

Baumeister, R. F. (1997). *Evil: Inside human violence and cruelty.* New York: Freeman.

Berkowitz, L. (1999). Evil is more than banal: Situationism and the concept of evil. *Personality and Social Psychology Review, 3,* 246–253.

Browning, C. R. (1992). *Ordinary men: Reserve Police Battalion 101 and the Final Solution in Poland.* New York: HarperCollins.

Colman, A. M. (1991). Crowd psychology of South African murder trials. *American Psychologist, 46,* 1071–1079.

Darley, J. M. (1992). Social organization for the production of evil. *Psychological Inquiry, 3,* 199–218.

Darley, J. M., & Batson, D. (1973). "From Jerusalem to Jericho": A study of situational and dispositional variables in helping behavior. *Journal of Personality and Social Psychology, 27,* 100–108.

Devine, P. G. (1989). Stereotypes and prejudice: Their automatic and controlled components. *Journal of Personality and Social Psychology, 56,* 5–18.

Diener, E., & Wallbom, M. (1976). Effects of self-awareness on antinormative behavior. *Journal of Research in Personality, 10,* 107–111.

Fenigstein, A. (1998). Were obedience pressures a factor in the Holocaust? *Analyse & Kritik, 20,* 1–20.

Fiske, S. (1987). On the road: Comment on the cognitive stereotyping literature in Pettigrew and Martin. *Journal of Social Issues, 43,* 113–118.

Fiske, S. (1992). Thinking is for doing: Portraits of social cognition from daguerreotype to laserphoto. *Journal of Personality and Social Psychology, 63,* 877–889.

Gilbert, D. T. (1995). Attribution and interpersonal perception. In A. Tesser (Ed.), *Advanced social psychology* (pp. 99–148). New York: McGraw-Hill.

Gilbert, D. T., & Malone, P. S. (1995). The correspondence bias. *Psychological Bulletin, 117,* 21–38.

Goldhagen, D. J. (1996). *Hitler's willing executioners: Ordinary Germans and the Holocaust.* New York: Knopf.

Haney, C., & Zimbardo, P. (1998). The past and future of U.S. prison policy: Twenty-five years after the Stanford Prison Experiment. *American Psychologist, 53,* 709–727.

Jones, E. E. (1990). *Interpersonal perception*. New York: Freeman.

Jones, E. E., & Davis, K. (1965). From acts to dispositions: The attribution process in person perception. In L. Berkowitz (Ed.), *Advances in experimental social psychology* (Vol. 2, pp. 219–266). New York: Academic Press.

Kelley, H. H. (1992). Common-sense psychology and scientific psychology. *Annual Review of Psychology, 43,* 1–23.

Kelman, H. C. (1973). Violence without moral restraint: Reflections on the dehumanization of victims and victimizers. *Journal of Social Issues, 29,* 25–61.

Kelman, H. C., & Hamilton, V. L. (1989). *Crimes of obedience: Toward a social psychology of authority and responsibility*. New Haven, CT: Yale University Press.

Latane, B., & Darley, J. (1970). *The unresponsive bystander: Why doesn't he help?* Englewood Cliffs, NJ: Prentice-Hall.

Lifton, R. J. (1986). *The Nazi doctors: Medical killing and the psychology of genocide*. New York: Basic Books.

Lutsky, N. (1995). When is "obedience" obedience? Conceptual and historical commentary. *Journal of Social Issues, 51,* 55–65.

Mandel, D. R. (1998). The obedience alibi: Milgram's account of the Holocaust reconsidered. *Analyse & Kritik, 20,* 74–94.

Milgram, S. (1963). Behavioral study of obedience. *Journal of Abnormal and Social Psychology, 67,* 371–378.

Milgram, S. (1964). Issues in the study of obedience: A reply to Baumrind. *American Psychologist, 19,* 848–852.

Milgram, S. (1974). *Obedience to authority: An experimental view*. New York: Harper and Row.

Miller, A. G. (1995). Constructions of the obedience experiments: A focus upon domains of relevance. *Journal of Social Issues, 51,* 33–53.

Miller, A. G., Gordon, A. K., & Buddie, A. M. (1999). Accounting for evil and cruelty: Is to explain to condone? *Personality and Social Psychology Review, 3,* 254–268.

Novick, P. (1999). *The Holocaust in American life*. New York: Houghton Mifflin.

Rochat, F., & Modigliani, A. (1995). The ordinary quality of resistance: From Milgram's laboratory to the village of Le Chambon. *Journal of Social Issues, 51,* 195–210.

Rosenbaum, R. (1995, May 1). Explaining Hitler. *The New Yorker,* pp. 50–70.

Rosenbaum, R. (1999). *Explaining Hitler: The search for the origins of his evil*. New York: Random House.

Rosenthal, A. M. (1964). *Thirty-eight witnesses*. New York: McGraw-Hill.

Ross, L., & Nisbett, R. E. (1991). *The person and the situation: Perspectives of social psychology* New York: McGraw-Hill.

Sabini, J. P., & Silver, M. (1980). Destroying the innocent with a clear conscience: A sociopsychology of the Holocaust. In J. E. Dimsdale (Ed.), *Survivors, victims, and perpetrators: Essays on the Nazi Holocaust* (pp. 329–358). New York: Hemisphere.

Staub, E. (1989). *The roots of evil: The origins of genocide and other group violence*. New York: Cambridge University Press.

Weiner, B. (1995). *Judgments of responsibility: A foundation for a theory of social conduct*. New York: Guilford.

Weiner, B., Perry, R. P., & Magnusson, J. (1988). An attributional analysis of reactions to stigmas. *Journal of Personality and Social Psychology, 55,* 738–748.

Zillmer, E. A., Harrower, M., Ritzler, B. A., & Archer, R. P. (1995). *The quest for the Nazi personality: A psychological investigation of Nazi war criminals.* Hillsdale, NJ: Erlbaum.

Zimbardo, P. G. (1970). The human choice: Individuation, reason, and order versus deindividuation, impulse, and chaos. In W. J. Arnold & D. Levine (Eds.), *1969 Nebraska Symposium on Motivation* (pp. 237–307). Lincoln: University of Nebraska Press.

Zimbardo, P. G. (1995). The psychology of evil: A situationist perspective on recruiting good people to engage in anti-social acts. *Research in Social Psychology, 11,* 125–133.

Zimbardo, P. G., Haney, C., Banks, C., & Jaffe, D. (1973, April 8). The mind is a formidable jailer: A Pirandellian prison. *The New York Times Magazine,* pp. 38–60.

Zimbardo, P. G., Maslach, C., & Haney, C. (2000). Reflections on the Stanford Prison Experiment: Genesis, transformations, consequences. In T. Blass (Ed.), *Obedience to authority: Current perspectives on the Milgram paradigm* (pp. 193–238). Mahwah, NJ: Erlbaum.

14

Epilogue

Social Psychologists Confront the Holocaust

Leonard S. Newman and Ralph Erber

No analysis of the Holocaust, no matter how compelling, could possibly "normalize" it. Confronting the Holocaust will always be a terrifying and disorienting experience. The same could be said for other such tragedies—the attempted extermination of the Armenians, the Rape of Nanking, the massacre of the Tutsis in Rwanda, the genocidal project of the Khmer Rouge in Cambodia, and (unfortunately) many others. Contemplation of these events can be a devastating experience, no matter how extensively one understands the conditions that set the stage for one group to target another for extermination, and no matter how deeply one has thought about the processes that turn individuals into the perpetrators of genocide. But as Yehuda Bauer argues, the horror that genocide evokes in us "doesn't remove it from the realm of human nature or human comprehension; it makes it a disturbing fact of human nature, not necessarily a metaphysical mystery" (Rosenbaum, 1998, p. 281). In other words, it is the job of social and behavioral scientists to at least attempt to make sense of this form of collective human behavior at the extremes.

Of course, anyone who has spent time thinking about these issues (including the readers of this book) knows at least a few things about the nature of genocide. These include the idea that the mass killing of out-group members is especially likely to emerge when a nation is experiencing a crisis of some kind; that individuals and groups often respond to fear and threat by selecting scapegoats, and that the persecution of scapegoats can escalate to the point of genocide; that some cultural values more than others lend themselves to the justification and promotion of genocide, and that these values are more pronounced in some societies than others; that people can be remarkably compliant with orders from people they consider their superiors, even when those orders involve aggression against blameless people; that other people, even those morally opposed to the behavior of perpetrators, will very often neglect to intervene or even speak up in protest; that perpetrators of genocide deal with what they have done by lying to other people about their activities; and that even holding social and cultural factors constant, some people are more willing than others to aggress against members of stigmatized outgroups. In addition, it is not uncommon to believe that the kind of violence in which perpetrators engage represents a normally repressed "animal" side of human nature, and that it perhaps even literally entails a regression to primitive modes of behavior more common in "less evolved" species.

What, then, did readers of the preceding chapters learn? For the most part, they learned that genocide is historically associated with crisis, fear, and threat; that crisis, fear, and threat can lead to the targeting of scapegoats; that some cultural values more than others might lend themselves to genocide; that people's behavior is often a function of obedience and conformity; that bystanders to violence and cruelty are often passive; that perpetrators lie about what they have done; that some people might be more willing than others to brutalize and kill their fellow human beings; and that analyses of genocide might benefit from an evolutionary level of analysis.

In other words, at first glance few of the issues raised by the authors of the chapters in this book were remarkably novel. The value of their contributions, however, derives from a few *other* things that people who have spent just a little *more* time thinking about the Holocaust and genocide also know: that nations and other groups do not always respond to crises by seeking targets for extermination; that genocide has occurred in countries and societies that on the surface do not seem to have much in common; that people often *refuse* to comply with what are perceived to be immoral directives; that perpetrators' brutal behavior often seems to be self-initiated rather than ordered from above; that witnesses to genocide frequently *do* take the initiative and find ways to undermine extermination plans; that the ease with which perpetrators of genocide transition back to a normal existence suggests that they do not so much "lie" as engage in actual self-deception; that although individual people are maybe not all equally prone to becoming perpetrators, those who do become mass killers do not seem to fit a specific personality profile and often seem otherwise to be quite "normal"; and that many aspects of the Holocaust and other episodes of genocide are simply without precedent in the behavior of other species.

Our point is that the things that everyone "knows" about genocide are often contradictory and do not add up to a satisfying account of how and why societies mobilize to exterminate entire national, religious, racial, ethnic, or other groups. It is not a trivial thing to be familiar with the social, psychological, cultural, and historical variables that have been associated with past episodes of genocide. However, these variables do not in themselves reveal necessary or sufficient preconditions for those episodes' occurrence. In other words, commonly understood "causes" of genocide are little more than starting points for investigation and analysis. The chapters in this book represent some of that investigation and analysis.

What the reader of this volume will not find is a "grand theory" of the Holocaust or of genocide in general. No one chapter promises that, nor do the individual contributions add up to a complete and integrated model. It would also be a mistake to think of the different chapters as offering competing accounts or to try to decide which one offers the "best" account. Instead, this book should be understood to be a response to Christopher Browning's call (in the introduction) to make "readily accessible to both scholars and the reading public" many of the "recent developments in the discipline of social psychology" that promise to increase our understanding of "not only the perpetrators but other aspects of human behavior during the Holocaust." In responding to that call, the contributors focused on different aspects of genocide and approached them at different levels of analysis (individual, interpersonal, cultural, historical, etc.).

What follows is a summary of some of the key arguments presented in the preceding chapters. This summary by no means covers all or even most of the provocative ideas developed by the authors. Hopefully, though, it will serve the purpose of showing how the hypotheses they raised and the conclusions they reached have helped move us beyond the starting point of what "everyone knows."

CRISES AND DIFFICULT LIFE CONDITIONS

A number of contributors noted that crises, difficult life conditions, and other widely experienced negative events can lead a group of people down the path that ends with genocide (Baumeister; Frey & Rez; Mandel; Staub; Suedfeld & Schaller; Tindale, Munier, Wasserman, & Smith). While none argue that such crises are sufficient causes of genocide, all assume that they at least set the stage. In Frey and Rez's and Staub's views, they might even be necessary causes. A "crisis," of course, can involve any number of problems—economic, cultural, political, geopolitical—although typically such problems tend to be highly correlated. It is impossible, however, to specify the key features of such crises in concrete terms because, as a number of authors note (Frey & Rez, Staub, Tindale et al.), a given negative event or condition could precipitate a crisis in one culture but not another. The disorder of the interwar years, for example, might have been especially intolerable to people in Germany because of preexisting shared attitudes and cultural values. The more general points are that the proximal causes of societal crises are psychological, and the nature of the events that will trigger a crisis is culture-specific.

If economic, political, and other conditions are only distal causes, what is the nature of the psychological distress that plays a more direct role in triggering genocide? A number of contributors address this issue. In Staub's view, for example, difficult life conditions frustrate basic human needs, including "needs for security, for a positive identity, for effectiveness and control over important events in one's life, for positive connections to other people, and for a meaningful understanding of the world or comprehension of reality." Although for Staub, the need for control over one's outcomes is just one need among many others, Frey and Rez argue that control (the need to explain, predict, and influence the events in one's life) is a superordinate need, encompassing the others. People feel a loss of control when their other needs are not being met and when they find it hard or impossible to effect any meaningful changes in their condition. Frey and Rez further argue that the need for control might function as a general mediating variable; that is, they propose that wherever there is a genocide, it involves a nation or other group that is taking extreme measures in the belief that these actions will allow it to regain control over its fate. Baumeister (see also Mandel) emphasizes the importance of another aversive subjective state: humiliation. His research indicates that people with high but unstable levels of self-regard have a tendency to respond violently when their self-views are threatened. The Holocaust, he suggests, can be construed as an extreme collective response to threatened egotism. An implication of this analysis is that setbacks are more likely to trigger aggression and even genocide in strongly nationalistic countries, such as prewar Germany.

Crises, of course, are experienced by individuals, and individuals can seek out personal solutions to the problems that crises cause for them. But in Glick's and Frey and Rez's accounts, collective responses to negative conditions are initiated when individual solutions have failed. In such circumstances, they argue, people are motivated to seek external attributions for their problems and will be open to finding something outside of themselves to blame. Problems construed in this way, given their widespread effects, have to be tackled by groups of people.

Unfortunately, when a society has reached the point of a major crisis, the problems facing it are quite complex, and simple solutions are rarely within reach. Construction of a stable political or economic system generally cannot be accomplished overnight. In these difficult circumstances, groups may choose to focus on fulfilling the psychological needs threatened by difficult social, economic, or other more concrete problems rather than directly tackling the problems themselves (Glick, Staub). In other words, if economic or other problems decrease collective self-esteem, and those problems are intractable (at least in the short term), other avenues to enhancing self-esteem could be sought. And the simpler the solutions (and the more parsimonious the explanations that suggest those solutions), the easier it will be to mobilize action meant to help alleviate a group's psychological distress.

Frey and Rez also note that the need for quick and simple solutions encourages nations and other collectives to delegate authority to a strong leader who can more efficiently take whatever steps are necessary to address people's unfulfilled needs. When that happens, the characteristics of the leader become decisive, and he or she can become a direct instigator of genocide. As Mandel notes, instigators are not "initial causes of collective violence. Rather, they dramatically increase the propensity for violence, and they act to accelerate its pace once it has started." Thus, once in place, leaders can independently play a decisive role in the turn of events.

In sum, to say that "crises" lead to genocide is not to say much. As discussed by a number of contributors to this volume, there is no universal set of necessary or sufficient conditions that will trigger a crisis; local values, attitudes, and expectations will determine the degree of subjective distress associated with specific objective circumstances. In addition, two specific kinds of psychological discomfort—loss of control and threatened egotism—have been proposed as being key mediators of the relationship between unfavorable life circumstances and genocide. Finally, a number of authors note that people's general preference for simple explanations and solutions to problems can have tragic implications in conditions of societal crisis. The need for simple solutions for widespread psychological distress might lead people to a particular simple solution: selecting a group of scapegoats and targeting those scapegoats for violence.

SCAPEGOATS

Why does the simple solution that societies seek to alleviate distress and suffering so often involve scapegoating? Suedfeld and Schaller present a provocative answer to this question. People seek out scapegoats, they suggest, because they are essentially programmed to do so. According to evolutionary psychologists, selection pressures have led human beings to develop a set of species-general psychological mechanisms that help people cope with specific adaptational problems. Mechanisms are context-specific and might not ever be activated (or activated very strongly) unless the environment poses specific challenges to the person. For example, evolutionary psychologists argue that jealousy is a psychological mechanism that is triggered by cues associated with partner infidelity and that it serves the purpose of both increasing the chances that one's genetic material will be passed on and that one's offspring will thrive.

Suedfeld and Schaller, summarizing decades of social psychology research, note that if one divides people "into two groups on the basis of even the most arbitrary of distinctions," then "those individuals will come to perceive their in-group members more favorably than out-group members." They also suggest that "this phenomenon may have its roots in our evolutionary past." For most of the history of our species, they argue, it would have been quite reasonable and adaptive to mistrust outsiders and seek to minimize encounters with them. It also would have been functional to have a psychological process in place that would allow one to quickly construct stereotypes emphasizing the dangerousness of out-group members. Suedfeld and Schaller also argue for the possible existence of an independent psychological mechanism that promotes the rejection of in-group members who differ from the norm in some salient way. Such a mechanism could have evolved because historically, differences of various kinds were often associated with diseases or other characteristics that could undermine a group of people's chances for survival. And "given the tendency to err on the side of overexclusion, it may be that perceived vulnerability may lead individuals to attempt to remove people who are 'different' on even the most superficial characteristics." Finally, Suedfeld and Schaller point out that these different kinds of prejudice will be enhanced by a specific kind of psychological situation: circumstances that cause people to feel fear and vulnerability. In sum, Suedfeld and Schaller suggest that psychological mechanisms that were functional in our evolutionary past might now unfortunately encourage the sorts of intergroup and interpersonal processes that all too often serve as a prelude to genocide.

This account, it should be noted, does not compete with the one outlined in general terms in the previous section; instead, it complements it. What Suedfeld and Schaller's analysis implies is that when people band together to seek simple solutions to complicated problems, evolution has essentially "primed the pump" for them to lash out at people they perceive to be different from themselves. And once they do, according to Staub (see also Frey & Rez, Glick), they are likely to continue doing so. Why? Because it feels good. More precisely, scapegoating can serve to satisfy basic human needs (albeit in a way that is ultimately self-defeating). Devaluing out-groups can make people feel better about themselves by comparison; blaming those groups for severe problems can alleviate feelings of responsibility for those problems; and acting against the scapegoats can restore a sense of control. In addition, by bringing in-group members together in a common cause, scapegoating can fulfill needs for connection with other people.

Frey and Rez suggest that "any out-group can potentially serve as a scapegoat" as long as that group is not powerful enough to retaliate, although, along with Staub and Mandel, they note that previous beliefs about some groups make them more likely to be scapegoated. But it is Glick's ideological model that makes the most important contribution to our understanding of how groups are targeted as scapegoats. As Glick notes, previous influential theories of scapegoating have suffered from their inability to specify which groups in a given society are more likely than others to be targeted for violence. Those theories did, however, suggest that scapegoated groups are singled out because of their vulnerability and helplessness. Glick agrees that scapegoated groups such as Jews in Nazi Germany (or Tutsis in Rwanda in the 1990s and ethnic Chinese in Indonesia in the 1960s) are typically quite vulnerable and

limited in their ability to defend themselves. However, he argues that they are selected for scapegoating because they are *perceived* to be the *opposite*— that is, powerful and dangerous. Otherwise, he notes, the scapegoats could not be plausibly seen as a cause for a society's problems, because "weak, unsuccessful groups are much less likely to be viewed as plausible causes of a dominant group's loss of status and power, their failure at war, or the meltdown of their economy than are successful minorities, who are viewed as wielding power and influence disproportionate to their numbers." Once a group has been identified that can be construed as being the cause of a crisis, people do not need much encouragement to treat members of that group with maximal brutality; after all, at that point they will not be "victimizing others" but "fighting for survival."

Glick also explains why persecution of a scapegoat—and even genocidal projects—can be expected to outlast the crisis that scapegoating was meant to resolve. Older models typically conceptualized scapegoating as always being a displacement of inhibited aggressive urges, which in turn were said to be caused by frustrating conditions. Those models could not explain why persecution would outlast a crisis and persist even when the perpetrators of genocide were no longer experiencing difficult life circumstances. As Glick notes, once a ideology supporting scapegoating is adopted, it takes on a life of its own; that is, "ideological commitment develops its own legs." In part, this occurs because once people engage in the violent behavior suggested by the ideology, they will want to justify that behavior. Justification will then serve to deepen their ideological commitment. Ultimately, unfavorable beliefs about an out-group become proximal causes of aggression, outweighing even pragmatic concerns. This account, of course, sheds light on why Nazi Germany's political and military leaders devoted so much time and energy to continuing their attempt to exterminate Europe's Jews, even when resources could have been redirected to the war effort.

People do indeed often respond to fear and threat by selecting scapegoats. As noted at the outset of this chapter, that much is obvious. But the factors leading to that tendency, how groups are targeted for scapegoating, and the processes determining how violent behavior toward the scapegoats unfolds are all far from obvious.

CULTURE

Although the processes described in the preceding section can potentially unfold in any intergroup context, some contributors to this volume suggest that they are prone to occur in some societies more than others. For example, Oyserman and Lauffer describe a distinction that has become very prominent in theorizing about cross-cultural differences in thinking and behavior: individualism versus collectivism. Individualism is a set of values or a "cultural frame" that emphasizes individual goals and achievement, independence, freedom of choice, and the importance of personal happiness and fulfillment. Collectivism, on the other hand, encourages a focus on groups instead of individuals. Obedience, tradition, conformity, and social harmony are among the central values associated with collectivism. Societies differ significantly in terms of whether collectivism or individualism is more salient and valued. Hence, one can speak loosely of individualistic and collectivistic societies. More specifically, research indicates that North America, Western Europe, and Australia (along with New Zealand) are highly individualistic, whereas collectivism characterizes much of Africa, Asia, and South America.

Oyserman and Lauffer do not directly address the question of whether it is in any way "better" to be a member of an individualistic or collectivistic culture; in fact, they suggest that a blend of collectivism and individualism would be ideal. They do, however, note that out-group status can be particularly precarious in collectivistic societies. They argue, "In a collectivist cultural frame, out-groups, groups one does not belong to, are viewed with suspicion, and their members are seen as very different, even alien from oneself. The out-group is a source of threat, and in-group members believe that only in-group members can be trusted." Even more provocatively, they suggest that due to the focus on groups over individuals in collectivistic cultures, "the individuality of out-group members, even their humanity, becomes suspect." Individualism, on the other hand, because it promotes individual rights and democratic political systems, "highlights the common humanity in all individuals." As a consequence, Oyserman and Lauffer conclude that a tendency toward intergroup violence and, more than that, the kind of dehumanization of out-groups that is characteristic of genocide will be more pronounced in societies that are dominated by collectivism. Nazism, they argue, was a radical collectivistic movement, in which one's identity as an individual was subordinated to one's identity as a German Aryan.

Although this analysis seems to lend itself to predictions about where future genocides are likely to occur, such predictions should be made with great caution. One can indeed categorize nations in terms of whether collectivistic or individualistic frames are dominant. But as Oyserman and Lauffer note, "Rather than thinking about societies and the individuals living within them as valuing either individual or group goals, it is more accurate to describe cultures in terms of the relative frequency that values pertaining to group versus individual good are evoked." All societies subscribe to a mix of values, and at least some level of collectivism is necessary for any society or other group to remain intact. As a result, mass movements capitalizing on the collectivist values that exist in a given society could potentially mobilize people for genocidal projects anywhere. Nonetheless, Oyserman and Lauffer clearly suggest that extreme intergroup violence is more likely to occur when individualistic values are less prevalent and thus less available to countervail collectivistic ones.

Tindale et al. provide another way of thinking about why culture matters. A number of contributors point out that even if preexisting cultural beliefs about specific groups' unfavorable characteristics do not directly trigger genocidal behavior, they do create enabling conditions for such tragedies. But how do these beliefs and associated attitudes develop? And how do they spread throughout a population? Tindale et al. provide some answers to these questions, with an account derived from an overarching conceptualization of attitudes and beliefs as social phenomena that are produced by groups by means of basic social-psychological processes.

Cognitively oriented perspectives in psychology assume that individuals have mental representations of their worlds, including mental representations of their own and other groups. Tindale et al., however, emphasize the importance of social representations—that is, beliefs and attitudes that not only are widely shared within a culture but also are formulated by groups in the context of social interaction. Social representations make up a group's shared reality. They do not require much or any supportive evidence to survive because they are constantly validated by other group members. In fact, they may come to be seen as so "obviously" correct that people rarely reflect on them. But even if people do not consciously examine them, social representations play an important role in the lives of the people who share them. Tindale et al. review quite a bit of research revealing that shared information and attitudes strongly influence the judgments and decisions made by groups—and, presumably, the behavior resulting from those judgments and decisions. Thus, when groups need to reach consensus, social representations shape that consensus.

A particularly important class of social representations consists of negative stereotypes about other groups. Stereotypes are constructed whenever people categorize themselves and others in terms of groups. Unfortunately, one of the major motives shaping group categorizations is self-esteem enhancement. That means that social representations of out-groups are likely to consist of unfavorable characteristics, because those types of representations are the ones that will help people feel better about themselves. In sum, whenever distinctions between groups of people are made salient, those groups are very likely to collectively create unflattering representations of each other. An interesting aspect of this process is that such representations can develop in the absence of much intergroup contact; groups of people can reach consensus on stereotypes even when most members of the group have little direct experience with the stigmatized outgroup. Thus, in the late nineteenth century, anti-Semitism was rampant in Germany even though Jews accounted for only approximately 1% of the total population.

Tindale et al., of course, do not assume that a typical social representation of an out-group would be so negative as to lead a society to mobilize for extermination of that group. That kind of hatred, they implicitly assume, is usually restricted to a small minority. How, then, can an extreme minority view overwhelm the consensus, spread through the population, and ultimately become a majority opinion? Tindale et al. review research showing that minority preferences can be influential when they are framed in terms of other social representations that are widely shared by other group members, even when those preferences are self-defeating and based on faulty assumptions. For example, Tindale et al. explain the Nazi Party's meteoric rise in the early 1930s in Germany in these terms. Although the Nazis proposed extreme and radical solutions for Germany's problems, the problems that they promised to address were indeed seen as problems by the vast majority of the population. In addition, the way in which their message was framed—in terms of the ineffectualness of the Weimar Republic, the humiliation suffered by Germany after World War I, the need for a strong leader, and, of course, anti-Semitism—was consistent with widely shared attitudes and beliefs. Minorities can thus take advantage of social representations, promote extreme versions of them, and mobilize violent action on that basis. The resulting transformation of a society can occur suddenly and with great rapidity. Overall, Tindale et al.'s analysis is sobering for those interested in preventing episodes of genocide and identifying where they will occur in the future.

Culture does indeed play a role in the emergence of genocide. But some of the aspects of culture that make a difference are not ones that at first glance would seem to so obviously have much to do with intergroup conflict. In addition, although the nature of the attitudes toward out-groups that are characteristic of a given culture at a specific point in time can be an indication of future trouble, such attitudes are far from perfect predictors.

OBEDIENCE AND CONFORMITY

As Miller, Buddie, and Kretschmar note, "When one considers the contribution of social psychology to an understanding of the Holocaust, invariably it will be the obedience experiments of Stanley Milgram (1963, 1974) that first come to mind." Milgram's research is summarized by Miller et al., Newman, and especially Blass, a leading authority on Milgram's life and work. As detailed in those chapters, Milgram found that in certain situations, most people will comply with the directives of an authority figure, even when they are asked to do things that they would otherwise find to be morally questionable—such as harming another human being. In addition, although one might be able to generate hypotheses about how people in individualistic and collectivistic cultures differ in terms of obedience, Milgram's findings have been replicated in a variety of European, Asian, and Middle Eastern countries.

Miller et al. note that what is most distinctive about social psychology is its emphasis on the power of the situation, and as Blass points out, it is for this reason that social psychologists embraced Milgram's research as a way to understand the behavior of genocide perpetrators: "Milgram's approach is situational in the sense that the external pressures of the moment exerted by an authority—rather than internal instigators of action such as hostility or hatred—are seen as the major determinants of the subject's harsh actions." Social psychologists are not the only people to find Milgram's analysis to be compelling; for example, prominent Holocaust historian Christopher Browning (1992; introduction, this volume) has also framed many of his findings in terms of the obedience experiments.

As Blass notes, a frightening implication of Milgram's research is that any-one, even "ordinary" people, could be a potential participant in genocide—not just Nazis and other people with attitudes that most readers of this book would probably find to be objectionable. Recently, however, a number of scholars have expressed skepticism about the relevance of the obedience studies to the behavior of Holocaust perpetrators. Daniel Goldhagen's book *Hitler's Willing Executioners* (1996) was perhaps the most prominent of those critiques, but the skeptics also include social psychologists (e.g., Berkowitz, 1999; Fenigstein, 1998; Mandel, 1998). A thorough review of these critiques is beyond the scope of this chapter, but what all have in common is the argument that Holocaust perpetrators engaged in a great deal of cruel and gratuitously sadistic behavior that was self-initiated and clearly not ordered by an authority figure. Blass also suggests that "historical details of the destruction of European Jewry raise questions about the degree of fit between Milgram's conceptual model of obedience to authority and the actualities of the Holocaust." In other words, Milgram might have shed light on an interesting aspect of human behavior, but the phenomenon he studied might have little to do with what happened to the victims of the Holocaust or with the behavioral dynamics involved in any episode of genocide. Indeed, the idea that all, most, or even many of the acts of cruelty perpetrated during the Holocaust were carried out by people who were grimly following orders is remarkably easy to disprove.

Milgram's critics have made an important contribution by warning against oversimplistic applications of the obedience research to understanding how and why people participate in genocide. Newman, however, argues that even if one were to show that the violent actions of Holocaust perpetrators were for the most part self-initiated and self-directed, that would not be sufficient for ruling out obedience as an important cause of many perpetrator behaviors. Nor, he argues, would it rule out obedience as an important factor underlying the behavior of the very people shown to have engaged in unsupervised sadistic behavior. The basis for this argument is research showing that how people behave affects their future behavior. This happens in large part because people's behavior not only is *caused* by their attitudes and beliefs but also *shapes and transforms* their attitudes and beliefs. For example, one might aggress against a group of people because of one's negative attitudes toward that group, but it is also possible that one's negative attitudes toward a group could be adopted as a consequence of one's aggression toward the people in that group. This occurs because people tend to want to justify their behaviors, and an easy way to justify hurting or killing a person is to convince oneself that he or she deserved it. Each act of aggression toward members of a group could in this way further intensify one's hatred for that group, and one's intensified hatred could lead to even more severe aggression. Staub calls this process "the continuum of destruction," whereas Miller et al. follow Darley (1992) in referring to it as the "conversion process" (see also Blass's final conclusions).

Thus, one cannot infer from the nature of a perpetrator's behavior—no matter how violent it is—how that behavior evolved. Even brutal perpetrators might have been at one point less than enthusiastic killers, and external pressure could well have played a role in their initial acts of aggression. Obedience (and conformity) pressure could play an important role in triggering the dynamic process that turns people from "ordinary men" (Browning, 1992) into "willing executioners" (Goldhagen, 1996).

To reiterate, it is now common knowledge that people are often more obedient than we expect them to be, and social-psychological research showing that people will comply with even objectionable requests from superiors has helped advance our understanding of how genocides unfold. But the role of obedience in genocide is far from straightforward, and understanding that role involves a consideration of the complex interrelationship between situational pressures, attitudes, and behaviors. Social psychology is uniquely positioned to inform us about how situations constrain behavior, how behaviors shape attitudes, and how attitudes affect behavior. Consideration of all these processes—and how they interact—is necessary for appreciating the precise way in which obedience pressure might shape perpetrator behavior.

BYSTANDERS AND HELPERS

Analyses of the dynamics of genocide typically focus not only on active killers but also on those who stand by and do nothing to stop or dissuade the perpetrators. For a variety of straightforward reasons, including fear of retribution and perceived powerlessness, people are often reluctant to intervene to stop interpersonal violence, even when they feel morally opposed to the brutal behavior of their fellow group members (see Latane & Darley, 1970, for an extended treatment of the predicament of bystanders). But history shows that when people witnessing persecution transform themselves from bystanders into resisters, they can be very effective in slowing down (and even diverting) their fellow group members as they march down the path to genocide. Staub describes a number of examples of this kind of heroic helping.

The decision to intervene or not intervene has important implications—and not just for the target of violence but also for the person making that decision. The psychological processes that propel a person along the continuum of destruction (described in the previous section) can also play themselves out and transform passive bystanders and heroic helpers. As Staub notes, people who act to help scapegoats in the face of pressures that would make it easier to do nothing may ultimately progress along a continuum of *benevolence*. Each altruistic act can serve to further convince the altruist that the targets of his or her benevolence are worthy of compassion and assistance. Staub argues that the actions of two legendary rescuers, Oskar Schindler and Raoul Wallenberg, followed this pattern of increasing commitment. Similarly, the inaction of those who choose to do nothing could be said to launch them down a continuum of *passivity*; each failure to act in the face of persecution and genocide creates psychological pressure to conclude that the targets of violence deserve their fate. Of course, that phenomenon dovetails tragically with the continuum of destruction. Seeing a lack of resistance or even protest in the face of the victimization of an out-group further emboldens perpetrators as the intensity of their brutality continues to escalate.

What motivates people to help individual targets of genocide or to even attempt to undermine an entire genocidal project? Staub mentions a number of personal attributes that have been found to characterize many heroic helpers: strong moral and humanitarian values, a prosocial orientation, empathy, an independent perspective, feelings of competence, fearlessness, and a high tolerance for risk. More surprising, though, is Suedfeld and Schaller's suggestion that the characteristics and motivations of resisters in some cases can be eerily similar to those of perpetrators. It seems safe to assume that few people would think to characterize any of the heroic people who rescued Jews during the Holocaust as being conformist, obedient to authority, and cognitively simple. But Suedfeld and Schaller's review of the literature led them to conclude that a "substantial subgroup" of those who resisted the Nazis' efforts to exterminate Europe's Jews did so primarily because a respected religious or community leader told them to do so. In other words, these people had the same cognitive and behavioral predispositions as others who murdered rather than sheltered Jews, and they were responsive to the same kinds of social pressures.

In sum, it is indeed the case that some people are passive in the face of genocide while others actively resist. That much is clear to anyone, but the psychological and behavioral consequences of being an unresponsive bystander or a heroic helper are much less obvious. In addition, bystanders and resisters might differ in many ways, but the relationship between individual difference variables and different responses to genocide are far from straightforward. Some of those people who (at great personal risk) go out of their way to help potential victims of genocide have a fairly peculiar personality profile, similar to the one said to characterize people with high levels of authoritarianism. Authoritarianism has long been thought to be associated with a propensity for prejudice and intergroup hostility, and so we turn next to the evidence for the relationship between authoritarianism (and other individual differences) and genocidal behavior.

INDIVIDUAL DIFFERENCES

One of social psychology's most well-established principles is that people tend to assume that others' behaviors are directly caused by underlying personality traits (Jones, 1990; Ross & Nisbett, 1991). Even when other possible causes for a behavior are obvious, there is a tendency to assume that acts of honesty reflect stable dispositions to be honest, that dishonest behaviors reflect dishonesty, that altruistic actions stem from altruism, that cruel behaviors can be explained in terms of the traits of cruelty and sadism, and so on. In light of this tendency, it is not surprising that after World War II many of the earliest efforts to understand both the Nazi leaders (Zillmer, Harrower, Ritzler, & Archer, 1995) and the rank and file (Adorno, Frenkel-Brunswik, Levinson, & Sanford, 1950) involved attempts to specify the kinds of personality traits that would predispose people to become attracted to the kinds of social movements that launch genocidal projects. In light of that research tradition, a number of contributors to this volume address the question of whether perpetrators of genocide can be distinguished from other people in terms of broad personality traits. Overall, they seem to conclude that attempts to identify and describe a unique perpetrator personality profile will not meet with much success.

As discussed by Suedfeld and Schaller, research on the authoritarian personality style (Adorno et al., 1950)—a style characterized by punitiveness, an emphasis on power and toughness, and ethnocentrism—was motivated by a desire to shed light on "people's susceptibility to the siren call of fascism." But Suedfeld and Schaller argue at length that the evidence for that link has never been very compelling (cf. Altemeyer, 1988, 1996). And, as noted earlier, they also suggest that a simple and rigid cognitive style, traditionally a central aspect of authoritarianism, was a characteristic shared by significant subsets of both perpetrators *and* people who rescued and hid targets of the Nazis' extermination efforts. Indeed, Suedfeld and Schaller propose that "the much-denigrated and stereotypically authoritarian characteristics of simple cognitive style and a tendency to conformity and obedience are largely process-based and content-free." In sum, even assuming that authoritarianism is a valid personality variable that can be reliably identified, the behavior of authoritarians is the result of a complicated interaction between their cognitive and motivational predispositions and the social influences to which they are exposed.

There is currently no compelling evidence that attempted genocides have historically been carried out or abetted by groups of people made up of large numbers of authoritarians.

Frey and Rez note that studies of perpetrators in the immediate postwar era were often also guided by the hypothesis that the behavior of people actively involved in the Holocaust was a function of psychiatric abnormalities predisposing them to sadism. Psychological testing of SS members, concentration camp guards, and Nazi leaders, however, yielded little evidence in support of this idea. Baumeister also discusses the role of sadism. He concludes that only a small percentage of perpetrators become involved in persecution and murder for the purpose of deriving pleasure from harming other people. (As he notes in reference to those killed during World War II, "It does not seem plausible that 11 million people were murdered for the fun of it.") At the same time, Baumeister acknowledges that sadism *did* play an important role in the Holocaust (and, presumably, in other episodes of genocide). These conclusions might at first seem contradictory, but Baumeister's argument is that although perpetrators are not initially motivated by sadism, as the brutality in which they are engaged escalates, they *learn* to derive pleasure from their activities. Thus, like other contributors to this volume, Baumeister emphasizes the transforming power of participation in genocide. His precise theoretical model of the development of sadism (opponent-process theory) is not identical to the one used by Newman and Staub and others to explain how initially ambivalent people could become enthusiastic and creative murderers. Nonetheless, it represents another way of understanding why the behaviors of perpetrators do not necessarily indicate what they were like before they became involved in such activities.

The point of these contributors is not that perpetrators do not differ in any meaningful way from those who refuse to participate in genocide or those who actively resist plans to exterminate an out-group. There is no reason to believe that, and no research that would support such a conclusion. In addition, Mandel's chapter reminds us that the personality of a *leader* of a nation or other community can have an enormous impact on how a conflict between groups unfolds. Although it is disturbing to contemplate, the quirks of an individual person who happens to be in power at a decisive moment in history could well play a crucial role in determining whether or not mass murder is triggered.

Instead, the overriding lessons seem to be that (a) when it comes to the factors that lead people to participate in genocide, individual differences in personality are less crucial than one might suppose, and (b) whatever those important individual differences are, they are unlikely to be broad and context-free personality traits. Contemporary personality theory (Caprara & Cervone, 200) conceptualizes personality in terms of a complex blend of underlying attitudes, beliefs, goals, and competencies, many of which are specific to given contexts. An implication of this perspective—and one supported by the data—is that it is unlikely that a unique genocidal personality style could be identified even in principle. (For a related argument, see, Frey and Rez's proposed typology of German Holocaust perpetrators.)

LYING AND SELF-DECEPTION

Everyone who has ever tried to imagine the reality of being a Holocaust perpetrator is struck by one puzzling question: How could the hangmen carry out their gruesome tasks and then go home to pet the dog and tuck in the children? Undoubtedly, there is no one definitive answer to this question, but several chapters shed at least some light on it. Erber, Newman, and Baumeister suggest that perpetrators may have deceived themselves about the nature of their actions in a number of ways.

Even though the Nazi death machine required the active cooperation of thousands of executioners (as well as the passive cooperation of an even larger number of bystanders), relatively few of them were involved in actual killings. In addition to making the Holocaust extremely efficient, the high division of labor so characteristic of Adolph Eichmann's assembly line of death may have allowed many to convince themselves that they were doing something other than death work. Instead, many may have construed their activities as loading boxcars, setting switches, assigning people to quarters, and so on. Eichmann himself was a master at this, pointing out repeatedly that he never did anything more than coordinate train schedules. As discussed by Erber, construing behavior at such concrete levels of action identification (see Vallacher & Wegner, 1987) not only divorces it from its larger context but also may provide the comforting illusion that one has committed no wrongdoing. Construing behavior at highly abstract levels of action identification may be comforting for very different reasons. As Baumeister and Newman point out, many perpetrators of genocide approach their task out of a sense of idealism. Instead of focusing on the concrete aspects of their behavior, perpetrators guided by idealism look at it in terms of its larger meaning. Instead of killing scores of people, idealistic perpetrators look at what they do as a contribution to a greater good, such as cleansing the world of people who have been declared undesirables.

Both of these self-deceptive strategies follow very different principles. In one case they involve the construal of behavior in very concrete ways. In the other case they involve the construal of behavior in very abstract ways. Nonetheless, they ultimately accomplish the same goal: a subjective lack of guilt in the face of having committed horrendous crimes. It is probably safe to speculate that those Holocaust perpetrators who issued orders were perhaps largely motivated by idealism, whereas those who carried them out construed their actions in more concrete terms. Either way, the research described by Erber suggests that perpetrators of genocide may acquire their beliefs about the nature of their actions to some extent by lying to others. Erber found that the mere repetition of a lie led to its being believed. This was true even when the liars had no a priori reason to want to believe the lies they were telling. In light of these findings, it is not hard to imagine that the more perpetrators tell themselves *self-serving* lies ("I'm merely filing papers"), the more they become convinced that these lies constitute the truth. This may aid them in carrying out their otherwise grim duties without being haunted by their conscience. And after the fact, it may promote a sense of innocence among people who by all objective standards are clearly guilty of crimes against humanity.

Much of the Holocaust was justified as being directed toward the elimination of inferior peoples. But as if a mere pronouncement to that effect was not enough, many aspects of the extermination had the effect of actually rendering the victims inferior in the eyes of the perpetrators. The brutality of the Nazi persecution and the desperate living conditions in the ghettos, on the trains, and in the death camps were such that the majority of the victims appeared dehumanized to their killers. Of course, what the killers ignored was the extent to which they themselves had contributed to this dehumanization. As discussed by Newman, not taking into account how one's behavior shapes the behavior of others can be looked at as another form of self-deception. In the context of the Holocaust, it may have helped grease the many parts of the Nazi death machine and ultimately contributed to its remarkable efficiency. More generally, motivated inattention to what Gilbert and Jones (1986) called "perceiver-induced constraint" might play a role in sustaining all campaigns of extermination once they have started.

PERPETRATORS AS "WILD ANIMALS"

Of course, declaring that a group or race of people is inferior may in itself not provide sufficient justification for genocide. If it is just a matter of inferiority, a number of less lethal ways could be pursued to remove such people from one's community. Moreover, inferiority may elicit nonhostile responses. The Nazis seemed to have been aware of this to some extent, as evidenced by their insistence that Jews, in addition to being inferior, were also dangerous. The Jews' alleged tight connections with both Bolshevism and international finance, along with their propensity to undermine the purity of the "Aryan race," were considered threats severe enough to warrant drastic measures. Constant appeals to the danger posed by the Jews allowed for the formation of exaggerated mental representations that ultimately aided in their destruction. Although the Nazis' characterizations of Jews seem in many ways to be absurd, the "inferior-yet-evil" message was unfortunately quite sensible given their goal of mobilizing people for violent action. As Suedfeld and Schaller argue, a readiness to perceive out-groups as being dangerous is deeply rooted

341

in our ancestral history. Exaggerating the threat posed by other groups thus capitalizes on psychological mechanisms that evolved to deal with the problems inherent in intergroup relations.

Evolutionary arguments of this kind have received increasing acceptance in psychology over the past couple of decades, and they often seem very compelling. As discussed earlier, we believe that an evolutionary psychology approach (such as the one presented by Suedfeld and Schaller) could have much to offer attempts to understand the dynamics of genocide. Some evolutionary or sociobiological accounts of human behavior, though, rest not only on comparisons within species over a period of time but also on comparisons across species. For example, it has long been argued that humans and other animals share an evolved instinct for aggression. It is tempting, then, to speculate about whether mass killers are simply responding to instinctual urges. But as Zajonc vividly points out, many of the atrocities that took place during the Holocaust and other massacres and genocides entailed actions that are hard to equate with a male fish's attack on a conspecific that approaches his nest. Animal aggression and human massacres differ both quantitatively (i.e., in terms of their scope) and qualitatively (i.e., in terms of the degree of organization and planning they require). The human violence observed during the Holocaust and the Rape of Nanking, for example, seems to have little in common with the violence that is part of the ritual involved in settling leadership issues among chimpanzees. Zajonc forcefully argues against facile analogies between human and animal behavior.

One cannot simply point to the genetic material shared between chimps and humans and then draw the conclusion that behavior that looks similar is caused by a common genetic mechanism. Such conclusions are based on the erroneous assumption that genes directly cause behavior. The issue of whether genes can actually do that seems far from settled. In fact, as neurobiologists remind us, genes merely manufacture proteins. Those proteins, of course, help determine the makeup of such things as one's appearance, metabolism, and nervous system. They also play at least an indirect role in determining social behavior, but we are far from being able to understand the precise mechanisms involved. Thus, as Zajonc concludes, "the attempt to construct an animal model of human collective violence faces so many discontinuities that only very superficial generalizations can be drawn."

SOCIAL-PSYCHOLOGICAL EXPLANATIONS AS EXONERATION

This chapter began with Yehuda Bauer's exhortation to treat genocide as a manifestation of human nature that is amenable to analysis and, ultimately, comprehension. Another (and not uncommon) perspective is represented by the French intellectual and filmmaker Claude Lanzmann. As discussed by Rosenbaum (1998), Lanzmann has vigorously opposed attempts to understand the causes of the Holocaust and the motives of its perpetrators. His fear is that understanding will lead to empathy for the perpetrators and even forgiveness.

A number of contributors to this volume (e.g., Baumeister, Tindale et al.) discuss the possibility that their accounts might serve to reduce the perceived culpability of perpetrators and that the processes they describe will be seen as justifications for engaging in mass killing. But these difficult issues are addressed most directly by Miller et al., who make the case that social-psychological explanations are especially likely to convey a condoning attitude toward perpetrators. Indeed, Miller et al. have collected data to back up this claim. Although their research did not directly focus on explanations for genocide, they have found that when people are presented with explanations for wrongdoing that emphasize situational influences or individual differences in personality, the former are seen as more exonerating. In other words, people presented with the more typical social-psychological explanations see the researcher as being more forgiving of people who engage in socially undesirable behavior. Although the causal mechanisms suggested to the research participants did not affect their *own* condemnatory attitudes, an implication of these studies is that in the long run social-psychological explanations could lead people to adopt what they perceive (mistakenly, most often) to be the researchers' more "forgiving" perspective.

Miller et al.'s findings are perhaps a premonition of the way in which many readers will react to some of the arguments presented in this book. Two caveats are in order, though. First, social-psychological explanations give the impression of exoneration only when the mechanisms involved suggest a lack of responsibility. As Miller et al. themselves note, social-psychological explanations are not unique in this respect; personality-based explanations (e.g., the insanity defense in a criminal trial) can also have this feature. In addition, many of the social-psychological accounts presented in this book are not purely situational but involve an intertwining of contextual, dispositional, and motivational factors.

Nonetheless, Miller et al. are undoubtedly right in predicting that a number of the ideas presented in this book will seem offensive to people who construe them as efforts not only to humanize perpetrators but also to inspire forgiveness toward them. We are willing to run that risk. The overall purpose of this book is to use social-psychological principles to increase our understanding of why individuals and collectives initiate and maintain attempts to exterminate other groups of people. By "understanding," we mean "making sense of the meaning and causes of genocide," not "sympathy for and tolerance of perpetrators." But developing "understanding" in the first sense described arguably requires one to take into account the perspective of the perpetrators to some extent (see Baumeister, 1997). Doing that is not always easy or pleasant—do we really want to imagine ourselves or the people we know in the shoes of an Auschwitz guard?—but that act of imagination might be necessary for gaining insight into the circumstances that could lead to future Holocausts. If this book makes people more aware of the social situations that could lead them to become participants in mass murder—and if in so doing, it makes even a tiny contribution toward preventing that from happening—it will have been worth it. Indeed, it is safe to say that all the contributors to this book were motivated by their hopes for a world where forgiving perpetrators will be moot.

NOTE

We would like to thank Maureen Wang Erber and Linda Skitka for their helpful comments on an earlier version of this chapter.

REFERENCES

Adorno, T. W., Frenkel-Brunswik, E., Levinson, D. J., & Sanford, R. (1950). *The authoritarian personality*. New York: Harper.

Altemeyer, B. (1988). *Enemies of freedom: Understanding right-wing authoritarianism*. San Francisco: Jossey-Bass.

Altemeyer, B. (1996). *The authoritarian specter*. Cambridge, MA: Harvard University Press.

Baumeister, R. F. (1997). *Evil: Inside human violence and cruelty*. New York: Freeman.

Berkowitz, L. (1999). Evil is more than banal: Situationism and the concept of evil. *Personality and Social Psychology Review, 3*, 246–253.

Browning, C. R. (1992). *Ordinary men: Reserve Police Battalion 101 and the Final Solution in Poland*. New York: HarperCollins.

Caprara, G. V., & Cervone, D. (2000). *Personality: Determinants, dynamics, and potentials*. New York: Cambridge University Press.

Darley, J. M. (1992). Social organization for the production of evil. *Psychological Inquiry, 3*, 199–218.

Fenigstein, A. (1998). Were obedience pressures a factor in the Holocaust? *Analyse & Kritik, 20*, 54–73.

Gilbert, D. T., & Jones, E. E. (1986). Perceiver-induced constraint: Interpretations of self-generated reality. *Journal of Personality and Social Psychology, 50*, 269–280.

Goldhagen, D. J. (1996). *Hitler's willing executioners: Ordinary Germans and the Holocaust*. New York: Knopf.

Jones, E. E. (1990). *Interpersonal perception*. New York: Macmillan.

Latane, B., & Darley, J. (1970). *The unresponsive bystander: Why doesn't he help?* Englewood Cliffs, NJ: Prentice-Hall.

Mandel, D. R. (1998). The obedience alibi: Milgram's account of the Holocaust reconsidered. *Analyse & Kritik, 20*, 74–94.

Milgram, S. (1963). Behavioral study of obedience. *Journal of Abnormal and Social Psychology, 67*, 371–378.

Milgram, S. (1974). *Obedience to authority*. New York: Harper and Row.

Rosenbaum, R. (1998). *Explaining Hitler: The search for the origins of his evil*. New York: Random House.

Ross, L., & Nisbett, R. E. (1991). *The person and the situation: Perspectives of social psychology*. New York: McGraw-Hill.

Vallacher, R. R., & Wegner, D. M. (1987). What do people think they're doing? Action identification and human behavior. *Psychological Review, 94,* 3–15.

Zillmer, E. A., Harrower, M., Ritzler, B. A., & Archer, R. P. (1995). *The quest for the Nazi personality: A psychological investigation of Nazi war criminals*. Hillsdale, NJ: Erlbaum.

Author Index

347

Author Index

Goodwin, S. A., 265
Gordon, A. K., 243, 261, 304, 305, 307
Goto, S., 175
Gourevich, P., 27, 35, 43
Granneman, B. D., 249
Green, D. P., 114, 137
Green, J. A., 122
Greenberg, J., 82, 83, 84, 85, 269
Greene, F. D., 23, 264
Greenwald, A. G., 268, 317, 321
Grossman, D., 106
Grossman, R., 62
Grusec, J. E., 22
Gur, C. R., 290
Gurin, P., 167, 190
Gurr, T. R., 11, 15
Gushee, D. P., 73, 76

Hains, S. C., 156
Hallie, P. P., 28
Hamilton, D., 168
Hamilton, V. L., 95, 264, 321
Hamilton, W. D., 226, 231
Haney, C., 73, 259, 313, 314, 321
Hardin, C., 149
Harff, B., 11, 15
Haritos-Fatouros, M., 21
Harris, M. B., 22
Harris, V. A., 57
Harrower, M., 208, 305, 309, 338
Harter, S., 191
Harvey, O. J., 73, 76, 273
Hashtroudie, S., 295
Haslam, S., 175
Hass, J., 81
Hastie, R., 153
Heider, F., 25
Herbert, U., 54, 56, 209, 211, 212, 214, 298
Herman, D., 54
Herman, J. 17, 22
Hertwig, R., 265, 273
Herz, M. J., 229
Herzstein, R. E., 101
Hewitt, J., 178
Higgins, E. T., 149, 278
Hilberg, R., 3, 15, 19, 23, 25, 26, 28, 73, 97, 98, 103, 104, 105, 209, 259, 260
Himmelfarb, M., 262
Hinde, R. A., 227
Hinsz, V. B., 152
Hirsch, J. U., 228

Hirsh, H., 95
Hitchcock, R. K., 29
Hitler, A., 267, 268, 269, 270, 271, 272, 274, 275, 277, 278
Hobsbawn, E. J., 43, 265
Hoffrage, U., 265, 273
Hofstede, G., 162, 165, 166, 167, 176
Hogg, M. A., 144, 145, 147, 148, 149, 152, 156, 175
Höhne, H., 210
Holliday, L., 73
Hood, W., 73, 273
Höss, R., 213
Hoss, R., 58
House, P., 264
Hsu, F., 169, 170
Hughes, M., 175
Huneke, D., 77
Hunt, D. E., 76
Hurtado, A., 167
Hutton, D. G., 249

Ickes, W., 57
Ignatieff, M., 55
Irving, D., 234

Jackman, M. R., 131
Jaffe, D., 259, 313
Jankowski, M. S., 81
Janoff-Bulman, R., 14
Janowitz, M., 116, 121
Joffe, J., 62
Johnson, M. K., 295
Jonas, E., 189, 193, 205
Jones, E. E., 57, 58, 59, 302, 306, 338, 341

Kadushin, C., 18
Kagitcibasi, C., 163
Kahneman, D., 261, 263
Kameda, T., 144, 152, 153
Kampe, N., 198
Kaplan, H., 78, 179
Kassin, S. M., 44
Kasulis, T., 168
Kater, M., 212
Katona, G., 216
Katz, F. E., 95
Katz, J., 256
Kelley, H. H., 306
Kelman, H. C., 30, 95, 264, 321
Kemmelmeier, M., 170, 172, 176

Author Index

Moscovici, S., 26, 144, 148, 150, 198, 202, 205
Mosse, G. L., 198
Mowrer, O. H., 116, 117, 125
Moyer, K. E., 226
Muckensturm, B., 229
Mullaly, P., 169
Mullin, B. A., 145, 147

Nathan, O., 17
Naumann, B., 289
Nemeth, C. J., 144, 155, 156
Neuberg, S. L., 75, 81
Newcomb, T. M., 273
Newman, L. S., 135
Newsom, J. T., 75
Nightingale, E. O., 28
Nisbett, R. E., 50, 60, 115, 259, 270, 271, 302, 304, 338
Niven, T. S., 154, 156
Norden, H., 17
Norfolk, S., 55
Novick, P., 95, 310
Nowak, A., 151
Nunca, M., 13, 16

O'Brien, D., 167
O'Brien, M., 75
Oakes, P. J., 175
Ohtsubo, Y, 153
Oliner, P., 32, 33, 35, 76, 86
Oliner, S. B., 32, 33, 35, 76, 86
Operario, D., 265
Opotow, S., 194
Orth, K., 209, 211, 213
Osnabrügge, G., 189, 204, 205
Oyserman, D., 163, 165, 166, 167, 168, 169, 170, 172, 175, 176, 178, 179

Palmer, C. T., 222, 231
Parry, R. L., 43
Paulhus, D. L., 292
Pearlman, L. A., 17, 35
Peeke, H. V., 229
Pelham, B. W., 59
Peng, T., 167, 168
Perry, R. P., 306
Pervin, L. A., 50
Peters, E., 23
Peterson, D., 223, 233
Peterson, R., 75

Pettigrew, T. F., 36, 137, 205
Petty, R. E., 74
Phinney, J., 168
Pinel, E., 179
Platt, G. M., 20
Pratto, F., 72
Prentice, D. A., 60, 61
Proctor, R. N., 73, 212, 276
Pruitt, D. G., 206
Prunier, G., 35, 234
Puxton, G., 278
Pyszczynski, T., 82, 83, 84, 85, 269

Rappoport, L., 18, 19, 20, 21, 208
Rauschning, H., 275
Reddaway, P., 12, 25, 28
Reed, G. M., 191
Reeves, R., 100
Reichel, P., 203
Reicher, S. D., 175
Rescorla, R. A., 273
Rhodewalt, F., 249
Rich, A., 114, 137
Ring, K., 99
Ritzler, B. A., 208, 305, 309, 338
Roberts, J., 163, 177
Robinson, J., 99
Rochat, F., 316
Roiphe, K., 299
Rokeach, M., 74
Rosenbaum, R., 59, 80, 235, 260, 305, 308, 321, 325, 342
Rosenberg, T., 43
Rosenberger, N., 167
Rosenblatt, A., 83
Rosenthal, A. M., 315
Rosenthal, L., 24
Rosenzweig, M., 167, 177
Ross, G. R., 216
Ross, L., 50, 57, 60, 115, 259, 264, 269, 271, 274, 275, 302, 304, 338
Ross, M., 204, 269
Roth, C., 253
Rothbart, G., 18
Rouhana, N. N., 30, 163
Rubenstein, R. L., 122, 125, 129
Rummel, R. J., 16, 260, 263, 276
Runciman, W. G., 130
Rushton, J. P., 22
Russell, B., 264
Ryan, R. M., 191

General Index

Abraham, biblical parable of, 245
Action identification, 55–56, 296–297, 340
Agentic state, 104–105
Allocentrism. *See* Culture
Altruism, 222 (*see also* Resistors/rescuers)
  antecedents of, 22
  banality of, 316, 337
  and the continuum of benevolence, 34 63 n.3, 337
  effects of contextual factors on, 302
Animal behavior, 80–81, 222–236, 242, 326, 342 (*see also* Sociobiology)
Anti-Semitism, 212, 316
  among partisan groups, 77
  Christian, 15, 26, 82, 86, 122, 129–130, 146–147, 155, 164, 168
  under communism, 71
  eliminationist, 45–46, 51, 63 n.1, 72, 289
  German, 3, 15, 45–46, 51, 85, 146–151, 155–157, 163–164, 198, 206, 215, 263, 269, 272, 333–334
  redemptive, 134
Argentina, disappearances in, 11, 23
  as a response to difficult life conditions, 13, 17, 20
  role of bystanders in, 24–27, 35
  role of military in, 16, 18
Armenian genocide, 11, 23, 325
  background factors, 15–16, 18–19
  as a response to difficult life conditions, 13, 17
  role of bystanders in, 24, 26–27

role of collectivism in, 177
role of scapegoating in, 139
Arousal, 125–126
Attitude-behavior consistency, 45–46
Attitude change, 151–152, 154, 271–274
Auschwitz, 34, 91, 100, 102, 188, 299
  conditions in, 58, 82, 213
  doctors in, 212
Austria, 286–287, 289
Authoritarian personality, 68–72, 74–78, 86–87, 338–339 (*see also* F scale)
  and cognitive style, 74–77, 275–276
  correlates of, 69–70, 317
  definition of, 68–69
  history of research on, 62, 68–71, 116–117, 143
  methodological problems of early research on, 69–70
  and obedience, 21, 70, 75–77,119
  and political ideology, 70–71
  as a predisposition to Nazism, 3, 121
  redefinitions of, 71–72, 86–87, 140 n.2

Berlin Psychoanalytic Institute, 25–26
Blacks, prejudice toward, 131, 150, 317–318
Browning, Christopher, 124, 255–256, 327
  and debate with Goldhagen, 47, 140 n.1
  on perpetrators as ordinary people, 47, 214–215, 302
  views on perpetrator conformity, 49, 289
  views on perpetrator obedience, 47, 97, 335

355